Political Strategies in Pre-Columbian Mesoamerica

Political Strategies in Pre-Columbian Mesoamerica

EDITED BY
Sarah Kurnick and Joanne Baron

UNIVERSITY PRESS OF COLORADO
Louisville

Published by University Press of Colorado
245 Century Circle, Suite 202
Louisville, Colorado 80027

First paperback edition 2020
Printed in the United States of America

The University Press of Colorado is a proud member of the Association of University Presses.

The University Press of Colorado is a cooperative publishing enterprise supported, in part, by Adams State University, Colorado State University, Fort Lewis College, Metropolitan State University of Denver, Regis University, University of Colorado, University of Northern Colorado, University of Wyoming, Utah State University, and Western Colorado University.

∞ This paper meets the requirements of the ANSI/NISO Z39.48-1992 (Permanence of Paper).

ISBN: 978-1-60732-415-7 (cloth)
ISBN: 978-1-64642-079-7 (paperback)
ISBN: 978-1-60732-416-4 (ebook)

Library of Congress Cataloging-in-Publication Data

Political strategies in pre-Columbian Mesoamerica / edited by Sarah Kurnick and Joanne Baron.
pages cm
ISBN 978-1-60732-415-7 (hardback) —ISBN 978-1-64642-079-7 (paperback) —
ISBN 978-1-60732-416-4 (ebook)
1. Indians of Mexico—Antiquities. 2. Indians of Central America—Antiquities. 3. Indians of Mexico—Politics and government. 4. Indians of Central America—Politics and government. 5. Authority—Political aspects—Mexico—History—To 1500. 6. Authority—Political aspects—Central America—History—To 1500. 7. Social archaeology—Mexico. 8. Social archaeology—Central America. 9. Ethnoarchaeology—Mexico. 10. Ethnoarchaeology—Central America. I. Kurnick, Sarah. II. Baron, Joanne.
F1219.3.P7P66 2015
972'.01—dc23

2015010767

Cover illustrations: detail from the *Codex Zouche-Nuttall* © the Trustees of the British Museum (*foreground*); detail of the *Lienzo de Ocotepec,* courtesy, Vanderbilt University Publications in Anthropology (*background*).

In memory of Robert J. Sharer.

Contents

Figures

Tables

Acknowledgments

This volume originated in a session we organized at the 77th annual meeting of the Society for American Archaeology, held in Memphis, Tennessee, in 2012. Our goal was to bring together archaeologists working throughout Mesoamerica to discuss and debate the processes associated with the creation, perpetuation, and negation of politically authoritative relationships.

We would like to thank the authors for their thoughtful chapters, as well as those who presented a paper at the SAAs but were unable to contribute to the volume: David Anderson, Susan Evans, Federico Paredes, Nancy Peniche, Adam Smith, Timothy Sullivan, and Lorraine Williams-Beck. It has been a pleasure to work with each of these scholars.

The University Press of Colorado has supported this volume from the outset, and we are gratified to have worked with Acquisitions Editor Jessica d'Arbonne, whose assistance and advice have proven invaluable, and with Director Darrin Pratt. We are also grateful to two anonymous reviewers for their constructive criticisms on the first draft of the manuscript and their insightful suggestions for improvement. This volume is better because of their comments.

Finally, we have benefited from the support of colleagues, friends, and family. To them, we say thank you.

Political Strategies in Pre-Columbian Mesoamerica

1

Paradoxical Politics

Negotiating the Contradictions of Political Authority

Sarah Kurnick

This volume examines the operation of political authority in pre-Columbian Mesoamerica. It considers, in other words, the creation, reproduction, and negation of politically authoritative relationships in several of the world's early complex societies. How did rulers acquire and maintain, or fail to maintain, political authority? And why did subjects choose to acknowledge or reject that authority? A primary goal of this volume is to advance the negotiation of contradictions as a fruitful avenue to explore the exercise of political authority in pre-Columbian Mesoamerica and in other parts of the world both past and present. In brief, rulers reinforce social inequality and bolster their own unique position at the top of the sociopolitical hierarchy yet simultaneously emphasize social similarities and the commonalities shared by all. Rulers also emphasize their differences from, and their similarities to, not only their followers, but also rulers of other contemporary communities and past leaders of their own communities. Followers, in turn, may choose to participate in politically authoritative relationships because of the appeal of an individual who is at the same time different and familiar, exceptional and relatable. They may recognize, in other words, the authority of an individual who is utterly distinct yet at the same time like them, like other contemporary rulers, and like past leaders.

In this introductory chapter, I will define political strategies and pre-Columbian Mesoamerica and

DOI: 10.5876/9781607324164.c001

consider why their intersection is an important and useful locus of study. I will then review previously proposed explanations and advance an analytical framework for understanding how rulers rule and why followers often choose to follow—generally, and in pre-Columbian Mesoamerica specifically. Through this introduction and the case studies that follow, this volume aims to bring the negotiation of contradictions to the fore of studies of political authority.

POLITICAL STRATEGIES AND PRE-COLUMBIAN MESOAMERICA

The following chapters examine the formation, perpetuation, and negation of politically authoritative relationships—relationships that are prominent and persistent features of past, other, and our own lives. Each chapter considers, in different ways, two fundamental questions: What strategies do rulers use to acquire and maintain political authority? And for what reasons do subjects choose to recognize or to reject the authority of rulers? These questions are, and have been, a primary concern of political philosophers from Aristotle to Hobbes, to contemporary scholars such as Giorgio Agamben (1998; Smith 2011a). For these and other thinkers, the "central problem of political life is to define—and reshape—the logic of authorization and subjection that assembles the polity and differentiates the terrain of personal will from that of sovereign power" (Smith 2011a:358). Put differently, the questions of how rulers rule and why followers often choose to obey lie at the core of politics and political association (Smith 2011a, 2011b).

Importantly, individuals do not always choose to recognize the authority of a self-styled leader or to obey her or his commands. Indeed, attempts to acquire and maintain political authority are not always successful and, even when successful, the authority acquired is not necessarily long-lived. Nevertheless, in various places and at various times, rulers did exercise political authority and individuals did choose to obey, and it is important to understand how and why.

There exists, however, no single or simple answers to these questions. Rulers use a wide variety of strategies to induce their followers to obey, and followers have many different reasons for choosing to acknowledge authority. These strategies and reasons vary across time and space, according to local conditions and circumstances, and with a polity's size, degree of political influence, and position in regional sociopolitical hierarchies. One goal of this introductory chapter is to advance a model that is all-inclusive yet allows for the great inherent variability in human practices. A goal of each case study is to ascertain and delineate the specific acts and practical actions—in other words, the political strategies—that engendered and reproduced politically authoritative relationships among a particular group in a particular place during a particular time. This volume thus aims to advance a framework that will be useful to those studying political authority in any and all societies and also to understand how actual, specific social groups created and maintained—or rejected—political relationships.

Why study political authority through archaeology, and why take pre-Columbian Mesoamerican societies as examples? The exercise of political authority is an intensely physical process that operates through the built environment and through tangible objects—the subjects of archaeological inquiry (Meskell 2005; Smith 2003; Davenport and Golden, this volume). Because of their reliance on material culture, archaeologists can thus provide a "vision of politics . . . steadfastly centered on the intense physicality of power and governance" (Smith 2003:21). Indeed, the material mediation of sovereignty is currently a hotly debated topic within the discipline (see Smith 2011a, 2011b, 2012; Johansen and Bauer 2011).

Many different types of scholars, however, study objects and are able to emphasize the intensely physical nature of authority. Perhaps the more important and unique contribution archaeologists make to the study of the political is our ability to provide temporal depth and geographic breadth to modern practices. As Adam T. Smith (2003:22) writes, the "temporal distance that separates early complex polities from the modern can . . . be understood as providing a unique lens for viewing political life that lends our gaze a greater critical refinement." Pierre Bourdieu (1994) similarly argues that studies of the origins, or genesis, of social institutions provide a means by which to understand and question those institutions. For Bourdieu (4) this "reconstruction of genesis" brings "back into view the conflicts and confrontations of the early beginnings and therefore all the discarded possibilities, [and] retrieves the possibility that things could have been (and still could be) otherwise." Put differently, an understanding of political authority in the past enhances an understanding of, and stimulates reflection on, political authority in the present.

Why then study political authority in pre-Columbian Mesoamerica? Mesoamerica can usefully be understood as a heuristic concept scholars use to study diverse groups of people who lived in a particular area, spoke a particular set of languages, and shared a common set of beliefs and practices (R. Joyce 2004). Although its boundaries remain inexact, Mesoamerica is generally recognized as encompassing the land occupied by the modern nations of Belize and Guatemala, and parts of Mexico, Honduras, and El Salvador (figure 1.1). Ancient Mesoamerican peoples are thought to have

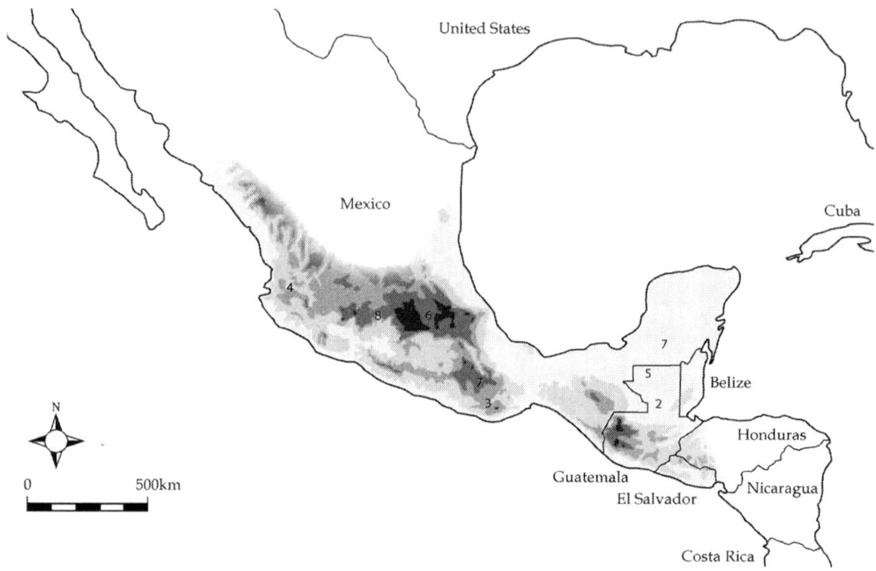

FIGURE 1.1. *Map of Mesoamerica showing locations of case studies from this volume by chapter number: (2) Ceibal, Guatemala; (3) coastal Oaxaca; (4) central Jalisco; (5) La Corona, Guatemala; (6) Teotihuacan; (7) Maya area and Mixteca Alta; (8) central Michoacán.*

spoken languages belonging to one of several families, including Mixe-Zoque, Totonac, Mayan, and Oto-Manguean. And Mesoamerican peoples developed similar, though not identical, subsistence practices, economic systems, and religious beliefs. Common characteristics include the cultivation of maize, the development of complex calendar systems, and participation in a form of the ballgame (Adams 2006; Blanton et al. 1993; Carmack, Gasco, and Gossen 1996; Evans 2004; R. Joyce 2004; Kirchhoff 1952; Spinden 1917; Weaver 1993).

Importantly, Mesoamerica was one of a handful of regions in the world where individuals independently developed agriculture as a means of subsistence and established sedentary villages and socially complex, hierarchical societies. Pre-Columbian Mesoamerican societies—those in existence from the initial occupation of the region to the arrival of Europeans—thus provide a prime example of the development of social complexity among early agricultural societies and of the operation of institutionalized political authority among early complex polities (Blanton et al. 1993; Evans 2004; Masson and Smith 2000; Sanders and Price 1968).

POLITICAL AUTHORITY

I adopt a Weberian perspective on authority. Max Weber (1978:212) classically defined authority as the "probability that certain specific commands . . . will be obeyed by a given group of persons" and argued that authority necessarily implies a "minimum of voluntary compliance, that is, an interest . . . in obedience." Authority, in other words, is the ability to give commands that others choose to obey. Weber's definition has three principal components. First, it suggests a separation between those who give commands and those who opt to follow them, between those who exercise authority and those who do not. Second, Weber recognizes that authority is situational and that only certain people under certain circumstances will obey commands. As other theorists (Bourdieu 1991; Lincoln 1994) have noted, to be obeyed, commands must be given by the correct speaker, with the correct delivery and staging, in the correct places, at the correct times, and before the correct audiences. Finally, and perhaps most importantly, Weber's definition suggests that authority cannot exist without explicit recognition and voluntary compliance. Rather than passively accepting authority, powerful individuals, for whatever reasons, actively choose to comply.

This definition of authority is a naturalistic one, consistent with theories of human agency. Agency theories recognize that all individuals exercise power and that all individuals make choices that have meaningful consequences (for an overview of agency theory in archaeology, see Dobres and Robb 2000; Dornan 2002). Humans do not merely react; they act, making decisions that influence their own lives and the lives of others. As Anthony Giddens (1984:14) writes, agents are "able to intervene in the world, or to refrain from such intervention . . . An agent is able to deploy . . . a range of causal powers, including that of influencing those deployed by others." By adopting a Weberian definition of authority, I acknowledge the importance of the agency of all to the exercise of authority by a few. I also continue an archaeological trend of "agency-centered examinations that increasingly seek to situate elements of deliberate action within a multivocalic and polythetic prehistoric past" (Lohse 2007:2).

Takeshi Inomata (this volume, 2006a) raises important questions about the applicability of modern political theory—such as a Weberian understanding of authority—to archaeological contexts. He notes that much political theory was developed to explain modern, and often Western, contexts and argues that archaeologists need to participate in reflexive theoretical discourses with social theory rather than passively borrow and apply it. Other authors have similarly noted the tendency of archaeologists to project their own biases, prejudices, and pre-conceived notions onto the past. As Julian Thomas (2004) argues, modernity tends to create a past in its own image.

Can a Weberian concept of authority illuminate political relationships in ancient societies? Specifically, does authority, as Weber asserts, necessarily imply legitimacy? And is authority still deemed legitimate when followers express discontent, discretely disapprove, or subtly resist (see Scott 1990)? As Inomata (this volume) asks, is the modern construct of legitimate authority applicable to archaeological contexts?

Smith (2003:108) defines legitimacy as "the ability of a regime to synchronize practices that perpetuate the existing political order within a discursive framework that generates the allegiance of subjects." Stated simply, legitimacy is the ability of rulers to maintain their position in a way that engenders the support of their followers. Following Smith and others, I argue that authoritative relationships, past or present, necessarily imply legitimacy. As Smith (2003:109) writes, a "regime without legitimacy, based solely on domination, may be described as piratical or extortionist, but not authoritative." Or, as Antonio Gramsci (1999:384) writes, "recourse to arms and coercion . . . can be nothing more than a methodological hypothesis . . . Force can be employed against enemies, but not against . . . one's own side . . . whose 'good will' and enthusiasm one needs."

I maintain that such a view does not negate legitimacy in the presence of dissent, disapproval, or subtle resistance. As many scholars have noted, dissatisfaction is likely to be present in all unequal social relationships. Indeed, "expressions of resistance of political domination are a component of all complex societies characterized by institutionalized power differentials" (Joyce and Weller 2007:144). Legitimacy is therefore best understood not as a condition that is either present or absent but as an ongoing process. Not all followers will agree with every act or decision a ruler makes, and those who do agree on some occasions will not agree on others. Rather, rulers must continually work toward legitimacy—through the use of political strategies—and followers continually choose to accept, subtly resist, or revolt against authority. At times of increasing dissatisfaction and dissent, regimes may either radically alter themselves or become illegitimate and fail. Arthur A. Joyce and colleagues (this volume), in their examination of the Terminal Formative Period lower Río Verde Valley, provide one example of a regime's inability to maintain legitimate authority.

Several other questions arise from a Weberian definition of authority. How do rulers induce their followers to obey? What techniques and tactics do rulers use to promote their legitimacy and encourage their subjects to participate in politically authoritative relationships? In *The German Ideology*, Karl Marx and Friedrich Engels (1970:64) assert that the "ideas of the ruling class are in every epoch the ruling ideas" and that the "class which is the ruling material force of society is at the same time its ruling intellectual force." Put differently, those controlling the means of production also control the ideas that prevail in society. By propagating ideas that reinforce their own position at the top of the sociopolitical hierarchy, those in charge can prevent others from seeing clearly the conditions of their existence and thus from revolting to change those conditions.

Several scholars have adopted a Marxist understanding of ideology to explain how ruling classes maintain their social positions and prevent revolt. Antonio Gramsci (1999), for one, offers the notion of cultural hegemony, or ideological control that represents an existing social order as natural and to the benefit of all rather than arbitrary and to the benefit of a few. Louis Althusser (1971), to take another example, distinguishes two coexisting types of state apparatuses: repressive and ideological. Repressive state apparatuses, such as the army and the police, function primarily through physical violence and exploitation and secondarily through the creation and propagation of imaginary and distorted representations of the world. Ideological state apparatuses, such as schools and churches, function primarily by producing and reproducing such representations and secondarily through coercive force. But for Althusser, it is ideology that allows rulers to generate obedient subjects: for him, rulers create followers by propagating an inaccurate understanding of social relations.

Much like Althusser, Pierre Bourdieu (1977, 1990) argues for dual processes of subjectification and frames rulers' strategies in terms of two coexisting types of violence: overt and symbolic. The creation of subjects through overt violence involves physical tactics, such as the use of force, or economic tactics, such as usury or excessive taxation. Acts of symbolic violence also serve to create subjects but in a way that is perceived as more humane and that occurs when overt violence must be concealed and the real basis of authoritative relationships masked. Symbolic violence is thus a way of establishing and preserving unequal relationships in a more socially acceptable manner.

Michel Foucault (1979, 2003, 2007) has suggested a number of ways that rulers create and reproduce subjects, including torture and punishment, discipline, and biopower. Foucault distinguishes premodern corporeal control, based on torture and punishment, from modern corporeal control, based on discipline and biopower. To torture or punish, rulers create a public spectacle during which they exact revenge on the body of an individual who has committed a crime and consequently challenged authority. Such spectacles allow rulers to restore their authority over disobedient individuals and demonstrate to others the consequences of refusing to comply. Torture and punishment function less to bring a perpetrator to justice and more to exhibit political authority in its most extreme form, to hurt or kill those who have disobeyed orders, and to dissuade others from similar acts of disobedience.

Discipline, on the other hand, is a positive, or constructive, political strategy whereby rulers create docile bodies—bodies that can be "subjected, used, transformed and improved" (Foucault 1979:136). Unlike punishment, discipline relies not on retribution for crimes but on the constitution and judgment of individuals. Discipline targets not actions but people, and it relies not on spectacle but on surveillance, observation, and subtle control over bodies. Biopower is exercised at the level of the population and transforms many unique individuals into a single, easily controlled, homogenous mass. Biopower is the "power of regularization," a de-individualizing "technology in which bodies are replaced by general biological processes (Foucault 2003:247, 249).

Archaeologists disagree whether these two modern "technologies of the body" can and should be applied to non-modern societies. Inomata (2006a:188–89; see also Davenport and Golden, this volume), for example, argues that in ancient societies, disciplinary mechanisms like those described by Foucault "did not exist and were not fully developed." Scott R. Hutson (2002:59), to take another example, uses Foucault's notion of discipline but sparingly, as it brings "a distinctively modern conception of subjectivity that may not be appropriate for pre-modern societies." Following Ian Hodder (2006) and others, I suggest that punishment and discipline can be coeval, rather than necessarily sequential, strategies and that discipline can be a useful concept to understand premodern politically authoritative relationships. Discipline does not necessarily require modern institutions such as the judiciary and psychiatric hospitals. As Hodder (2006:83) writes, "family, clan, and lineage can . . . be seen as mechanisms every bit as disciplining and pervasive as the structures of the modern state. Docile bodies were produced by the mechanisms of power working within the daily practices of social life."

Much like Foucault, James C. Scott (1998) suggests that rulers create and reproduce subjects through regularizing processes. Rather than biopower, Scott focuses on the notion of legibility—the ability to "arrange the population in ways that simplified the classic state functions of taxation, conscription, and prevention of rebellion" (Scott 1998:2). Scott thus argues that rulers imposed certain organizational structures on their followers in attempts to simplify, keep track of, and ultimately affect, their actions.

Perhaps the most common framework archaeologists use to understand how rulers create subjects is Michael Mann's (1986) IEMP model of organized power. Mann suggests four sources of social power—ideological, economic, military, and political—and outlines the sociospatial organization of each. According to Mann (23), ideological power is a monopoly over that which is beyond the realm of the everyday, over that which "cannot be totally tested by experience." Economic power is the monopolization over the production, distribution, exchange, and consumption of goods and resources. Military power is the monopolization over the legitimate use of force and political power is the monopolization over centralized, institutionalized, territorial regulation of social relations. For Mann, it is through these different forms of monopolization that rulers manifest their authority and prevail on followers to obey. Perhaps because of its utility, the IEMP model has become a common classification scheme for understanding the ways rulers induce their followers to obey. Waging wars against enemies—or threatening to do so—is often categorized as a primarily military strategy. Control over natural resources and trade routes is often categorized as a primarily economic strategy. And the performance of rituals, commissioning of monuments, and veneration of ancestors are often categorized as primarily ideological strategies.

But another question arises from a Weberian definition of authority. Why do individuals often choose to comply with authority? Why do they choose to participate in politically authoritative relationships? And under what circumstances do they refuse to comply? As mentioned, a Weberian perspective requires consideration of the actions of the ruler as well as those who choose to follow or to reject rulership. As many scholars (e.g., Hutson 2002; Joyce, Bustamante, and Levine 2001; Pauketat 2000) have noted, "political relationships are produced through social negotiations involving commoners as well as elites" (Joyce, Bustamante, and Levine 2001:343).

Answers as to why individuals chose to—or not to—comply can be divided into three general categories: those that emphasize negative or repressive reasons, those that emphasize positive or constructive reasons, and those that posit either uncritical habituation or a lack of other conceivable options. Scholars who suggest negative or repressive reasons maintain that individuals choose to obey authority because there will be adverse consequences if they do not. Refusal to comply with authority may result, for example, in a fine, social ostracism, or a more extreme penalty such as torture or punishment, as discussed above.

Those who suggest positive or constructive reasons argue that individuals choose to acknowledge authority because they believe in the validity and virtue of that authority or because they have grown, or have been conditioned, to accept it. Weber (1978), for one, emphasizes the notion of belief, be it based on charismatic grounds, or the exceptional character of an individual leader; traditional grounds, or long-standing customs; or rational grounds, or the legality of enacted rules and laws. Bourdieu and Scott also adopt constructive theories but suggest that subordination can be self-legitimizing and that belief can result from learned patterns of behavior. Bourdieu (1977:93–94) discusses such patterns in his consideration of bodily hexis—a "political mythology realized, em-bodied, turned into a permanent disposition, a durable manner of standing, speaking, and thereby of feeling and thinking." Scott similarly argues that the performance of repetitive actions can engender belief. As he writes, "those obliged by domination to act a mask will eventually find that their faces have grown to fit that mask. The practice of subordination in this case produces, in time, its own legitimacy" (Scott 1990:10).

Finally, several theorists argue that individuals choose to comply with authority because of either uncritical habituation or a lack of other conceivable options. Bourdieu's (1977:166; 1991) notion of doxa, or "that which is taken for granted," provides perhaps the best example of this approach. As Bourdieu (1977:164) writes, "schemes of thought and perception can produce the objectivity that they do produce only by producing misrecognition of the limits of the cognition that they make possible, thereby founding immediate adherence, in the doxic mode, to the world of tradition experienced as a 'natural world.'" Put simply, individuals take for granted the social conditions of their existence and do not realize that other possible alternatives exist. For Bourdieu (1977:168), this "recognition of legitimacy through misrecognition of arbitrariness" is the basis of all authority. Individuals conceive of particular authoritative relationships as the only options and believe those relationships to be normal and natural rather than debatable and arbitrary.

It must be emphasized, however, that individuals do not always choose to recognize the authority of a potential leader or obey commands. Attempts to acquire and maintain political authority are not always successful and, even when successful, acquired authority rarely endures. Notably, individuals who choose to reject authority and disobey orders often do so by appropriating the same mechanisms rulers use to foster legitimacy. As scholars recognize, political authority is "inherently problematic, as it is contingent on multiple factors that can be used against central authority as well as being used by it" (Earle 1997:10). David I. Kertzer (1988) has shown that particular symbols, and the rituals that employ them, serve to both bolster and question authority. As he writes, such "symbolism is necessary to prop up the governing political order, but it is also essential in overthrowing it" (Kertzer 1988:174). Similarly, Foucault has suggested that spectacles of terror and punishment afford opportunities not only for a ruler to demonstrate her or his authority but also for the community to question and reject that authority. A group "drawn to the spectacle intended to terrorize it, could express its rejection of the punitive power and sometimes revolt" (Foucault 1979:59).

POLITICAL AUTHORITY IN PRE-COLUMBIAN MESOAMERICA

Inquiries into Pre-Columbian Mesoamerican politics have frequently focused on political organization. The literature is replete with debates about how and to what degree pre-Columbian Mesoamerican polities were centralized and how best to model these polities—as strong states, weak states, city states, segmentary states, theater states, etc. (e.g., Chase and Chase 1996; Fox et al. 1996; Iannone 2002; Marcus 1993; Sharer and Golden 2004; Sharer and Traxler 2006). Political organization and integration, however, are only two aspects of politics. Also important are the strategies used to create, perpetuate, and resist authoritative relationships.

Over the last two decades, many scholars have offered explanations of how various pre-Columbian Mesoamerican societies created, maintained, and negated political authority. Perhaps the most prominent framework is Richard E. Blanton and colleagues' (1996) overarching model of dual-processual theory. Other, more specific explanations are wide ranging but can usefully be divided into those that emphasize supernatural mediation and those that focus on the relationships between rulers and followers.

DUAL-PROCESSUAL THEORY

In 1996 Blanton and colleagues proposed the notion of dual-processual theory to understand the operation of political authority throughout pre-Columbian Mesoamerica. In an effort to move away from neoevolutionary approaches, and specifically ideal-type stages, Blanton and colleagues identify two primary types of power strategies: exclusionary and corporate. Following Mann (1986), they define exclusionary strategies as attempts to monopolize control over various sources of social power and corporate strategies as those employed when, for whatever reasons, such attempts at monopolization are precluded. Although these two strategies coexist to some degree, according to Blanton and colleagues, one will always be paramount at any given place and time.

Dual-processual theory makes an important contribution by affirming the importance of communal political strategies rather than focusing solely on the monopolization of sources of social power (Blanton 1998; Feinman 2001). Dual-processual theory also creates an artificial and unnecessary dichotomy and forces those who rely on it to choose one of two possible dominant types of power strategies. The imposition of dichotomies, however, is not a useful way to understand complex social processes. Smith (2011b:419; see also Martin, this volume) offers a similar critique, writing that the primary influence of dual-processual theory has been to "reignite typological debates by substituting new terms rather than to open an inquiry into the practices of authorization and subjection at the heart of the political." Furthermore, and as others have noted (Murakami, this volume:151; Drennan, Peterson, and Fox 2012), political interactions are complex, nuanced, and multifaceted and must be understood along multiple axes of variability, not "subsumed in a single dimension of leadership strategies."

SUPERNATURAL MEDIATION

Despite the prominence of dual-processual theory, perhaps the greatest number of scholars have argued that pre-Columbian Mesoamerican rulers derived their authority from their exclusive knowledge about, and thus ability to monopolize control over, esoterica, be it supernatural entities, time, or the cosmos in general. The most prevalent view in the literature is that pre-Columbian Mesoamerican rulers acquired and maintained political authority through their unique ability to communicate with the supernatural and act as intermediaries between their followers and deities—a view sometimes, though not always, couched in terms of shamanism.

Beginning in the 1960s, Peter T. Furst (1968, 1981, 1995) published a series of articles interpreting various Mesoamerican artifacts as evidence of shamanism (see Eliade 1972). Mining ethnographic accounts, Furst (1968:160) noted that members of certain South American societies believed in "shaman-jaguar equivalence and transformation." Furst then used ethnographic analogy to argue that Olmec figures displaying a combination of human and jaguar characteristics depicted shamans transforming into their jaguar animal familiars. Drawing on the arguments presented by Furst, Michael Coe (1972) suggested it unlikely that a hierarchical society such as the Olmec would have produced an entire corpus of art that depicted shamans. For Coe, it was much more likely that these figures depicted not shamans themselves, but rulers who had appropriated shamanic attributes, including the ability to transform into jaguars.

In the ensuing decades, many scholars embraced the notion of "shamanistic paths to power" (Reilly 1989:17) within various Mesoamerican societies, including not only the Olmec (Reilly 1989, 1991, 1994, 1995; but also see Clark 1997) but also the people of Izapa (Guernsey 2006; Guernsey Kappelman 1997, 2001; Guernsey and Love 2005), the Zapotec (A. Joyce 2004; Masson and Orr 1998), the Mixtec (Joyce and Winter 1996), and the Maya (Freidel 2008; Freidel and Schele 1988; Freidel, Schele, and Parker 1993; Oakley 2006; Schele and Freidel 1990).

Not all scholars who argue that ancient Maya rulers derived their authority from their exclusive control over esoterica suggest that rulers monopolized communication with deities. Some contend instead that rulers monopolized control over time. In 1996 David Stuart hypothesized an ancient Maya "belief that rulers were themselves embodiments of time and its passage—a role that was fundamental to the cosmological underpinnings of divine kingship" (Stuart 1996:165–66). In the past decade, Prudence M. Rice (2004, 2007, 2008) has championed this idea, arguing that Maya rulers derived their authority from their exclusive knowledge about, and thus illusion of control over, calendric knowledge. As she states, "the foundation of Maya kings' power and divinity was esoteric knowledge about time" (Rice 2008:275). According to Rice, this esoteric knowledge would have afforded rulers the unique ability to make scheduling decisions, such as determining the most auspicious day for farmers to plant or harvest crops. And, for Rice (2008:279), "those who hold authority over the calendar of daily and seasonal economic and ritual activities also hold authority over individuals' daily lives."

Arguments asserting that rulers acquired and maintained authority through the monopolization of esoterica are problematic in several respects. First, despite the epigraphic evidence of the various ways in which pre-Columbian Mesoamerican rulers linked themselves with the divine (Houston and Stuart 1996), there is little to suggest—as Christopher S. Beekman (this volume) notes—that those rulers were either shamans or shamanic (Klein et al. 2002; McAnany 2001; Sanders 1995; Stuart 2005; Webster 1995, 2002; Zender 2004). Marc Zender (2004:77), for example, has refuted the archaeological, epigraphic, and iconographic evidence in support of ancient Maya shamanic rulership and concludes that "there is little contemporary support for . . . arguments in favor of the 'shaman king' concept." Stuart (2005:263) has similarly asserted a lack of epigraphic evidence for the concept, writing that a "shamanic model of Maya kingship . . . is difficult to discern through the Classic texts."

More broadly, it often remains unclear—and unquestioned—to what degree followers believed rulers' claims of association with divinity. Importantly, an assertion of supernatural mediation may be an ineffective strategy "if the messages that actors get . . . are quite different from the authoritarian propaganda intended by their senders" (Hutson 2002:65). One crucial aspect of Stephen D. Houston and David Stuart's work is their consideration not only of how rulers presented themselves but also of how the rest of the population would have perceived them. As Houston and Stuart (1996:308; see also 2001) write,

> We have described a system of legitimation predicated on dynastic assertions of divinity and monopolistic attempts to control divine mediation. These efforts may have met with variable success . . . Power derives from social and political discourse involving assertion, on the one hand, and acceptance or rejection on the other . . . The system of beliefs about Maya kings studied here is only one part of that equation. Whether it was widely held, whether it was believed firmly by the larger population, is another.

Monuments reflect not how things are but how their creators would like them to be. Indeed, monuments do not necessarily reflect accepted ideas but may be attempts to communicate and impose contested ones, and rulers often try hardest to communicate the ideas their subjects are least likely to accept (Bell 2007). Archaeologists thus cannot assume that subjects were receptive to rulers' assertions. Rather, we must ask whether, and demonstrate that, rulers' claims were accepted—as Joanne Baron (this volume) does in her consideration of the introduction of patron deity shrines at the Classic Maya site of La Corona.

THE RELATIONSHIPS BETWEEN RULERS AND FOLLOWERS

Another approach taken by scholars is to examine the various relationships between rulers and followers. Scholars adopting this approach emphasize that rulers and ruled formed part of a single, cohesive community and contend that the specific ways in which rulers and followers constituted and interacted within that community was essential to the exercise of political authority.

Some maintain that rulers fostered legitimacy by appropriating practices familiar to their followers, such as household rituals (Lucero 2003; see also McAnany and Plank 2001), and specifically ancestor veneration (McAnany 1995, 1998). Patricia A. McAnany (1995), for example, cogently argues that the practice of ancestor veneration emerged in an agrarian milieu during the Middle and Late Preclassic Periods (1000 BCE to 100 CE) and was later appropriated by Classic Maya rulers to legitimize their authority. As McAnany explains, the ancient Maya buried their dead in locations regularly inhabited by living members of their community. By doing so, the living could—through the dead—legitimize their claims to land and other resources. By the beginning of the Classic Period, however, the practice of using ancestors to substantiate proprietary claims to land was "appropriated . . . politicized, and used as means to sanction elite power and authority" (McAnany 1995:127). According to McAnany (1995:125), rulers thereby subverted "ancestor veneration from a practice that linked family and lineage to landholdings to one that validated the semidivinity of the royal lines . . . and in general sanctioned kingly prerogative"[1]—a process Baron (this volume) illustrates at La Corona. Classic Period rulers could thus reinforce their own authority by referencing the authority of their progenitors—through recording their dynastic genealogies in hieroglyphic texts and iconography and by maintaining their family shrines.

Others suggest the importance of activities that created communal identities and fostered a communal sense of belonging. Robert J. Sharer and Charles W. Golden (2004:32), for example, in a discussion of moral authority, emphasize the importance of a community's shared vision of socially correct behavior, and specifically the "shared view among both rulers and the ruled in the sanctions that gave rulers the rights to exercise authority over their subjects." Warren D. Hill and John E. Clark (2001) similarly focus on the importance of shared, communal identities to the exercise of political authority and look to competitive sports as a catalyst for creating and contesting communal identities. They argue that team sports, such as the ballgame, would have engendered a heightened sense of community identity, a polarization of community loyalties, and the emergence of community leaders. And Inomata (2006b, 2006a) stresses the importance not of competitive sports specifically, but of theatrical events more generally—any and all public spectacles that include an audience acting as observers and evaluators (Inomata 2006b:806; Inomata and Coben 2006:15). For Inomata (2006a:189), Classic Period Maya "mass spectacles constituted a key mechanism for the cohesion of polities and for the imposition and subversion of power."

One of the most important aspects of Inomata's argument is the pivotal role he assigns to the audience that watched and evaluated theatrical events. Scholars studying the emergence of institutionalized politically authoritative relationships have often focused on aggrandizers—self-interested political entrepreneurs vying for prestige (Clark and Blake 1994:17; Hayden 2011; but also see Blanton and Fargher 2008). For those who adopt models centered on the actions of aggrandizers, "leadership is a creation—a creation of followership" (Sahlins 1963:290). Inomata (2006b:809) questions this approach and argues instead that the "archaeological study of the development of large centralized polities should direct its attention not only to the political maneuvering of a small number of 'aggrandizers' but to the motivation and roles of an audience or the masses." Inomata also raises the possibility that the gathering of an audience may prefigure and produce authority figures. In this sense, his argument recalls that of Bruce Lincoln (1994), discussed below, who suggests that large audiences may fall quiet not to listen to the voice of another but to hear themselves through a speaker they take as one of their own. As Inomata (2006b:808) writes, "public events may have created a condition in which the emergence of central figures in the form of dramatic protagonists was tolerated or even desired and demanded by an audience." He thus suggests not that ambitious individuals became rulers by acquiring followers but that large groups of individuals may have preceded and allowed for the existence of rulers.

Still others argue that ancient Maya rulers tied themselves to their followers not by creating communal identities or fostering a communal sense of belonging but by making themselves essential to the daily lives of all (Freidel and Reilly 2009; Masson and Freidel 2013). Specifically, these scholars suggest that rulers proved themselves vital to a community by administering regional markets and ensuring supplies of food, water, and other goods. Lisa J. Lucero (2006a; 2006b), to take one example, emphasizes the politicization of environmental needs, specifically water. She notes the difficulties presented by the extreme seasonal variation in rainfall and the importance of available water in the dry season. Consequently, she suggests the possibility that "a ruler's ability to provide clean water during the dry season served as a key means for the political elite to acquire and maintain political power at some centers" (Lucero 2006a:127).

THE NEGOTIATION OF CONTRADICTIONS

The notion of contradictions has a long history in anthropological and archaeological thought, particularly in the form of the dialectic. Georg Wilhelm Friedrich Hegel (2004) originally posited the notion of the dialectic and argued that change occurs through contradictions. A proposition, or thesis, contains within itself, and leads to the expression of, its opposite, or antithesis. The struggle between the thesis and the antithesis leads to a new proposition, or synthesis (Moberg 2013:71). As Hegel (2004:647) wrote, "we are dealing with forms of consciousness each of which in realizing itself at the same time abolishes and transcends itself, [and] has for its result its own negation—and so passes into a higher form."

Marx adopted from Hegel the notion that history progresses through dialectical change, and that every historical epoch contains within itself the seeds of its own destruction. Whereas Hegel argued that dialectical change is driven by ideas, Marx stood Hegel on his head, arguing instead that change is driven by the forces and relations, or mode, of production. Furthermore, for Marx, the antithesis, or contradictory source of change, is class struggle. The capitalist epoch of history, for example, contains within it and gives rise to the proletariat, which will overturn the system and usher in a communist epoch (Marx and Engels 1970, 1967; Moberg 2013).

Practice theorists have also made use of the concept of the dialectic to describe the relationship between structure and agency. Bourdieu (1977:84), for one, argues for a dialectical relationship between structuring principles and the habitus. As outlined by Bourdieu, change to the structure and the habitus occurs because each influences and alters the other. By producing, and being produced by, the habitus, the structure contains within itself that which changes it. Similarly, by producing, and being produced by, the structure, the habitus also contains within itself that which changes it. Structuration theorists too use the notion of the dialectic, and of contradictions more generally, to explain social change. Giddens (1984), for example, like Bourdieu, posits a reflexive relationship between social rules and the actions of human agents.

Like social theorists more generally, archaeologists have emphasized contradictions as integral aspects of social relationships. Marxist archaeologists in particular have asserted the importance of the dialectic and of contradictions to an understanding of human societies, and particularly social change (McGuire 1993, 2002; McGuire and Saitta 1996; McGuire and Wurst 2002; Trigger 1993; Tilley 1984; Marqardt 1992; Spriggs 1984). Randall H. McGuire and Dean J. Saitta (1996), to take one example, argue that the contradictions between egalitarianism and hierarchy were a critical impetus for change in pre-Hispanic social organization in the southwestern United States. Christopher Tilley (1984), to take a second example, argues that contradictions between represented and actual social relationships fueled the change from the Funnel Neck Beaker tradition to the Battle-Axe/Corded-Ware tradition in southern Sweden.

Drawing on the theoretical and archaeological literature summarized in this chapter, I argue that the operation of political authority can usefully be understood in terms of the negotiation of contradictions. Although "conflict and contradictions are [often] viewed as major sources of social change" (Trigger 1993:176), I contend such paradoxes and incongruities can also be sources of stability. They can aid in the ongoing process of legitimation and "bind individuals and social groups with conflicting interests together" (McGuire, O'Donovan, and Wurst 2005:366).

Specifically, I maintain that the operation of political authority involves the negotiation of a series of contradictions. Generally speaking, rulers must simultaneously reinforce social inequality and promote social solidarity and social similarities. Anthropologists have long questioned the nature and function of centralized political authority, and they debate whether such authority is primarily coercive and maintains the privilege of the few or whether it is primarily integrative and coordinates and regulates societies for the benefit of all (Claessen and Skalník 1978; Cohen 1978; Engels 1970; Fried 1967, 1978; Gailey and Patterson 1987; Haas 1982; Jones and Krautz 1981; Service 1975, 1978; Yoffee 2005). Several scholars (e.g., Cohen 1978; Haas 1982) have suggested that authority need not have one true purpose and that it can simultaneously be coercive and integrative. I argue that it is not just that societies with centralized political authority are often both coercive and integrative. Rather, those exercising authority must adopt strategies that are at the same time coercive and integrative, that at once strengthen social differences and bolster social solidarity and similarities. Rulers, in other words, must adopt strategies that reinforce their own exclusive position at the top of the sociopolitical hierarchy and at the same time promote social cohesiveness and recognize the similarity of all. And individuals may recognize authority, at least in part, because they accept social inequality but still believe in social similarities and a communal identity.

More specifically, I maintain that rulers must emphasize the ways in which they are unique and distinct from all others yet at the same time demonstrate their commonalities with their subjects, rulers of other polities, and past rulers of their own polities. Followers, in turn—though their specific motivations must necessarily remain unknown to us—may choose to recognize authority because of the appeal of individuals who are unlike all others yet who simultaneously tie themselves to their community and to other leaders both present and past (Kurnick 2013).

By definition, political authority involves a separation between those who give commands and those who choose to obey them. To communicate and demonstrate their authority successfully, rulers must create and perpetuate dissimilarities between themselves and their followers. Perhaps for this reason, scholars studying the acquisition and maintenance of authority have tended to focus on the establishment and institutionalization of difference: there is a long tradition of understanding difference as the essence of authority. That trend is particularly evident in studies of kingship (Feeley-Harnik 1985; Helms 1998;

Hocart 1927; Quigley 2005; Sahlins 1981, 1985, 2008). Such an emphasis on difference is also an important component of Mann's IEMP model of social power, which frames authority in terms of the monopolization over various sources of social power and thus in terms of exclusivity and uniqueness: those who hold monopolies are necessarily distinct from all others.

Difference is unquestionably an integral component of rulership. Authority would cease to exist if rulers did not actively work to distinguish themselves. But the processes associated with acquiring, legitimizing, and exercising political authority are more complex, nuanced, and multifaceted. It is not enough for rulers merely to set themselves apart. They must also emphasize their sameness. Houston and Tom Cummins (2004:384–85) make just this point in their consideration of Mesoamerican and Andean royal bodies, arguing that "the regal frame had to be made into a paradox" that "undertakes at once common yet unique acts." The regal body wears clothing, has five senses, and exists as a material, earthly entity, yet simultaneously is unlike and distinct from all other bodies. Inomata and Houston (2001:13; see also Inomata 2001) also note the "inherently contradictory nature of kingship: at once remote and close: sacred and secular, protective and dangerous." And Houston and Stuart (2001:61) suggest that authority be understood in terms of such paradoxes, noting the existence of a "ruler who forms a collectivity with his people and yet is existentially distinct."

Emphasizing difference is thus not enough. On the one hand, rulers must emphasize their similarities to other members of their community. To demonstrate successfully their legitimacy and to engender the allegiance of subjects, rulers make manifest the ways in which they and their subjects are alike. Put differently, one method by which rulers garner the support of others is to be, in some respects, like them. And one reason subjects might choose to acknowledge authority is the appeal of an individual who is exceptional yet nevertheless relatable. Indeed, an increasing number of scholars have emphasized the importance of subjects in the constitution and reconstitution of authoritative relationships (Joyce, Bustamante, and Levine 2001; Inomata 2006b; Lucero 2003), and some assert a reflexive relationship in which rulers and followers influence one another, albeit to substantially different degrees (Lohse 2007). Put differently, "not only do commoners react to elite strategies, but elites react to commoner strategies as well" (Yaeger and Robin 2004:149).

To take one example, Jason Yaeger (2003) argues that, at Xunantunich, Belize, a "Xunantunich identity" shared by rulers and followers alike was crucial to the exercise of authority. As he writes,

> This identity was overtly and implicitly fostered and reinforced in political and religious celebrations at Xunantunich, but its creation was not a top-down process. Politically charged practices in hinterland settlements helped define the criteria of membership in this community and the rights and responsibilities of its members, and the community's existence was implicitly accepted and reinforced through daily practices throughout the Xunantunich hinterland. (Yaeger 2003:135–36)

Commonalities between rulers and subjects thus facilitate the operation of political authority.

In a discussion of authoritative speech, Lincoln makes a similar point. He asks,

> When an authorized speaker advances to an authorized and authorizing place, the audience falls quiet . . . How does this silence come to be? . . . What does the absence of speech signify? More pointedly, one might ask if it is the speaker . . . who silences an audience, or if an audience silences itself in order that the speaker might speak? Further, is it really the speaker who speaks to the audience in such situations, or does an audience speak to itself through the medium of the speaker? . . . We are led to wonder if, at least in those situations where the audience is most respectfully attentive, it might not be silencing itself in order to hear itself speak to itself through a speaker it takes to be its own representative, delegate, or incarnation? (Lincoln 1994:9–10)

Individuals may thus acknowledge authority because they are recognizing someone who is distinct, but also because they are recognizing someone who is like them.

On the other hand, rulers must also emphasize their similarities to, and differences from, their counterparts in other communities as well as their predecessors in their own communities. Many scholars have stressed the importance of foreign ties to the operation of political authority. In a consideration of leadership in Melanesia and Polynesia, Marshall David Sahlins (1963:290), for one, notes the importance not only of community relations but of foreign affiliations, writing that leaders must not only interact with their supporters but must also "fac[e] outward from [her or] his own faction." In a discussion of ancient Mesoamerica specifically, John E. Clark and Michael Blake (1994:19) similarly emphasize the importance of both intra- and inter-communal relations and argue that aspiring or successful leaders must "traffic outside their home communities and establish ties to individuals elsewhere."

Other scholars have stressed the importance of the past to the operation of authority. In a discussion of Classic Maya temple architecture, Karl Taube (1998:469) considers one function of temple facades "to portray what is enduring and constant in Maya kingship and religion, linking the generations of the living to the honored dead." And, as already discussed, many (e.g., Freidel and Schele 1988), particularly McAnany (1995, 1998), have documented the importance of ancestor veneration to Mesoamerican rulership.

Like these and other scholars, I maintain that politically authoritative relationships involve not just rulers and followers but other contemporary rulers and lines of past rulers. Importantly, political communities do not exist in isolation, either geographically or temporally. Rather, they are part of broader cultures and have their own lengthy histories. To be successful, rulers must show that they are part of the already-established customs and traditions of rulership yet maintain that they are nevertheless exceptional. They must demonstrate their likeness to rulers of other polities and to past leaders of their own polity yet still communicate their uniqueness. The force of already-established customs and traditions of rulership suggests another reason why individuals might have chosen to comply with authority: individuals may be more likely to accept established ideas rather than completely novel ones. Numerous scholars (e.g., Connerton 1989; Hobsbawm 1983; Pocock 1971; but see also Appadurai 1981) have emphasized this force of tradition. As Lucero (2003:525, 544) puts it, "abrupt or extreme change is much less likely to succeed because new ideas, beliefs, and practices are foreign and unacceptable," but "adopting and expanding familiar, traditional rites allow[s] . . . rulers to connect to those with whom they [wish] to build and maintain an unequal relationship."

In sum, in addition to understanding the exercise of political authority as the creation and maintenance of difference through the monopolization of sources of social power, scholars should also consider the exercise of political authority as attempts by rulers to emphasize their differences from, and similarities to, their subjects, rulers of other polities, and past leaders of their own polities. In addition to classifying political strategies as attempts by rulers to monopolize ideological, economic, or military power, scholars should also consider the importance of community, of extra-local connections, and of the past to the operation of political authority.

THE PURVIEW OF THE VOLUME

In the following chapters, contributors will present seven case studies that span the geographic breadth and temporal depth of pre-Columbian Mesoamerica. These case studies will consider societies ranging from Formative Period groups in coastal Oaxaca to the Classic Period Maya in the Petén region of Guatemala, to the Postclassic Period Tarascans in Michoacán, Mexico. The case studies will also use a variety of different data types, incorporating information from excavations, surveys, architectural configurations, and ethnohistoric documents, among other sources. Each case study, however, will grapple with the same two fundamental issues: how those exercising authority compel others to obey and why individuals choose to recognize, or to reject, such authority. And each case study will use the proposed framework along with newly gathered data to ascertain and understand the specific strategies and practical actions that engendered and reproduced, and sometimes negated, politically authoritative relationships in pre-Columbian Mesoamerica.

In chapter 2, using the Formative Period Maya community of Ceibal as a case study, Takeshi Inomata questions the applicability of concepts such as authority and legitimacy to premodern contexts. He rightly suggests that authority and legitimacy are not monolithic, coherent concepts and that scholars can and should consider various types of authority and various types of legitimacy, especially within the premodern world. He also cogently argues for a shift in scholarly emphasis from the actions of individual rulers to the interactions between the many different social groups that constitute communities.

In chapter 3, Arthur A. Joyce and colleagues examine the negotiations among the diverse social groups within the Formative Period lower Río Verde Valley in Oaxaca and consider how that polity emerged as well as how and why its existence was both tenuous and transient. Much like Inomata, Joyce and colleagues argue that authority is not singular and that an understanding of the dynamic and ever-changing relationships between various social groups is critical to an understanding of political authority.

In chapter 4, Christopher S. Beekman reassesses traditional arguments that Late Formative and Early Classic Period rulers in the Tequila valleys of central Jalisco were shaman kings who ruled through their ability to monopolize sacred power. He focuses instead on the co-occurrence of social institutions that contributed to the aggrandizement of individual lineages and those that addressed the needs of the entire community.

Joanne Baron, in chapter 5, examines the importance of religious ritual, and specifically practices of patron deity veneration, to the negotiation of politically authoritative relationships among the Classic Period Maya. She uses the community of La Corona as a case study to address how followers received claims of divine sanction and supernatural mediation made by rulers.

In chapter 6, Tatsuya Murakami focuses on the Classic Period city of Teotihuacan. He emphasizes the physical, tangible nature of political authority and communal identity and considers how similarities and differences in architecture reflect the complex and changing nature of relationships between Teotihuacan's rulers, bureaucracy, and intermediate elites.

In chapter 7, Bryce Davenport and Charles Golden, much like Murakami, emphasize the material nature of authority and examine the relationships between authority and territory. Through an exploration of the Mixteca Alta and Maya regions, they consider the connections between Mesoamerican rulership and landscape and argue that, although the bodies of rulers and commoners were fundamentally different, the actions those bodies performed to delimit the landscape were essentially similar.

Helen Perlstein Pollard, in chapter 8, argues for the importance of a new ideology to the creation of the Tarascan state in Michoacán during the Middle Postclassic Period. Central to this new ideology was a founding cultural hero, Tariacuri, who was simultaneously a member of the local Purépecha and the foreign Chichimec ethnic populations. Notably, Tarascan rulers expressed their similarities to, and differences from, those they ruled by, like Tariacuri, claiming both Chichimec and Purépecha ancestry.

In chapter 9, Simon Martin concludes the volume by placing into historical and theoretical context the key themes raised within the various chapters and considering potential future avenues for research.

Together, this introductory chapter, the case studies, and the concluding chapter aim to place the negotiation of contradictions at the fore of studies of political authority and promote an all-inclusive model that allows for variability in human practices across time and space. In doing so, the volume emphasizes not only the importance of difference but also of similarities. It eschews the notion of shaman kingship and suggests an alternative to the classic categorization of political strategies as ideological, economic, or military. Taken as a whole, the volume offers a theoretically based inquiry into political life in pre-Columbian Mesoamerica. It seeks to address fundamental questions and to speak to both the past and the present political moment.

ACKNOWLEDGMENTS

I would like to thank Takeshi Inomata and two anonymous reviewers for their constructive and invaluable comments on an earlier draft of this chapter. I would also like to thank the Louis J. Kolb Society of Fellows for their generous financial support.

NOTE

1. This statement does not mean, however, that farmers no longer venerated their ancestors. Rather, practices of ancestor veneration continued throughout the Classic Period at the family, lineage, and house level.

REFERENCES

Adams, Richard E. W. 2006. *Prehistoric Mesoamerica*. Third edition. Norman: University of Oklahoma Press.

Agamben, Giorgio. 1998. *Homo Sacer: Sovereign Power and Bare Life*. Translated by Daniel Heller-Roazen. Stanford: Stanford University Press.

Althusser, Louis. 1971. *Lenin and Philosophy and Other Essays*. Translated by Ben Brewster. New York: Monthly Review Press.

Appadurai, Arjun. 1981. "The Past as a Scarce Resource." *Man* 16(2): 201–19.

Bell, Ellen Elizabeth. 2007. "Early Classic Ritual Deposits Within the Copan Acropolis: The Material Foundations of Political Power at a Classic Period Maya Center." PhD diss., University of Pennsylvania.

Blanton, Richard E. 1998. "Beyond Centralization: Steps Toward a Theory of Egalitarian Behavior in Archaic States." In *Archaic States*, edited by Gary M. Feinman and Joyce Marcus, 137–72. Santa Fe: School of American Research Press.

Blanton, Richard E., and Lane F. Fargher. 2008. *Collective Action in the Formation of Pre-Modern States*. New York: Springer.

Blanton, Richard E., Gary M. Feinman, Stephen A. Kowalewski, and Peter N. Peregrine. 1996. "A Dual-Processual Theory for the Evolution of Mesoamerican Civilization." *Current Anthropology* 37(1): 1–14.

Blanton, Richard E., Stephen A. Kowalewski, Gary M. Feinman, and Laura M. Finsten. 1993. *Ancient Mesoamerica: A Comparison of Change in Three Regions*. Second edition. Cambridge: Cambridge University Press.

Bourdieu, Pierre. 1977. *Outline of a Theory of Practice*. Translated by Richard Nice. Cambridge: Cambridge University Press.

Bourdieu, Pierre. 1990. *The Logic of Practice*. Translated by Richard Nice. Stanford: Stanford University Press.

Bourdieu, Pierre. 1991. *Language and Symbolic Power*. Edited by John B. Thompson. Translated by Gino Raymond and Matthew Adamson. Cambridge, MA: Harvard University Press.

Bourdieu, Pierre. 1994. "Rethinking the State: Genesis and Structure of the Bureaucratic Field." Translated by Loic J. D. Wacquant and Samar Farage. *Sociological Theory* 12(1): 1–18.

Carmack, Robert M., Janine Gasco, and Gary H. Gossen. 1996. *The Legacy of Mesoamerica: History and Culture of a Native American Civilization*. Upper Saddle River, NJ: Prentice Hall.

Chase, Arlen F., and Diane Z. Chase. 1996. "More Than Kin and King: Centralized Political Organization among the Late Classic Maya." *Current Anthropology* 37(5): 803–10.

Claessen, Henri J. M., and Peter Skalník. 1978. "The Early State: Theories and Hypotheses." In *The Early State*, edited by Henri J. M. Claessen and Peter Skalník, 3–29. The Hague: Mouton.

Clark, John E. 1997. "The Arts of Government in Early Mesoamerica." *Annual Review of Anthropology* 26: 211–34.

Clark, John E., and Michael Blake. 1994. "The Power of Prestige: Competitive Generosity and the Emergence of Rank Societies in Lowland Mesoamerica." In *Factional Competition and Political Development in the New World*, edited by Elizabeth M. Brumfiel and John W. Fox, 17–30. Cambridge: Cambridge University Press.

Coe, Michael D. 1972. "Olmec Jaguars and Olmec Kings." In *The Cult of the Feline: A Conference in Pre-Columbian Iconography*, edited by Elizabeth P. Benson, 1–12. Washington, DC: Dumbarton Oaks.

Cohen, Ronald. 1978. Introduction to *Origins of the State: The Anthropology of Political Evolution*, edited by Ronald Cohen and Elman R. Service, 1–20. Philadelphia: Institute for the Study of Human Issues.

Connerton, Paul. 1989. *How Societies Remember*. Cambridge: Cambridge University Press.

Dobres, Marcia-Anne, and John E. Robb. 2000. *Agency in Archaeology*. New York: Routledge.

Dornan, Jennifer L. 2002. "Agency and Archaeology: Past, Present, and Future Directions." *Journal of Archaeological Method and Theory* 9(4): 303–29.

Drennan, Robert D., Christian E. Peterson, and Jake R. Fox. 2012. "Degrees and Kinds of Inequality." In *Pathways to Power: New Perspectives on the Emergence of Social Inequality*, edited by Price T. Douglas and Gary M. Feinman, 45–76. New York: Springer.

Earle, Timothy. 1997. *How Chiefs Come to Power: The Political Economy in Prehistory*. Stanford: Stanford University Press.

Eliade, Mircea. 1972. *Shamanism: Archaic Techniques of Ecstasy*. Princeton: Princeton University.

Engels, Friedrich. 1970. *The Origin of the Family, Private Property, and the State*. New York: International Publishers.

Evans, Susan Toby. 2004. *Ancient Mexico and Central America: Archaeology and Culture History*. London: Thames & Hudson.
Feeley-Harnik, Gillian. 1985. "Issues in Divine Kingship." *Annual Review of Anthropology* 14: 273–313.
Feinman, Gary M. 2001. "Mesoamerican Political Complexity: The Corporate-Network Dimension." In *From Leaders to Rulers*, edited by Jonathan Haas, 151–75. New York: Kluwer Academic/Plenum.
Foucault, Michel. 1979. *Discipline and Punish: The Birth of the Prison*. Translated by Alan Sheridan. New York: Vintage.
Foucault, Michel. 2003. *"Society Must Be Defended": Lectures at the Collège de France, 1975–1976*. Edited by Mauro Bertani and Alessandro Fontana. Translated by David Macey. New York: Picador.
Foucault, Michel. 2007. *Security, Territory, Population: Lectures at the Collège de France, 1977–1978*. Edited by Michel Senellart. Translated by Graham Burchell. New York: Picador.
Fox, John W., Garrett W. Cook, Arlen F. Chase, and Diane Z. Chase. 1996. "Questions of Political and Economic Integration: Segmentary Versus Centralized States among the Ancient Maya." *Current Anthropology* 37(5): 795–801.
Freidel, David. 2008. "Maya Divine Kingship." In *Religion and Power: Divine Kingship in the Ancient World and Beyond*, edited by Nicole Brisch, 191–206. Chicago: Oriental Institute of the University of Chicago.
Freidel, David, and F. Kent Reilly III. 2009. "The Flesh of God: Cosmology, Food, and the Origins of Political Power in Ancient Southeastern Mesoamerica." In *Pre-Columbian Foodways: Interdisciplinary Approaches to Food, Culture, and Markets in Ancient Mesoamerica*, edited by John Edward Staller and Michael D. Carrasco, 635–80. New York: Springer.
Freidel, David, and Linda Schele. 1988. "Kingship in the Late Preclassic Maya Lowlands: The Instruments and Places of Ritual Power." *American Anthropologist* 90(3): 547–67.
Freidel, David, Linda Schele, and Joy Parker. 1993. *Maya Cosmos: Three Thousand Years on the Shaman's Path*. New York: William Morrow.
Fried, Morton H. 1967. *The Evolution of Political Society: An Essay in Political Anthropology*. New York: Random House.
Fried, Morton H. 1978. "The State, the Chicken, or the Egg; Or, What Came First?" In *Origins of the State: The Anthropology of Political Evolution*, edited by Ronald Cohen and Elman R. Service, 35–47. Philadelphia: Institute for the Study of Human Issues.

Furst, Peter T. 1968. "The Olmec Were-Jaguar Motif in the Light of Ethnographic Reality." In *Dumbarton Oaks Conference on the Olmec: October 28th and 29th, 1967*, edited by Elizabeth P. Benson, 143–74. Washington, DC: Dumbarton Oaks.

Furst, Peter T. 1981. "Jaguar Baby or Toad Mother: A New Look at an Old Problem in Olmec Iconography." In *The Olmec and Their Neighbors: Essays in Memory of Matthew W. Stirling*, edited by Matthew Williams Stirling, Michael D. Coe, and David C. Grove, 149–62. Washington, DC: Dumbarton Oaks.

Furst, Peter T. 1995. "Shamanism, Transformation, and Olmec Art." In *The Olmec World: Ritual and Rulership*, 69–81. Princeton: Art Museum, Princeton University.

Gailey, Christine W., and Thomas C. Patterson. 1987. "Power Relations and State Formation." In *Power Relations and State Formation*, edited by Thomas C. Patterson and Christine W. Gailey, 1–26. Washington, DC: American Anthropological Association.

Giddens, Anthony. 1984. *The Constitution of Society: Outline of the Theory of Structuration*. Berkeley: University of California Press.

Gramsci, Antonio. 1999. *Selections from the Prison Notebooks of Antonio Gramsci*. Edited by Quentin Hoare and Geoffrey Nowell Smith. London: ElecBook.

Guernsey, Julia. 2006. *Ritual & Power in Stone: The Performance of Rulership in Mesoamerican Izapan Style Art*. Austin: University of Texas Press.

Guernsey, Julia, and Michael Love. 2005. "Late Preclassic Expressions of Authority on the Pacific Slope." In *Lords of Creation: The Origins of Sacred Maya Kingship*, edited by Virginia M. Fields and Dorie Reents-Budet, 37–43. London: Scala.

Guernsey Kappelman, Julia. 1997. "Of Macaws and Men: Late Preclassic Cosmology and Political Ideology in Izapan-Style Monuments." PhD diss., University of Texas at Austin.

Guernsey Kappelman, Julia. 2001. "Sacred Geography at Izapa and the Performance of Rulership." In *Landscape and Power in Ancient Mesoamerica*, edited by Rex Koontz, Kathryn Reese-Taylor, and Annabeth Headrick, 81–135. Boulder: Westview.

Haas, Jonathan. 1982. *The Evolution of the Prehistoric State*. New York: Columbia University Press.

Hayden, Brian 2011. "Big Man, Big Heart? The Political Role of Aggrandizers in Egalitarian and Transegalitarian Societies." In *For the Greater Good of All: Perspectives on Individualism, Society, and Leadership*, edited by Donelson R. Forsyth and Crystal L. Hoyt, 101–18. New York: Palgrave Macmillan.

Hegel, G.W.F. 2004. "Dialectics." In *Literary Theory: An Anthology*, edited by Julie Rivkin and Michael Ryan, 647–49. Malden, MA: Blackwell.

Helms, Mary W. 1998. *Access to Origins: Affines, Ancestors, and Aristocrats*. Austin: University of Texas Press.

Hill, Warren D., and John E. Clark. 2001. "Sports, Gambling, and Government: America's First Social Compact?" *American Anthropologist* 103(2): 331–45.

Hobsbawm, Eric. 1983. "Introduction: Inventing Traditions." In *The Invention of Tradition*, 1–14. Cambridge: Cambridge University Press.

Hocart, A. M. 1927. *Kingship*. London: Oxford University Press.

Hodder, Ian. 2006. "The Spectacle of Daily Performance at Çatalhöyük." In *Archaeology of Performance: Theaters of Power, Community, and Politics*, edited by Takeshi Inomata and Lawrence S. Coben, 81–102. Lanham, MD: AltaMira.

Houston, Stephen D., and Tom Cummins. 2004. "Body, Presence, and Space in Andean and Mesoamerican Rulership." In *Palaces of the Ancient New World*, edited by Susan Toby Evans and Joanne Pillsbury, 359–98. Washington, DC: Dumbarton Oaks.

Houston, Stephen D., and David Stuart. 1996. "Of Gods, Glyphs, and Kings: Divinity and Rulership Among the Classic Maya." *Antiquity* 70: 289–312.

Houston, Stephen D., and David Stuart. 2001. "Peopling the Classic Maya Court." In *Royal Courts of the Ancient Maya*, vol. 1, *Theory, Comparison, and Synthesis*, edited by Takeshi Inomata and Stephen D. Houston, 54–83. Boulder: Westview.

Hutson, Scott R. 2002. "Built Space and Bad Subjects: Domination and Resistance at Monte Alban, Oaxaca, Mexico." *Journal of Social Archaeology* 2(1): 53–80.

Iannone, Gyles 2002. "Annales History and the Ancient Maya State: Some Observations on the 'Dynamic Model.'" *American Anthropologist* 104(1): 68–78.

Inomata, Takeshi. 2001. "King's People: Classic Maya Courtiers in a Comparative Perspective." In *Royal Courts of the Ancient Maya*, vol. 1, *Theory, Comparison, and Synthesis*, edited by Takeshi Inomata and Stephen D. Houston, 27–53. Boulder: Westview.

Inomata, Takeshi. 2006a. "Politics and Theatricality in Mayan Society." In *Archaeology of Performance: Theaters of Power, Community, and Politics*, edited by Takeshi Inomata and Lawrence S. Coben, 187–221. Lanham, MD: AltaMira.

Inomata, Takeshi. 2006b. "Plazas, Performers, and Spectators: Political Theaters of the Classic Maya." *Current Anthropology* 47(5): 805–42.

Inomata, Takeshi, and Lawrence S. Coben. 2006. "Overture: An Introduction to Archaeological Theater." In *Archaeology of Performance: Theaters of Power, Community, and Politics*, edited by Takeshi Inomata and Lawrence S. Coben, 11–44. Lanham, MD: AltaMira.

Inomata, Takeshi, and Stephen D. Houston. 2001. "Opening the Royal Maya Court." In *Royal Courts of the Ancient Maya*, vol. 1, *Theory, Comparison, and

Synthesis, edited by Takeshi Inomata and Stephen D. Houston, 3–23. Boulder: Westview.

Johansen, Peter G., and Andrew M. Bauer. 2011. "Reconfiguring the 'Political' in the Reconstruction of Past Political Production." In *The Archaeology of Politics: The Materiality of Political Practice and Action in the Past*, edited by Peter G. Johansen and Andrew M. Bauer, 1–19. Newcastle upon Tyne: Cambridge Scholars.

Jones, Grant D., and Robert R. Krautz. 1981. "Issues in the Study of New World State Formation." In *The Transition to Statehood in the New World*, edited by Grant D. Jones and Robert R. Krautz, 3–34. Cambridge: Cambridge University Press.

Joyce, Arthur A. 2004. "Sacred Space and Social Relations in the Valley of Oaxaca." In *Mesoamerican Archaeology: Theory and Practice*, edited by Julia A. Hendon and Rosemary A. Joyce, 192–216. Oxford: Blackwell.

Joyce, Arthur A., Laura Arnaud Bustamante, and Marc N. Levine. 2001. "Commoner Power: A Case Study From the Classic Period Collapse on the Oaxaca Coast." *Journal of Archaeological Method and Theory* 8(4): 343–85.

Joyce, Arthur A., and Errin T. Weller. 2007. "Commoner Rituals, Resistance, and the Classic-to-Postclassic Transition in Ancient Mesoamerica." In *Commoner Ritual and Ideology in Ancient Mesoamerica*, edited by Nancy Gonlin and Jon C. Lohse, 143–84. Boulder: University Press of Colorado.

Joyce, Arthur A., and Marcus Winter. 1996. "Ideology, Power, and Urban Society in Pre-Hispanic Oaxaca." *Current Anthropology* 37(1): 33–47.

Joyce, Rosemary A. 2004. "Mesoamerica: A Working Model for Archaeology." In *Mesoamerican Archaeology: Theory and Practice*, edited by Julia A. Hendon and Rosemary A. Joyce, 1–42. Oxford: Blackwell.

Kertzer, David I. 1988. *Ritual, Politics, and Power*. New Haven: Yale University Press.

Kirchhoff, Paul 1952. "Meso-America." In *Heritage of Conquest: The Ethnology of Middle America*, edited by Sol Tax, 17–30. New York: Free Press.

Klein, Cecelia F., Eulogio Guzmán, Elisa C. Mandell, and Maya Stanfield-Mazzi. 2002. "The Role of Shamanism in Mesoamerican Art: A Reassessment." *Current Anthropology* 43(3): 383–419.

Kurnick, Sarah. 2013. "Negotiating the Contradictions of Political Authority: An Archaeological Case Study from Callar Creek, Belize." PhD diss. University of Pennsylvania.

Lincoln, Bruce. 1994. *Authority: Construction and Corrosion*. Chicago: University of Chicago Press.

Lohse, Jon C. 2007. "Commoner Ritual, Commoner Ideology: (Sub-) Alternate Views of Social Complexity in Prehispanic Mesoamerica." In *Commoner Ritual and Ideology in Ancient Mesoamerica*, edited by Nancy Gonlin and Jon C. Lohse, 1–32. Boulder: University Press of Colorado.

Lucero, Lisa J. 2003. "The Politics of Ritual: The Emergence of Classic Maya Rulers." *Current Anthropology* 44(4): 523–58.

Lucero, Lisa J. 2006a. "The Political and Sacred Power of Water in Classic Maya Society." In *Precolumbian Water Management: Ideology, Ritual, and Power*, edited by Lisa J. Lucero and Barbara W. Fash, 116–28. Tucson: University of Arizona Press.

Lucero, Lisa J. 2006b. *Water and Ritual: The Rise and Fall of Classic Maya Rulers*. Austin: University of Texas Press.

Mann, Michael. 1986. *The Sources of Social Power*. Vol. 1, *A History of Power from the Beginning to A.D. 1760*. Cambridge: Cambridge University Press.

Marcus, Joyce. 1993. "Ancient Maya Political Organization." In *Lowland Maya Civilization in the Eighth Century A.D.: A Symposium at Dumbarton Oaks 7th and 8th October 1989*, edited by Jeremy A. Sabloff and John S. Henderson, 111–83. Washington, DC: Dumbarton Oaks.

Marqardt, William H. 1992. "Dialectical Archaeology." *Archaeological Method and Theory* 4: 101–40.

Marx, Karl, and Friedrich Engels. 1967. *Manifesto of the Communist Party*. London: Penguin.

Marx, Karl, and Friedrich Engels. 1970. *The German Ideology*. Edited by C. J. Arthur. New York: International Publishers.

Masson, Marilyn A., and David Freidel. 2013. "Wide Open Spaces: A Long View of the Importance of Maya Market Exchange." In *Merchants, Trade and Exchange in the Pre-Columbian World*, edited by Kenneth G. Hirth and Joanne Pillsbury, 201–28. Washington, DC: Dumbarton Oaks.

Masson, Marilyn A., and Heather Orr. 1998. "The Writing on the Wall: Political Representation and Sacred Geography at Monte Alban." In *The Sowing and the Dawning: Termination, Dedication, and Transformation in the Archaeological and Ethnographic Record of Mesoamerica*, edited by Shirley Boteler Mock, 165–75. Albuquerque: University of New Mexico Press.

Masson, Marilyn A., and Michael E. Smith. 2000. "Introduction: Mesoamerican Civilizations." In *The Ancient Civilizations of Mesoamerica: A Reader*, edited by Michael E. Smith and Marilyn A. Masson, 1–14. Oxford: Blackwell.

McAnany, Patricia A. 1995. *Living with the Ancestors: Kinship and Kingship in Ancient Maya Society*. Austin: University of Texas Press.

McAnany, Patricia A. 1998. "Ancestors and the Classic Maya Built Environment." In *Function and Meaning in Classic Maya Architecture: A Symposium at Dumbarton Oaks*, edited by Stephen D. Houston, 271–98. Washington, DC: Dumbarton Oaks.

McAnany, Patricia A. 2001. "Cosmology and the Institutionalization of Hierarchy in the Maya Region." In *From Leaders to Rulers*, 125–50. New York: Kluwer Academic/Plenum.

McAnany, Patricia A., and Shannon Plank. 2001. "Perspectives on Actors, Gender Roles, and Architecture at Classic Maya Courts and Households." In *Royal Courts of the Ancient Maya*, vol. 1, *Theory, Comparison, and Synthesis*, edited by Takeshi Inomata and Stephen D. Houston, 84–129. Boulder: Westview.

McGuire, Randall H. 1993. "Archaeology and Marxism." *Archaeological Method and Theory* 5: 101–57.

McGuire, Randall H. 2002. *A Marxist Archaeology*. Second edition. Clinton Corners, NY: Percheron.

McGuire, Randall H., Maria O'Donovan, and LouAnn Wurst. 2005. "Probing Praxis in Archaeology: The Last Eighty Years." *Rethinking Marxism* 17(3): 355–72.

McGuire, Randall H., and Dean J. Saitta. 1996. "Although They Have Petty Captains, They Obey Them Badly: The Dialectics of Prehispanic Western Pueblo Social Organization." *American Antiquity* 61(2): 197–216.

McGuire, Randall H., and LouAnn Wurst. 2002. "Struggling with the Past." *International Journal of Historical Archaeology* 6(2): 85–94.

Meskell, Lynn. 2005. "Object Orientations." In *Archaeologies of Materiality*, edited by Lynn Meskell, 1–17. Oxford: Blackwell.

Moberg, Mark. 2013. *Engaging Anthropological Theory: A Social and Political History*. London: Routledge.

Oakley, Francis. 2006. *Kingship: The Politics of Enchantment*. Oxford: Wiley-Blackwell.

Pauketat, Timothy R. 2000. "The Tragedy of the Commoners." In *Agency in Archaeology*, edited by Marcia-Anne Dobres and John E. Robb, 113–29. London: Routledge.

Pocock, J. G. A. 1971. "Time, Institutions and Action: An Essay on Traditions and Their Understanding." In *Politics, Language and Time: Essays on Political Thought and History*, 233–72. New York: Atheneum.

Quigley, Declan. 2005. "Introduction: The Character of Kingship." In *The Character of Kingship*, edited by Declan Quigley, 1–23. Oxford: Berg.

Reilly, F. Kent. 1989. "The Shaman in Transformation Pose: A Study of the Theme of Rulership in Olmec Art." *Record of the Art Museum, Princeton University* 48(2): 4–21.

Reilly, F. Kent. 1991. "Olmec Iconographic Influences on the Symbols of Maya Rulership: An Examination of Possible Sources." In *Sixth Palenque Round Table, 1986*, edited by Virginia M. Fields, 151–66. Norman: University of Oklahoma Press.

Reilly, F. Kent. 1994. "Visions to Another World: Art, Shamanism, and Political Power in Middle Formative Mesoamerica." PhD diss., University of Texas at Austin.

Reilly, F. Kent. 1995. "Art, Ritual, and Rulership in the Olmec World." In *The Olmec World: Ritual and Rulership*, 27–45. Princeton: Art Museum, Princeton University.

Rice, Prudence M. 2004. *Maya Political Science: Time, Astronomy, and the Cosmos*. Austin: University of Texas Press.

Rice, Prudence M. 2007. *Maya Calendar Origins: Monuments, Mythistory, and the Materialization of Time*. Austin: University of Texas Press.

Rice, Prudence M. 2008. "Time, Power, and the Maya." *Latin American Antiquity* 19(3): 275–98.

Sahlins, Marshall David. 1963. "Poor Man, Rich Man, Big-Man, Chief: Political Types in Melanesia and Polynesia." *Comparative Studies in Society and History* 5(3): 285–303.

Sahlins, Marshall David. 1981. "The Stranger-King or Dumézil among the Fijians." *Journal of Pacific History* 16(3): 107–32.

Sahlins, Marshall David. 1985. *Islands of History*. Chicago: University of Chicago Press.

Sahlins, Marshall David. 2008. "The Stranger-King or, Elementary Forms Of The Politics Of Life." *Indonesia and the Malay World* 36(105): 177–99.

Sanders, William T. 1995. "A Skeptical Response." *Cambridge Archaeological Journal* 5(1): 130–33.

Sanders, William T., and Barbara J. Price. 1968. *Mesoamerica: The Evolution of a Civilization*. New York: Random House.

Schele, Linda, and David Freidel. 1990. *A Forest of Kings: The Untold Story of the Ancient Maya*. New York: William Morrow.

Scott, James C. 1990. *Domination and the Arts of Resistance: Hidden Transcripts*. New Haven: Yale University Press.

Scott, James C. 1998. *Seeing Like a State: How Certain Schemes to Improve the Human Condition Have Failed*. New Haven: Yale University Press.

Service, Elman R. 1975. *Origins of the State and Civilization: The Process of Cultural Evolution*. New York: W. W. Norton.

Service, Elman R. 1978. "Classical and Modern Theories of the Origin of Government." In *Origins of the State: The Anthropology of Political Evolution*, edited by Ronald Cohen and Elman R. Service, 1–20. Philadelphia: Institute for the Study of Human Issues.

Sharer, Robert J., and Charles W. Golden. 2004. "Kingship and Polity: Conceptualizing the Maya Body Politic." In *Continuities and Changes in Maya*

Archaeology: Perspectives at the Millennium, edited by Charles W. Golden and Greg Borgstede, 23–50. New York: Routledge.
Sharer, Robert J., and Loa P. Traxler. 2006. *The Ancient Maya*. Sixth edition. Stanford: Stanford University Press.
Smith, Adam T. 2003. *The Political Landscape: Constellations of Authority in Early Complex Polities*. Berkeley: University of California Press.
Smith, Adam T. 2011a. "Figuring the Political: The Stuff of Sovereignty in a Post-Evolutionary Archaeology." In *The Archaeology of Politics: The Materiality of Political Practice and Action in the Past*, edited by Peter G. Johansen and Andrew M. Bauer, 354–61. Newcastle upon Tyne: Cambridge Scholars.
Smith, Adam T. 2011b. "Archaeologies of Sovereignty." *Annual Review of Anthropology* 40: 415–32.
Smith, Adam T. 2012. "The Political Machine: Sense, Sensibility, and Sentiment in the Late Bronze Age Caucasus." Paper presented at the University of Pennsylvania Department of Anthropology Colloquium, Philadelphia.
Spinden, Herbert Joseph. 1917. *Ancient Civilizations of Mexico and Central America*. New York: American Museum of Natural History.
Spriggs, Matthew. 1984. "Another Way of Telling: Marxist Perspectives in Archaeology." In *Marxist Perspectives in Archaeology*, edited by Matthew Spriggs, 1–9. Cambridge: Cambridge University Press.
Stuart, David. 1996. "Kings of Stone: A Consideration of Stelae in Ancient Maya Ritual and Representation." *Res* 29/30: 148–71.
Stuart, David. 2005. "Ideology and Classic Maya Kingship." In *A Catalyst for Ideas: Anthropological Archaeology and the Legacy of Douglas Schwartz*, edited by Vernon L. Scarborough, 257–85. Santa Fe: School of American Research Press.
Taube, Karl. 1998. "The Jade Hearth: Centrality, Rulership, and the Classic Maya Temple." In *Function and Meaning in Classic Maya Architecture*, edited by Stephen D. Houston, 427–78. Washington, DC: Dumbarton Oaks.
Thomas, Julian. 2004. *Archaeology and Modernity*. New York: Routledge.
Tilley, Christopher. 1984. "Ideology and the Legitimation of Power in the Middle Neolithic of Southern Sweden." In *Ideology, Power and Prehistory*, edited by Daniel Miller and Christopher Tilley, 111–46. Cambridge: Cambridge University Press.
Trigger, Bruce G. 1993. "Marxism in Contemporary Western Archaeology." *Archaeological Method and Theory* 5: 159–200.
Weaver, Muriel Porter. 1993. *The Aztecs, Maya, and Their Predecessors: Archaeology of Mesoamerica*. Third edition. San Diego: Academic Press.
Weber, Max. 1978. *Economy and Society: An Outline of Interpretive Sociology*. Edited by Guenther Roth and Claus Wittich. Berkeley: University of California Press.

Webster, David L. 1995. "Maya Shaman-Kings: Some Evolutionary Implications." *Cambridge Archaeological Journal* 5(1): 120–22.

Webster, David L. 2002. "Groundhogs and Kings: Issues of Divine Rulership among the Classic Maya." In *Incidents of Archaeology in Central America and Yucatan: Essays in Honor of Edwin M. Shook*, edited by Michael Love, Marion Popenoe de Hatch, and Héctor L. Escobedo, 433–58. Lanham, MD: University Press of America.

Yaeger, Jason. 2003. "Untangling the Ties That Bind: The City, Countryside, and the Nature of Maya Urbanism at Xunantunich, Belize." In *The Social Construction of Ancient Cities*, edited by Monica I. Smith, 121–46. Washington, DC: Smithsonian Institution Press.

Yaeger, Jason, and Cynthia Robin. 2004. "Heterogeneous Hinterlands: The Social and Political Organization of Commoner Settlements near Xunantunich, Belize." In *Ancient Maya Commoners*, edited by Jon C. Lohse and Fred Valdez, 147–73. Austin: University of Texas Press.

Yoffee, Norman. 2005. *Myths of the Archaic State: Evolution of the Earliest Cities, States and Civilizations*. Cambridge: Cambridge University Press.

Zender, Marc. 2004. "A Study of Classic Maya Priesthood." PhD diss., University of Calgary.

2

Theories of Power and Legitimacy in Archaeological Contexts

The Emergent Regime of Power at the Formative Maya Community of Ceibal, Guatemala

Takeshi Inomata

In her stimulating introductory chapter of this volume, Sarah Kurnick urges us to examine theoretical questions of politics in pre-Columbian Mesoamerica. I strongly agree with her proposal that archaeologists should engage with political theory more explicitly and that in doing so, archaeologists have to think about the implications and potential contributions of our work to the present. In examining the theoretical issues that Kurnick raises, I address an archaeological case from the early Middle Formative Period (1000–700 BCE) at the lowland Maya site of Ceibal, Guatemala. It was a time when the first fully sedentary communities with ceramic use emerged in the Maya lowlands. At Ceibal, a formalized spatial plan was established at the beginning of the site's occupation. Some form of social inequality with emergent elites was already present, but it took several more centuries before the establishment of what we might call Maya rulership. In other words, I am interested in the origin, or genesis, of social intuitions and in how such studies contribute to the understanding of what came after, as discussed by Pierre Bourdieu and raised by Kurnick.

An important concern of mine is the applicability of modern political theory to archaeological contexts. We should not forget that most political theories have been developed specifically for modern, and often Western, contexts. As we apply these theories to vastly different contexts that Mesoamerican archaeologists typically deal with, we need to evaluate critically the

DOI: 10.5876/9781607324164.c002

appropriateness and limitation of such operations. We need to examine which concepts and assumptions may be applicable to specific archaeological cases and which ones should be modified or left out. By saying this, I am not questioning the importance of modern political theory. Unlike some of my colleagues who advocate the development of archaeologists' own theory (Sullivan 2008), I do not see necessity or validity to create a different set of social or political theory just for archaeology. While archaeologists offer unique perspectives through long time scales and explicit engagement with materiality, archaeological information is typically fragmentary and our interpretation of the past is built with explicit or implicit references to our knowledge of our own society and of historically closely related ones. Engagement with modern social theory is of critical importance for archaeologists.

At the same time, this does not mean that archaeologists should be simple borrowers of theory. As Kurnick notes, we should think about how we might contribute to the understanding of the contemporary world. To me, the central aspect for archaeologists in this regard is participation in reflexive theoretical discourse rather than providing concrete "lessons" from the past. Evaluating the applicability of modern social theories means explicating hidden assumptions held in their proposals about our own society and humanity in general. In this regard, the archaeological study of origin is not really about when and where the earliest forms of our social institutions emerged. Some past institutions may look similar to ours, and archaeologists may apply the same terms such as *state*, *authority*, and *ruler*. But we should not uncritically project back to the past our own concepts embedded in the modern society. The critical part of archaeological studies should be to examine how these institutions might be different from ours, and how they have transformed over time. Such an exercise should also reveal our own assumptions tied to the modern world in which we live. An important contribution of archaeology should be disclosing—or at least providing materials through which to explore—the historical situatedness of our taken-for-granted ideas about humanity and human society.

More specifically, my theoretical concerns revolve around the following points: (1) the construction of historical or archaeological narratives and the dangers of imposing our own preexisting views, particularly regarding relations between action, motivation, and strategy; (2) the applicability of concepts derived from modern political theory, including authority and legitimacy; and (3) the theoretical and analytical balance between individual and society, which may be highlighted in the discussion of power and rulers. In discussing these issues, I address what I perceive as common problems in theoretical perspectives held by many archaeologists. The original version of Kurnick's introductory chapter guided my discussion. Although she subsequently made revisions to her chapter, I have decided to keep the original structure of my discussion, hoping that our chapters provide a sense of dialog among archaeologists.

CONSTRUCTIONS OF HISTORICAL NARRATIVES

It is impossible not to project our own preexisting narratives onto the past to a certain degree. Our task should be to evaluate critically our own implicit assumptions. In this regard, a particularly important issue is the relation between action, motivation, and strategy. Many archaeologists ask what strategies rulers used in attempts to acquire and maintain political authority, as Kurnick notes. I have to wonder if this is the right question to ask. This question appears to assume that gaining and maintaining political authority is a goal of all rulers and that they actively and rationally strategize for this purpose. A resulting narrative would be, "rulers did this and that to acquire and maintain authority." This is a typical course of action for modern politicians, but did all rulers in the past think and act in a similar manner?

I have to wonder to what degree this question is framed in the notions of personhood and agency deeply embedded in our own modern experience. To me, this is not simply a question of language. It concerns some of the central theoretical issues that we need to confront. Such a narrative would essentialize human action in a one-dimensional, highly functionalist explanation that is probably not unrelated to modern society's strong emphasis on functionality, rationality, and goal-seeking behavior. Historically known rulers include diverse personalities, ranging from highly capable and motivated ones to reluctant rulers who did not have other choices but to take the throne, to incapable or disengaged ones whose royal status was maintained only by the efforts of councilors, and even to mentally challenged ones. If so, can we assume that it is the ruler who is making strategies?

For a few decades, many cultural anthropologists have highlighted negotiation among diverse personalities, views, ideas, and perceptions, leading to the critique of traditional anthropological concepts of culture and emic views as homogeneous or coherent entities, which may indeed be impositions of researchers' own views, or at least researchers' selective extraction and simplification of diversity in what natives say and do (Abu-Lughod 1991). Feminist and gender studies have further highlighted differences in views and perceptions that exist in a single "culture." Many archaeologists have embraced these theoretical developments and the notion of multivocality, but the temptation of essentializing narratives of the past remains strong.

An aspect of this issue may be the assumption of one-directional causality from motivation to strategy to action. The aforementioned question starts from the archaeologically or textually observable external state (a ruler achieving or staying in the position of authority) and assumes that there were specific internal conditions in the individual—that is, motivation and planning leading to the resulting state. In addition, it is assumed that some of these internal states are recoverable. The diversity in motivations and perceptions that exists among different individuals puts the recovery of internal states in question. Moreover, various scholars have come to question the assumption of one-directional causality from motivation to action. We need to consider and examine how people's actions also shape their ideas, perceptions, and motivations. This recursive relation between action and thought is the central premise of practice theory (Bourdieu 1977; Giddens 1984) and has also been elaborated by performance theory (Austin 1962; Bell 1997; Inomata and Coben 2006; Inomata 2006a; Inomata and Tsukamoto 2014). Practice theory has been particularly influential among archaeologists, but its central premise appears to be often left out.

A recent exciting development is the convergence of social sciences, cognitive sciences, and philosophy that further emphasizes the recursive relation of thought and action. Cognitive sciences, in particular, provide a scientific grounding to the philosophical perspective of practice theory (Shore 1996; Strauss and Quinn 1997). Antonio R. Damasio (1994, 1999, 2003), for example, stresses the duality and inseparability of mind and body, and thus of thought and action, by demonstrating that emotion, which according to him is tied to physical conditions of the body, plays a central role in this duality. Even more suggestive for archaeologists interested in practice theory is the growing understanding of the unconscious in human cognitive processes, which helps us explain how what Bourdieu calls practical knowledge works. Humans process a substantial part of our daily routine, including fairly complex operations, at an unconscious level and make a series of decisions without consciously evaluating them. In other words, a social agent does not have access to a substantial part of his or her mental process, and we are often unable to explain specific reasoning, motivations, and logics behind many of our actions and decisions (Hassin et al. 2005; Wegner 2002; Wilson 2002). More importantly, people are, in most cases, unaware of this inaccessibility to their own mental process, holding an illusion of conscious will (Galdi et al. 2008; Wegner 2002). Various experiments and studies demonstrate that people often give explanations for motives and reasons for their decisions and actions retrospectively, without noticing their retrospective nature (Johansson et al. 2005; Johansson et al. 2006; Nisbett and Wilson 1977). Instead of motivations and reasoning leading to actions and outcomes, people often perceive or reconstruct their motivations retrospectively based on the outcomes of the action, and often by referring to commonly accepted forms of discourse. Various philosophers, linguists, and anthropologists are incorporating such results to build a broader understanding of the relation between thought and action (Johnson 2006; Lakoff and Johnson 1999; Searle 2000), but archaeologists have been slow to incorporate this significant interdisciplinary trend (for an important exception, see Boivin 2008). A central problem appears to be that many archaeologists continue to hold the illusion of conscious will and extend it to their narratives of the past.

These understandings compel us to explore different perspectives. We need to be cautious and critical in assuming people's motivations and reasons. Such practices often fall into the imposition of researchers' own narratives. We need to focus more on the observable dimensions of action and speech and explore how they shaped, and were shaped by, prevailing forms of practice and discourse. This means that we have to shift our emphasis from assumptions on the attempts and objectives of rulers to their practice and performance and the social institution of rulership.

AUTHORITY AND LEGITIMACY

If our purpose is theoretical refinement, I think that before asking how rulers achieved authority, we should probably ask whether concepts such as authority and legitimacy are appropriate for the study of premodern contexts, and what kinds of assumption are embedded in these terms. The applicability of some anthropological concepts to different historical contexts has always been an important focus of scholarly debate. Among archaeologists, a prominent issue involved those of political organization, such as chiefdom and state. The concept of chiefdom, in particular, has been heavily criticized (Yoffee 1993), and some even chose to abandon the term. Many archaeologists are not ready to throw away the term of *state*, but it is now commonly recognized that there is a substantial diversity in different historical contexts among what we call states (Smith 2003; Yoffee 2004). In comparison, there has been surprisingly little discussion among archaeologists about the applicability and appropriateness of the concepts of authority and legitimacy in different historical contexts. Are they so self-evident and universally applicable?

It is probably fair to say that many archaeologists, including Kurnick, use explicitly or implicitly the classic version of authority and legitimacy formulated by Max Weber (see, for example, Smith 2003:105–9). There have been substantial debates and critiques of Weber's conceptualization in political science, sociology, and philosophy, but most of this scholarship has not been incorporated in archaeological discussion. In the most succinct manner, Weber (1978:212–15) defines authority as legitimate domination. Thus, in his view, authority and legitimacy are inseparably tied together. Following Weber, Kurnick (this volume:7) states that "authority cannot exist without explicit recognition and voluntary compliance. Rather than passively accepting authority . . . individuals, for whatever reasons, actively choose to comply." However, this is just one version of authority among diverse scholarly conceptualizations, and in my opinion, it is not an adequate one for many archaeological cases. In political philosophy, the question of authority is often discussed in terms of the relation between *de jure* authority and *de facto* authority; the former refers to legally justified legitimate authority, the latter is authority by the fact that subjects follow orders even in the absence of such justification (Christiano 2013). An important question is whether authority always needs the voluntary compliance of subjects or their consensus on its legitimacy (Lassman 2000:89; Lukes 1978:641–44). Many contemporary theorists think that voluntary or active compliance, and thus the belief in its legitimacy, are not a necessary condition of authority (Christiano 2013). Rather, a fundamental question in political philosophy is "when is political authority legitimate?" We should note that this perspective derives strongly from modern concerns, but such theoretical discussion forces us to reconsider the applicability of Weber's concepts.

The question of authority may become clearer as we discuss the closely related concept of legitimacy. Many archaeologists who follow Weber appear to equate the maintenance of legitimacy with that of authority (see, for example, Smith 2003:108–9). To me, a fundamental problem lies in the monolithic, one-dimensional conceptualization of legitimacy and thus, of authority. Various scholars have noted that the most problematic aspect of Weber's formulation of authority and legitimacy is his view of people's belief as their ultimate source (Weber 1978:213): a ruler's regime is legitimate when the subjects express their belief in its legitimacy (Beetham 1991; Friedrich 1963; Malešević 2002; Pitkin 1972). In this conceptualization, legitimacy is equated with acquiescence; as long as the regime remains stable and people do not express dissent, it is considered legitimate, although in reality people may covertly disapprove of the regime (Blau 1963; Grafstein 1981; Schaar 1970). This creates a tautological argument in which stable authority and political order are conflated with legitimacy, and thus, the explanations of cause and effect depend on each other (Grafstein 1981:469). Jürgen Habermas (1975:97–102) has argued that Weber's conceptualization presents ethical and moral problems and that the study of legitimacy needs to question people's beliefs themselves. As alternatives to Weber's formulation, various scholars have proposed that legitimacy needs to be examined on the basis of normative measures (Beetham 1991; Schaar 1970).

Problems in the application of Weber's version of legitimacy to archaeological contexts should be evident. As discussed above, we should not simply equate the condition of a polity or people's behavior, as estimated from the archaeological records, with common beliefs in legitimacy. This would inevitably lead to the problem of imposition of researchers' own narratives, discussed above. A prominent proponent of discrepancy between externally or publicly visible behavior of conformity and internal or covert dissent is James C. Scott. He argues that while in the public domains nonelites typically follow the "public transcripts" that conform to elites' views, they often express their "hidden transcripts" behind the scenes, thus demonstrating dissent with the authorities (Scott 1990). As I understand it, Scott's view is largely incompatible with Weber's conceptualization of authority.

We should again note that many of the alternative views of authority are deeply embedded in modern conditions in which codified laws and specific notions of justice play an important role, and we need to be cautious in using them. In modern society the concepts of authority and legitimacy are part of common public discourse, and they are largely internalized in the mind of modern political subjects. This observation most likely does not apply well to most premodern contexts. Did pre-Columbian Mesoamerican commoners discuss or evaluate the "legitimacy" of their rulers? More likely, their attitudes varied by specific directives and actions of rulers and other elites; different individuals may have reacted differently to the same action of the ruler, and the same individual may have reacted differently to different directives of the ruler. The most important point to keep in mind is that authority and legitimacy are not necessarily monolithic and coherent. This point concerns any historical contexts, but it is particularly important in the study of premodern contexts. We need to examine the multilayered, fragmentary, and inconsistent nature of legitimacy (Beetham 1991). The recognition of multiple layers of legitimacy implies that complex processes of negotiation exist. An important question may not be simply whether rulers maintained or failed to maintain authority. We probably should ask what kind of authority, with its layers and inconsistencies, was constituted in specific historical contexts.

POWER, RULERS, AND SOCIETY

An underlying issue is the eternal anthropological and sociological question of the relation between individual and society. This is not a simple question of one or the other, and my point is that if we want to refine our theory, we need to examine our position in this regard reflexively. Many archaeologists focus on how rulers rule. We probably need to ask to what degree the explicit focus on the ruler might be rooted in the modern, and possibly Western, thought that strongly emphasizes the role of individuals as political game-players. This issue may come into clearer focus as we discuss the concept of power. Like that of authority, many archaeologists appear to follow the classic conceptualization of power by Weber. For Weber, power has a broader reach than authority, as it does not require consent or belief in its legitimacy, and it is a capacity possessed and exercised by individuals and groups. This formulation probably has a better utility for archaeologists than his concept of authority because archaeologists can approach power in a more straightforward manner through the observation of its effects and avoid the problematic ground of guessing about belief in the legitimacy of authority. For our theoretical interest, we need to keep in mind that Weber focuses on individuals as the starting point of his theoretical formulation (Elster 2000; Keyes 2002).

One of the scholars who tried to advance Weber's theory of power is Michael Mann (1986). As noted by Kurnick, Mann's concept of power appears to be most popular among archaeologists. In my opinion, however, this is one of the most inadequate conceptualizations of power for many archaeologists. His narrative of power is highly categorical, as seen in the division among ideological, economic, military, and political power, and is highly mechanistic, as seen in the assumption of "sources" of power. It allows little room for the complexity and nuance in social process. Shouldn't all power be political for most anthropologists? To be fair to Mann, his scholarship and analysis is about modern European history (despite the ambitious subtitle of *The Sources of Social Power*, "the history of power from the beginning"), and his conceptualization probably has utility in this historical context. His categorical division of power corresponds to a certain level of separation in economic, political, ideological, and military institutions in the modern world. His narrow definition of *political power* gains analytical validity only with the rise of specialized governmental institutions. I probably do not need to repeat many anthropological arguments about why such categorical divisions are problematic in the study of different historical contexts. Mann (1986:34) states that "in the true beginning there was neither power nor history." The validity of this statement aside, he appears to acknowledge that his concepts are not applicable to contexts that interest many archaeologists. The most fundamental problem is his basic theoretical premise. He states that "the original source of power" is human nature that is "restless, purposive, rational, striving to increase their enjoyment of the good things of life and capable of choosing and pursuing appropriate means for doing so" (4). A strong modern and Western bias in his basic assumption is clear. The rationally maximizing actor is the starting point of his causal analysis, and consequently, he essentially rejects any consideration of human agency and cultural contexts (Bryant 2005; Kiser 2005:61). As a result, despite his claim of not being materialist (Mann 2005), his conceptualization of ideological power is mostly materialist (Kiser 2005:65; Reus-Smit 2002), and despite his criticism of evolutionism, his narrative of history of power looks much like a simplistic version of evolutionism (Schroeder 2005:5).

Weber's writing is highly complex, but simplified or extreme forms of neo-Weberian theory may have led to the overemphasis on individuals as the sole starting point of theoretical constructs or analysis. Without going back to the other extreme of Durkheimian notion—seeing society as an organic whole—we probably should pay more explicit attention to the dynamics emerging from relations among people. In this sense, it is probably useful to revisit the theory of Michel Foucault. He seeks a theory of power and domination that does not presume the centrality of the ruler, and thus advocates cutting off the king's head (Foucault 1980:121,1978:89). While Weber defines power as an entity possessed and exercised by individuals and groups, Foucault advances the concept of power that is not localized in individuals or groups but circulates through social relations. In his analysis, biopower and disciplinary power are not conceived as strategies of rulers but as techniques of power that operated in a broader web of society in specific historical eras (Foucault 1978,1977). Governmental institutions are not so much the possessors of such power as products of the scheme of power. Like most theorists, Foucault's main interest lies in the modern period, in which, according to him, disciplinary power has come to prevail, and he contrasts it to the pre-eighteenth-century Europe characterized by sovereign power tied to kings and spectacles of public execution. This overly categorical division—in addition to his reluctance to give much credit to human agency—probably contributed to the limited influence of Foucault among archaeologists compared to the wide popularity of Bourdieu. In this regard, the work of Giorgio Agamben (2005, 1998) encourages us to explore the intersection of sovereign power and biopower in premodern eras as well as the intertwined nature of disciplinary power and sovereign power in modern times (Hansen and Stepputat 2006; Smith 2011). Thus, Foucault provides a useful framework through which to explore the operation of power not directly tied to specific individuals, but the direct, uncritical application of his ideas to archaeological contexts would be problematic.

If we question the assumption of individualism, we probably need to pay closer attention to collective dynamics, including the roles of nonelites, in making social institutions. At the same time, we should also pay attention not only to practices and strategies of rulers but to the social institution of rulership and the historical contexts in which the agency of individual rulers were embedded. Elsewhere I have suggested that the notion of divine kingship is a useful concept in examining the rulership in Classic Maya society (Inomata 2001, 2006a, 2008). An important implication we might draw from broad cross-cultural studies is that the central property of the divine king is not so much his ability, will, or strategy to rule but his symbolic nature as the embodiment of the political community (Fortes and Evans-Pritchard 1940; Feeley-Harnik 1985). It is commonly observed that the divine king is at once at the center of the community as a patriarchal and exemplary symbol and outside of it as a liminal figure, which relates to Kurnick's statement that the political authority at the same time emphasizes both its uniqueness and commonalities with others. The paradox of the divine king is that this supreme figure may be ridiculed in public ceremonies and may be even killed when his health or sexual potency deteriorates (Hicks 1996; Hocart 1970). The classic concept of regicide reported from Africa and Asia may not directly apply to Classic Maya society, but Maya kings were sacrificed in a somewhat figurative manner through a bloodletting ritual and in a more direct, decisive manner through torture and decapitation when their polities were defeated in war. This nature of divine kings suggests that their characterization as ones holding authority or power over others is not enough. I have to wonder whether the common use of agentive nouns (*ruler*, *leader*, etc.) to denote these figures inadvertently makes us focus excessively on their nature as the ones who rule, lead, attempt, and strategize. We need to explore the other side of recursive process that is not addressed by extreme versions of the Weberian account of power; we probably should examine how the collective dynamics caught rulers and other elites in the history and structure of their own actions. Important elements in this process include nonelites who may not voluntarily comply or commit to the monolithic belief of legitimacy.

Obviously, this approach does not make Maya kings neutral to power. On the contrary, they were inseparably tied to violence and death. They presided over public ceremonies in which captive enemies were sacrificed, and kings themselves were the primary figures that needed to be sacrificed. This pattern resonates with Agamben's (1998:94–103) observation that the king's body may be indistinguishable from that of *homo sacer*, those who were placed outside of the Roman laws and could be killed by anybody. In both Maya and Roman cases, sovereignty was inseparably tied to violence situated outside the ordinary domain of society. This power, the one that kills captive enemies and the king himself, cannot be understood as a property possessed by the king alone. We need to examine a broader regime of power. Elsewhere I have argued that in Classic Maya society mass spectacles of public rituals and ceremonies were important settings for the operation of power (Inomata 2006a, 2006b). My point was that these public events were not simply strategies of rulers or elites but arenas of negotiation and contestation among diverse parties. They were settings where the king could show his ability to communicate with supernaturals and take credit for military success but could also be ignored, ridiculed, or killed. Studies of earlier periods show that this pattern of negotiation took shape long before the emergence of rulership.

CEIBAL DURING THE MIDDLE PRECLASSIC PERIOD

Our investigations at the lowland Maya site of Ceibal (figure 2.1) have revealed the earliest known E-Group assemblage, dating to 950 BCE (Inomata et al. 2013) (figure 2.2). The E-Group was a standardized ceremonial group, consisting of a western square building, a central plaza, and an eastern long platform, which later spread to many Maya sites. The residents of Ceibal also built large platforms, first to the southwest of the E-Group, around 950 BCE, then to the northeast of it, around 800 BCE, and eventually forming a spatial plan extending along the north-south axis of the site after 700 BCE. This highly formalized plan was also found in Middle Formative (1000–400 BCE) sites in central Chiapas; John Clark (Clark and Hansen 2001) has called it the Middle Formative Chiapas (MFC) pattern (figure 2.3). Before 1000 BCE, the Maya lowlands appear to have been occupied sparsely by small mobile groups that combined small-scale horticulture with hunting and gathering without the use of substantial buildings or ceramics. Chiapas and other areas surrounding the Maya lowlands had earlier sedentary settlements with ceramics, but these settlements did not have comparable formal ceremonial complexes prior to 1000 BCE. Michael W. Love (1999) has pointed out that the establishment of these complexes marked both a major architectural innovation and a significant change in social practice. These well-marked spaces probably defined proper actions for people who entered them and helped create disciplinary power comparable to the one described by Foucault for modern society. Excavations along the center lines of the E-Group assemblage at Ceibal, as well as at the

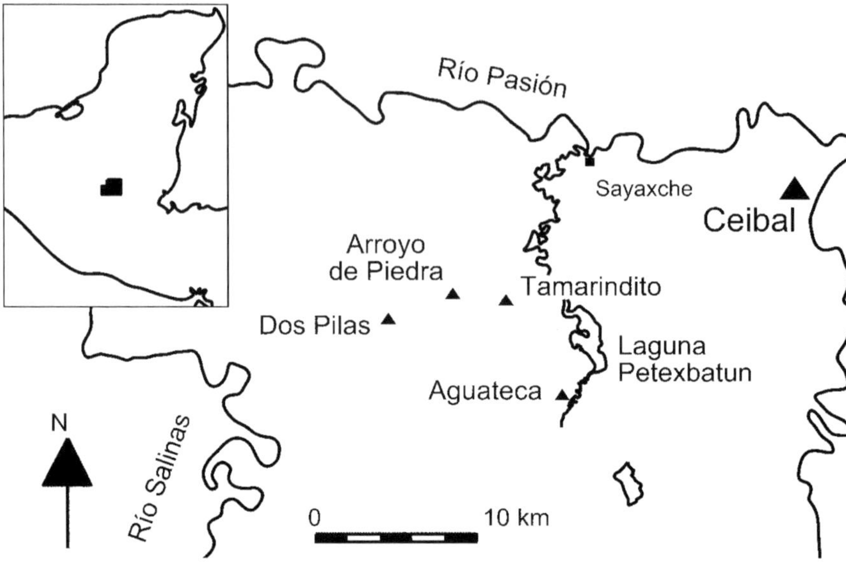

FIGURE 2.1. *Map showing the location of Ceibal.*

Chiapan centers of San Isidro and Chiapa de Corzo, revealed greenstone axe caches similar to each other (Bachand and Lowe 2012; Inomata and Triadan forthcoming; Lowe 1981), indicating that these complexes were indeed associated with highly standardized ritual practice. Ceibal Cache 108, dating to around 800 BCE, contained a carved shell pendant representing a decapitated head (figure 2.4). It appears that human sacrifice was already part of public ritual held in the plaza. Around 400 BCE, human sacrifice appears to have become a primary theme of public ceremonies, and a series of decapitated or dismembered bodies were deposited in the plaza (Inomata 2014; Palomo 2013).

Despite the highly standardized spatial pattern and associated social practices across various regions, the degree of social inequality appears to have varied. The excavation of the western building of the E-Group assemblage at Chiapa de Corzo by Bruce R. Bachand and Lynneth S. Lowe (2012) revealed rich tombs with numerous jade ornaments, but our tunnel excavation through the basal level of the corresponding building at Ceibal did not encounter any burials. The southwestern and northeastern platforms at Ceibal supported multiple buildings on top and appear to have served as residential complexes for the emergent elite. The excavation of the southwestern platform unearthed two greenstone axe caches comparable to those

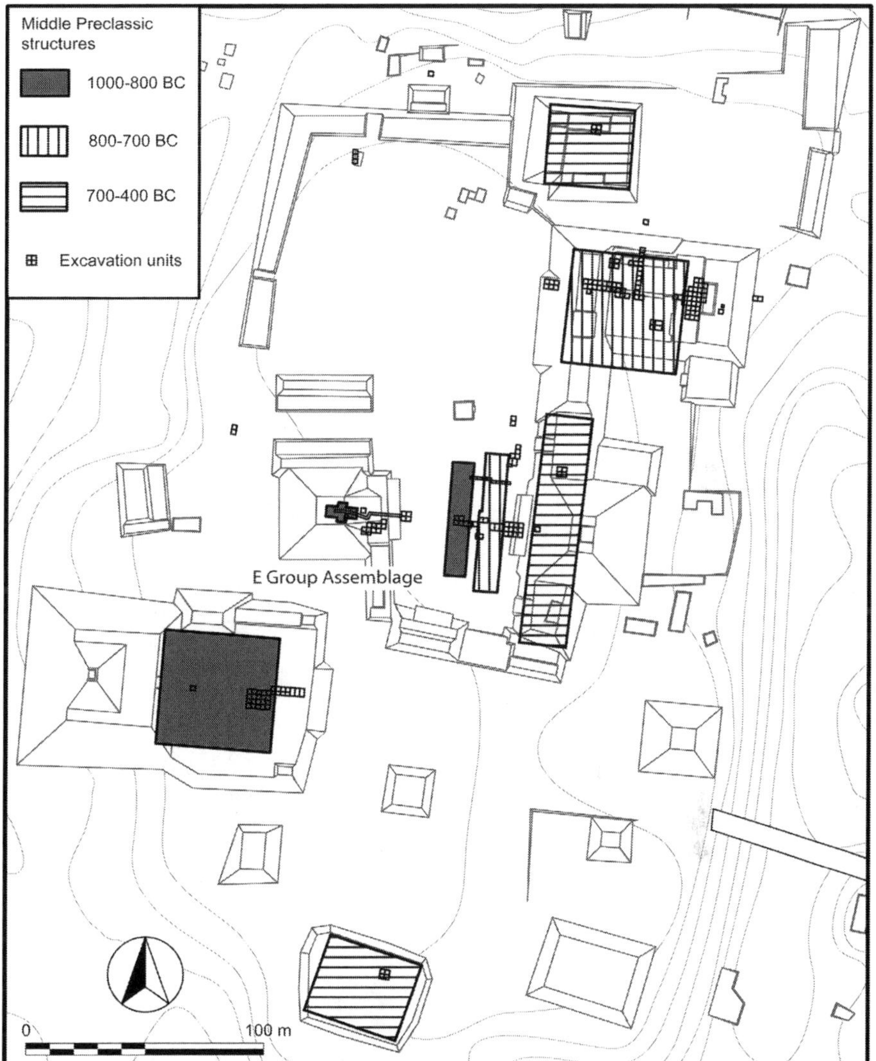

Figure 2.2. *Map of Ceibal (modified from Willey et al. 1975:figure 2), 1 meter contours. The eastern long mounds of the E-Group assemblage show sequential expansions; with the construction of a new long mound, the older one was covered by a plaza floor.*

found in the plaza. These finds suggest that, if the southwestern platform was indeed a residential complex, its inhabitants probably had privileged access to precious objects from afar, along with associated knowledge, and

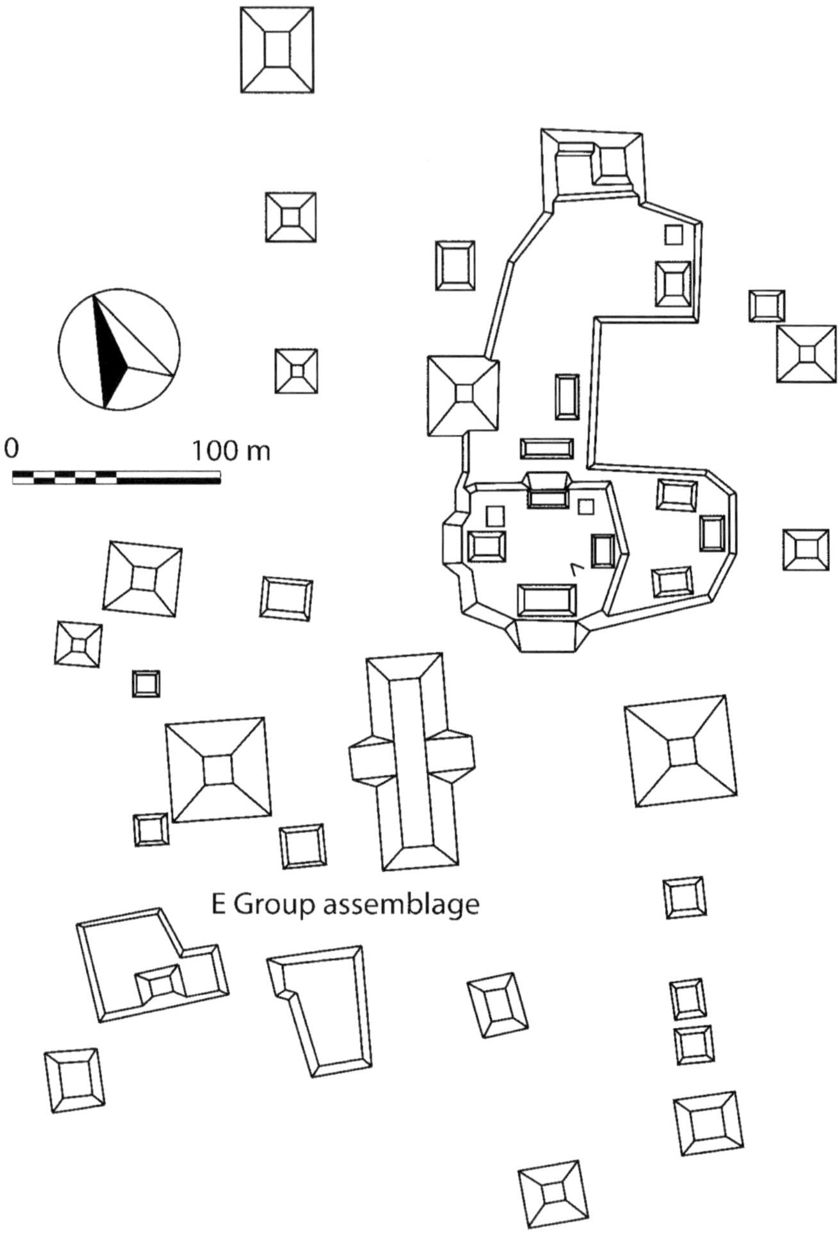

Figure 2.3. *Map of La Libertad, Chiapas, as an example of the Middle Formative Chiapas pattern (redrawn from Bryant et al. 2005:figure 1.5).*

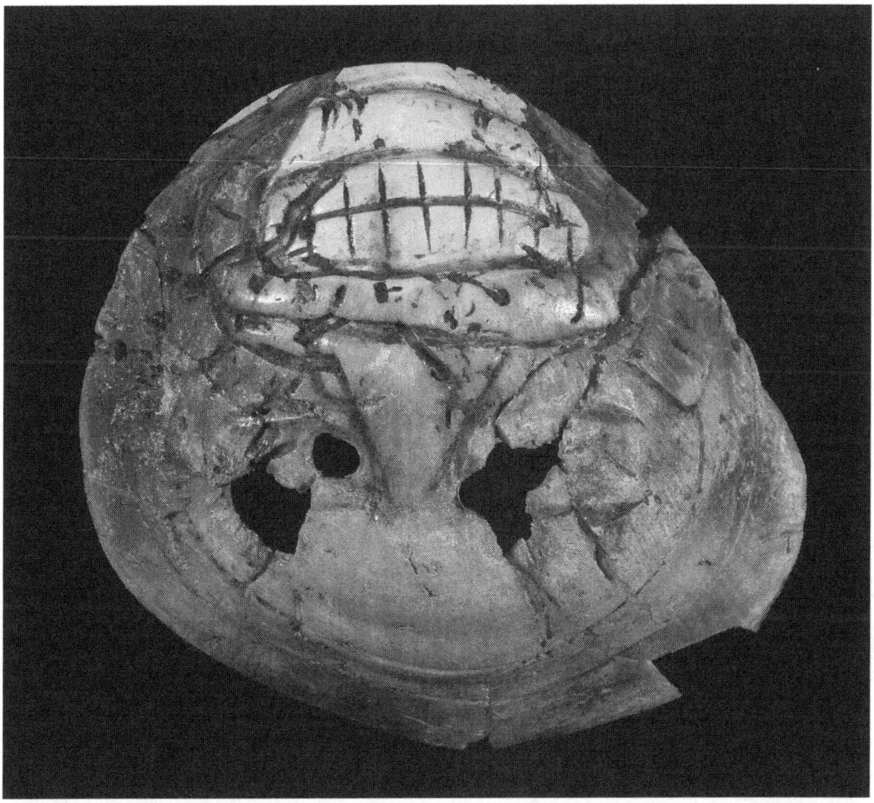

FIGURE 2.4. *A carved shell pendant representing a decapitated head, from Ceibal Cache 108 (ca. 800 BCE).*

acted as main ritual performers in communal ceremonies held in the plaza. However, there is no clear indication that these emergent elites had strong power to impose their will on others by coercion. It appears that mobile horticulturalists persisted in the areas around Ceibal until 800 or 700 BCE, and returning to the traditional mobile lifeway was probably an easy, viable option for most Ceibal residents if they wanted to escape from the imposition of elite power (Inomata et al. 2015a, 2015b).

It is unlikely that the formation of the standardized architectural plan and the associated operation of disciplinary power resulted from imposition by the elite. In examining this issue, we need to distinguish analytically the choice of a specific physical form (in this case, the spatial plan consisted of an E-Group and large platforms) from the broader domain of spatial and social practice. The emerging elites most likely played a leading role in the former through their interactions with other privileged groups in other regions. This does not mean that elites initiated the whole social change. Before the creation of a new physical form of ceremonial complex was realized, a new structure of spatial and social practice tied to aggregated sedentary settlements and a stronger commitment to agriculture must have already been emerging. New perceptions of the world and society associated with novel practices possibly made the conceptualization of a new ceremonial complex feasible. When a proposition of a new construction project was made, a consensus and agreement among diverse community members, rather than coercion or imposition by the elite, must have been critical. In addition, even the elite who conceptualized the specific new physical form of architecture possibly did not foresee much of its social effect (Joyce 2004). Moreover, the very existence of the elite would not have been possible without such new perceptions of the world. It is well recognized that egalitarian societies maintain a strong egalitarian ethos to prevent the excessive accumulation of wealth and power by certain individuals (Ingold 1999; Lee 1979; Woodburn 1982). Prior to the emergence of elites, a different perception of society must have been developing. Once a proposition of a new physical form was made and accepted, the resulting ceremonial complex probably enhanced and perpetuated the already developing form of new social and spatial practices and lay the groundwork for its later transformation.

In this sense, nonelite members of the community possibly contributed substantially to the creation of a new form of society and its later transformations. We may even need to consider the possibility that a broad body of community members desired or demanded the increasing specialization of public performers who also acted as political figures. This process was probably not a smooth, coherent one. The constant possibility of some Ceibal residents fleeing back to the mobile lifeway implies that division, contestation, and negotiation were inevitable parts of this trajectory. This emergent regime of power seen at Ceibal appears to have left a strong legacy for later Maya society. Rulers of the Classic Period closely followed the template of public interaction that we see at Middle Preclassic Ceibal. Although later rulers lived in elaborate palaces and were buried in rich tombs, their primary duty to the community was to perform in public ceremonies and to be sacrificed either in a figurative way or in a direct manner. In this sense, Classic Maya kings were tightly caught in this historical tradition and the social institution.

CONCLUSION

The establishment of a formal ceremonial complex around 950 BCE at Ceibal indicates that the basic form of collective interaction that would continue through the pre-Columbian history of the lowland Maya people emerged as soon as they began to adopt the sedentary way of life. The role of the emergent elite in public ceremonies and the centrality of spectacle of violence at the Middle Preclassic community of Ceibal foretold the institutionalized performance of rulership in later periods. I do not mean to argue that Maya rulership had a timeless nature or that public performance was its most important aspect. Many other social dimensions are left out of this short essay, including governmental institutions, gender relations, domestic organization, daily life of various groups, subsistence and other technologies, etc. In addition, the symbolic contents of public events most likely changed substantially from the strong emphasis on communal values during the Middle Formative Period to the focus on rulership and dynastic history during the Classic Period. Through changes in these diverse social dimensions and symbolic contents, the lowland Maya continued to recreate the basic external form of collective interaction. This commonality shared through many centuries and across many communities cannot be explained in terms of strategies of individual rulers alone. Intersections between the perspectives focusing on individuals and those stressing collectives need to be explored, and we also have to examine how broader social processes may have made rulers. In doing so, engagement with social theories is critical, but we need to evaluate the historical situatedness of the modern theories. Such exercise makes us consider potential contributions of archaeological research to today's world.

ACKNOWLEDGMENTS

I thank Sarah Kurnick and Joanne Baron for inviting me to participate in this volume. Investigations at Ceibal were carried out with permits generously issued by the Instituto de Antropología e Historia de Guatemala and were supported by grants from the National Geographic Society, the National Science Foundation (BCS-0750808), the National Endowment for the Humanities (RZ-51209-10), and the Alphawood Foundation awarded to myself and Daniela Triadan, as well as funds from the Ministry of Education, Culture, Sports, Science and Technology–Japan KAKENHI (21101003 and 21101002) and the Japan Society for the Promotion of Science KAKENHI (21402008) awarded to Kazuo Aoyama.

REFERENCES

Abu-Lughod, Lila. 1991. "Writing Against Culture." In *Recapturing Anthropology: Working in the Present*, edited by Richard G. Fox, 137–62. Santa Fe: School of American Research Press.

Agamben, Giorgio. 1998. *Homo Sacer: Sovereign Power and Bare Life*. Stanford: Stanford University Press.

Agamben, Giorgio. 2005. *State of Exception*. Chicago: University of Chicago Press.

Austin, J. L. 1962. *How to Do Things with Words*. Oxford: Oxford University Press.

Bachand, Bruce R., and Lynneth S. Lowe. 2012. "Chiapa De Corzo's Mound 11 Tomb and the Middle Formative Olmec." In *Arqueología reciente de Chiapas: Contribuciones del encuentro celebrado en el 60^0 aniversario de la Fundación Arqueológica Nuevo Mundo*, edited by Lynneth S. Lowe and Mary E. Pye, 45–68. Papers of the New World Archaeological Foundation No. 72. Provo, UT: Brigham Young University.

Beetham, David. 1991. "Max Weber and the Legitimacy of the Modern State." *Analyse & Kritik* 13: 34–45.

Bell, Catherine M. 1997. *Ritual: Perspectives and Dimensions*. Oxford: Oxford University Press.

Blau, Peter M. 1963. "Critical Remarks on Weber's Theory of Authority." *American Political Science Review* 57(2): 305–16.

Boivin, Nicole. 2008. *Material Cultures, Material Minds: The Impact of Things on Human Thought, Society, and Evolution*. Cambridge: Cambridge University Press.

Bourdieu, Pierre. 1977. *Outline of a Theory of Practice*. Cambridge: Cambridge University Press.

Bryant, Douglas B., John E. Clark, and David Cheetham. 2005. "Ceramic Sequence of the Upper Grijalva Region, Chiapas, Mexico." Papers of the New World Archaeological Foundation No. 67. Provo, UT: Brigham Young University.

Bryant, Joseph. 2005. "Grand, Yet Grounded: Ontology, Theory, and Method in Michael Mann's Historical Sociology." In *An Anatomy of Power: The Social Theory of Michael Mann*, edited by John A. Hall and Ralph Schroeder, 71–98. Cambridge: Cambridge University Press.

Christiano, Tom. 2013. "Authority." In *The Stanford Encyclopedia of Philosophy*, edited by Edward N. Zalta. Last modified March 19, 2013. http://plato.stanford.edu/archives/spr2013/entries/authority/.

Clark, John E., and Richard D. Hansen. 2001. "The Architecture of Early Kingship: Comparative Perspectives on the Origins of the Maya Royal Court." In *Royal Courts of the Ancient Maya*, vol. 2, *Data and Case Studies*, edited by Takeshi Inomata and Stephen D. Houston, 1–45. Boulder: Westview.

Damasio, Antonio R. 1994. *Descartes' Error: Emotion, Reason, and the Human Brain*. New York: Putnam.

Damasio, Antonio R. 1999. *The Feeling of What Happens: Body and Emotion in the Making of Consciousness*. New York: Harcourt.

Damasio, Antonio R. 2003. *Looking for Spinoza: Joy, Sorrow, and the Feeling Brain*. New York: Harcourt.

Elster, Jon. 2000. "Rationality, Economy, and Society." In *The Cambridge Companion to Weber*, edited by Stephen T. Turner, 21–41. Cambridge: Cambridge University Press.

Feeley-Harnik, Gillian. 1985. "Issues in Divine Kingship." *Annual Review of Anthropology* 14: 273–313.

Fortes, Meyer, and Evans-Pritchard, E. E., eds., 1940. *African Political Systems*. Oxford: Oxford University Press.

Foucault, Michel. 1977. *Discipline and Punish: The Birth of the Prison*. Translated by Alan Sheridan. New York: Pantheon.

Foucault, Michel. 1978. *The History of Sexuality*. Vol. 1, *An Introduction*. Translated by Robert Hurley. New York: Pantheon.

Foucault, Michel. 1980. *Power/Knowledge: Selected Interviews and Other Writings, 1972–1977*. Edited by Colin Gordon. Brighton: Harvester Press.

Friedrich, Carl J. 1963. *Man and His Government: An Empirical Theory of Politics*. New York: McGraw-Hill.

Galdi, Silvia, Luciano Arcuri, and Bertram Gawronski. 2008. "Automatic Mental Associations Predict Future Choices of Undecided Decision-Makers." *Science* 321: 1100–2.

Giddens, Anthony. 1984. *The Constitution of Society: Outline of the Theory of Structuration*. Cambridge: Polity Press.

Grafstein, Robert. 1981. "The Failure of Weber's Conception of Legitimacy: Its Causes and Implications." *Journal of Politics* 43(2): 456–72.

Habermas, Jürgen. 1975. *Legitimation Crisis*. Boston: Beacon.

Hansen, Thomas Blom, and Finn Stepputat. 2006. "Sovereignty Revisited." *Annual Review of Anthropology* 35: 295–315.

Hassin, Ran R., James S. Uleman, and John A. Bargh. 2005. *The New Unconscious*. Oxford: Oxford University Press.

Hicks, David. 1996. "Making the King Divine: A Case Study in Ritual Regicide from Timor." *Journal of the Royal Anthropological Institute* 2(4): 611–24.

Hocart, A. M. 1970. *Kings and Councillors: An Essay in the Comparative Anatomy of Human Society*. Chicago: University of Chicago Press.

Ingold, Tim. 1999. "On the Social Relations of the Hunter-Gatherer Band." In *The Cambridge Encyclopedia of Hunters and Gathers*, edited by Richard B. Lee and Richard Daly, 399–440. Cambridge: Cambridge University Press.

Inomata, Takeshi. 2001. "King's People: Classic Maya Royal Courtiers in a Comparative Perspective." In *Royal Courts of the Ancient Maya*, vol. 1, *Theory, Comparison, and Synthesis*, edited by Takeshi Inomata and Stephen D. Houston, 27–53. Boulder: Westview.

Inomata, Takeshi. 2006a. "Plazas, Performers, and Spectators: Political Theaters of the Classic Maya." *Current Anthropology* 47(5): 805–42.

Inomata, Takeshi. 2006b. "Politics and Theatricality in Maya Society." In *Archaeology of Performance: Theaters of Power, Community, and Politics*, edited by Takeshi Inomata and Lawrence S. Coben, 187–222. Lanham, MD: AltaMira.

Inomata, Takeshi. 2008. "Women in Classic Maya Royal Courts." In *Servants of the Dynasty: Palace Women in World History*, edited by Anne Walthall, 45–64. Berkeley: University of California Press.

Inomata, Takeshi. 2014. "War, Violence, and Society in the Maya Lowlands." In *Embattled Bodies, Embattled Places: War in Pre-Columbian Mesoamerica and the Andes*, edited by Andrew K. Scherer and John W. Verano, 25–56. Washington, DC: Dumbarton Oaks.

Inomata, Takeshi, and Lawrence S. Coben, eds. 2006. *Archaeology of Performance: Theaters of Power, Community, and Politics*. Lanham, MD: AltaMira.

Inomata, Takeshi, and Daniela Triadan. forthcoming. "Middle Preclassic Caches from Ceibal, Guatemala." *Maya Archaeology* 3.

Inomata, Takeshi, Jessica MacLellan, and Melissa Burham. 2015a. "The Construction of Public and Domestic Spheres in the Preclassic Maya Lowlands." *American Anthropologist* 117: 519-34.

Inomata, Takeshi, Jessica MacLellan, Daniela Triadan, Jessica Munson, Melissa Burham, Kazuo Aoyama, Hiroo Nasu, Flory Pinzon, and Hitoshi Yonenobu. 2015b. "Development of Sedentary Communities in the Maya Lowlands: Coexisting Mobile Groups and Public Ceremonies at Ceibal, Guatemala." *Proceedings of the National Academy of Sciences of the United States of America* 112(14): 4268-73.

Inomata, Takeshi, Daniela Triadan, Kazuo Aoyama, Victor Castillo, and Hitoshi Yonenobu. 2013. "Early Ceremonial Constructions at Ceibal, Guatemala, and the Origins of Lowland Maya Civilization." *Science* 340(6131): 467–71.

Inomata, Takeshi, and Kenichiro Tsukamoto. 2014. "Gathering in an Open Space: Introduction to Mesoamerican Plazas." In *Mesoamerican Plazas: Practices, Meanings, and Memories*, edited by Kenichiro Tsukamoto and Takeshi Inomata, 3–17. Tucson: University of Arizona Press.

Johansson, Petter, Lars Hall, Sverker Sikström, and Andreas Olsson. 2005. "Failure to Detect Mismatches between Intention and Outcome in a Simple Decision Task." *Science* 310(5745): 116–19.

Johansson, Petter, Lars Hall, Sverker Sikström, Betty Tärning, and Andreas Lind. 2006. "How Something Can Be Said about Telling More Than We Can Know: On Choice Blindness and Introspection." *Consciousness and Cognition* 15: 673–92.

Johnson, Mark. 2006. "Mind Incarnate: From Dewey to Damasio." *Daedalus* 135(3): 46–54.

Joyce, Rosemary A. 2004. "Unintended Consequences? Monumentality As a Novel Experience in Formative Mesoamerica." *Journal of Archaeological Method and Theory* 11(1): 5–29.

Keyes, Charles F. 2002. "Weber and Anthropology." *Annual Review of Anthropology* 31: 233–55.

Kiser, Edgar. 2005. "Mann's Microfoundations: Addressing Neo-Weberian Dilemmas." In *An Anatomy of Power: The Social Theory of Michael Mann*, edited by John A. Hall and Ralph Schroeder, 56–70. Cambridge: Cambridge University Press.

Lakoff, George, and Mark Johnson. 1999. *Philosophy in the Flesh: The Embodied Mind and Its Challenge to Western Thought*. New York: Basic Books.

Lassman, Peter. 2000. "The Rule of Man over Man: Politics, Power and Legitimation." In *The Cambridge Companion to Weber*, edited by Stephen T. Turner, 81–98. Cambridge: Cambridge University Press.

Lee, Richard Borshay. 1979. *The !Kung San: Men, Women, and Work in a Foraging Society*. Cambridge: Cambridge University Press.

Love, Michael W. 1999. "Ideology, Material Culture, and Daily Practice in Pre-Classic Mesoamerica: A Pacific Coast Perspective." In *Social Patterns in Pre-Classic Mesoamerica*, edited by David C. Grove and Rosemary A. Joyce, 127–53. Washington, DC: Dumbarton Oaks.

Lowe, Gareth W. 1981. "Olmec Horizon Defined in Mound 20, San Isidro, Chiapas." In *The Olmec and Their Neighbors*, edited by Michael D. Coe and David Grove, 231–56. Washington, DC: Dumbarton Oaks.

Lukes, Steven. 1978. "Power and Authority." In *A History of Sociological Analysis*, edited by Tom Bottomore and Robert Nisbet, 633–76. London: Heinemann.

Malešević, Siniša. 2002. *Ideology, Legitimacy and the New State: Yugoslavia, Serbia and Croatia*. Oxford: Routledge.

Mann, Michael. 1986. *The Sources of Social Power*. Vol. 1, *A History of Power from the Beginning to A.D. 1760*. Cambridge: Cambridge University Press.

Mann, Michael. 2005. "The Sources of Social Power Revisited: A Response to Criticism." In *An Anatomy of Power: The Social Theory of Michael Mann*, edited by John A. Hall and Ralph Schroeder, 343–96. Cambridge: Cambridge University Press.

Nisbett, Richard E., and Timothy DeCamp Wilson. 1977. "Telling More than We Can Know: Verbal Reports on Mental Processes." *Psychological Review* 84(3): 231–59.

Palomo, Juan Manuel. 2013. "Mortuary Treatments at the Ancient Maya Center of Ceibal, Guatemala." PhD diss., University of Arizona.

Pitkin, Hanna. 1972. *Wittgenstein and Justice*. Berkeley: University of California Press.

Reus-Smit, Chris. 2002. "The Idea of History and History with Ideas." In *Historical Sociology of International Relations*, edited by Stephen Hobden and John M. Hobson, 120–40. Cambridge: Cambridge University Press.

Schaar, John. 1970. "Legitimacy in the Modern State." In *Power and Community*, edited by Philip Green and Sanford Levinson, 276–327. New York: Pantheon.

Schroeder, Ralph. 2005. "Introduction: The IEMP Model and Its Critics." In *An Anatomy of Power: The Social Theory of Michael Mann*, edited by John A. Hall and Ralph Schroeder, 1–16. Cambridge: Cambridge University Press.

Scott, James C. 1990. *Domination and the Arts of Resistance: Hidden Transcripts*. New Haven: Yale University Press.

Searle, John R. 2000. "Consciousness." *Annual Review of Neuroscience* 23: 557–78.

Shore, Bradd. 1996. *Culture in Mind: Cognition, Culture, and the Problem of Meaning*. Oxford: Oxford University Press.

Smith, Adam T. 2003. *The Political Landscape: Constellations of Authority in Early Complex Polities*. Berkeley: University of California Press.

Smith, Adam T. 2011. "Archaeologies of Sovereignty." *Annual Review of Anthropology* 40: 415–32.

Strauss, Claudia, and Naomi Quinn. 1997. *A Cognitive Theory of Cultural Meaning*. Cambridge: Cambridge University Press.

Sullivan, Alan P., ed. 2008. *Archaeological Concepts for the Study of the Cultural Past*. Salt Lake City: University of Utah Press.

Weber, Max. 1978. *Economy and Society*. Berkeley: University of California Press.

Wegner, Daniel M. 2002. *The Illusion of Conscious Will*. Cambridge: MIT Press.

Willey, Gordon R., A. Ledyard Smith, Gair Tourtellot III, and Ian Graham. 1975. *Excavations at Seibal, Department of Peten, Guatemala: Introduction: The Site and Its Setting*. Peabody Museum Memoirs 13. Cambridge, MA: Harvard University Press.

Wilson, Timothy D. 2002. *Strangers to Ourselves: Discovering the Adaptive Unconscious*. Cambridge, MA: Belknap Press of Harvard University Press.

Woodburn, James C. 1982. "Egalitarian Societies." *Man* 17(3): 431–51.

Yoffee, Norman. 1993. "Too Many Chiefs? (or, Safe Texts for the '90s)." In *Archaeological Theory: Who Sets the Agenda?*, edited by Norman Yoffee and Andrew Sherratt, 60–78. Cambridge: Cambridge University Press.

Yoffee, Norman. 2004. *Myths of the Archaic State: Evolution of the Earliest Cities, States and Civilizations*. Cambridge: Cambridge University Press.

Scott, James C. 1998. *Seeing Like a State: How Certain Schemes to Improve the Human Condition Have Failed*. New Haven: Yale University Press.

Service, Elman R. 1975. *Origins of the State and Civilization: The Process of Cultural Evolution*. New York: W. W. Norton.

Service, Elman R. 1978. "Classical and Modern Theories of the Origin of Government." In *Origins of the State: The Anthropology of Political Evolution*, edited by Ronald Cohen and Elman R. Service, 1–20. Philadelphia: Institute for the Study of Human Issues.

Sharer, Robert J., and Charles W. Golden. 2004. "Kingship and Polity: Conceptualizing the Maya Body Politic." In *Continuities and Changes in Maya Archaeology: Perspectives at the Millennium*, edited by Charles W. Golden and Greg Borgstede, 23–50. New York: Routledge.

Sharer, Robert J., and Loa P. Traxler. 2006. *The Ancient Maya*. Sixth edition. Stanford: Stanford University Press.

Smith, Adam T. 2003. *The Political Landscape: Constellations of Authority in Early Complex Polities*. Berkeley: University of California Press.

Smith, Adam T. 2011a. "Figuring the Political: The Stuff of Sovereignty in a Post-Evolutionary Archaeology." In *The Archaeology of Politics: The Materiality of Political Practice and Action in the Past*, edited by Peter G. Johansen and Andrew M. Bauer, 354–61. Newcastle upon Tyne: Cambridge Scholars.

Smith, Adam T. 2011b. "Archaeologies of Sovereignty." *Annual Review of Anthropology* 40: 415–32.

Smith, Adam T. 2012. "The Political Machine: Sense, Sensibility, and Sentiment in the Late Bronze Age Caucasus." Paper presented at the University of Pennsylvania Department of Anthropology Colloquium, Philadelphia.

Spinden, Herbert Joseph. 1917. *Ancient Civilizations of Mexico and Central America*. New York: American Museum of Natural History.

Spriggs, Matthew. 1984. "Another Way of Telling: Marxist Perspectives in Archaeology." In *Marxist Perspectives in Archaeology*, edited by Matthew Spriggs, 1–9. Cambridge: Cambridge University Press.

Stuart, David. 1996. "Kings of Stone: A Consideration of Stelae in Ancient Maya Ritual and Representation." *Res* 29/30: 148–71.

Stuart, David. 2005. "Ideology and Classic Maya Kingship." In *A Catalyst for Ideas: Anthropological Archaeology and the Legacy of Douglas Schwartz*, edited by Vernon L. Scarborough, 257–85. Santa Fe: School of American Research Press.

Taube, Karl. 1998. "The Jade Hearth: Centrality, Rulership, and the Classic Maya Temple." In *Function and Meaning in Classic Maya Architecture*, edited by Stephen D. Houston, 427–78. Washington, DC: Dumbarton Oaks.

Thomas, Julian. 2004. *Archaeology and Modernity*. New York: Routledge.

Tilley, Christopher. 1984. "Ideology and the Legitimation of Power in the Middle Neolithic of Southern Sweden." In *Ideology, Power and Prehistory*, edited by Daniel Miller and Christopher Tilley, 111–46. Cambridge: Cambridge University Press.

Trigger, Bruce G. 1993. "Marxism in Contemporary Western Archaeology." *Archaeological Method and Theory* 5: 159–200.

Weaver, Muriel Porter. 1993. *The Aztecs, Maya, and Their Predecessors: Archaeology of Mesoamerica*. Third edition. San Diego: Academic Press.

Weber, Max. 1978. *Economy and Society: An Outline of Interpretive Sociology*. Edited by Guenther Roth and Claus Wittich. Berkeley: University of California Press.

Webster, David L. 1995. "Maya Shaman-Kings: Some Evolutionary Implications." *Cambridge Archaeological Journal* 5(1): 120–22.

Webster, David L. 2002. "Groundhogs and Kings: Issues of Divine Rulership among the Classic Maya." In *Incidents of Archaeology in Central America and Yucatan: Essays in Honor of Edwin M. Shook*, edited by Michael Love, Marion Popenoe de Hatch, and Héctor L. Escobedo, 433–58. Lanham, MD: University Press of America.

Yaeger, Jason. 2003. "Untangling the Ties That Bind: The City, Countryside, and the Nature of Maya Urbanism at Xunantunich, Belize." In *The Social Construction of Ancient Cities*, edited by Monica I. Smith, 121–46. Washington, DC: Smithsonian Institution Press.

Yaeger, Jason, and Cynthia Robin. 2004. "Heterogeneous Hinterlands: The Social and Political Organization of Commoner Settlements near Xunantunich, Belize." In *Ancient Maya Commoners*, edited by Jon C. Lohse and Fred Valdez, 147–73. Austin: University of Texas Press.

Yoffee, Norman. 2005. *Myths of the Archaic State: Evolution of the Earliest Cities, States and Civilizations*. Cambridge: Cambridge University Press.

Zender, Marc. 2004. "A Study of Classic Maya Priesthood." PhD diss., University of Calgary.

3

Negotiating Political Authority and Community in Terminal Formative Coastal Oaxaca

Arthur A. Joyce, Sarah B. Barber, Jeffrey Brzezinski, Carlo J. Lucido, and Víctor Salazar Chávez

Mesoamerican archaeologists have traditionally viewed complex polities as highly integrated with well-developed hierarchies led by powerful rulers (e.g., Charlton and Nichols 1997; Flannery 1972; Lucero 2006:155–62; Marcus 1998:63–73; Martin and Grube 2000; Spencer and Redmond 2001). Over the past twenty-five years, however, archaeologists have begun to challenge these assumptions by considering a range of forms of political authority (e.g., Beekman 2008, this volume; Blanton et al. 1996; Blanton and Fargher 2008; Fargher et al. 2010) along with exploring the ways in which social processes within polities complicate and limit integration (Barber 2005; Barber and Joyce 2007; Brumfiel 1992; Joyce 2010; Joyce et al. 2001; Robin 2002; Yaeger 2003). Archaeologists are increasingly viewing complex polities as the result of dynamic and ongoing negotiations among people across salient lines of social difference—elite and nonelite, urban and rural, center and periphery (Ashmore et al. 2004; Barber and Joyce 2007; Beekman, this volume; Gonlin and Lohse 2007; Inomata, this volume; Joyce 2009, 2013a). The resulting perspective creates a more dynamic and contingent understanding of the history of complex societies in Mesoamerica and beyond.

In this chapter, we build on more than a decade of research concerning the negotiation of political authority in complex societies (Barber 2005, 2013; Barber and Joyce 2007; Joyce 2000, 2004, 2009, 2010, 2013a; Joyce et al. 2001) to examine initial political centralization

DOI: 10.5876/9781607324164.c003

during the Terminal Formative Period (150 BCE–250 CE) in the lower Río Verde Valley on the Pacific coast of Oaxaca (figure 3.1). Based on excavations at the early urban center of Río Viejo, along with regional survey and excavations at several outlying sites, we examine the historical context for early political centralization. Rather than focusing on the emergence of a polity whose ruling ideas, practices, and institutions came to be established and have a degree of historical durability, Terminal Formative Río Viejo allows us to explore an instance where hierarchy and regional rulership were tenuous and short-lived. Río Viejo therefore provides insights into the kinds of tensions, contradictions, and conflicts that must be negotiated and worked out for regional political authority to become institutionalized.

We argue that incipient regional political authority in the lower Río Verde Valley was the outcome of negotiations among the diverse social groups that inhabited the region. These negotiations involved political and religious practices, ideas, and materials focused on the civic-ceremonial center of Río Viejo, located on the site's massive acropolis. By the late Terminal Formative (100–250 CE), the acropolis became a regionally significant place that embodied the history of the many communities in the valley that participated in its construction and use, thereby facilitating a process through which the kinds of acts that had for generations defined local places and social groups came to define a polity (Barber and Joyce 2007). We argue, however, that the diverse entanglements centered on the acropolis were insufficiently differentiated from practices, places, people, objects, and beliefs that defined local communities and more traditional, corporate, and egalitarian forms of leadership. We contrast Terminal Formative Río Viejo with the early history of the Monte Albán polity, which persisted in one form or another for over a millennium (Blanton 1978; Joyce 2010). This comparison leads us to conclude that perhaps the most significant reason why the Río Viejo polity collapsed after only a handful of generations was the inability of regional elites to become focal nodes in the kinds of complex and far-reaching networks of ritual, politics, and economy that led to more cohesive, integrated, and long-lived polities in other parts of Mesoamerica, such as at Monte Albán.

THE LATE FORMATIVE ROOTS OF THE RÍO VIEJO POLITY

Archaeological research over the past thirty years on the Formative Period in the lower Río Verde Valley has provided a detailed, diachronic database that forms the basis of this chapter (Barber 2005, 2013; Barber and Joyce 2007, 2011, 2012; Joyce 1991a, 1991b, 1993, 2008, 2010, 2013a; Joyce and Barber 2011, n.d.; Joyce and Levine 2009; Joyce and Winter 1989; Joyce et al. 1998; Levine 2002,

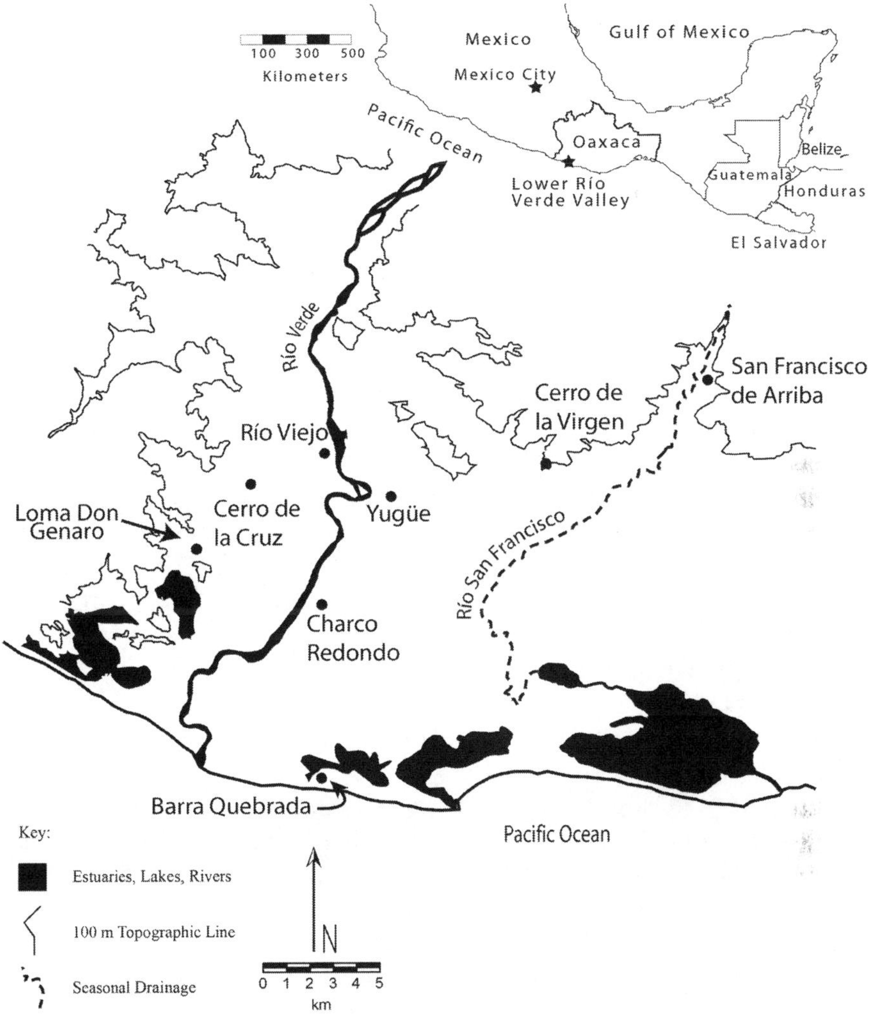

FIGURE 3.1. *Map of the lower Río Verde, showing archaeological sites mentioned in the text (drawn by Sarah Barber).*

2013; Workinger 2002). Archaeological research has included excavation at the Terminal Formative political seat of Río Viejo and lower-order sites such as Cerro de la Cruz, Cerro de la Virgen, San Francisco de Arriba, Yugüe, Charco Redondo, Loma Don Genaro, and Barra Quebrada. Over the past ten years, our research has focused on large-scale excavations on the acropolis of Río

Viejo (Barber and Joyce 2011, 2012; Barber et al. 2013a; Joyce and Barber 2011, n.d.). A full-coverage regional survey carried out over 164 square kilometers has yielded data on changes in settlement patterns and social organization (Hedgepeth and Koukopoulos 2012; Joyce et al. 2001). Finally, paleoenvironmental research has provided data on changes in floodplain and coastal environments that inform the history of human resource use (Goman et al. 2005, 2010, 2013; Joyce and Goman 2012; Mueller et al. 2013).

The archaeological evidence shows that trends toward population growth and increasing social complexity that culminated with the Terminal Formative Río Viejo polity can be traced back to the Middle Formative. During the latter part of the Middle Formative a regional demographic center emerged at Charco Redondo, which grew to 62 hectares. Current evidence is insufficient to determine whether the site was a political center or to assess the nature of social inequality in the region at this time. Population as measured by the occupational area in the full-coverage survey increased from 64 hectares in the late Middle Formative (700–400 BCE) to 344 hectares by the Late Formative (400–150 BCE) (Hedgepeth and Koukopoulos 2012). Evidence from sediment cores suggests that environmental changes, including the expansion of the lower Verde's floodplain and the creation of coastal estuaries, contributed to population growth during the latter part of the Formative (Goman et al. 2005, 2013; Mueller et al. 2013).

Two demographic centers developed during the Late Formative on the east side of the river: Charco Redondo at 70 hectares and San Francisco de Arriba at 95 hectares (Workinger 2002). Monumental construction occurred at both sites (Butler 2011; Workinger 2002), although evidence for social inequality is limited (Joyce 1991a, 1994; 2010:180–86). Most inhabitants of the valley lived in small sites where communal practices like ritual feasting, cemetery burial, and collective labor projects defined local groups consisting of multiple households and perhaps entire communities (Barber 2005:95–101; Barber and Joyce 2007; Barber et al. 2013b; Joyce 1991a, 1994; 2005, 2010:180–86; Joyce et al. 1998). At the 1.5-hectare site of Cerro de la Cruz, for example, horizontal excavations exposed a communal cemetery in a modest public building on the site's upper terrace (Joyce 1991a, 1991b, 1994). The remains of forty-nine individuals were recovered from the cemetery. Most of the burials (86 percent) were adults, and none were accompanied by offerings. Adjacent to the public building, excavations revealed a granite flagstone patio. Three small storerooms were discovered on the west side of the patio opposite the public building. Within one of the storerooms was a thin organic deposit containing over 1,000 fragments of charred maize (Woodard 1991:869). A hearth of 3 square meters, which far exceeds the size of cooking features typically associated with residences, intruded into the surface of the patio. We interpret the hearth, midden, and storerooms as evidence for ritual feasting that brought together multiple households.

The evidence for communal rituals and labor projects and the lack of indications of pronounced inequality therefore suggests that Late Formative authority and identity were defined in terms of horizontal, communal social relationships rather than hierarchical, exclusionary ones (Barber and Joyce 2007; Joyce 2005, 2010). At both large and small sites, people created socially meaningful places through the construction and use of shared public spaces and monumental facilities that embedded collective actions and histories in specific locations on the landscape. The inhabitants of these places, who probably would have included the living, the dead, and other animate entities, engaged in feasting, mortuary ceremonies, other rituals, and communal labor. Late Formative public spaces thus were loci of entanglement where practices, people, and things became intertwined in ways that constituted a particular form of community that included a shared history and identity. As discussed in the next section, the working out of tensions and contradictions between new and preexisting forms of community and authority would be a major site of struggle, negotiation, and contradiction during the Terminal Formative.

COMMUNITY AND AUTHORITY IN THE TERMINAL FORMATIVE

Political complexity culminated during the Terminal Formative with the emergence of an urban center at Río Viejo on the west bank of the river (Joyce 2013b). Río Viejo increased in size from a 25-hectare town in the Late Formative to a 225-hectare urban center by the early Terminal Formative (150 BCE–100 CE). Applying formulae developed elsewhere in Mesoamerica to estimate population from site area (e.g., Blanton 1978:29–30; Kowalewski et al. 2009:24–25; Sanders et al. 1979), we estimate Río Viejo's maximum Terminal Formative population at about 8,500. Regional population grew through this period based on the area occupied in the survey zone, which reached 775 hectares by the late Terminal Formative. Other large sites included Charco Redondo, Cerro de la Virgen, Tututepec, and San Francisco de Arriba, all of which ranged in size from 60 to 72 hectares. Increased inequality is evident in mortuary offerings, domestic architecture, ceremonial caches, and monumental buildings (Barber 2005, 2013; Barber and Olvera 2012; Barber et al. 2009; Joyce 2005, 2006, 2010:186–95, 2013b; Joyce and Barber 2011; Mayes and Barber

2008). The evidence from Río Viejo and outlying sites in the region show that during the Terminal Formative, community continued to be constituted through the construction and use of shared public spaces and monumental buildings as they had been in the Late Formative.

Communal Ceremony

Communal ceremonies associated with monumental public buildings and spaces continued and expanded in scale from the Late Formative, including mortuary rituals in cemeteries, feasting, and communal caches. At Yugüe, during the early Terminal Formative, people constructed a public building on the site's mixed-use platform (Substructure 1) (Barber 2005:150–206; 2013). Feasting is indicated by a cooking feature just outside the public building that included three large jars, burned on their exterior surfaces; one still contained whole shells of estuarine mussels. An early Terminal Formative midden containing sherds, ash, bone, and estuarine shells resulted from a number of distinct feasting events, while a late Terminal Formative sheet midden was likely deposited as the result of one or a small number of feasts. During the late Terminal Formative, Substructure 1 at Yugüe became the location of a communal cemetery (Barber 2005; Barber et al. 2013b). Unlike the earlier cemetery at Cerro de la Cruz, the one at Yugüe included people of varying status levels and a broader range of ages. Additional evidence for the repetitive use of the public building at Yugüe is in the form of ritual caches. During the early Terminal Formative, a cache of twenty ceramic vessels was placed in the fill of Substructure 1 (Barber 2005:164–65; 2013:173–76), and by the late Terminal Formative, at least fifty cylindrical vessels were cached in the building over an extended period of time (figure 3.2a).

At other sites in the region, public buildings are also associated with evidence of feasting, cemeteries, and caching ceremonies. For example, at Charco Redondo, Butler (2011) excavated part of an early Terminal Formative cemetery located in a probable public building. At San Francisco de Arriba, people left ritual caches in the fill of different building phases of the site's acropolis (Workinger 2002:185–214). One cache, however, was much more impressive than the others, consisting of 356 greenstone beads, 27 rock crystal beads, 109 beads of an unidentified stone, 2 greenstone bird head pendants, 2 rock crystal pendants, fragments of iron ore, 9 locally produced miniature grayware jars, and disarticulated animal bone. Higher proportions of fancy grayware serving vessels in nonelite ceramic inventories suggest an increase in ritual feasting in the region as a whole (Levine 2002, 2013).

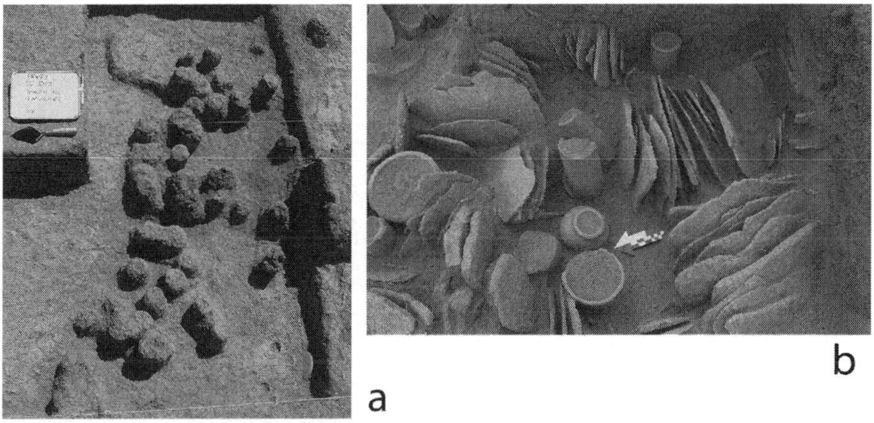

FIGURE 3.2. *Terminal Formative Period ritual offerings in public buildings: (a) cache of cylindrical vessels at Yugüe (after Barber 2005:figure 6.12); (b) part of the Complex A offering at Cerro de la Virgen, showing ceramic vessels and vertical stone slabs (courtesy of Jeff Brzezinski).*

At Cerro de la Virgen, evidence of both feasting and caching rituals were associated with the ceremonial center located around the site's large public plaza. Along the northeast edge of the plaza, investigations during the 2013 field season recorded an architectural complex (Complex A) consisting of two low platforms built at right angles to one another, with patios to the north and south (Brzezinski n.d.). Dug into the surface of both patios were several hearths, possibly for feasting events; a large hearth far exceeding typical cooking features found in residences was also present in the plaza. Beneath the northern patio of Complex A, excavations exposed an impressive series of caches. The offerings covered an area of 62 square meters and included 260 ceramic vessels placed in granite-slab compartments (figure 3.2b). The stratigraphy and position of the caches and slabs indicate that they consisted of numerous individual offerings emplaced over an extended period of time.

Communal Labor Projects

Major communal works projects during the Terminal Formative included the construction of monumental buildings at Río Viejo and at least nine other sites, including Charco Redondo, San Francisco de Arriba, Cerro de la Virgen, and Yugüe (Barber 2005:117–18; Butler 2011; Joyce 2006, 2010:187–91; Joyce et al. 2013; Workinger 2002:147–230). The scale of construction was considerable, even at some smaller settlements. For example, at the 10-hectare site of Yugüe, on the east side of the river a multiuse platform was built that measured 300 meters by 150 meters and reached 10 meters at its highest point. The summit of the structure supported public ceremonial space while the flanks supported residences (Barber 2005). At the 60-hectare hilltop site of Cerro de la Virgen, northeast of Yugüe, monumental constructions included a ceremonial precinct that contained a public plaza measuring approximately 2,800 square meters surrounded by a ballcourt and several public buildings (Barber 2005:138–40).

The largest Terminal Formative Period public buildings in the lower Río Verde Valley were located at Río Viejo. The ceremonial core of the site consisted of two monumental earthen architectural complexes. The earlier was Mound 9-Structure 4, which was probably begun at the very end of the Late Formative and then raised incrementally through subsequent building episodes during the early Terminal Formative (Joyce 1991a:364–74). Structure 4 consisted of a massive rectangular platform, measuring 125 meters by 200 meters and at least 5 meters high, raised over the site's Late Formative residential areas (A. Joyce 1999). The platform supported four substructures, one of which today rises 12 meters above the floodplain.

Toward the end of the early Terminal Formative, the ceremonial center was shifted approximately 600 meters to the west of Mound 9-Structure 4. The new ceremonial center was an even larger acropolis that we have designated Mound 1 (Joyce 2006; Joyce and Barber 2011; Joyce et al. 2013). In its final form, the acropolis covered an area of 350 meters by 200 meters and supported two large substructural platforms rising at least 17 meters above the floodplain, a sunken patio, and a plaza (figure 3.3). The acropolis was begun late in the early Terminal Formative, but a major occupation is not evident until the late Terminal Formative. At this time, the Mound 1 acropolis consisted of a platform rising at least 6 meters above the floodplain and supporting two large substructures on its northwestern and eastern sides (Structures 1 and 2, respectively) both of which stood at least 16 meters high. South of Structures 1 and 2 was a large open space located beneath the area that would become the sunken patio in the Late Classic. Excavations suggest that during the late Terminal Formative this space was at the level of the floodplain (Joyce and Barber 2011). The use of this space cannot be determined because Formative Period occupational surfaces are now below groundwater, but we suspect that it was a large public plaza. The possible plaza was bounded to the south and west by a 5- to 7-meter-high platform or platforms that may have been continuous with the main part of the acropolis.[1] Our estimated total volume for Mound 1 is 560,050 cubic meters, which is about half the volume of the Sun

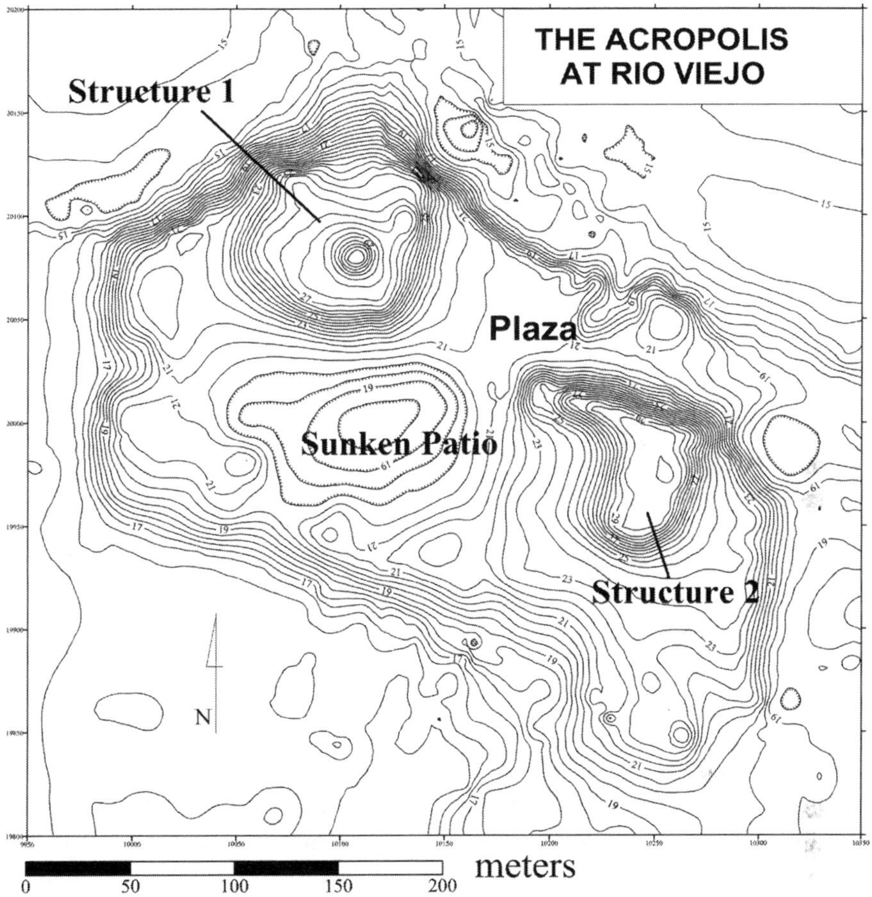

FIGURE 3.3. *Plan of the acropolis at Río Viejo (after Joyce 2005:figure 6).*

Pyramid at Teotihuacan, or slightly smaller than Monk's Mound at Cahokia (Joyce et al. 2013:table 5.1). Our conservative estimate of the volume of the Terminal Formative version of the acropolis is 455,050 square meters.

Evidence that construction of the acropolis required the mobilization of a large labor force from multiple communities comes from excavations in the platform fill and retaining walls on the acropolis (Joyce et al. 2013). The stratigraphy exposed by the excavations indicates that the acropolis was raised by a small number of massive fill deposits, likely emplaced over a relatively short period of time rather than being the result of frequent but smaller scale construction episodes involving numerous superimposed periods of building remodeling, such as observed with the acropolis at San Francisco de Arriba (Workinger 2002:147–222), Substructure 1 at Yugüe (Barber 2005:150–94), and Mound 9-Structure 4 at Río Viejo (Joyce 1991a; Salazar Chávez et al. n.d.). Although the initial fill layers in the acropolis consisted of unconsolidated sediment, the majority of the fill revealed unexpectedly diverse and labor-intensive construction techniques. We have identified at least five distinct forms of fill, including unconsolidated basket loads of sediment, rammed earth, sheet fills, and two types of fill utilizing adobe blocks (for more detailed discussions, see Joyce and Barber 2011; Joyce et al. 2013). We use the term *structured-fill* to describe adobe and rammed-earth deposits, since they would have required greater organization and labor to construct in comparison with basket loads of unconsolidated sediment or rubble. The variability in fill construction is mirrored in more formal architectural features, especially retaining walls, which include adobe bricks and stone masonry (see Barber and Joyce 2011, 2012; Frederick n.d.; Joyce and Barber 2011, 2013, n.d.; Joyce et al. 2013; Joyce and Levine 2009). Even within individual walls we see considerable variability in construction techniques. For example, an adobe retaining wall exposed on the western end of the acropolis contained bricks made from two different clay sources that varied in shape and size and were emplaced both horizontally and vertically (Egan 2012:367) (figure 3.4).

We have found no architectural explanation for the different construction techniques on the acropolis. Instead, the variability in construction fill and retaining walls suggests to us that at least five distinct work groups were involved in building the acropolis (e.g., Hastings and Moseley 1975). We hypothesize that each group used slightly different materials and strategies to create the stable interior fill of the structure (i.e., basket loads of unconsolidated fill plus the four types of structured fill). The construction techniques also indicate that the acropolis was not built by a permanent work force, since we would expect to see greater consistency in construction methods, but was the result of a rotation of work groups carrying out their jobs in slightly different ways. Based on estimates of the labor needed to construct the acropolis, we have argued that workers must have been drawn from both Río Viejo and the surrounding settlements who were fulfilling obligations to the community and the nobility at Río Viejo (Joyce et al. 2013). We have also tentatively linked some of the specific construction techniques to earlier buildings at Río Viejo and to buildings at other sites. For example, early Terminal Formative construction fill on Mound 9-Structure 4 at Río Viejo included a rammed earth wall that retained unconsolidated fill (Salazar Chávez et al. n.d.). In contrast, at the site of Loma Don Genaro, located about 6 kilometers southwest

Figure 3.4. *Adobe retaining wall on the western end of the acropolis with bricks made from three different clay sources (photo by Sarah Barber).*

of Río Viejo, we have documented unconsolidated fill and sheet fill construction techniques dating to the late Terminal Formative (Lucido et al. n.d.). At Yugüe, Barber (2005) noted unconsolidated fill and stone and adobe walls in Terminal Formative architecture.

We argue that the diversity of construction techniques found in the acropolis, which exceeds that of other sites, resulted from a labor pool drawn from multiple communities. Participation of people in the construction of the acropolis, as well as the rituals carried out there, would have acted as practices that affiliated people with the symbols, institutions, and rulers at Río Viejo. It is not clear, however, if people from the entire region were engaged physically and symbolically in practices of affiliation centered on Río Viejo and its politico-religious institutions and authorities. Although regional data indicate that social inequality increased during the Terminal Formative, evidence pertaining to the rulers of Río Viejo has remained illusory.

Hierarchy and Authority

Excavations throughout the lower Verde region indicate that inequality and the power of local leaders increased during the Terminal Formative. At Cerro de la Virgen, Barber (2005, 2013) excavated a high-status house, which was considerably larger and architecturally more elaborate than typical residences in the region. The house was located on a large terrace near the summit of the hill directly above the public plaza, Structure 1, and Complex A, suggesting an association between elites and public space. The scale of Terminal Formative monumental buildings also suggests that rulers had considerable power to mobilize labor (Barber 2005; Barber and Joyce 2007; Joyce 2013b; Joyce and Barber 2011; Joyce et al.2013).

Mortuary evidence suggests rising inequality as well. While most people interred in the Yugüe cemetery did not have offerings or were accompanied by a few ceramic vessels or beads made of greenstone or shell, some burials were marked by exotic offerings or adornments. For example, an adult female (Burial 8-Individual 8) showed evidence for pyrite incrustations in her upper incisors. Although dental modification was not necessarily an indicator of high status in pre-Columbian Mesoamerica (Krejci and Culbert 1995), iron pyrite is sufficiently rare in the lower Verde that it was likely a socially valued material. A juvenile (Burial 11-Individual 12) was buried with a string of 36 greenstone and white stone or shell beads as well as a greenstone pendant carved in the shape of a human face. The most elaborate burial (Burial 14-Individual 16) in the cemetery was an adolescent male who was interred wearing a plaster-backed iron ore pectoral and holding an incised flute made from a deer femur (Barber 2005; Barber and Olvera 2012; Mayes and Barber 2008). Based on analyses of the iconography on the flute, Barber and Olvera (2012) argue that this individual was likely a local elite and a ritual specialist with the ability to contact important nonhuman beings such as divinities and ancestors.

Evidence that elites had specialized ritual roles and knowledge also comes from ritual caches in more restricted and exclusive public buildings. For example, an unusual offering was recovered beneath the center of Structure 1 at Cerro de la Virgen, a small public building reached by a stairway ascending from Complex A. The cache was emplaced on bedrock just prior to the construction of Structure 1 and consisted of several ceramic vessels, a small stone figure, 2 miniature stone thrones, fragments of a stone mask, and a nearly complete stone mask depicting a rain deity or rain deity impersonator that was broken prior to deposition (figure 3.5). Another unusual offering associated with a restricted ceremonial building comes from a subfloor cache in a small public platform at Yugüe (Substructure 2). The cache consisted of a

FIGURE 3.5. *Offering in Structure 1 from Cerro de la Virgen with stone rain deity mask (courtesy of Jeff Brzezinski).*

coarse brownware cooking jar, grayware sherds, including one from a Valley of Oaxaca import, half of an incised local grayware bowl, ash, estuarine shell, fragments of 16 different ceramic earspools, a ceramic figurine, and burned earth. The incised design on the grayware bowl included an anthropomorphic image depicting a regional variant of the Zapotec *xicani* or the Mixtec *yahui* (Brzezinski 2011:107–9), a high-status sacrificial specialist who wears a mask with a long, upturned snout (Urcid 2005:56). The inclusion of the earspools indicates an association with elite status (R. Joyce 1999).

Although excavation data from outlying sites demonstrate inequality in the Terminal Formative Period, evidence for the nature of rulership and political authority at Río Viejo has proved difficult to come by, even from the extensive excavations on the acropolis. We have found no domestic architecture that might indicate the location of a noble residence or ruler's palace. There is no evidence for tombs or elaborate burials of nobility. We have yet to find stone monuments with portraits of rulers that date to the Terminal Formative, as have been recorded in many other regions of Mesoamerica (Joyce 2010; Love 1999; Pool 2007). We have investigated at least one elaborate and spatially restricted ceremonial space on the acropolis that indicates a degree of exclusivity that presumably marked status distinctions. Structure 2 was a large, stepped platform that supported an adobe superstructure that had remnants of the only architectural stucco ever found in the valley and a massive stone retaining wall that would have supported a narrow elevated platform (Joyce 2006; Joyce et al. 2013). The absence of domestic artifacts or refuse in association with Structure 2 indicates that it was a public building, possibly a temple. Yet there are fewer direct indications of elites on the acropolis than at many of the public buildings we have excavated elsewhere in the region. Instead, we see evidence for regional political authority in the distribution of the population, in the coordination required to underwrite monument construction, and in the sponsorship of large-scale ritual feasts and presumably other rituals on the acropolis. As discussed in the next section, the evidence suggests to us that regional authority and political identity were both tenuous and contradictory to local authority and community identity.

THE RÍO VIEJO POLITY: CONTRADICTION, NEGOTIATION, AND COLLAPSE

We see the construction and use of the acropolis at Río Viejo during the late Terminal Formative as key processes in the constitution of regional political identity and authority. The relocation of Río Viejo's site center from Mound 9-Structure 4 to the acropolis would have detached the new ceremonial center from the long-standing material, symbolic, and practical focus of Rio Viejo's local community. Limited excavations in Mound 9-Structure 4 suggest that it was not used during the late Terminal Formative (Joyce 1991a; Salazar Chávez et al. n.d.). By purging the ceremonial center of its exclusively local entanglements, the acropolis created the potential for the construction of a regionally significant place that could have become a material and ideational focal point in a multi-community polity. Our data suggest, however, that the scaling-up of communal practices and the emergence of incipient forms of regional authority created points of contradiction and tension relative to long-standing communal practices and forms of authority at the local level (Barber 2013; Barber and Joyce 2007; Joyce 2008, 2010:194–96, 2013b; Joyce et al. 2013). The polity that resulted was tenuous, contested, and short lived.

The Contradictions of Local Community and Polity

The construction of the acropolis was a massive communal project that drew on labor from multiple communities in the valley. Yet there is only limited evidence for practices that would have continued to draw large numbers of people to Río Viejo after the acropolis was built. The best documented practice was ritual feasting, the evidence for which is abundant across the acropolis. Feasting-related features demonstrate that both food preparation and discard took place at much larger scales than has been found at outlying communities (Lucido et al. 2013). Ten refuse deposits were recovered on the south and west sides of the acropolis. Nine of these deposits were located in pits that had been excavated into Terminal Formative construction fill. The two largest pits were more than 1.5 meters deep and one was more than 4 meters in diameter. These features spanned the entire period from the completion of the acropolis, probably early in the second century CE, to the time of the area's abandonment at ca. 250 CE. The middens contained ash, thick lenses of estuarine mussel shell, dense deposits of sherds, and organic sediments. Five of these features were internally stratified, demonstrating that they were formed by multiple depositional events. The lack of domestic architecture and other features and artifacts normally associated with residences (e.g., Barber 2005; Gaxiola 1984; Joyce et al. 1998; Robles García 1988; Winter 1986) on the acropolis indicates that the middens were formed as the result of nondomestic commensal activities. The size and number of most of these features is well beyond that of a domestic refuse deposit. At least some of the food consumed at feasts was probably prepared in a huge earth oven discovered at the base of Structure 2 on the acropolis (Barber et al. 2013a; Joyce and Barber 2013). Refuse from the oven consisted of ash, burned sherds, and burned rock that covered an area with a diameter of at least 10 meters (figure 3.6). The burned rock and sherds were used to retain heat. Despite the oven's large size, it is unlikely that it was sufficient to cook all foods used in feasting, and the absence of storage facilities on the acropolis indicates that people attending feasts brought food there.

The size and contents of the middens suggests that both large-scale and repeated food consumption was taking place on the acropolis (Lucido et al. 2013). The evidence available thus far does not indicate that feasting on the acropolis was restricted to the elite. The scale and distribution of commensal activities makes restricted feasting seem unlikely to us. The ceramics themselves do not include unusual decorations, surface treatments, or vessel forms that might indicate elite wares of restricted circulation (cf. Elson and Sherman 2007; LeCount 2001). These data indicate that large groups of people were brought together not only in the construction of Río Viejo's monumental spaces but also in their subsequent use. The feasting activities can be considered a scaled-up version of practices that had brought together people in ritually charged ways at other public buildings in the region and a means through which new

Figure 3.6. *Photo of a section of the earth oven on the acropolis at Río Viejo (photo by Arthur Joyce).*

social ties were forged (cf. Monaghan 1995). Yet ritual feasting would have also drawn people away from ritual activities at public buildings in their home communities, which clearly continued as an important focus of ritual action at this time (Barber 2005; Levine 2002). The increase in obligations of feast sponsors at both the local and regional level could have taxed people's abilities to generate surpluses and led to social tensions and conflicts, just as feasting can do in modern Mixtec communities in Oaxaca (Monaghan 1995:167–89).

Despite the scale of communal construction and feasting on the acropolis, evidence from outlying communities suggests that practices of affiliation at the regional level did not result in an overarching political identity centered on Río Viejo and its rulers. In fact, the regional evidence suggests that practices of affiliation and community identity did not extend much beyond local communities. For example, site orientations, including those of public buildings, varied from site to site (Barber 2005:210–11). Construction techniques of monumental architecture also varied from community to community, with both rubble fill and unconsolidated sediment used at San Francisco de Arriba (Workinger 2002) and Cerro de la Virgen (Barber 2005) and various forms of earthen architecture dominant at other sites, including Cerro de la Cruz, Yugüe, Loma Don Genaro, Barra Quebrada, and Río Viejo (Barber 2005; Joyce 1991a; Joyce and Barber 2011; Joyce et al. 2013; Lucido et al. n.d.; Winter and Joyce 1987). Data from ceremonial caches at Yugüe, San Francisco de Arriba, Cerro de la Virgen, and Loma Don Genaro suggest a pattern of regional idiosyncrasy in the use of public buildings (Barber 2005, 2013; Barber et al. 2014; Brzezinski n.d.; Lucido et al. n.d.; Workinger 2002). The contents and positioning of caches, for instance, was quite variable across the valley. The San Francisco de Arriba cache, which included crystal and greenstone artifacts, contained a number of valuable imported items as well as a wide range of raw materials. At Cerro de la Virgen, the Complex A cache consisted almost entirely of cylindrical ceramic vessels, some of which are similar to those found at San Francisco de Arriba. However, the Cerro de la Virgen vessels were deposited without associated valuables and within granite slab compartments—a formation seen nowhere else in the region. Exotic stone objects were found in Structure 1 at the site, including the stone mask and thrones, but were quite distinct from those deposited at San Francisco de Arriba. Caches at Yugüe, on the other hand, did not contain valuable items. In fact, the two largest caches at the site contained dozens of crudely made ceramic cylinders that look as if they may have been amateur copies of the cylindrical offering vessels found at San Francisco de Arriba and Cerro de la Virgen (Barber et al. 2014). The evidence therefore suggests that, while there was a regionally shared set of ideas regarding how communities were defined, there were clear distinctions among sites in the materials and practices through which specific community identities were instantiated. Contrary to the expectations of many models of early complex societies (e.g., Flannery 1998; Redmond and Spencer 2008), the construction and use of the acropolis at Río Viejo does not seem to have led to uniformity in religious practices and architectural canons across the region.

There is also evidence for points of tension surrounding increasing inequality and the emergence of regional political authorities at Río Viejo. Even though local leaders were still tied to their communities, as shown by the excavations at Yugüe, Cerro de la Virgen, and Charco Redondo (Barber 2005, 2013; Barber and Joyce 2007; Barber et al. 2013b; Joyce 2010:186–95), they were also increasingly distinguishing themselves from others through mortuary practices, prestige goods, and elaborate residences. Social valuables obtained through long-distance exchange linked lower Verde elites to those in other parts of Mesoamerica and contributed to the creation of a high-status identity. Although prestige goods may have had complex life histories that included use as adornments and gifts exchanged among prominent people, many were ultimately consumed in burials and caches and so became entangled with the community via collective ceremonies. The interment of socially valued goods in burials and offerings in public buildings contributed to status inequality because these objects demonstrated the unique social ties of their donors. However, the deposition of such materials in nondomestic contexts converted valuable items into collective resources, thereby transforming hierarchical social distinctions into expressions of traditional communal principles. Cached valuables thus became inalienable objects that materialized corporate identities and histories (Barber et al. 2014; see also Weiner 1992). The marking of elite bodies via adornment and prestigious objects, as well as the elaborate architecture and spatial setting of the high-status house at Cerro de la Virgen, demonstrate the increasing visibility of high status at the local level. Their interment in community cemeteries upon death, however, in turn highlighted elites' membership in a local collectivity. Likewise, since evidence for the celebration of rulers and rulership has not been found, it appears that the construction of monumental buildings with voluntary labor emphasized corporate action and identity rather than the authority of rulers. The evidence suggests that rulership and hierarchy were embedded in and constrained by communal principles, practices, and obligations, resulting in a form of political authority that Blanton (1998:151) defines as egalitarian.

The only possible evidence we see for a regional political identity tied to the rulers of Río Viejo is in the form of imagery on widely available grayware vessels. Brzezinski (2011) shows that the most common iconography on Terminal Formative Period grayware bowls (figure 3.7) included images pertaining to widespread Mesoamerican religious themes such as maize, clouds, lightning, wind, and rain (Jansen and Pérez Jiménez 2007; Monaghan 1990; Sellen 2011; Taube 1996). Images of skulls and dead humans, especially on anthropomorphic vessel appliqués, also suggest the important role of death, and perhaps

FIGURE 3.7. *Late Terminal Formative iconographic gray wares: (a) conical bowl from Yugüe with incised maize icon (after Brzezinski 2011:figure 10a); (b) conical bowl from Cerro de la Cruz with incised cloud icon (after Brzezinski 2011:figure 15); (c) incurving wall bowl from Yugüe with lightning iconography (after Brzezinski 2011:figure 33a).*

sacrifice, in pre-Columbian religion (Brzezinski 2011:105; Hepp and Joyce 2013:277–79). At Yugüe, the imagery on the bone flute from the cemetery and the grayware bowl fragment from the cache in Substructure 2 suggest that elites may have taken on more important roles as religious specialists, as has been seen in other regions of Mesoamerica at this time (Freidel and Schele 1988; Joyce 2000). It is possible that the widely available iconographic ceramics materialized an ideology that legitimated the central role of rulers in religious belief and practice in the lower Río Verde Valley, although there is no evidence suggesting that elites controlled the production or distribution of these vessels. Rather than the results of an ideology imposed on common people by the nobility, the wide distribution of iconographic graywares could be a function of the communal nature of political authority and religious practice.

Overall, the evidence suggests to us that people from different communities in the region participated in the construction and use of the acropolis and rulers of Río Viejo gained some degree of political influence over multiple communities. These multi-community links, however, appear to us to have been tenuous and unstable such that Terminal Formative Río Viejo challenges the limits of what might be defined as a polity. The evidence suggests that authority in the region was not singular, and it is likely that newer, more regional and hierarchical forms of authority existed alongside traditional, community-based and less hierarchical leadership. Points of tension and negotiation probably surrounded issues such as participation in feasts and other rituals on public buildings and the centrality of regional rulers rather than local communities in important ceremonies. We suspect that while Río Viejo was the most powerful political center, people of other communities had considerable independence and were able to strategically strengthen ties with or create distance from rulers and ruling institutions at Río Viejo.

The Collapse of Río Viejo

The collapse of the late Terminal Formative polity around 250 CE was followed by a period of political fragmentation in the Early Classic Period (250–500 CE), showing that Terminal Formative authority was indeed tenuous and short lived (Joyce and Barber 2011; Joyce 2005, 2008:234–240). At ca. 250 CE the archaeological record indicates a dramatic change in regional settlement and sociopolitical organization. Río Viejo decreased in size from 200 hectares in the late Terminal Formative to 75 hectares in the Early Classic. Several other large Terminal Formative floodplain sites with mounded architecture, including Yugüe, declined significantly in size or were abandoned. Regional surveys in the lower Río Verde region show a shift to defensible piedmont locations. During the Early Classic, the region contained perhaps as many as eight demographic centers of roughly equivalent size. There is little evidence for monumental building activities, suggesting that leaders were unable to mobilize large labor forces as they did in the Terminal Formative. The data indicate that during the Early Classic, multiple, perhaps competing, polities occupied the lower Río Verde Valley.

As a focus of the tenuous regional entanglements that constituted the Río Viejo polity, it is not surprising that our excavations on the site's acropolis show that it was abandoned at ca. 250 CE. While we are still working to understand this important social and political transition, our excavations on the acropolis suggest that people may have formally dismantled or "closed" this monumental public space as the Formative Period came to an end. Burning of superstructures and platform surfaces is indicated in the ceremonial building atop Structure 2 and in a substantial wattle-and-daub public building on the south edge of the acropolis (Arellano 2012; Joyce et al. 2013; Rivas 2012). In both areas we recovered burned earthen floors; and in one instance we found burned daub detritus from no fewer than three separate superstructures. We cannot rule out the possibility that violence was the cause of this burning and potentially part of the reason Río Viejo collapsed. Evidence from subsequent deposits indicates, however, that the acropolis went through a period of ritual termination, and the final and most extensive episode of burning may have initiated these ceremonies.

At the very end of the late Terminal Formative, immediately following the burning of these buildings, much of the structure was covered by thin fill layers and/or deposits of refuse containing high densities of broken ceramics that resemble the results of termination ceremonies found in other parts of Mesoamerica (Elson and Smith 2001; Hamann 2008; Stanton et al. 2008; Stross 1998; Walker 1998). Most importantly, there were changes in the kinds of activities taking place on the acropolis at this time. Stones were removed from masonry features and superstructures covered by fill were not rebuilt. At the base of Structure 2, colluvial deposits suggest that the structure was not being maintained and began to erode. In several areas of the acropolis, sherds and partial vessels overlay these fill deposits or were placed into pits that had been excavated into the final layers of earthen fill. These pits varied significantly in size, but their contents were consistently sherds; whole and partial vessels, some of which appeared to have been broken in place; and sand. One pit consisted of sherds and an organic incendiary that were burned *in situ*. The fill deposits that overlay the final Terminal Formative strata throughout the acropolis date to the Late Classic, reiterating that the actions must have been among the very last undertaken on the acropolis until the area was reoccupied around 500 CE.

Activity on the acropolis changed dramatically in the Early Classic Period, during which time there was no construction or modification of monumental spaces. Indeed, some areas may have been mined for sediment to use in construction elsewhere given the presence of large pits that were refilled in the Late Classic Period. During the Late Classic, the acropolis was reoccupied and once again became the focus of important ceremonies (Baillie 2012; Joyce et al. 2001). At this time, Río Viejo reemerged as an urban center and political seat for the region.

We are not entirely sure what led to the collapse of the Río Viejo polity and the ritual termination and abandonment of the acropolis. Although we cannot entirely rule out interaction and perhaps conflict with distant polities such as Teotihuacan (Joyce 2003; cf. Workinger 2013), we increasingly see evidence for the sorts of tensions and contradictions that developed from regional historical processes, such as those surrounding community and authority that we have delineated in this chapter (Joyce 2008, 2010, 2013b; Joyce and Barber 2011). In particular, we see fracture points created by new forms of political authority as well as the more encompassing sets of practices, beliefs, and identities centered on the acropolis at Río Viejo. Contradictions developed during the Terminal Formative between the newer, more hierarchical and regional forms of authority and identity that were beginning to emerge at Río Viejo and long-standing local and communal forms of authority and identity centered on public buildings at places like Yugüe, Cerro de la Virgen, and San Francisco de Arriba. We see contradictions between peoples' obligations to their local communities and to the rulers of Río Viejo. At the same time, Río Viejo's rulers were faced with the conflicting demands of hierarchy and community. To extend their political power, the rulers of Río Viejo needed to set themselves apart so as to supersede the authority of local leaders and become a focal point of a new scaled-up regional community. Yet they were operating in a cultural setting where authority was tightly constrained by local communal identity and obligations. Similar kinds of contradictions and points of tension existed at this time in other parts of Mesoamerica and were worked through in diverse ways, leading to a variety of forms of political organization and divergent political histories.

INSTITUTIONALIZING REGIONAL AUTHORITY: THE VIEW FROM MONTE ALBÁN

Our archaeological research in the lower Río Verde Valley shows that Río Viejo exhibits many of the hallmarks that archaeologists have traditionally attributed to the kinds of politically centralized and tightly integrated societies normally defined as states. In the case of Río Viejo, these characteristics include a five-tiered settlement hierarchy, urbanism, monumental public architecture, and rulers who were sufficiently powerful to sponsor large labor projects and public ceremonies. Yet a closer reading of the evidence shows that people in outlying communities like Yugüe, Cerro de la Virgen, San Francisco de Arriba, and Loma Don Genaro exhibited considerable independence from the regional center in ritual practices and architectural techniques and styles. In contrast to traditional archaeological models of complex political formations as strongly hierarchical and tightly integrated, our view of the later Formative Río Viejo polity is that it was neither highly integrated nor significantly coercive. While Río Viejo challenges assumptions about complex polities, it was far from being an isolated case. Throughout much of later Formative Mesoamerica, people in complex polities were struggling over competing forms of political authority (e.g., Cowgill 1997; Joyce 2010; Love 1999; Pool 2008; Sugiyama 1993). In some cases, such as at Teotihuacan and Monte Albán, the outcome led to the institutionalization of regional political authority, although the form of that authority varied from region to region. Likewise, while these polities persisted for centuries, their ruling ideas, practices, and institutions were far from stable. In other cases, including Río Viejo and probably many of the polities of the Mixteca Alta of Oaxaca, regional political authority was tenuous and short lived (Joyce 2010:195).

The later Formative Monte Albán polity in the highlands of Oaxaca offers a comparative case to explore some of the factors that could have contributed to the institutionalization of regional political authority (also see Joyce 2010; Joyce and Barber 2013). We see a number of points of divergence between

Monte Albán and Río Viejo that may have had significant consequences in the history of these polities, especially as they relate to the ability of rulers to extend their authority across multiple communities throughout a broader region. In the Valley of Oaxaca, evidence suggests that the rulers of Monte Albán were initially successful in negotiating shared forms of political control with more traditional communal forms of leadership. Although we see political authority in the Late Formative Valley of Oaxaca as largely communal, Monte Albán's rulers were successful in linking their authority and identity to a series of innovations in politico-religious belief and practice that served to set them apart from local leaders as well as commoners. These innovations included the increasing control over ritual knowledge and authority centered on Monte Albán's Main Plaza as well as the manufacture of social valuables and the use of coercive force.

A focal point in this new relational field was the Main Plaza of Monte Albán, which was a socially significant place marked by architecture and imagery that was clearly distinct from previous ceremonial precincts (e.g., Blanton 1978; Joyce 2000, 2004; Winter 2001). The Main Plaza had been a symbol of collective identity and authority during the Late Formative, but by the Terminal Formative it was increasingly controlled by and restricted to the nobility (Joyce 2004:205–7). Associations of elite residences and burials with religious symbols, spaces, and artifacts, especially the monumental art and architecture found on the Main Plaza, indicate that the nobility increasingly came to control ritual knowledge and authority, although high-ranking commoners may have also achieved positions of political and religious power (Joyce 2010:143; Urcid 2011).

Rulers at Monte Albán were successful in gaining control over the manufacture of a variety of social valuables through which debts and obligations could be established and political institutions funded. These items included fancy creamware ceramics often with post-fire scratch incising and large hollow supports (Elson and Sherman 2007; Kowalewski et al. 1989:180, 199; Markens and Martínez 2009). Like the iconographic graywares in the lower Río Verde Valley, the creamwares often exhibited step-fret designs symbolizing the rain-lightning deity and were part of a pan-Mesoamerican system of elite display. Unlike the lower Verde graywares, the distribution of creamwares in the Valley of Oaxaca was markedly status linked. These symbols may have been another indication of the increasing control of important religious symbols and ceremonies by powerful elites. Excavations in a nonresidential architectural complex on the northwestern corner of the Main Plaza recovered evidence of the production of shell ornaments and prismatic obsidian blades, suggesting that the rulers of Monte Albán may have also controlled the manufacture of these items (Markens and Martínez 2009).

Finally, the rulers of Monte Albán had recourse to coercive force to bring communities in the valley into compliance. For example, although we question the degree to which areas outside the valley were conquered (e.g., Joyce 2013c; Workinger and Joyce 2009; Zeitlin and Joyce 1999), there is evidence that the site of El Palenque, south of Monte Albán, was defeated and incorporated into the Monte Albán polity at ca. 30 BCE (Redmond and Spencer 2006). Warfare included elements of religious ritual through human sacrifice and ritual preparations for battle (Joyce 2000; Urcid 2011; Urcid and Joyce 2014). There are also indications that conflict may have been part of what eventually contributed to the declining influence of communal forms of leadership and the institutionalization of more hierarchical, exclusionary, and regional forms of authority centered at Monte Albán (Joyce 2010:159; Urcid 2011; Urcid and Joyce 2014). Evidence from the end of the Terminal Formative suggests that these tensions may have erupted in a political upheaval at Monte Albán around 200 CE. At this time, several major iconographic programs on the Main Plaza were dismantled and some monuments were defaced and buried under new buildings. A temple on the North Platform was burned and a defensive wall was built around parts of the site. One access point onto the Main Plaza was probably monitored through military force. Since these iconographic programs downplay the power of rulers, and in some cases probably represent communal forms of leadership, their dismantling and destruction may directly reflect the suppression of communal authority that had existed alongside the hierarchical rulers of the polity (Joyce 2010; Urcid 2011; Urcid and Joyce 2014). Evidence for the increasing formalization of status distinctions by the Early Classic Period and iconography celebrating the religious and political power of rulers suggest that the more exclusionary and hierarchical forms of authority gained prominence over competing forms of leadership (Joyce 2004, 2010).

CONCLUSIONS

In contrast to Monte Albán, in the lower Río Verde Valley regional political identity and authority were never extended across multiple communities at the end of the Formative Period. Despite the scale of monumental construction at Río Viejo, the regional polity seems to have been weakly integrated and tenuous. There are few indications of innovations in religious, political, and economic practices that would have distinguished rulers from followers and created sources of goods or specialized knowledge not available at the local level. Instead, what seems to have been new in terms of political relationships was limited to a scaling-up of traditional practices that had previously materialized notions of local community identity, including monumental construction programs and ritual feasting. The active maintenance of strong community identities limited the degree to which the authority of the rulers of Río Viejo could be extended across the region. The Río Viejo polity was never a cohesive political formation and lasted no more than a century or two at most. Because the contradictions and tensions that contributed to the collapse of the Río Viejo polity were never overcome, sites of struggle and negotiation are more accessible to archaeological study. Unlike in the Valley of Oaxaca, victorious regional rulers never suppressed the evidence of competing forms of authority and internal political conflict. Río Viejo therefore has the potential to provide important insights on the kinds of political struggles, negotiations, and conflicts that are inherent to all complex political formations.

We agree with Inomata (this volume) that the negotiation of political authority extends well beyond the strategies that polity rulers take to work out contradictions surrounding inequality and social solidarity as well as those pertaining to the balance between coercion and integration (also see Barber 2005; Barber and Joyce 2007; Joyce 2000, 2008, 2010; Joyce et al. 2001; Murakami, this volume; cf. Baron, this volume; Kurnick, this volume). Likewise, we view contradictions that crosscut salient social distinctions involving belief and socioeconomic interest and opportunity as more significant in social negotiations than those faced by polity rulers in political decision-making (see Brumfiel 1996; Giddens 1979; Marx and Engels 1998). We argue that in the lower Río Verde Valley, as in all complex societies, the negotiation of political authority was far more complex than elite power strategies or simple polarities surrounding the interests and agency of elites and commoners (also see Beekman, this volume). For example, we cannot be sure of the reasons for the construction of the acropolis at Río Viejo. Those reasons may have involved some sort of political strategy by rulers or instead might have been motivated by issues related to religion. What is more important and archaeologically accessible, however, is how the ramifying effects of the construction of the acropolis created contradictions and tensions between the newer, more hierarchical and regional forms of authority and identity that were beginning to emerge at Río Viejo and long-standing local and communal forms of authority and identity centered on public buildings at outlying sites. Our research leads us to argue that the negotiation of these contradictions was focused on the centrality of Río Viejo's rulers versus local communities in the construction and ceremonial use of public buildings through which community was constituted. From this perspective, the most acute tensions may have surrounded contradictions between the interests of Río Viejo's rulers and those of elites at outlying communities as well as between elites and commoners. As early as the Late Formative, if not before, public buildings at outlying sites were loci of entanglement, where ceremonial practices, people, bodies interred in cemeteries, and emplaced offerings became intertwined in ways that constituted a particular form of community that included a shared history and identity. Regardless of what may have motivated the construction of the acropolis at Río Viejo, our evidence shows that such entanglements were never scaled-up to the regional level. Although the rulers of Río Viejo were probably able to mobilize labor from surrounding communities for the construction of the acropolis, in contrast to Monte Albán, these regional political relationships were never institutionalized in ways that contributed to the creation of a polity with a degree of durability. Instead, incipient regional authority was tightly constrained by local communal identity and obligations. The working out of these contradictions and tensions contributed to the abandonment of the acropolis and the decline of Río Viejo in size and regional prominence.

ACKNOWLEDGMENTS

We would like to thank the people of the lower Río Verde Valley for their friendship and assistance through the years as well as the Consejo de Arqueología and Centro INAH Oaxaca of the Mexican Instituto Nacional de Antropología e Historia. Funding for our archaeological research discussed in this chapter has been provided by grants from the following organizations: National Science Foundation (BCS-0096012, BNS-8716332, BCS-1123388, BCS-1123377), Historical Society (Religion and Innovation in Human Affairs grant funded by the Templeton Foundation), Foundation for the Advancement of Mesoamerican Studies (99012 with Stacie King), National Geographic Society (3767-88), Wenner-Gren Foundation (GR. 4988), University of Colorado Boulder (CARTSS, CRCW, Norton Anthropology Fund, and Dean's Fund for Excellence), University of Central Florida Office of Research and Commercialization In-House research grant and start-up fund, Vanderbilt University Research Council and Andrew W. Mellon Foundation, Fulbright Foundation, H. John Heinz III Charitable Trust, Explorers Club, Sigma Xi, Association for Women in Science, Women's Forum Foundation of Colorado, Colorado Archaeological Society, and Rutgers University.

NOTE

1. Excavations in six different locations along the southern and western edges of the acropolis have failed to find evidence of separate Terminal Formative buildings.

REFERENCES

Arellano González, Gabriela. 2012. "Análisis de bajareque." In "El proyecto Río Verde: Informe técnico de la temporada de 2012," edited by Sarah B. Barber and Arthur A. Joyce, 650–62. Final report submitted to the Consejo de Arqueología, Instituto Nacional de Antropología e Historia, Mexico City.

Ashmore, Wendy, Jason Yaeger, and Cynthia Robin. 2004. "Commoner Sense: Late and Terminal Classic Social Strategies in the Xunantunich Area." In *The Terminal Classic in the Maya Lowlands: Collapse, Transition, and Transformation*, edited by Arthur A. Demarest, Prudence M. Rice, and Donald S. Rice, 302–23. Boulder: University Press of Colorado.

Baillie, Harold Barry Andrew. 2012. "Late Classic Río Viejo Mound 1 Construction and Occupation, Oaxaca, Mexico." MA thesis, University of Colorado Boulder.

Barber, Sarah. 2005. "Identity, Tradition, and Complexity: Negotiating Status and Authority in Pacific Coastal Mexico." PhD diss., University of Colorado Boulder.

Barber, Sarah. 2013. "Defining Community and Status at Outlying Sites During the Terminal Formative Period." In *Polity and Ecology in Formative Period Coastal Oaxaca*, edited by Arthur A. Joyce, 165–92. Boulder: University Press of Colorado.

Barber, Sarah B., and Arthur A. Joyce. 2007. "Polity Produced and Community Consumed: Negotiating Political Centralization in the Lower Río Verde Valley, Oaxaca." In *Mesoamerican Ritual Economy*, edited by E. Christian Wells and Karla L. Davis-Salazar, 221–44. Boulder: University Press of Colorado.

Barber, Sarah B., and Arthur A. Joyce, eds. 2011. "El proyecto Río Verde: Informe técnico de la temporada de 2009." Report submitted to the Consejo de Arqueología, Instituto Nacional de Antropología e Historia, Mexico City.

Barber, Sarah B., and Arthur A. Joyce, eds. 2012. "El Proyecto Río Verde: Informe técnico de la temporada de 2012." Report submitted to the Consejo de Arqueología, Instituto Nacional de Antropología e Historia, Mexico City.

Barber, Sarah, Arthur Joyce, and Jeffrey Brzezinski. 2013a. "Recent Excavations at the Rio Viejo Acropolis, Oaxaca, Mexico." Paper presented at the 78th Annual Meeting of the Society for American Archaeology, Honolulu, HI, April 4.

Barber, Sarah B., Arthur A. Joyce, Arion T. Mayes, José Aguilar, and Michelle Butler. 2013b. "Formative Period Burial Practices and Cemeteries." In *Polity and Ecology in Formative Period Coastal Oaxaca*, edited by Arthur A. Joyce, 97–134. Boulder: University Press of Colorado.

Barber, Sarah B., and Mireya Olvera Sánchez. 2012. "A Divine Wind: The Arts of Death and Music in Terminal Formative Oaxaca." *Ancient Mesoamerica* 23(1): 9–24.

Barber, Sarah B., Gonzalo A. Sanchez Santiago, and Mireya Olvera. 2009. "Sounds of Death and Life in Mesoamerica: The Bone Flutes of Ancient Oaxaca." *Yearbook of Traditional Music* 41: 40–56.

Barber, Sarah B., Andrew Workinger, and Arthur A. Joyce. 2014. "Situational Inalienability and Social Change in Formative Period Coastal Oaxaca." *Archaeological Papers of the American Anthropological Association* 23(1): 38–53.

Beekman, Christopher S. 2008. "Corporate Power Strategies in the Late Formative to Early Classic Tequila Valleys of Central Jalisco." *Latin American Antiquity* 19(4): 414–34.

Blanton, Richard E. 1978. *Monte Albán: Settlement Patterns at the Ancient Zapotec Capital.* New York: Academic Press.

Blanton, Richard E. 1998. "Beyond Centralization: Steps Toward a Theory of Egalitarian Behavior in Archaic States." In *Archaic States*, edited by Gary M. Feinman and Joyce Marcus, 135–72. Santa Fe: School of American Research Press.

Blanton, Richard, and Lane F. Fargher. 2008. *Collective Action in the Formation of Pre-Modern States.* New York: Springer.

Blanton, Richard E., Gary M. Feinman, Stephen A. Kowalewski, and Peter N. Peregrine. 1996. "A Dual-Processual Theory for the Evolution of Mesoamerican Civilization." *Current Anthropology* 37(1): 1–14.

Brumfiel, Elizabeth M. 1992. "Distinguished Lecture in Archaeology: Breaking and Entering the Ecosystem—Gender, Class, and Faction Steal the Show." *American Anthropologist* 94(3): 551–67.

Brumfiel, Elizabeth M. 1996. "Figurines and the Aztec State: Testing the Effectiveness of Ideological Domination." In *Gender and Archaeology*, edited by Rita P. Wright, 143–66. Philadelphia: University of Pennsylvania Press.

Brzezinski, Jeffrey S. 2011. "Worldview, Ideology, and Ceramic Iconography: A Study of Late Terminal Formative Graywares from the Lower Río Verde Valley of Oaxaca, Mexico." MA thesis, University of Central Florida.

Brzezinski, Jeffrey S. n.d. "Excavaciones en Cerro de la Virgen." In "El proyecto Río Verde: Informe técnico de la temporada de 2013," edited by Arthur A. Joyce and Sarah B. Barber. Final report to be submitted to the Consejo de Arqueología, Instituto Nacional de Antropología e Historia, Mexico City.

Butler, Michelle. 2011. "Excavaciones en Charco Redondo, 2009." In "El proyecto Río Verde: Informe técnico de la temporada de 2009," edited by Sarah B. Barber and Arthur A. Joyce, 185–221. Final report submitted to the Consejo de Arqueología, Instituto Nacional de Antropología e Historia, Mexico City.

Charlton, Thomas H., and Deborah L. Nichols. 1997. "Diachronic Studies of City-States: Permutations on a Theme." In *The Archaeology of City-States: Cross-Cultural Approaches*, edited by Deborah L. Nichols and Thomas H. Charlton, 169–207. Washington, DC: Smithsonian Institution Press.

Cowgill, George L. 1997. "State and Society at Teotihuacan, Mexico." *Annual Review of Anthropology* 26: 129–61.

Egan, Rachel. 2012. "Excavaciones en la Operación E." In "El proyecto Río Verde: Informe técnico de la temporada de 2012," edited by Sarah B. Barber and Arthur A. Joyce, 336–421. Final report submitted to the Consejo de Arqueología, Instituto Nacional de Antropología e Historia, Mexico City.

Elson, Christina M., and R. Jason Sherman. 2007. "Crema Ware and Elite Power at Monte Albán: Ceramic Production and Iconography in the Oaxaca Valley, Mexico." *Journal of Field Archaeology* 32(3): 265–82.

Elson, Christina M., and Michael E. Smith. 2001. "Archaeological Deposits from the Aztec New Fire Ceremony." *Ancient Mesoamerica* 12: 157–74.

Fargher, Lane F., Richard E. Blanton, and Veronica Y. Heredia Espinoza. 2010. "Egalitarian Ideology and Political Power in Prehispanic Central Mexico: The Case of Tlaxcallan." *Latin American Antiquity* 21(3): 227–51.

Flannery, Kent V. 1972. "The Cultural Evolution of Civilizations." *Annual Review of Ecology and Systematics* 3: 399–426.

Flannery, Kent V. 1998. "The Ground Plans of Archaic States." In *Archaic States*, edited by Gary M. Feinman and Joyce Marcus, 15–58. Santa Fe: School of American Research Press.

Frederick, Charles. n.d. "Análisis micromorfológico de arquitectura de tierra en el valle bajo del Río Verde." In "El proyecto Río Verde: Informe técnico de la temporada de 2013," edited by Arthur A. Joyce and Sarah B. Barber. Final report to be submitted to the Consejo de Arqueología, Instituto Nacional de Antropología e Historia, Mexico City.

Freidel, David A., and Linda Schele. 1988. "Kingship in the Late Preclassic Maya Lowlands." *American Anthropologist* 90(3): 547–67.

Gaxiola González, Margarita. 1984. *Huamelulpan: Un centro urbano de la Mixteca Alta.* Mexico City: Instituto Nacional de Antropología e Historia.

Giddens, Anthony. 1979. *Central Problems in Social Theory: Action, Structure and Contradiction in Social Analysis.* Berkeley: University of California Press.

Goman, Michelle, Arthur A. Joyce, and Raymond G. Mueller. 2005. "Stratigraphic Evidence for Anthropogenically Induced Coastal Environmental Change from Oaxaca, Mexico." *Quaternary Research* 63(3): 250–60.

Goman, Michelle, Arthur A. Joyce, and Raymond G. Mueller. 2013. "Paleoecological Evidence for Early Agriculture and Forest Clearance in Coastal Oaxaca." In *Polity and Ecology in Formative Period Coastal Oaxaca*, edited by Arthur A. Joyce, 43–64. Boulder: University Press of Colorado.

Goman, Michelle, Arthur Joyce, Raymond Mueller, and Larissa Paschyn. 2010. "Multi-Proxy Paleoecological Reconstruction of Prehistoric Land Use History in the Western Region of the Lower Río Verde Valley, Oaxaca, Mexico." *Holocene* 20(5): 761–72.

Gonlin, Nancy, and Jon C. Lohse, eds. 2007. *Commoner Ritual and Ideology in Ancient Mesoamerica*. Boulder: University Press of Colorado.

Hamann, Byron Ellsworth. 2008. "Chronological Pollution: Potsherds, Mosques, and Broken Gods before and after the Conquest of Mexico." *Current Anthropology* 49(5): 803–36.

Hastings, C. Mansfield, and M. Edward Moseley. 1975. "The Adobes of Huaca del Sol and Huaca de la Luna." *American Antiquity* 40(2): 196–203.

Hedgepeth, Jessica, and John Robert Morgan Koukopoulos. 2012. "Proyecto Río Verde 2012: Recorrido Regional de Superficie." In "El proyecto Río Verde: Informe técnico de la temporada de 2012," Sarah B. Barber and Arthur A. Joyce, eds., 490–537. Report submitted to the Consejo de Arqueologia, Instituto Nacional de Antropología e Historia, Mexico City.

Hepp, Guy David, and Arthur A. Joyce. 2013. "From Flesh to Clay: Formative Period Iconography from Oaxaca's Lower Río Verde Valley." In *Polity and Ecology in Formative Period Coastal Oaxaca*, edited by Arthur A. Joyce, 265–300. Boulder: University Press of Colorado.

Jansen, Maarten, and Gabina Aurora Pérez Jiménez. 2007. *Encounter with the Plumed Serpent: Drama and Power in the Heart of Mesoamerica*. Boulder: University Press of Colorado.

Joyce, Arthur A. 1991a. "Formative Period Occupation in the Lower Río Verde Valley, Oaxaca, Mexico: Interregional Interaction and Social Change." PhD diss., Rutgers University–New Brunswick.

Joyce, Arthur A. 1991b. "Formative Period Social Change in the Lower Río Verde Valley, Oaxaca, Mexico." *Latin American Antiquity* 2(2): 126–50.

Joyce, Arthur A. 1993. "Interregional Interaction and Social Development on the Oaxaca Coast." *Ancient Mesoamerica* 4(1): 67–84.

Joyce, Arthur A. 1994. "Late Formative Community Organization and Social Complexity on the Oaxaca Coast." *Journal of Field Archaeology* 21(2): 147–68.

Joyce, Arthur A. 1999. "Mapeo de sitios." In "El proyecto patrones de asentamiento del Río Verde," edited by Arthur A. Joyce, 37–50. Final report submitted to the Consejo de Arqueología, Instituto Nacional de Antropología e Historia, Mexico City.

Joyce, Arthur A. 2000. "The Founding of Monte Albán: Sacred Propositions and Social Practices." In *Agency in Archaeology*, edited by Macia-Anne Dobres and John Robb, 71–91. London: Routledge.

Joyce, Arthur A. 2004. "Sacred Space and Social Relations in the Valley of Oaxaca." In *Mesoamerican Archaeology*, edited by Julia A. Hendon and Rosemary A. Joyce, 192–216. Oxford: Blackwell.

Joyce, Arthur A. 2005. "La arqueología del bajo Río Verde." *Acervos* 29(7): 16–36.

Joyce, Arthur A. 2006. "The Inhabitation of Río Viejo's Acropolis." In *Space & Spatial Analysis in Archaeology*, edited by Elizabeth C. Robertson, Jeffrey D. Seibert, Deepika C. Fernández, and Marc U. Zender, 83–96. Albuquerque: University of New Mexico Press; Calgary: University of Calgary Press.

Joyce, Arthur A. 2008. "Domination, Negotiation, and Collapse: A History of Centralized Authority on the Oaxaca Coast." In *After Monte Albán: Transformation and Negotiation in Oaxaca, Mexico*, edited by Jeffrey P. Blomster, 219–54. Boulder: University Press of Colorado.

Joyce, Arthur A. 2009. "Theorizing Urbanism in Ancient Mesoamerica." *Ancient Mesoamerica* 20(2): 189–96.

Joyce, Arthur A. 2010. *Mixtecs, Zapotecs, and Chatinos: Ancient Peoples of Southern Mexico*. Malden, MA: Wiley-Blackwell.

Joyce, Arthur A., ed., 2013a. *Polity and Ecology in Formative Period Coastal Oaxaca*. Boulder: University Press of Colorado.

Joyce, Arthur A. 2013b. "Polity and Ecology in Formative Period Coastal Oaxaca: An Introduction." In *Polity and Ecology in Formative Period Coastal Oaxaca*, edited by Arthur A. Joyce, 1–42. Boulder: University Press of Colorado.

Joyce, Arthur A. 2013c. "Warfare in Late/Terminal Formative Period Oaxaca." In *Embattled Bodies, Embattled Places: War in Pre-Columbian America*, edited by Andrew K. Scherer and John W. Verano, 117–42. Washington, DC: Dumbarton Oaks.

Joyce, Arthur A., Laura Arnaud Bustamante, and Marc N. Levine. 2001. "Commoner Power: A Case Study from the Classic Period Collapse on the Oaxaca Coast." *Journal of Archaeological Method and Theory* 8(4): 343–85.

Joyce, Arthur A., and Sarah B. Barber. 2011. "Excavating the Acropolis at Río Viejo, Oaxaca, Mexico." *Mexicon* 33(1): 15–20.

Joyce, Arthur A., and Sarah B. Barber. 2013. "Alternative Pathways to Power in Formative Oaxaca." Paper presented at the 78th Annual Meeting of the Society for American Archaeology, Honolulu, HI, April 5.

Joyce, Arthur A., and Sarah B. Barber, eds. n.d. "El proyecto Río Verde: Informe técnico de la temporada de 2013." Final report to be submitted to the Consejo de Arqueología, Instituto Nacional de Antropología e Historia, Mexico City.

Joyce, Arthur A., and Michelle Goman. 2012. "Bridging the Theoretical Divide in Holocene Landscape Studies: Social and Ecological Approaches to Ancient Oaxacan Landscapes." *Quaternary Science Review* 55: 1–22.

Joyce, Arthur A., Marc N. Levine, and Sarah B. Barber. 2013. "Place-Making and Power in the Terminal Formative: Excavations on Río Viejo's Acropolis." In *Polity and Ecology in Formative Period Coastal Oaxaca*, edited by Arthur A. Joyce, 135–64. Boulder: University Press of Colorado.

Joyce, Arthur A., and Marcus Winter. 1989. "Investigaciones arqueológicas en la cuenca del Río Verde inferior, 1988." *Notas Mesoamericanas* 11: 249–62.

Joyce, Arthur A., Marcus Winter, and Raymond G. Mueller. 1998. *Arqueología de la costa de Oaxaca: Asentamientos del periodo formativo en el Valle del Río Verde Inferior*. Oaxaca: Centro INAH Oaxaca.

Joyce, Rosemary A. 1999. "Social Dimensions of Pre-Classic Burials." In *Social Patterns in Pre-Classic Mesoamerica*, edited by David C. Grove and Rosemary A. Joyce, 15–47. Washington, DC: Dumbarton Oaks.

Kowalewski, Stephen A., Andrew K. Balkansky, Laura R. Stiver Walsh, Thomas J. Pluckhahn, John F. Chamblee, Verónica Pérez Rodríguez, Verenice Y. Heredia Espinoza, and Charlotte A. Smith. 2009. *Origins of the Ñuu: Archaeology in the Mixteca Alta, Mexico*. Boulder: University Press of Colorado.

Kowalewski, Stephen, Gary Feinman, Laura Finsten, Richard Blanton, and Linda M. Nicholas. 1989. *Monte Albán's Hinterland, Part II: Prehispanic Settlement Patterns in Tlacolula, Etla, and Ocotlán, the Valley of Oaxaca, Mexico*. Memoirs of the Museum of Anthropology No. 23. Ann Arbor: University of Michigan.

Krejci, Estella, and T. Patrick Culbert. 1995. "Preclassic and Classic Burials and Caches in the Maya Lowlands." In *The Emergence of Lowland Maya Civilization: The Transition from the Preclassic to the Early Classic*, edited by Nikolai Grube, 103–16. *Acta Mesoamericana* 8. Möckmühl: Anton Saurwein.

LeCount, Lisa J. 2001. "Like Water for Chocolate: Feasting and Political Ritual among the Late Classic Maya at Xunantunich, Belize." *American Anthropologist* 103(4): 935–53.

Levine, Marc N. 2002. "Ceramic Change and Continuity in the Lower Río Verde Region of Oaxaca Mexico: The Late Formative to Early Terminal Formative Transition." MA thesis, University of Colorado Boulder.

Levine, Marc N. 2013. "Examining Ceramic Evidence for the Zapotec Imperialism Hypothesis in the Lower Río Verde Region of Oaxaca, Mexico." In *Polity and*

Ecology in Formative Period Coastal Oaxaca, edited by Arthur A. Joyce, 227–64. Boulder: University Press of Colorado.

Love, Michael. 1999. "Ideology, Material Culture, and Daily Practice in Pre-Classic Mesoamerica: A Pacific Coast Perspective." In *Social Patterns in Pre-Classic Mesoamerica*, edited by David C. Grove and Rosemary A. Joyce, 127–54. Washington, DC: Dumbarton Oaks.

Lucero, Lisa J. 2006. *Water and Ritual: The Rise and Fall of Classic Maya Rulers*. Austin: University of Texas Press.

Lucido, Carlo, Sarah Barber, and Arthur Joyce. 2013. "Pottery, Feasting, and Urbanism in the Lower Rio Verde Valley, Oaxaca." Paper presented at the 78th Annual Meeting of the Society for American Archaeology, Honolulu, HI, April 5.

Lucido, Carlo, Sarah Barber, and Arthur Joyce. n.d. "Excavaciones en Loma Don Genaro." In "El proyecto Río Verde: Informe técnico de la temporada de 2013," edited by Arthur A. Joyce and Sarah B. Barber. Final report to be submitted to the Consejo de Arqueología, Instituto Nacional de Antropología e Historia, Mexico City.

Marcus, Joyce. 1998. "The Peaks and Valleys of Ancient States: An Extension of the Dynamic Model." In *Archaic States*, edited by Gary M. Feinman and Joyce Marcus, 59–94. Santa Fe: School of American Research Press.

Markens, Robert, and Cira Martínez López. 2009. "El sistema de producción cerámica en Monte Albán durante el Preclásico Tardío y el Clásico Tardío." In *Bases de la complejidad social en Oaxaca: Memoria de la cuarta Mesa Redonda de Monte Albán*, edited by Nelly Robles García, 123–52. Mexico City: Instituto Nacional de Antropología e Historia.

Martin, Simon, and Nikolai Grube. 2000. *Chronicle of the Maya Kings and Queens*. London: Thames & Hudson.

Marx, Karl, and Friedrich Engels. (1932) 1998. *The German Ideology*. Amherst: Prometheus Books.

Mayes, Arion, and Sarah B. Barber. 2008. "Osteobiography of a High-Status Burial from the Lower Río Verde Valley of Oaxaca, Mexico." *International Journal of Osteoarchaeology* 18(6): 573–88.

Monaghan, John. 1990. "Sacrifice, Death, and the Origins of Agriculture in the Codex Vienna." *American Antiquity* 55(3): 559–69.

Monaghan, John. 1995. *The Covenants with Earth and Rain: Exchange, Sacrifice, and Revelation in Mixtec Sociality*. Norman: University of Oklahoma Press.

Mueller, Raymond G., Arthur A. Joyce, Aleksander Borejsza, and Michelle Goman. 2013. "Anthropogenic Landscape Change and the Human Ecology of the Lower

Río Verde Valley." In *Polity and Ecology in Formative Period Coastal Oaxaca*, edited by Arthur A. Joyce, 65–96. Boulder: University Press of Colorado.

Pool, Christopher A. 2007. *Olmec Archaeology and Early Mesoamerica*. Cambridge: Cambridge University Press.

Pool, Christopher A. 2008. "Architectural Plans, Factionalism, and the Protoclassic-Classic Transition at Tres Zapotes." In *Classic Period Cultural Currents in Southern and Central Veracruz*, edited by Philip J. Arnold III and Christopher A. Pool, 121–57. Washington, DC: Dumbarton Oaks.

Redmond, Elsa M., and Charles S. Spencer. 2006. "From Raiding to Conquest: Warfare Strategies and Early State Development in Oaxaca, Mexico." In *The Archaeology of Warfare: Prehistories of Raiding and Conquest*, edited by Elizabeth N. Arkush and Mark W. Allen, 336–93. Gainesville: University Press of Florida.

Redmond, Elsa M., and Charles S. Spencer. 2008. "Rituals of Sanctification and the Development of Standardized Temples in Oaxaca, Mexico." *Cambridge Archaeological Journal* 18(2): 239–66.

Rivas, Alexander E. 2012. "Excavaciones en la Operación E." In "El proyecto Río Verde: Informe técnico de la temporada de 2012," edited by Sarah B. Barber and Arthur A. Joyce, 280–335. Final report submitted to the Consejo de Arqueología, Instituto Nacional de Antropología e Historia, Mexico City.

Robin, Cynthia. 2002. "Outside of Houses." *Journal of Social Archaeology* 2(2): 245–67.

Robles García, Nelly M. 1988. *Las unidades domésticas del preclásico superior en la Mixteca Alta*. BAR International Series 407. Oxford: British Archaeological Reports.

Salazar, Victor, Cuauhtémoc Vidal-Guzmán, Karla López Carranco, and Victoria Menchaca. n.d. "Excavaciones en Río Viejo." In "El proyecto Río Verde: Informe técnico de la temporada de 2013," edited by Arthur A. Joyce and Sarah B. Barber. Final report to be submitted to the Consejo de Arqueología, Instituto Nacional de Antropología e Historia, Mexico City.

Sanders, William T., Jeffrey R. Parsons, and Robert S. Santley. 1979. *The Basin of Mexico: Ecological Processes in the Evolution of a Civilization*. New York: Academic Press.

Sellen, Adam T. 2011. "Sowing the Blood with the Maize: Zapotec Effigy Vessels and Agricultural Ritual." *Ancient Mesoamerica* 22(1): 71–90.

Spencer, Charles S., and Elsa M. Redmond. 2001. "Multilevel Selection and Political Evolution in the Valley of Oaxaca, 500–100 B.C." *Journal of Anthropological Archaeology* 20: 195–229.

Sugiyama, Saburo. 1993. "Worldview Materialized in Teotihuacán, Mexico." *Latin American Antiquity* 4(2): 103–29.

Stanton, Travis W., M. Kathryn Brown, and Jonathan B. Pagliaro. 2008. "Garbage of the Gods? Squatters, Refuse Disposal, and Termination Rituals among the Ancient Maya." *Latin American Antiquity* 19(3): 227–47.

Stross, Brian. 1998. "Seven Ingredients in Mesoamerican Ensoulment: Dedication and Termination in Tenejapa." In *The Sowing and the Dawning: Termination, Dedication, and Transformation in the Archaeological and Ethnographic Record of Mesoamerica*, edited by Shirley Boteler Mock, 31–39. Albuquerque: University of New Mexico Press.

Taube, Karl A. 1996. "The Rainmakers: The Olmec and Their Contribution to Mesoamerican Belief and Ritual." In *The Olmec World: Ritual and Rulership*, edited by Jill Guthrie, 83–103. Princeton: Art Museum, Princeton University.

Urcid, Javier. 2005. *The Zapotec Scribal Tradition: Knowledge, Memory, and Society in Ancient Oaxaca*. Coral Gables, FL: Foundation for the Advancement of Mesoamerican Studies. http://www.famsi.org/zapotecwriting/.

Urcid, Javier. 2011. "Los oráculos y la guerra: El papel de las narrativas pictóricas en el desarrollo temprano de Monte Albán (500 a.c.–200 d.c.)." In *Monte Albán en la encrucijada regional y disciplinaria: Memoria de la Quinta Mesa Redonda de Monte Albán*, edited by Nelly M. Robles García and Ángel Rivera Guzmán, 163–240. Mexico City: Instituto Nacional de Antropología e Historia.

Urcid, Javier, and Arthur A. Joyce. 2014. "Early Transformations of Monte Albán's Main Plaza and Their Political Implications (500 BC–AD 200)." In *Mesoamerican Plazas*, edited by Kenichiro Tsukamoto and Takeshi Inomata, 149–67. Tucson: University of Arizona Press.

Walker, Debra S. 1998. "Smashed Pots and Shattered Dreams: The Material Evidence for an Early Classic Maya Site Termination at Cerros, Belize." In *The Sowing and the Dawning: Termination, Dedication, and Transformation in the Archaeological and Ethnographic Record of Mesoamerica*, edited by Shirley Boteler Mock, 81–99. Albuquerque: University of New Mexico Press.

Weiner, Annette B. 1992. *Inalienable Possessions: The Paradox of Keeping-While-Giving*. Berkeley: University of California Press.

Winter, Marcus. 1986. "Unidades habitacionales prehispánicas en Oaxaca." In *Unidades habitacionales mesoaméricanas y sus áreas de actividad*, edited by Linda Manzanilla, 325–74. Mexico City: Universidad Nacional Autónoma de México.

Winter, Marcus. 2001. "Palacios, templos y 1300 años de vida urbana en Monte Albán." In *Reconstruyendo la ciudad maya: El urbanismo en las sociedades antiguas*, edited by Andrés Ciudad Ruiz, María Josefa Iglesias Ponce de Léon, and María del Carmen Martínez, 253–301. Madrid: Sociedad Española de Estudios Mayas.

Winter, Marcus, and Arthur A. Joyce. 1987. "Excavaciones en Barra Quebrada, 1986: Un informe preliminar." Report submitted to the Centro Regional de Oaxaca, Instituto Nacional de Antropología e Historia, Oaxaca, Mexico.

Woodard, S. Justine. 1991. "Appendix 3: Paleobotanical Study Río Verde Formative Project." In "Formative Period Occupation in the Lower Río Verde Valley, Oaxaca, Mexico: Interregional Interaction and Social Change," by Arthur A. Joyce, 840–82. PhD diss., Rutgers University–New Brunswick.

Workinger, Andrew. 2002. "Coastal/Highland Interaction in Prehispanic Oaxaca, Mexico: The Perspective from San Francisco de Arriba." PhD diss., Vanderbilt University.

Workinger, Andrew. 2013. "Coastal/Highland Interaction in Oaxaca, Mexico: The Perspective from San Francisco de Arriba." In *Polity and Ecology in Formative Period Coastal Oaxaca*, edited by Arthur A. Joyce, 193–226. Boulder: University Press of Colorado.

Workinger, Andrew, and Arthur A. Joyce. 2009. "Reconsidering Warfare in Formative Period Oaxaca." In *Blood and Beauty: Organized Violence in the Art and Archaeology of Mesoamerica and Central America*, edited by Heather Orr and Rex Koontz, 3–38. Los Angeles: Cotsen Institute of Archaeology Press.

Yaeger, Jason. 2003. "Untangling the Ties that Bind: The City, the Countryside, and the Nature of Maya Urbanism at Xunantunich, Belize." In *The Social Construction of Ancient Cities*, edited by Monica L. Smith, 121–55. Washington, DC: Smithsonian Books.

Zeitlin, Robert N., and Arthur A. Joyce. 1999. "The Zapotec Imperialism Argument: Insights from the Oaxaca Coast." *Current Anthropology* 40(3): 383–92.

4

Conflicting Political Strategies in Late Formative to Early Classic Central Jalisco

Christopher S. Beekman

The archaeology of the Tequila valleys of central Jalisco (figure 4.1) is ripe for a shift in perspective, after five decades of approaches that either eschewed political organization altogether or relied on older political economic models that associated power with the monopolization of resources. The editors of this volume instead ask us to consider the evidence for political strategies that contradict one another and are not resolved (Fogelin 2011)—political strategies whose contradictions presented opportunities for the powerful to negotiate the authority to rule and allowed followers to rationalize their decision to follow. After considering past research into political strategies in western Mexico, I discuss recent analyses that associate different types of formal built space in the Tequila valleys with conflicting political strategies by virtue of their spatial characteristics as well as iconographic and archaeological evidence. Despite their strategic associations, the architectural forms share close proximity, even physical integration, that suggest that the same elites were practicing both strategies at different times. I follow this with a consideration of ethnographic data that help to elucidate how the balance between these conflicting strategies may have changed over time. I round this out with a discussion of the major foci for conflict and how both elites and nonelites could have navigated these issues.

DOI: 10.5876/9781607324164.c004

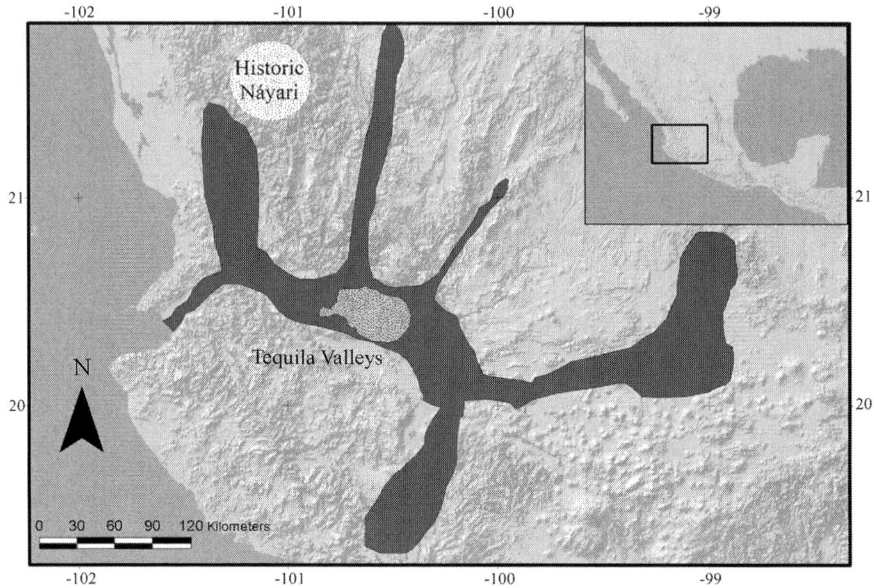

FIGURE 4.1. *Map of western highland Mexico, indicating the groups discussed in this chapter. The darkly shaded and irregular area depicts the distribution of the Teuchitlán culture, ca.* CE *400, with the Tequila valleys of central Jalisco marked in its center. The Náyari culture of highland Nayarit is also noted.*

PAST RESEARCH INTO THE POLITICAL ORGANIZATION OF THE LATE FORMATIVE/EARLY CLASSIC

Western highland Mexico (the modern states of Jalisco, Colima, and Nayarit) is one of the regions of Mesoamerica that has been most negatively affected by the shamanism model discussed in Kurnick's introductory chapter. Peter Furst (1966) introduced the model in the mid-1960s as an alternative to what he stated was the strongly secular approach used at the time to interpret the ceramic figures looted from the shaft tombs of the western states (ca. 300 BCE–500 CE). According to Furst, the hollow figures that populate museum and private collections worldwide depict an all-pervading shamanism enacted through peyote-induced animal transformations (e.g., Furst 1972, 1974, 1975). The academic and nonacademic influences on this model have been dissected elsewhere (Fikes 1993; Klein et al. 2002), but these critiques have made disappointingly limited headway among academics or museum exhibitors. Yet empirically speaking, the shamanism model always broke upon the shoals of local data. Interpretations of the shaft tomb figures in terms of Mesoamerican beliefs and practices had been made since at least the 1940s (Bernal 1949; Corona Nuñez 1955; Toscano 1946). Furthermore, other interpretations of the proposed shamanic features are more in accordance with what we know of Mesoamerican ethnography, archaeology, and belief systems that avoid the imprecision of the shaman concept (Beekman in preparation).

Alternate explanations for the emergence of complex societies in western highland Mexico emerged in the 1980s, stemming primarily from archaeological fieldwork that found substantial public architecture associated with the shaft tombs. Phil C. Weigand's archaeological research in central Jalisco took a decidedly political economic perspective and associated the emergence of complex society there with the availability of obsidian and other less prominent minerals (e.g., Weigand 1985a). He became particularly interested in obsidian as a potentially strategic resource whose access, production, or exchange may have been under political control (Spence et al. 2002). Weigand and other researchers however have recorded the presence of several dozen easily accessible quality obsidian sources within the Tequila valleys alone (Esparza López 2004, 2008; Esparza López and Ponce Ordaz 2005; Weigand et al. 2002); direct control over sources would have been impossible. The highly expedient nature of lithic technology in the region (e.g., prismatic blade technology was not adopted until the Postclassic Period [900–1600 CE]) also argues against any special production techniques that might have been monopolized.

Mark Miller Graham (1998) was the first art historian to incorporate the updated archaeology into his interpretations, and he brought more current approaches to iconographic analysis to bear on the hollow figures. He argued that political elites may have associated themselves with agricultural fertility and success, drawing upon a familiar Mesoamerican political formula in which political elites claimed the position of exclusive mediator between humans and the supernatural (Houston and Stuart 1996; Joyce 2000).

I initially drew upon this perspective in my studies of the symbolism of the public architecture of central Jalisco (Beekman 2003a, 2003b). The *guachimontón* temple groups are distinctive circular arrangements of usually eight rectangular platforms facing a circular patio with a central round altar or pyramid. As in many areas of Mesoamerica (e.g., Joyce 2000; Sugiyama 1993), the architecture represents the Mesoamerican cosmos. The patio symbolizes the current world, the shaft tombs occasionally beneath the surrounding platforms vividly represent the underworld, and the central pyramid (sometimes the base for a vertical pole) was a link to the heavens (Kelley 1974; Beekman 2003a). I further interpreted the guachimontones as representations of a form of maize known to have emerged in western Mexico around the Late Formative Period

(300 BCE–200 CE) (Beekman 2003b, 2009). In accord with these interpretations, ceramic dioramas looted from the shaft tombs depict the architecture of the site as places of public performance, particularly feasting and a maize ceremony associated with the central pole (Beekman 2000, 2003a, 2003b; Butterwick 1998). In sum, there is good reason to see the guachimontón form as a highly sacred space appropriate for public ritual. As the argument goes elsewhere in Mesoamerica, those elites who controlled such spaces through the possession of sacred knowledge could claim to be the mediators between humans and the supernatural. A Classic Lowland Maya ruler could reasonably make this claim, as only a single royal dynast held power at any one time. The situation in the Tequila valleys was considerably more complex and should lead archaeologists in other areas to reassess current assumptions about a royal monopoly on sacred authority on the one hand, and the room for resistance possessed by commoners on the other.

THE TEQUILA VALLEYS OF CENTRAL JALISCO

During the Late Formative and Classic Periods (300 BCE–500 CE), social complexity in the Tequila valleys accelerated in a manner not seen in neighboring areas of western highland Mexico. The local environment is distinctive for its concentration of both extensive farmland and lakes or wetlands around the Tequila Volcano. The region experiences a strongly dichotomized rainy season and a dry season that focused most agricultural activity into the period from June through November (Beekman and Baden 2011). Fish and fowl associated with the Laguna Magdalena and wetlands provided other subsistence opportunities throughout the year. Out of a hazily understood Middle Formative base of family tombs and burial mounds, the Teuchitlán culture emerged (see figure 4.1). The ceremonial centers known from the Tequila valleys include residential architecture, ballcourts, circular temple groups known as guachimontones, and deep shaft and chamber family tombs occurring as isolates or in cemeteries (figure 4.2).

In a companion piece to this chapter (Beekman in press), I analyzed the spatial characteristics and performance activities associated with each type of formal architecture in terms of the exclusionary and corporate political strategies defined by Blanton et al. (1996). In their original model, the former strategy seeks to aggrandize a family, dynasty, ruler, etc. through the expression of difference, using myth, material culture, social rules, group endogamy, etc. The corporate strategy stresses inclusiveness and ideologies that promote community well-being through reference to cosmic values, though not necessarily by

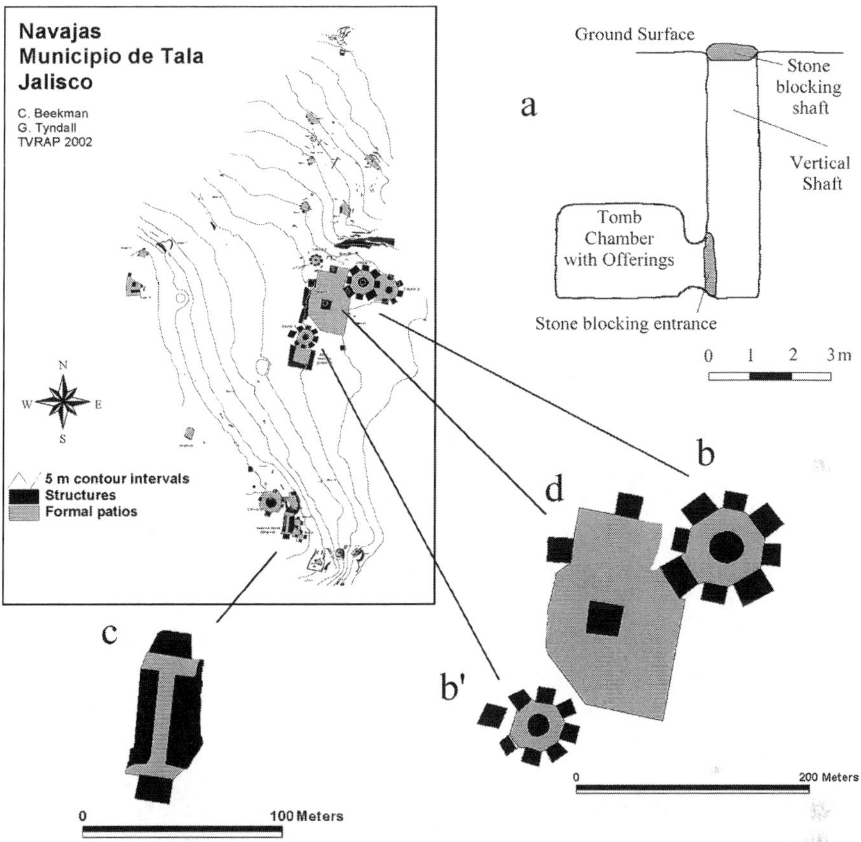

FIGURE 4.2. *Examples of each of the forms of built space proposed to be associated with specific social institutions and strategies: (a) shaft tomb; (b) guachimontón; (c) ballcourt; (d) elite residential group (images taken from Beekman 2005a:figures 4.2, 4.4, courtesy of the Tequila Valley Regional Archaeological Project).*

eschewing social hierarchy. The authors of the original study stress the incompatibility of the two strategies and their concomitant temporal or spatial separation (Blanton et al. 1996:7).

Maurice Bloch (1975) examined a similar contradiction; he questioned how traditional political oratory that drew upon the formalized rules of speech could propose novel plans that required divergence from those same rules. Bloch found that the contradictions between them required some kind of separation between the two speech events. The separation could be temporal, with both formal and informal parts to a speech. The two roles could be separated into two individuals, as between priests and rulers or between presidents and prime ministers. The first option is inaccessible to archaeologists and the second might potentially be addressed through studies of burials or imagery. But a third option is the separation of traditional and novel political oratory into entirely separate speech events (Bloch 1975:26–28). Bloch's focus is on language and oratory, of course, and not necessarily on the material and spatial component that draws the attention of archaeologists. But, we can consider the possibility that traditional and more innovative speech events took place in different dedicated spaces. This possibility is available to us archaeologically, and my analysis of built space in terms of distinct strategies can be summarized briefly.

Those forms of architectural space that I (Beekman in press) associated with an exclusionary strategy were places in which lineages were celebrated in dramatic fashion. Mortuary ritual was a public event depicted in ceramic models from the region (figure 4.3). The family tombs were often reused and could include offerings quantitatively and qualitatively superior to anything known from other excavated contexts (Galván Villegas 1991; Ramos de la Vega and López Mestas 1996). Burial furniture included fine vessels such as the Oconahua Red on Cream type, objects made of imported jade or marine shell, and the hollow ceramic figures that were used for decades to define the archaeology of western highland Mexico (e.g., Kan et al. 1989). Descent group ritual thus incorporated rare materialized cultural capital that exhibited the wealth and social connections of the family associated with the tomb (Beekman 2000).

Habitation areas are known from the rural hinterland and within the immediate environs of the ceremonial centers and provide another possible line of evidence for the aggrandizement of particular families. Drawing upon those published in the site maps for Llano Grande and Navajas (Beekman 2003a:figure 7, 2005b:figure 8), residential groups can be defined by the presence of those structures arranged around rectilinear patios and their immediate ancillary buildings (cf. Smith 2009, who focuses solely on those with four structures around a patio). These groups can have from two to eight structures and display a wide size range. Although one would hesitate to call them palaces, a handful of very large and more symmetrical residential groups exist within major ceremonial centers and, while unexcavated, suggest the efforts of particular lineages to express their power and access to labor.

In contrast, the ballcourts and guachimontones (which are typically attached to one another) are separate architectural spaces better associated

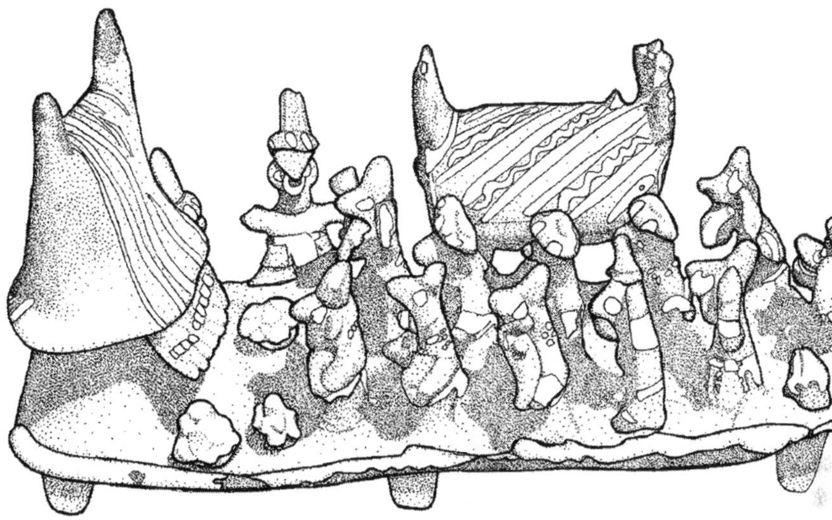

FIGURE 4.3. *Ceramic model depicting a burial procession, with pallbearers carrying the dead (drawing by Kathy Beekman, after von Winning and Hammer 1972:figure 89).*

with community rituals and interests. Ballcourts across Mesoamerica were arenas of controlled competition, in which conflicts could be resolved or compartmentalized in a socially acceptable manner (Blanco 2009; Gillespie 1991; Weigand 1991). Secular games could easily be played in open fields, but constructed ballcourts within the ceremonial centers imply a more public function—indeed, the ballgame across Mesoamerica had cosmic overtones in which the myths of the gods or the cycles of the cosmos were enacted through play (Scarborough and Wilcox 1991; Whittington 2001). Far from being associated with ancestors and the aggrandizement of a family, the ballgame was a material manifestation of community ritual oriented toward the higher goal of social and cosmic balance. Even impressive athletic prowess in the game would have been reinterpreted in cosmic terms, and excavations within the ballcourts have found modestly decorated ceramics focused on unelaborated food consumption and human remains associated with sacrifice (Blanco 2009:119–57). As discussed above, the guachimontón architecture was also the seat of community ritual. Ceramic models depict known agricultural ceremonies, and our excavations within the circles have recovered a considerably less elaborate assemblage than found in the shaft tombs (Beekman 2000, 2008). The contrast in associated artifacts is all the more striking when one considers that some of the lineage tombs are found beneath the guachimontón architecture (Beekman 1996:159–64, figure 4.4; Long 1966:248–78, figures 8–10; Ramos de la Vega and López Mestas 1996:126–29, figures 3, 4, 12; Weigand and Beekman 1998:40, figures 8, 9), underlining how particular forms of built space were used very differently, even when one was literally on top of the other. Each formal architectural space was a field in the sense of Pierre Bourdieu (1990), in which competition over power was bounded by social rules.

The circular guachimontón architecture presents an especially illustrative case. As noted, the architecture was used for agricultural ritual and replicated the Mesoamerican cosmos. But the elites who could claim a connection to the architecture and its symbolism were composed of multiple (usually eight) lineages who each constructed and maintained one of those structures that formed the outermost concentric circle of the guachimontón (Beekman 2008). In other words, the individual lineages that aggrandized themselves in ancestral ritual tied to the shaft tombs also participated in broader community ritual with distinct and even contradictory goals. Furthermore, since lineages shared privileged access to this sacred space, no one of them was in a position to monopolize the tie to the supernatural (for specific potential exceptions, see Beekman in press). Whether this was truly unique to this region or whether non-reigning elites in other areas of Mesoamerica may have held more clout than we usually assume is obscured by elite monopolization of writing, sculpture, and other forms of social mass media in those areas.

The social institutions present in the Late Formative to Early Classic Tequila valleys included both those oriented toward the aggrandizement of individual lineages and others that stressed the needs of the entire community, and they show intriguing patterns when one examines their distribution across the landscape (Beekman in press). While these contrasts were partly smoothed over through the separation of the opposing strategies into different forms of built space (cf. Fogelin 2011), this was not completely successful in the case of the shaft tombs and the guachimontones. Indeed, the presence of family tombs beneath the satellite structures of the guachimontones makes it very likely that the same families participated in both ritual series and thus had to represent lineage and community interests at different times. One may have even been dependent upon the other. For example, lineage elites may have been forced to link themselves to the community in some way to fully legitimize themselves as descent groups. The contradictions are evident, and the resulting cognitive dissonance (Festinger et al. 1955) would have impacted not only elites but also followers attempting to navigate these conflicting messages. While the archaeological record documents these opposing descent group and community strategies, ethnohistoric and ethnographic data from the region help explain how the tensions between them could produce their own internal dynamic over time, and how some of those contradictions might have been mitigated.

SOCIAL CONTRADICTIONS AMONG THE NÁYARI OF WESTERN MEXICO

Ethnographic research in western highland Mexico has diversified in recent years to consider more broadly the Náyari (Cora), Wixarika (Huichol), Tepecano, and others from northern Jalisco and Nayarit and to place them more effectively within a historic context (Coyle 2001; Fikes 1985; Jáuregui and Neurath 2003; Magriña 2002; Neurath 2005, 2008). Older sources have been rediscovered, republished, and incorporated into a more dynamic understanding of the social and ceremonial systems of these groups (Diguet 1992; Lumholtz 1902; Preuss 1998; Seler 1993; Zingg 1988).

The indigenous peoples of this mountainous region are the most plausible known descendants and heirs of the Teuchitlán culture to the south. A number of studies have compared archaeological and ethnographic evidence for specific rituals, religious symbolism, temple architecture, and sociopolitical organization (Beekman 2003a, 2003b, 2005b; Neurath 2000; Weigand 1985b, 1996). Among the better substantiated parallels is the practice of communal rituals in sacred spaces, subdivided into areas built by and/or associated with different lineages. Past comparisons focused heavily on the Wixarika to the exclusion of other groups (e.g., Furst 1966, 1972, 1974, 1977), but here I draw upon ethnographic work among the Náyari. This is not the place to delve into the specifics of past-present analogies, and my aim is merely to use a similar case of internal social conflict to illustrate the contradictions likely to have been present in the archaeological case described above. Anthropologists warn against using traditional societies in uncritical comparisons with the past. I strive to respect those issues here while simultaneously recognizing the value of understanding the descendants of those cultures being studied.

The Náyari occupy an isolated and dissected upland landscape in Nayarit known as the Gran Nayar. They live in scattered farmsteads and in the few communities of Mesa del Nayar, Santa Teresa, and Jesús María. Similar to their Maya counterparts at the opposite end of Mesoamerica (though receiving, sadly, much less scholarly attention), the Náyari were not conquered by the Spanish until 1722. Their temple to the Sun (Tonatí) was destroyed and the mummified remains of past rulers were taken from a nearby cave and burned (Malvido Miranda 2000). The temple to the sun may suggest a community-oriented role, while the physical separation of the remains of the ruling dynasty into a cave points to special treatment of a family and ancestral rituals, perhaps symbolically related to the burials in the much earlier artificial caves of the shaft tombs. In the following centuries, the Náyari continued to practice an annual ritual cycle very similar to that followed by descent groups today (Coyle 2001:76–86). By the end of the nineteenth century, however, descent group rituals existed in dynamic opposition with community-oriented ceremonies that closely interwove both traditional and Catholic elements. Philip E. Coyle suggests that similar community ceremonialism existed in the past but had been centered on the capital at Mesa del Tonatí, whereas today each town has its own complement of community ritual.

Coyle describes the tension between descent group and community-level authorities among the late twentieth-century Náyari of Santa Teresa and how external interference further fanned the flame. His (Coyle 2001:26–73) description of descent group ceremonialism invites comparison to the Late Formative to Early Classic ceremonies associated with lineages and their shaft tombs. Individual Náyari participate in the ceremonial cycle of one or more descent groups to which they can claim kinship. Members receive bundles of maize specific to their descent group(s) and participate in a series of three major annual ceremonies, or *mitotes*, that celebrate the planting and harvest of maize. Descent group rites of passage are nested within these maize ceremonies, and children, male and female adults, and group ancestors all play a role at different points of the year. Ancestors become equated with the rains that support maize farming, but specifically for the lands held by that descent group. Indeed, individuals obtain access to land through their attachment to one or more groups. Membership in a group and the concomitant participation in its descent group ceremonialism are therefore critical to the social identity and physical survival of people relying on subsistence agriculture.

Community rituals, on the other hand, are the primary route by which lineage elders can extend their authority to wider segments of the community. Community rituals incorporated two authority structures: one that "scales up" the metaphors of descent group ritual to the community level and another based on the well-known cargo system of Mesoamerica (Coyle 2001:96–176). The senior community elder is in charge of the first of these ritual series, which draws upon many of the same metaphors found in descent group ritual to bind individuals to their community rather than to their descent groups. For example, while the ritual actions of ceremonial elders of each of the lineages are responsible for bringing rain to their descent group territory, the ceremonial elders active in the community mitotes are considered responsible for ensuring the entire dry season-rainy season cycle. They are thus of another order with greater authority and responsibilities that are a closer match to the Late Formative and Early Classic temple rituals of central Jalisco. The cargo system rituals fuse Christian myths about Jesus with Náyari culture hero twins Xuráve and Sáutari (Coyle 2001:115–24). Descent group elders together form a council that runs the cargo system, and therefore hold leading roles in the ceremonies for their own descent groups and simultaneously for the larger community.

Both lineage and community rituals are associated with a complement of material objects, symbols, and sacred spaces with notable similarities to the archaeological record. Descent group rituals are performed in prepared plazas close to the home of the group's ceremonial elder. Decorated gourd bowls are used as containers for maize or sacred waters collected from throughout the group's territory and used in ritual. Much like the pre-Columbian vessels found in tombs or ritual centers, the gourd bowls are decorated with quadripartite motifs that are explicitly described by Náyari informants as nested representations simultaneously of the cosmos and of the circular mitote plazas (figure 4.4). The bowl becomes a means of communication with the ancestors during ritual by moving it up a series of steps over the course of a mitote, and one can easily see how something similar might have been done on the stepped guachimontón pyramids. Prayer arrows, maguey liquor, tobacco, quartz crystals, and beads all play a role in the ceremonies, and potential correlates exist for all of them either in the excavation record from Llano Grande or Navajas or in contemporary ceramic figures that depict individuals smoking or drinking (Beekman 2005b; Butterwick 2004; Cabrero García and López Cruz 1997).

The community-level mitotes are scaled up from the descent group rituals, in an attempt to stress their more universal claims. Mitotes are practiced in a sacred locale close to the town of Santa Teresa and separate from the homes of descent group elders (perhaps the plaza depicted in Lumholtz 1902, 2: 519). The water collected for the rites comes from different parts of the community territory rather than descent group lands. Descent group maize bundles are substituted with bundles of maize grown in the town's communal garden and greater use is made of the more cosmic symbol of the cross representing the four directions. *Chánaka* poles are raised in the center of sacred grounds as an explicit representation of the cosmos, in a clear parallel to the poles erected in the pre-Columbian guachimontones. Few of these materialized symbols are exclusive to either descent group or community ritual, and the expanded meanings attributed to them are most important to Coyle's analysis.

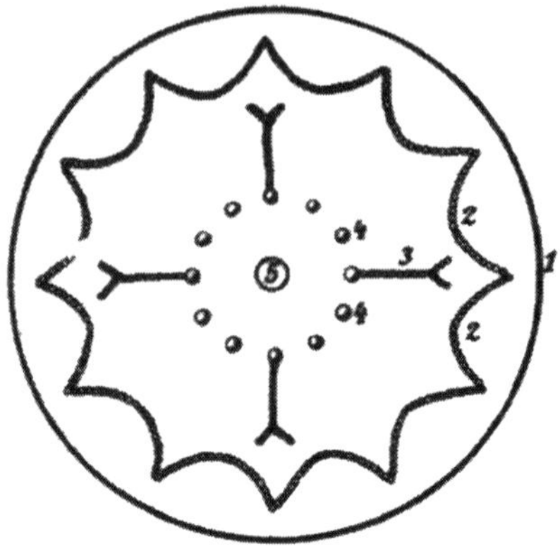

	The World	The Festival Patio
1)	The rim of the world, all the world, or the image of the world	The rim of the festival patio, or the gourd bowl that represents the world
2)	The 12 bows, that are the corral of the gods, are located close to the end or edge of the world	There is dancing between the rim of the world and the corral of the gods, between the singer and the altar
3)	The four directions of the universe, the abodes of the gods	The four directions of the festival patio where the gods live and where they receive offerings for their children
4)	The 12 ancients that correspond to the first inhabitants of the world	The ancients of the town, that is, the governor and the people of great prestige
5)	The center of the universe where lives our father the sun	The fire that represents the sun. It is located in the center of the patio

FIGURE 4.4. *A design within a votive bowl used in Náyari temples and the explicit symbolism embodied in the design (after the reprint of Preuss 1998:408–9, figure 3a).*

This summary only covers the essentials of Coyle's analysis but serves to demonstrate two major points: the notable parallels between the modern Náyari and the Teuchitlán culture of Jalisco and the origins in deep time of the conflict between descent group and community interests being acted out among the modern Náyari. Prior to the 1722 conquest of the Cora, descent group interests appear to have been paramount and focused on the central figure of the ruler at Mesa del Tonatí. Spanish authorities dismantled this layer of political organization and that of individual communities without replacing them with effective religious or political authority, allowing local descent group ceremonialism to dominate until a resurgence of community organization and ritual took place over the course of the nineteenth century. Coyle's (2001:177–240) research addresses how sharp but intermittent interference by federal agencies with U.S. backing during the twentieth century has increased the presence of the distant Mexican state and eroded the legitimacy of community authority structures, all while feeding local violence. The oscillations between different political interests have occurred on a historic or archaeological timescale and resemble the temporal cycling between strategies recognized earlier by Richard E. Blanton and his colleagues (Blanton et al. 1996). The twentieth century was marked by the addition of an entirely new scale of political activity, as the centuries-old field of conflict has been disrupted by the external demands of distant political authorities.

DISCUSSION AND CONCLUSIONS

The ethnographic example explored here provides a more dynamic view of the archaeological case study but without insisting that the modern Náyari are necessarily the direct descendants of the Teuchitlán culture. Rather, the community of Santa Teresa presents a similar field of power (Bourdieu 1990) to that from pre-Columbian central Jalisco, with sacred spaces dedicated to different forms of performative ritual that competed for followers' attention and support of different political authorities. Descent group elders carried out ceremonies that highlighted membership in the group, while community elders (who were, in turn, lineage elders as well) performed rituals that stressed broader unifying interests. Community support of one or the other could enable or deny ritual specialists' efforts to extend their authority over groups other than their own lineages. It is the clash between different political strategies that is held in common between the present and the past, and Coyle documents how the dominance of community or lineage interests may tip one way or the other over time due to both internal dynamics and external impacts.

In considering the relevance of this material to the goals of this volume, I will focus on three intertwined themes present in the archaeological and ethnographic cases presented here: access to property through group membership, appeals to symbolic meanings as the basis for legitimacy, and the affective qualities of performance. Outside of private ownership, individuals commonly obtain access to capital such as land, titles, sacred knowledge, hunting grounds, etc. through their membership in corporate groups (Beekman 2005a). Their primary mechanisms of recruitment (such as descent or alliance) have traditionally been used in anthropology to distinguish them as lineages (Evans-Pritchard 1940), houses (Lévi-Strauss 1982), etc., but the group's role in enabling access to corporate property (Carsten and Hugh-Jones 1995; Watanabe 2004) deserves more attention. Individuals could probably claim membership in the lineages described in my prehistoric case in much the same way that they could to the descent groups among the Náyari—by tracing ties of genealogy or fictive kinship to one or more groups. Some families held access to land while others held title to sacred knowledge; or perhaps it was a subset of a descent group that held myths and rituals in secret. But descent group rituals such as rite of passage ceremonies or mortuary ritual would have constantly reaffirmed the boundaries of that group and identified those who could continue to access corporate property by their active participation in group events and perhaps physical proximity to other members. The motivation for "followers" (or members) of the descent group was comparatively clear, as their continuing presence at events was necessary to ensure their access to capital, thereby reproducing the authority of group leaders. It is noteworthy that in the Náyari case, individuals traced descent via multiple pathways, allowing them some flexibility as to which groups they would continue to support. Therefore, the decision of these followers is not so much to follow as it is whether to maintain social ties to one group or another.

The inducements to identify with broader community interests and support community authorities are distinct. Coyle (personal communication 2014) notes that the Jesuits established a communal garden and cattle herd in the center of Santa Teresa, and these supplied maize and meat for the communal authorities. But this only establishes the source for financing the community ritual series rather than a form of capital that becomes accessible to participants. More important to my mind is Coyle's subsequent observation that participation in ritual at this scale is tied to one's very existence as a Náyari of Santa Teresa. Failure to participate marginalizes one as a member, though the ability of the authorities to enforce this in some concrete manner would seem to be a critical variable. For these reasons, I would argue that more durable community authority would require leaders to offer something more concrete for those who support community ritual (such as burial within the community gave access to formal citizenship in classical Athens [Morris 1991:157–58]). The useful part of this discussion is that it prompts us to ask what community leaders in the Late Formative/Early Classic provided that drew in followers who already had access to land through their lineage membership. Did community leaders obtain independent rights to conquered lands, convincingly establish exclusive links to higher ranks of the supernatural, as described by Joanne Baron (this volume), or provide other inducements to community members? We do not know, but these are worthy topics of research. The value of community affiliation, and hence the importance of civic leaders, can also be destabilized from above if a higher level of political organization were to abrogate community powers or resources to itself. In the case of the Náyari, distant governments with pretensions to authority in the area have frequently played a role in delegitimizing community leaders, actions that should result in a decline in participation in community ritual.

The second issue is the cross-legitimization of community and descent group interests. Coyle's Náyari example assumes that descent groups and their rituals are the more primal form of social organization and predate community authorities. Hence, community leaders draw upon prior descent group symbolism to legitimize their more expansive yet historically ephemeral positions. But archaeologists typically assume the opposite in their treatment of the rise of Mesoamerican elites. If a community already existed as a meaningful social entity, emerging descent group elites may have sought to legitimize their own positions through reference to the established suite of meanings associated with the community. We may or may not be able to identify the arrow of causality in this chicken-and-egg problem, but the close proximity of opposed forms of built space associated with distinct strategies suggests that some form of cross-legitimization was at work. Lineage-based shaft tombs have been found beneath some guachimontones, despite the very different interests represented—elites associated with one may have sought to draw upon the legitimacy of the other in order to achieve social acceptance as lineage elites sought to bootstrap their authority upward over the community as a whole. The same might be said for the very largest elite residential groups, which are prominently located within the central areas of ceremonial centers. Were these built only after one or more descent groups succeeded in making inroads toward acceptance, or did community leaders purporting to control wider aspects of the supernatural through ritual borrow from the authority previously associated with the elders of each descent group?

The final issue is the cultivation of affective ties between elites and followers through performance (Inomata, this volume; Inomata and Coben 2006; Smith 2000). Access to land or other capital is an important consideration in determining whether someone will associate with a group, but the fact that the Náyari of Santa Teresa are free to choose between different descent groups suggests that other factors play a role in their decision to select one or another. The aesthetic aspects of public performance may be one of these factors, and exclusionary or communal rituals could generate ties of affect through an appeal to small and familiar or large and inclusive audiences, respectively. Thus, the very limited space associated with shaft tombs in comparison to guachimontones or ballcourts implies that only a small subset of the community could ever have participated fully in ancestral rituals (Beekman 2000), and they, in fact, derived their power from that greater intimacy. Georg Simmel (1971[1908]) once suggested that the desires for imitation and differentiation are present in all individuals, and people could have been attracted equally to exclusive and inclusive rituals.

Whatever the size of the audience, ritual must be carried out in reference to tradition in order to be recognized by the supernatural powers to which it is addressed (Coyle 2001:14). But in order to meet with the approval of its human audience, ritual must be performed in ways that are novel, aesthetically interesting, and engaging. In the case of the Náyari, much the same symbolism exists in both descent group and community ritual, with the difference being primarily one of scale. Both sets of rituals propitiated rain, but the first does so through requests to the ancestors of the descent group while the second claims responsibility for the dry-rainy season cycle. This raises the question "When is ritual sufficiently different in its claims of efficacy to attract the participation of members?" Compliance can lead to further participation in ritual, reproducing the authority of the lineage or community leaders. But a failure to engage can lead to a decline in follower participation and legitimacy, just as is currently taking place in Santa Teresa. The most extreme result may be a catastrophic loss of support and physical relocation (Houston et al. 2003), and it is the perpetuation or cessation of performance that is our best archaeological evidence for the success or failure to engage the emotions of the audience.

The three themes considered here thus isolate potential areas of conflict between descent group and communal authorities and interests: socially defined access to resources, the concepts and meanings that legitimize the holders of these resources, and the theatrical attempts to create emotional bonds between leaders and supporters. Lineage and community leaders each likely sought to associate their groups with material or spiritual resources that were either different in scale or in kind. Newer groups likely borrowed from existing concepts of legitimacy in their attempts to establish themselves and achieve acceptance, whether by attempting to co-opt meanings or through associating themselves with acknowledged sacred spaces. Their use of performance and theater to create emotional bonds with audiences was a further area of potential conflict in the contrasting appeals that might be made toward exclusiveness or inclusiveness. Supporters were in the position of selecting among the options presented to them and thereby reproducing one form of authority or another, but they may have found it far more difficult to opt out of the system altogether if they wished to maintain access to land and social relationships. Theoretical arguments that emphasize the power held by commoners in social negotiation may be assuming independent access to lands and hence a degree of autonomy from the distant wranglings among political elites, but individuals may actually have been very dependent upon membership in communal groups for their social and physical survival.

Strategies that appear to contradict one another can be massaged through the efforts of both elites and members/followers so that those contradictions become less apparent even as they remain unresolved. They may be spatially separated into different forms of built space. Innovations in ritual can gradually fuse Christianity and native religion or appropriate and alter the claims of lineage elders to control aspects of the environment. Those elites seeking to establish competing claims to community leadership may need to offer something different from lineage elders in order to stabilize their authority. Conflicts do not need to be resolved, but neither are they left unaddressed.

ACKNOWLEDGMENTS

Thanks go to the National Science Foundation and the University of Colorado Denver for their support of field research in central Jalisco. I would like to thank Philip (Ted) Coyle for discussions of the Náyari and for his interest in bridging archaeology and cultural anthropology. I would also like to express my appreciation to the editors for presenting us with a stimulating framework for thinking about our data.

REFERENCES

Beekman, Christopher S. 1996. "The Long-Term Evolution of a Political Boundary: Archaeological Research in Jalisco, México." PhD diss., Vanderbilt University.

Beekman, Christopher S. 2000. "The Correspondence of Regional Patterns and Local Strategies in Formative to Classic Period West Mexico." *Journal of Anthropological Archaeology* 19(4): 385–412.

Beekman, Christopher S. 2003a. "Agricultural Pole Rituals and Rulership in Late Formative Central Jalisco." *Ancient Mesoamerica* 14(2): 299–318.

Beekman, Christopher S. 2003b. "Fruitful Symmetry: Corn and Cosmology in the Public Architecture of Late Formative and Early Classic Jalisco." *Mesoamerican Voices* 1: 5–22.

Beekman, Christopher S. 2005a. "Agency, Collectivities, and Emergence: Social Theory and Agent Based Simulations." In *Nonlinear Models for Archaeology and Anthropology: Continuing the Revolution*, edited by Christopher S. Beekman and William W. Baden, 51–78. Aldershot: Ashgate.

Beekman, Christopher S. 2005b. "Nuevos enfoques sobre la tradición Teuchitlán: Investigaciones actuales en Llano Grande y Navajas, Jalisco." In *El antiguo occidente de México: Nuevas perspectivas sobre el pasado prehispánico*, edited by Eduardo Williams, Phil C. Weigand, Lorenza López Mestas, and David C. Grove, 73–91. Zamora: Colegio de Michoacán.

Beekman, Christopher S. 2008. "Corporate Power Strategies in the Late Formative to Early Classic Tequila Valleys of Central Jalisco." *Latin American Antiquity* 19(4): 414–34.

Beekman, Christopher S. 2009. "Los Sistemas Políticos del Formativo en los Valles de Tequila, Jalisco y su Relación con la Subsistencia." In *Las sociedades complejas del occidente de México en el mundo mesoamericano: Homenaje a Dr. Phil C. Weigand*, edited by Eduardo Williams, Lorenza López Mestas, and Rodrigo Esparza, 75–95. Zamora: Colegio de Michoacán.

Beekman, Christopher S. Forthcoming. "Built Space as Political Fields: Community vs. Lineage Strategies in the Tequila Valleys." In *Alternative Pathways to Complexity: Households, Markets, World Systems, and Political Economy: Essays Honoring the Work of Richard E. Blanton*, edited by Lane Fargher and Verenice Heredia, Boulder: University Press of Colorado.

Beekman, Christopher S. Forthcoming. "Unseating the Shaman: Reinterpreting the Hollow Figures of Western Mexico.." In *Gods, Ancestors and Human Beings: Anthropomorphic Representations in the Mesoamerican Highlands*, edited by Brigitte Faugere and Christopher S. Beekman.

Beekman, Christopher S., and William W. Baden. 2011. "El cultivo del maíz y su impacto regional: Agotamiento de los suelos en el corredor de La Venta, Jalisco." In *Patrones de asentamiento y actividades de subsistencia en el Occidente de México: Reconocimiento a la Dra. Helen P. Pollard*, edited by Eduardo Williams and Phil C. Weigand, 351–82. Zamora: Colegio de Michoacán.

Bernal, Ignacio. 1949. "El Volador en Nayarit." *Tlalocan* 3(1): 92–93.

Blanco Morales, Ericka Sofía. 2009. "El juego de pelota en la tradición Teuchitlán: Hacia una propuesta sobre su función social." Tesis de maestría, Colegio de Michoacán.

Blanton, Richard E., Gary M. Feinman, Stephen A. Kowalewski, and Peter N. Peregrine. 1996. "A Dual-Processual Theory for the Evolution of Mesoamerican Civilization." *Current Anthropology* 37(1): 1–14.

Bloch, Maurice. 1975. Introduction to *Political Language and Oratory in Traditional Society*, edited by Maurice Bloch, 1–28. London: Academic Press.

Bourdieu, Pierre. 1990. *The Logic of Practice*. Translated by Richard Nice. Palo Alto: Stanford University Press.

Butterwick, Kristi. 1998. "Days of the Dead: Ritual Consumption and Ancestor-Worship in an Ancient West Mexican Society." PhD diss., University of Colorado Boulder.

Butterwick, Kristi. 2004. *Heritage of Power: Ancient Sculpture from West Mexico*. New York: Metropolitan Museum of Art.

Cabrero García, María Teresa, and Carlos López Cruz. 1997. "Catálogo de piezas de las tumbas de tiro del cañón de Bolaños." Mexico City: Universidad Nacional Autónoma de México / Instituto de Investigaciones Antropológicas.

Carsten, Janet, and Stephen Hugh-Jones, eds. 1995. *About the House: Lévi-Strauss and Beyond*. Cambridge: Cambridge University Press.

Corona Nuñez, José. 1955. "Tumba de El Arenal, Etzatlán, Jalisco." Mexico City: Instituto Nacional de Antropología e Historia.

Coyle, Philip E. 2001. *Náyari History, Politics, and Violence: From Flowers to Ash*. Tucson: University of Arizona Press.

Diguet, León. 1992. *Por tierras occidentales: Entre sierras y barrancas*. Mexico City: Centro de Estudios Mexicanos y Centroamericanos / Instituto Nacional Indigenista y Embajada de Francia en México.

Esparza López, Rodrigo. 2004. "Minería prehispánica de obsidiana en la región central de Jalisco." In *Tradiciones arqueológicas*, edited by Efraín Cárdenas García, 79–90. Morelia: Colegio de Michoacán.

Esparza López, Rodrigo. 2008. "Los yacimientos de obsidiana de El Pedernal–La Mora: Una explotación constante durante el desarrollo de la tradición Teuchitlán." In *La tradición Teuchitlán*, edited by Phil C. Weigand, Christopher Beekman, and Rodrigo Esparza, 143–66. Zamora: Colegio de Michoacán.

Esparza López, Rodrigo, and Carla Ponce Ordaz. 2005. "La obsidiana en el contexto arqueológico de Los Guachimontones, Teuchitlán, Jalisco." In *El antiguo occidente de México: Nuevas perspectivas sobre el pasado prehispánico*, edited by Eduardo Williams, Phil C. Weigand, Lorenza López Mestas, and David C. Grove, 145–70. Zamora: Colegio de Michoacán.

Evans-Pritchard, E. E. 1940. *The Nuer: A Description of the Modes of Livelihood and Political Institutions of a Nilotic People*. Oxford: Clarendon.

Festinger, Leon, Henry W. Riecken, and Stanley Schachter. 1956. *When Prophecy Fails*. Minneapolis: University of Minnesota Press.

Fikes, Jay Courtney. 1985. "Huichol Indian Identity and Adaptation." PhD diss., University of Michigan.

Fikes, Jay Courtney. 1993. *Carlos Castaneda, Academic Opportunism and the Psychedelic Sixties*. Victoria: Millennia Press.

Fogelin, Lars. 2011. "Ignoring the Problem: Spatial Strategies for Ameliorating Social Contradictions in Early South Asian Buddhism." *Journal of Social Archaeology* 11(2): 194–211.

Furst, Peter T. 1966. "Shaft Tombs, Shell Trumpets, and Shamanism: A Culture-Historical Approach to Problems in West Mexican Archaeology." PhD diss., University of California, Los Angeles.

Furst, Peter T. 1972. *Flesh of the Gods: The Ritual Use of Hallucinogens*. Prospect Heights, IL: Waveland.

Furst, Peter T. 1974. "Ethnographic Analogy in the Interpretation of West Mexican Art." In *The Archaeology of West Mexico*, edited by Betty Bell, 132–46. Ajijic: West Mexican Society for Advanced Study.

Furst, Peter T. 1975. "House of Darkness and House of Light: Sacred Functions of West Mexican Funerary Art." In *Death and the Afterlife in Pre-Columbian America*, edited by Elizabeth P. Benson, 33–68. Washington, DC: Dumbarton Oaks.

Galván Villegas, Luis Javier. 1991. *Las tumbas de tiro del Valle de Atemajac*. Mexico City: Instituto Nacional de Antropología e Historia.

Gillespie, Susan D. 1991. "Ballgames and Boundaries." In *The Mesoamerican Ballgame*, edited by Vernon L. Scarborough and David R. Wilcox, 317–45. Tucson: University of Arizona Press.

Graham, Mark Miller. 1998. "The Iconography of Rulership in Ancient West Mexico." In *Ancient West Mexico: Art and Archaeology of the Unknown Past*, edited by Richard F. Townsend, 191–203. New York: Thames & Hudson.

Headrick, Annabeth. 2007. *The Teotihuacan Trinity: The Sociopolitical Structure of an Ancient Mesoamerican City*. Austin: University of Texas Press.

Houston, Stephen, Héctor Escobedo, Mark Child, Charles Golden, and René Muñoz. 2003. "The Moral Community: Maya Settlement Transformation at Piedras Negras, Guatemala." In *The Social Construction of Ancient Cities*, edited by Monica L. Smith, 212–53. Washington, DC: Smithsonian Institution Press.

Houston, Stephen, and David Stuart. 1996. "Of Gods, Glyphs and Kings: Divinity and Rulership among the Classic Maya." *Antiquity* 70(268): 289–312.

Inomata, Takeshi, and Lawrence S. Coben, eds. 2006. *Archaeology of Performance: Theaters of Power, Community, and Politics*. Lanham, MD: AltaMira.

Jáuregui, Jesús, and Johannes Neurath, eds. 2003. *Flechadores de estrellas: Nuevas aportaciones a la etnología de coras y huicholes*. Mexico City: Instituto Nacional de Antropología e Historia / Universidad de Guadalajara.

Joyce, Arthur. 2000. "The Founding of Monte Albán: Sacred Propositions and Social Practices." In *Agency in Archaeology*, edited by Marcia-Anne Dobres and John Robb, 71–91. London: Routledge.

Kan, Michael, Clement W. Meighan, and Henry B. Nicholson. 1989. *Sculpture of Ancient West Mexico: Nayarit, Jalisco, Colima*. Los Angeles: Los Angeles County Museum of Art.

Kelley, J. Charles. 1974. "Speculations on the Culture History of Northwestern Mesoamerica." In *The Archaeology of West Mexico*, edited by Betty Bell, 19–39. Ajijic: Sociedad de Estudios Avanzados del Occidente de México.

Klein, Cecelia F., Eulogio Guzman, Elisa C. Mandell, and Maya Stanfield-Mazzi. 2002. "The Role of Shamanism in Mesoamerica Art: A Reassessment." *Current Anthropology* 43(3): 383–401.

Lévi-Strauss, Claude. 1982. *The Way of the Masks*. Translated by Sylvia Modelski. Seattle: University of Washington Press.

Long, Stanley V. 1966. "Archaeology of the Municipio de Etzatlán, Jalisco." PhD diss., University of California. Los Angeles.

Lumholtz, Carl. 1902. *Unknown Mexico: A Record of Five Years' Exploration among the Tribes of the Western Sierra Madre; in the Tierra Caliente of Tepic and Jalisco; and among the Tarascos of Michoacan*. 2 vols. New York: Charles Scribner's Sons.

Magriña, Laura. 2002. *Los coras entre 1531 y 1722*. Mexico City: Instituto Nacional de Antropología e Historia / Universidad de Guadalajara.

Malvido Mirando, Elsa. 2000. "La guerra contra las momias en Nueva España: El siglo XVIII, jesuitas, franciscanos, autoridades seculares e Inquisición." *Chungará* 32(2): 199–205.

Morris, Ian. 1991. "The Archaeology of Ancestors: The Saxe/Goldstein Hypothesis Revisited." *Cambridge Archaeological Journal* 1: 147–69.

Nedelmann, Birgitta. 1990. "Georg Simmel as an Analyst of Autonomous Dynamics: The Merry-Go-Round of Fashion." In *Georg Simmel and Contemporary Sociology*, edited by Michael Kaern, Bernard S. Phillips and Robert S. Cohen, 243–57. Dordrecht: Kluwer.

Neurath, Johannes. 2000. "Tukipa Ceremonial Centers in the Community of Tuapurie (Santa Catarina Cuexcomatitlan): Cargo Systems, Landscape, and Cosmovision." *Journal of the Southwest* 42(1): 81–110.

Neurath, Johannes, ed. 2005. "Etnografía del ritual, textos rituales y mitologías de la Sierra Madre Occidental, a cien años de la Expedición al Nayarit." *Dimensión Antropológica* 34(12): 7–21.

Neurath, Johannes, ed. 2008. *Por los caminos del maíz: Mito y ritual en la periferia septentrional de Mesoamérica*. Mexico City: Fondo de Cultura Económica / Consejo Nacional para la Cultura y las Artes.

Preuss, Karl Theodor. 1998. *Fiesta, literatura, y magia en el Nayarit: Ensayos sobre coras, huicholes, mexicaneros de Konrad Theodor Preuss*. Compiled by Jesús Jáuregui and Johannes Neurath. Mexico City: Instituto Nacional Indigenista / Centro Francés de Estudios Mexicanos y Centroamericanos.

Ramos de la Vega, Jorge, and Lorenza López Mestas. 1996. "Datos preliminares sobre el descubrimiento de una tumba de tiro en el sitio de Huitzilapa, Jalisco." *Ancient Mesoamerica* 7(1): 121–34.

Scarborough, Vernon L., and David R. Wilcox, eds. 1991. *The Mesoamerican Ballgame*. Tucson: University of Arizona Press.

Seler, Eduard. 1993. "The Huichol Indians of the State of Jalisco in Mexico." In *Collected Works in Mesoamerican Linguistics and Archaeology*, vol. 4, edited by J. Eric S. Thompson and Francis B. Richardson, 179–97. Culver City, CA: Labyrinthos.

Simmel, Georg. [1908] 1971. "Group Expansion and the Development of Individuality." In *Georg Simmel: On Individuality and Social Forms*, edited by Donald N. Levine, 251–93. Chicago: University of Chicago Press.

Smith, Adam T. 2000. "Rendering the Political Aesthetic: Political Legitimacy in Urartian Representations of the Built Environment." *Journal of Anthropological Archaeology* 19: 131–63.

Smith Marquez, Sean Montgomery. 2009. "El Caso Teuchitlán-Loma Alta: Un ejemplo de patron de patrón de asentamiento mesoamericano." Tesis de maestría, Colegio de Michoacán.

Spence, Michael W., Phil C. Weigand, and Maria de los Dolores Soto de Arechavaleta. 2002. "Production and Distribution of Obsidian Artifacts in Western Mexico." In *Pathways to Prismatic Blades: A Study in Mesoamerican Obsidian Core-Blade Technology*, edited by Kenneth Hirth and Bradford Andrews, 61–79. Cotsen Institute of Archaeology Monograph 45. Los Angeles: University of California, Los Angeles.

Sugiyama, Saburo. 1993. "Worldview Materialized in Teotihuacan, Mexico." *Latin American Antiquity* 4(2): 103–29.

Toscano, Salvador. 1946. "El arte y la historia del occidente de México." In *Arte precolombino del occidente de México*, edited by Salvador Toscano, 9–48. México City: Secretaria Educacíon Pública.

Watanabe, John M. 2004. "Some Models in a Muddle: Lineage and House in Classic Maya Social Organization. *Ancient Mesoamerica* 15(1): 159–66.

Von Winning, Hasso, and Olga Hammer. 1972. *Anecdotal Sculpture of Ancient West Mexico*. Los Angeles: Ethnic Arts Council of Los Angeles.

Weigand, Phil C. 1985a. "Evidence for Complex Societies during the Western Mesoamerican Classic Period." In *The Archaeology of West and Northwest Mesoamerica*, edited by Michael S. Foster and Phil C. Weigand, 47–91. Boulder: Westview.

Weigand, Phil C. 1985b. "Considerations on the Archaeology and Ethnohistory of the Mexicaneros, Tequales, Coras, Huicholes, and Caxcanes of Nayarit, Jalisco, and Zacatecas." In *Contributions to the Archaeology and Ethnohistory of Greater Mesoamerica*, edited by William J. Folan, 126–87. Carbondale: Southern Illinois University Press.

Weigand, Phil C. 1991. "The Western Mesoamerican Tlachco: A Two-Thousand-Year Perspective." In *The Mesoamerican Ballgame*, edited by Vernon L. Scarborough and David R. Wilcox, 73–86. Tucson: University of Arizona Press.

Weigand, Phil C. 1993. *Evolución de una civilización prehispánica: Arqueología de Jalisco, Nayarit y Zacatecas*. Zamora: Colegio de Michoacán.

Weigand, Phil C. 1996. "Las sociedades huicholas antes de la llegada de los españoles." In *Memoria 4 (agrupa los boletines correspondientes a 1996)*, edited by Maria del Pilar Sánchez Alfaro, 410–32. Guadalajara: Benemérita Sociedad de Geografía y Estadística del Estado de Jalisco.

Weigand, Phil C., and Christopher S. Beekman. 1998. "The Teuchitlán Tradition: Rise of a Statelike Society." In *Ancient West Mexico: Art and Archaeology of the Unknown Past*, edited by Richard F. Townsend, 35–51. New York: Thames & Hudson.

Weigand, Phil C., Acelia García de Weigand, and Michael D. Glascock. 2004. "La explotación de los yacimientos de obsidiana del centro-oeste de Jalisco." In *Bienes estratégicos del antiguo occidente de México: Producción e intercambio*, edited by Eduardo Williams, 113–35. Zamora: Colegio de Michoacán.

Whittington, E. Michael, ed., 2001. *The Sport of Life and Death: The Mesoamerican Ballgame*. New York: Thames & Hudson.

Zingg, Robert M. 1988. *La mitología de los huicholes*. Guadalajara: Colegio de Jalisco.

5

Patron Deities and Politics among the Classic Maya

Joanne Baron

Most modern scholars agree that religious belief played at least some role in the exercise and legitimization of political authority among the Classic Period Maya. Many have seen Maya rulership as a form of divine kingship, or a system in which the ruler draws his authority from a special relationship with the divine (e.g., Demarest 1992; Fields and Reents-Budet 2005; Freidel and Schele 1988; Freidel, Schele, and Parker 1993; Houston and Stuart 1996; Inomata, this volume; Schele and Miller 1986). For example, Arthur A. Demarest (1992) has drawn on African and Southeast Asian parallels to argue that Maya polities were "theater states" in which the ruler's display of his supernatural connections was the main force behind his political authority. Inomata (2006, this volume) similarly notes that the theatricality of ritual acts was responsible for drawing large masses of people to participate in community formation centered on the royal court. Others, particularly Linda Schele and David A. Freidel (e.g., Freidel and Schele 1988; Freidel, Schele, and Parker 1993; Schele and Freidel 1990; Schele and Miller 1986), have viewed the Maya ruler as shaman. According to these scholars, village-level ritual specialists of the Formative Period developed into a form of institutionalized shamanism during the Classic Period. Even scholars who take a primarily materialist perspective acknowledge the importance of ritual in the legitimacy of power and the mobilization of goods (e.g., Lucero 2003). These scholars all agree that religious belief and its behavioral

DOI: 10.5876/9781607324164.c005

expression, religious ritual, were used to legitimize social inequality and the authority of the ruler and his court.

In this chapter, I will also argue for the importance of religious ritual in the negotiation of political relationships among the Classic Maya. However, it is important to note some deficiencies with the ways previous scholars have dealt with this topic. First, as Sarah Kurnick notes in her introductory chapter to this volume, simply observing that rulers served a religious role within the polity does not go far enough to explain how that role was acquired and maintained, nor the particular ways in which it induced followers to obey. Secondly, as Kurnick also notes, studies of divine kingship among the Maya have focused on the ways rulers represented themselves in text and image and not enough on how those representations were received by non-rulers. In this chapter, I hope to address these questions by focusing more attention on the actual content of Classic Maya religious beliefs and rituals. For example, how can we understand and categorize "the divine" among the Maya? What did the Maya believe that particular supernatural entities did in the world and how did rulers act as intermediaries? How were the interests of followers served by the ruler's intercession? And how did that intercession play a role in the authority of particular rulers or royal lineages?

In her introductory chapter, Kurnick invites us to consider the many contradictions inherent in the negotiation of political authority. Rulership has often been thought of in terms of difference: those with authority are set apart from others in some way. At the same time, rulers must also emphasize the ways in which they are the same as their followers, because obedience to commands (Max Weber's classic definition of authority) is only likely to be long-lasting if followers feel that obedience is in their best interest. If a ruler is completely different from them, followers will lose incentives to obey.

In this chapter, I will apply this framework to a new consideration of Classic Maya divine kingship. Specifically, I will examine patron deities among the Classic Maya. Each Maya polity had its own set of patron gods. These gods were believed to belong to the whole community and serve the interests of all of its members. While scholars have recognized patron deities among the Maya and other Mesoamerican groups, certain misconceptions have impeded our understanding of their role in political relationships—namely, they are often considered an outgrowth of ancestor veneration. I will define patron deities and discuss the ways in which they differed from other supernatural beings. I will also discuss the importance of patron gods in the negotiation of Classic Maya political authority. I will end with a case study to illustrate these claims based on excavations at the site of La Corona, Guatemala.

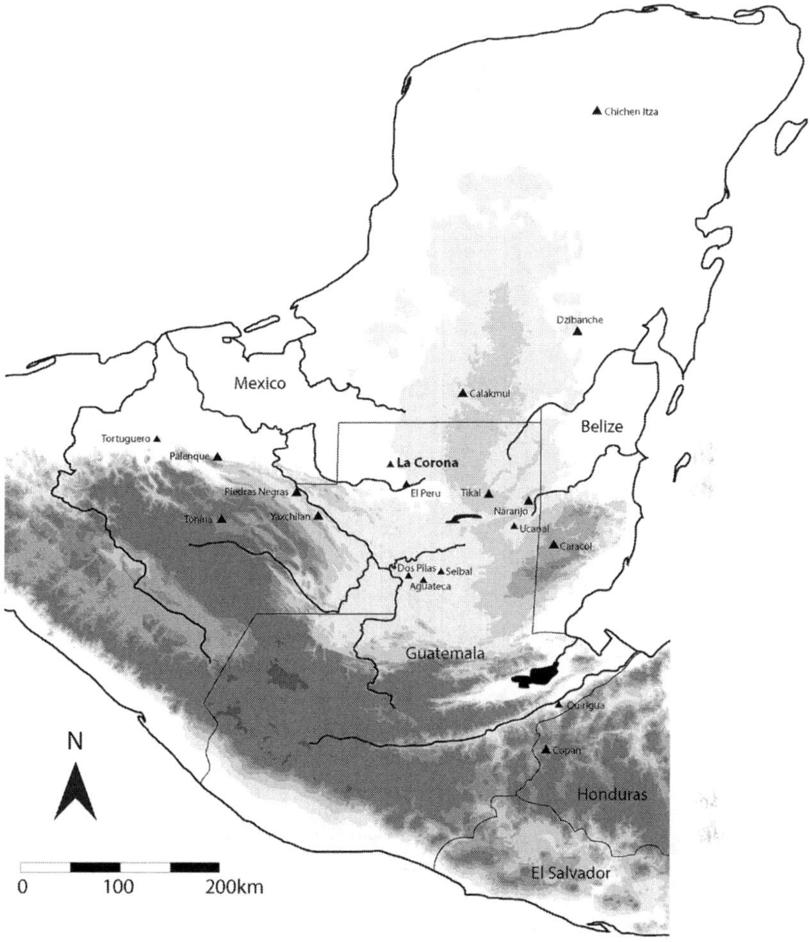

FIGURE 5.1. *Map of the Maya area showing the location of La Corona.*

LA CORONA

La Corona is a small site located in northwestern Petén (figure 5.1). The site was occupied for approximately the duration of the Classic Period, starting in the third or fourth century CE and continuing to the mid-ninth century CE. La Corona has an unusually rich historical record for a site of its size, providing a great deal of detail about the ruling family and its relationships. The La Corona Regional Archaeological Project has undertaken excavations since 2008 under the direction of Marcello A. Canuto and Tomás Barrientos.

Under its auspices, my excavations were focused on Structures 13R-2, 13R-3, 13R-4, and 13R-5, a set of patron deity temples in an architectural group known as Coronitas (figure 5.2). The function of these structures was identified as patron deity shrines by means of a carved hieroglyphic panel recovered from Structure 13R-5 (Canuto et al. 2006). The text of this panel makes it clear that Structure 13R-5 was a shrine constructed for a patron deity in the year 677 CE by ruler K'inich ? Yook (Guenter 2005). The panel also makes mention of an earlier construction of three temples for three other patron deities in the year 658 CE by K'inich? Yook's father, ruler Chakaw Nahb Chan (Guenter 2005). The best candidates for these three patron deity temples are Structures 13R-2, 13R-3, and 13R-4. Not only are they adjacent to the known patron deity shrine 13R-5, they are also of approximately the same size as one another and, in their final phase of construction, were built at the same time in a single architectural program. No other structures at La Corona obviously fit the criteria of a set of three temples built at the same time. The ability to identify Maya patron deity temples is rare. In fact, these circumstances exist at only four other sites: Chichen Itza, Palenque, Tikal, and Yaxchilan. And while some of these have been investigated, none of them have undergone a program of excavation designed to identify ritual activities or participants. At La Corona, my excavations explored the architectural phases of the temples as well as the remains of ritual activities left as middens and refuse.

Based on archaeological and epigraphic evidence, I argue that patron deity veneration was a strategy employed by Classic Maya rulers to negotiate the contradictions inherent in rulership. Rulers promoted the polity-wide veneration of patron gods as a way of emphasizing a shared ethnic or community identity. At the same time, rulers represented themselves as having a special relationship to patron deities, and thereby as uniquely suited to serve the community's interests through their intercession. Archaeological evidence at La Corona indicates that this strategy was successful in promoting institutionalized rulership. In fact, it was so successful that La Corona rulers introduced new patron gods in periods of dynastic upheaval. A close examination of patron deity veneration can fill in some of the gaps left by other studies of Maya divine kingship and help us see Classic Maya polities as complex entities in which authority was constantly under negotiation.

RECONSTRUCTING CLASSIC MAYA RELIGION

Understanding the role of religion in Classic Maya politics demands that we begin by understanding Maya religious beliefs. Numerous hieroglyphic

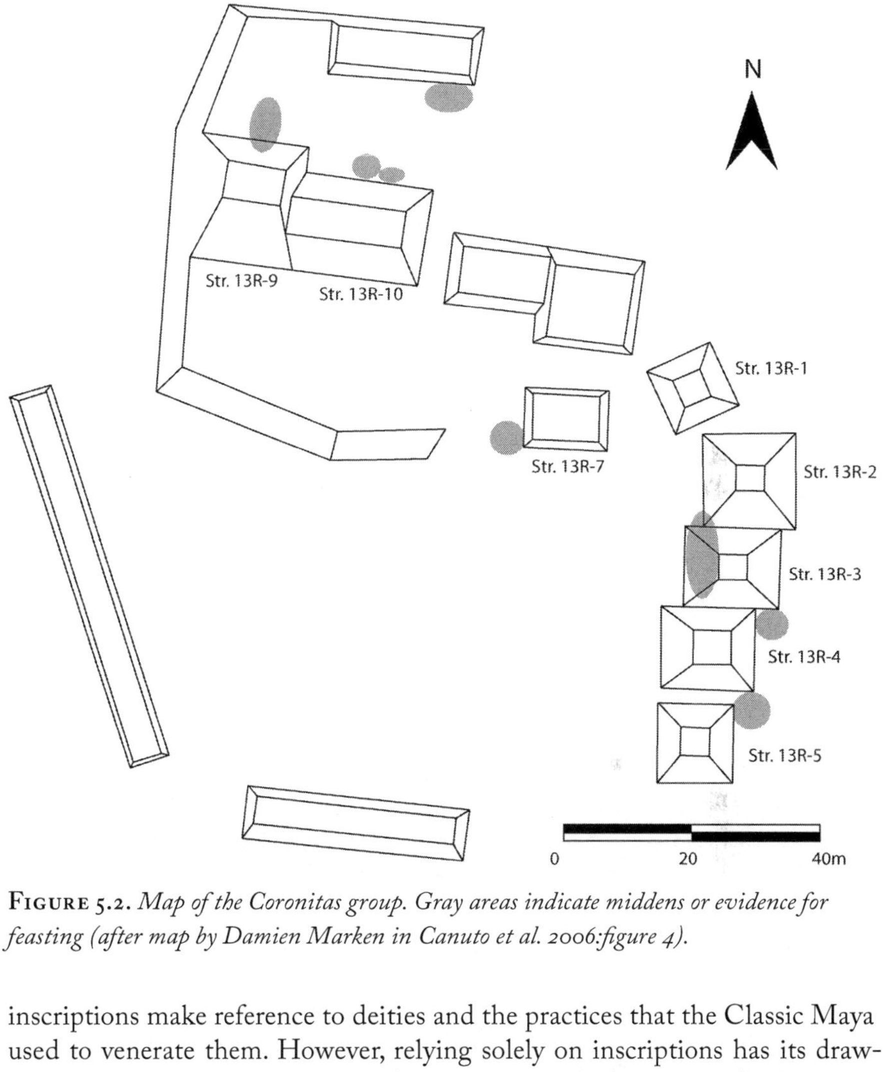

FIGURE 5.2. *Map of the Coronitas group. Gray areas indicate middens or evidence for feasting (after map by Damien Marken in Canuto et al. 2006:figure 4).*

inscriptions make reference to deities and the practices that the Classic Maya used to venerate them. However, relying solely on inscriptions has its drawbacks, since they represent a specific viewpoint and often a specific rhetorical purpose. In the case of the Classic Maya, inscriptions were almost always commissioned by rulers and occasionally by lesser elites. There are no known inscriptions commissioned by nonelite people. Thus, it is difficult to know whether inscriptions represent the religious beliefs of the whole society or simply that which its rulers most strongly promoted.

Archaeological evidence can be used to supplement these data by looking for the presence of religious ritual as practiced by different segments of society. Recent archaeological approaches to commoner ritual often focus on domestic contexts, where nonelites could more freely shape the content of religious rituals, beyond the watchful eyes of rulers (e.g., Gonlin 2007; Joyce and Weller 2007). These studies provide a contrast to elite-sponsored ideology and thus offer a theory of commoner resistance as shaped through ritual. However, commoner participation (or nonparticipation) in public rituals also played a role in shaping power relations among Mesoamerican groups (Joyce and Weller 2007:146–47, Joyce et al., this volume; Beekman, this volume). As I will discuss later in this chapter, there is archaeological evidence to suggest large-scale commoner participation in Classic Maya public patron deity rituals.

Finally, Maya religion can be examined by turning to the historical and ethnographic records from more recent periods. Ethnohistoric documents from the Maya area, such as the Popol Vuh, the Titulo de Totonicapan, and the Annals of the Kaqchikels describe the era immediately prior to the Spanish conquest. Furthermore, some religious beliefs and practices exist in syncretic form in contemporary Maya communities. The Maya area has a rich ethnographic record from the mid-twentieth century that reveals similarities between modern beliefs and those recorded on Classic Period monuments.

THE NATURE OF MAYA DEITIES

The exact nature of Maya gods has been a source of study for decades and continues to be debated. One line of study has been the identification of individual deities and the classification of these deities into different groupings (Schellhas 1904; Thompson 1950; Hellmuth 1987; Taube 1992). Other scholars have argued that a pantheon of deities in the Greco-Roman sense misunderstands Mesoamerican religion in general (Baudez 2002; Marcus 1978; 1983; Stuart 2005). They contend that ancient Mesoamericans viewed deities as a manifestation of "the vital force or power that inhabits the blood and energizes people and a variety of objects of ritual and everyday life" (Houston and Stuart 1996:292).

In fact, both views are true: Classic Maya gods behaved as specific personalities in the sense of a pantheon *and* as representations of vital natural forces. This is because the Classic Maya actually had two different categories of gods. These categories have already been recognized as "major gods that are the personifications of universal phenomena as well as natural and cosmological forces . . . and . . . local gods like tutelary deities" (Sachse 2004:9). In this chapter, I refer to these categories as general gods (those that represent natural forces such as the sun, rain, wind, etc.) and patron gods (those that belong to particular communities). The Classic Maya referred to both of types of entities as *k'uh* (Ringle 1988), and they were therefore clearly related to one another in some way. In fact, most patron gods can be identified as an aspect or local iteration of an original general deity. Thus, general deities actually became patron deities by forming special relationships with particular communities. As patron deities, their behavior differed from the impersonal general deities and more closely resembled the Western conception of gods, like those of ancient Greece.

At Palenque, the forging of this local relationship of supernatural patronage was made explicit and was referred to as the "arrival," the "earth-touching," and the "birth" of the site's three main patron gods during the ancient past (Lounsbury 1980:112–13). In fact, Palenque texts also include mythological activities of the patron god "GI" before this birth. For years scholars were confused as to how GI could perform mythological actions before his own birth and concluded that there must be two different GIs (Lounsbury 1980:112). However, Stuart (2006:173–74) has asserted more recently that there was simply one GI who took two forms: pre-birth and post-birth. This "birth"/"arrival"/"earth-touching" event corresponded to the descent of the general deity into his patron deity form, forging a new relationship with the Palenque community.

PATRON GODS VS. ANCESTORS

Many scholars have argued that patron deities among the Classic Maya were, in fact, simply deified ancestors (e.g., Proskouriakoff 1978:116–17; Marcus 1983, 1992; McAnany 1995:27; Wright 2011:232–33). But the Maya drew a clear distinction between these two categories. To begin, they had separate words referring to them: *k'uh* for "god" and *mam* for "ancestor." Furthermore, a close examination of epigraphic data demonstrates that Maya patron gods and ancestors behaved in very different ways from one another. For example, only patron deities appear to have existed in the form of effigies while ancestors did not. Furthermore, patron deities were active participants in the world of human beings. They were given credit for success in war, the overseeing of important rituals, and even the passage of time. Ancestors, on the other hand, were passive, merely gazing down from above upon their descendants (see Baron 2013:165–66). Thus, patron deities and ancestors should be seen as distinct categories of supernatural entities. Deceased ancestors did not become patron deities over time.

There are reasons for the confusion between patron deities and ancestors. One is that ancestors were often depicted with the attributes of general gods, specifically the Sun god (or Moon goddess in the case of female ancestors) and the Maize god. Nevertheless, ancestors were not depicted with attributes of their site's own patron gods and rulers hardly ever incorporated the names of their polity's own patron deities into their title strings. Another source of confusion is the fact that patron deities were often described as *ajaws*, or "rulers," making it seem as though they had once been living rulers of their home communities. They are sometimes even given accession statements. However, dynastic counts (numbered lists of rulers) never originated with patron deities but always with an identifiable human ancestor. Thus, the comparison of patron deities to ancestors should be seen as a rhetorical trope rather than a belief in their origins as human beings.

The integrity of the trichotomy I have outlined here (general deities-patron deities-deceased ancestors) is demonstrated by comparison to modern Maya religious beliefs. John Watanabe (1990) defines three types of supernatural beings among the modern Maya of Guatemala. First, patron saints are associated with community identity and sociality. Watanabe describes them as "accessible" and "worldly." They are not town founders or ancestors but were introduced to the community in the ancient mythic past. These can be distinguished from a second category, ancestors, who were once real living people and who founded the town and its traditions. Ancestors are believed to be the original owners of family lands, and offerings are made to them in order to establish continued claim to these plots. However, patron saints are not themselves considered ancestors, nor vice versa. A third type of supernatural being is Earth Lords, also referred to as "mountain owners" (Watanabe 1990, 1992; Siegel 1941), Satan (Warren 1978), Judas (Bunzel 1959; Warren 1978; Watanabe 1992), and Maximon (Christenson 2001; Mendelson 1965 in Watanabe 1992:122; Reina 1966). These supernatural entities are believed to own the mountains that surround the community. These mountains are seen as a source of great wealth, and thus Earth Lords control access to worldly success. They are associated with amoral intractability, sometimes stealing away souls, sometimes granting riches.

These three supernatural categories correspond to those I defined above. Patron saints are in many ways the modern equivalents of pre-Columbian patron deities. This link can be readily established by examining the history of the conquest, in which Spanish friars intentionally made use of beliefs in local patron gods to facilitate the introduction of patron saints (Baron 2013). General deities, on the other hand, include creator gods and underworld gods.

Allen Christenson (2001:186–87) argues that Maximon/Earth Lords closely correspond to the ancient Maya underworld deities, especially the one nicknamed "God L" by scholars: "Like [Maximon], God L was an aged deity famous for his lascivious nature . . . Both deities are closely associated with the sacrifice of gods and cosmic devastation . . . and cigars are part of their standard iconography. Also, both God L and [Maximon] are patrons of the underworld, jaguars and long-distance travel." These gods are aloof and do not represent specific communities or actively participate in human affairs. Finally, ancestors in both periods were once real, living people and thus distinct from the other two categories.

The distinctions between different types of supernatural entities among the Maya are interesting in their own right but are even more significant if we consider what these practices meant for social relationships within Maya communities. Each lineage, whether elite or common, had its own set of ancestors to venerate at the household level. Patricia A. McAnany (1995) has aptly described these practices as "living with the ancestors," in that they often involved burying lineage members beneath household floors and continuing to interact with them in certain ways after their death. By venerating these ancestors, each lineage in the community, no matter what its social status, maintained links to the past, which conferred privileges such as access to ancestral lands and social status. While Maya rulers also venerated ancestors, McAnany argues that kingship was more than simply kinship writ large. Instead, kingship was essentially an extractive institution that appropriated, politicized, and ultimately superseded kin-based social organization. Rather than a series of autonomous lineages, each with its own rights to land and resources, the institution of hereditary rulership promoted the claims of the ruler to these resources as superior to all lineage-based claims.

This was accomplished in several ways. First, royal ancestors were promoted as superior to all other ancestors within the community, thus conferring exceptional (royal) status upon their descendants. The practice of depicting royal ancestors as fused with the Sun god, Moon goddess, or Maize god was one way to accomplish this task. Another strategy was to neutralize the kinship-based claims of rival lineages: "An effective means of quelling dissent to centralized rule is to dismantle the organizational nexus of that dissent—the kinship structure—and thereby reduce factional conflict to simple class conflict, which yields a more easily controllable playing field since conflict is resolved in favor of those who have the power to resolve it" (McAnany 1995:150). McAnany suggests that the desecration of competing lineage shrines or the appropriation of lineage resources were effective ways of neutralizing competing lineages.

Finally, I propose that a third strategy for overcoming the lineage system was to promote the alternative practice of patron deity veneration. As I discuss below, patron deity veneration practices were ideal for negotiating the contradictions inherent in rulership. As rulers promoted themselves above all other lineages, they faced the task of demonstrating that their authority was advantageous to the community. The discourses associated with patron deity veneration presented the well-being of the entire community, regardless of lineage, as dependent on the benevolence of patron gods, thereby making their veneration more important than ancestor veneration. At the same time, rulers presented themselves as uniquely suited to intercede with patron deities on behalf of the community due to their personal relationships with these gods.

PATRON DEITY VENERATION: BELIEFS AND PRACTICES

Unlike ancestors, who belong to particular lineages, patron saints in modern Guatemala are identified with the whole community. Saint images are often dressed in each town's traditional clothing and are only prayed to in the indigenous language of the community rather than in Spanish (Watanabe 1990, 1992). In the Maya highland region, where language and dress differ substantially from town to town, both of these features serve as markers of ethnic/community identity to a strong degree. Thus, forms of dressing and speaking to the saint reinforce the notion that the saint is a member of the community although he/she may have a Spanish name. Maya community members say that their patron saints provide the community with protection and well-being (e.g., Reina 1966:122). In Santiago Chimaltenango, for example, it is said that the saint protected the community from the worst atrocities of the Guatemalan Civil War, while their immediate neighbors suffered far worse under the army occupation (Watanabe 1990:134). If, however, proper rituals for saints are not carried out, they are believed to punish the whole town (Reina 1966:18).

The associations between community well-being, ethnic identity, and patron saint/deity veneration can be traced back through time. For example, in Native histories from highland Guatemala, the gods that various groups received at the mythical city of Tulan before the first dawning of the sun defined ethnicity. The K'iche narrative presented in the Popol Vuh is most explicit in this regard. At the time it was written, the K'iches consisted of three political units—the Nima K'iches, the Tamub, and the Ilocab—that struggled for dominance. Written from the perspective of the Nima K'iches, the text describes a single ethnic, though not political, identity for the three groups, based on their worship of the patron god Tohil: "thus was the naming of the three Quichés. But . . . it was the same god's name, Tohil Quiché, for all of them. It was Tohil for the Tamub as well as for the Ilocab. There was only one name for the god among them. Therefore the three groups of Quichés were not divided" (Christenson 2003a:213). As with modern patron saints, Tohil was believed to provide benefits to the whole K'iche nation, such as agricultural abundance, human fertility, security, and protection from shame, misfortune, injury, illness, etc. (289–90).

Differences between the highland nations are also expressed in terms of their allegiance to certain patron gods. While the Popol Vuh describes the progenitors of the K'iches receiving the god Tohil, it specifies that the Kaqchikels received a different god. The Kaqchikels' own account (Otzoy 1999) names a pair of deities given to them at Tulan. These gods played an important role in subsequent conflicts in the region. The Popol Vuh foreshadows the eventual subjugation of competing ethnic groups by describing their defeat by the trickery of Tohil (Christenson:216–18). And the Kaqchikels' eventual capture of the effigy of Tohil constituted a major victory over the K'iches (Otzoy 1999:178).

The associations between patron deities and ethnic identity are harder to prove for the Classic Period, chiefly because ethnic designations are rare in hieroglyphic texts and references to commoners are entirely absent, let alone commoner ethnicity. Nevertheless, inscriptions indicate that patron deities were associated with particular places, which suggests that the ethnic associations seen in later periods were likely true of the Classic Period as well.

A good example of this phenomenon is a deity nicknamed "GI-K'awiil" of Ceibal. This deity was also venerated at other nearby sites of the Petexbatun region, including Aguateca, Cancuen, La Amelia, and Tamarandito (Houston and Stuart 1996:302). In the seventh century, an offshoot of the Tikal dynasty founded a new site in the region at Dos Pilas (Houston et al. 1992), apparently bringing its own patron gods from Tikal (Schele and Freidel 1990:389–90). Over time, the Dos Pilas dynasty conquered other sites in the area, including Ceibal, reducing them to client states. Then the Dos Pilas dynasty itself splintered, and one of its offshoots established a petty court at Ceibal, replacing the original dynasty (see Martin and Grube 2000:61–65). By the end of the eighth century, the Petexbatun region had collapsed entirely and Ceibal was depopulated. About thirty years later, a new Terminal Classic dynasty from Ucanal established itself at Ceibal (Schele and Mathews 1998) until the site was eventually abandoned completely. In spite of these dynastic changes, GI-K'awiil remained a patron deity of Ceibal throughout its history. References to his veneration can be found in each of the four periods mentioned: before Ceibal was conquered by Dos Pilas, after it was conquered, when a splinter of the Dos Pilas dynasty took over the site, and when it was ruled by a dynasty from Ucanal. This demonstrates that GI-K'awiil was associated with Ceibal itself, and presumably the entire community, rather than the ruling dynasty.

Another suggestive example comes from the inscriptions of Copan. There, a series of patron gods of the site were referred to as *koknoom Ux Witik*, "the guardians of Copan" (Lacadena and Wichmann, 2004:106). Rather than protecting a particular lineage, these gods were associated with the place itself, suggesting that they belonged to and protected all the people that lived there. Further evidence for the association of patron gods with entire communities was found during excavation at La Corona. As I will discuss shortly, midden deposits from the patron deity temples and other structures at the site indicate that elites and commoners alike carried out patron deity veneration rituals.

As in later periods, Classic Period patron deities were believed to provide supernatural services for their home communities. On hieroglyphic monuments, they are commonly stated to "oversee" important rituals such as period ending ceremonies (Baron 2013:205). In other cases, texts suggest that they actually caused time to elapse, using the verb *ukabjiiy* (roughly translatable as "to make happen"). Other examples of this verb attribute success in war to patron deities as well (205–6). Such divine intercession would have benefited the whole populace, not just the ruler alone.

In exchange for the benefits that patron saints and patron deities provided to their home communities, they required care, comfort, and maintenance. In the case of modern Maya communities, this usually requires providing the saint's altar with flowers (Bunzel 1959:166; Cancian 1965:34; Reina 1966:102; Siebers 1999:53; Wisdom 1940:376), incense and candles (Bunzel 1959:166; Cancian 1965:34; Oakes 1951:60; Valladares 1957:148; Vogt 1993:18; Watanabe 1992:124; Wisdom 1940:381), sweeping and maintaining the church building where the saints reside (Cancian 1965:34–35; Oakes 1951:60; Reina 1966:102; Siebers 1999:53; Watanabe 1992:109), making sure the clothes of the saint are washed and in good repair (Cancian 1965:34; Christenson 2001:92; Reina 1966:105, 145; Vogt 1993:118; Wisdom 1940:417), and making sure the saints are generally comfortable (Reina 1966:121).

The feeding of saints is also an important responsibility. Usually, saints are described as "eating" candles and incense, as if such items were food (e.g., Bunzel 1959:166; Vogt 1993:1). For example, one informant claimed that without candles, rum, and incense, God and the saints "would have no tortillas" (Wagley 1949 in Watanabe 1992:76). In other instances, however, saints are believed to actually partake of food and drink (e.g., Reina 1966:115; Wisdom

1940:376). Saint feeding involves the sharing of food between humans and saints within the context of the annual patron saint fiesta. At these public feasts, all members of the community are invited to participate and large amounts of food and alcohol are consumed (Bunzel 1959:254; Cancian 1965:38; Redfield and Villa Rojas 1962:150–56; Siebers 1999:64, 66; Siegel 1941:72; Watanabe 1992:124; Wisdom 1940:385, 387, 449–50).

Similar practices are also described in Native authored histories. The Popol Vuh, the Titulo de Totonicapan, and the Annals of the Kaqchikels all indicate that patron gods during the Postclassic Period existed in effigy form (Christenson 2003a:286; Carmack and Mondloch 1983:177; Otzoy 1999:156). The nations were required to feed these effigies with the hearts of captured enemy warriors as well as with auto-sacrificial blood (Christenson 2003a:219). Other offerings used to feed the gods included flowers, corn, incense, and animals (Carmack and Mondloch 1983:191; Otzoy 1999:155). In one passage from the Annals of the Kaqchikels, the founders of the nation are instructed that they must "carry, feed, and eat with" their gods (Otzoy 1999:156). This implies an obligation of ritual feasting: the Kaqchikels were not only responsible for sustaining the gods but also participated in commensal feasts with them in order for their veneration to be properly achieved. The Title of the Lords of Totonicapan, another K'iche account, also describes the dressing and adorning of the god Tohil: "The son of the ruler was the first to load the hand of Tohil with jades, metals, mirrors and offerings all around, and a loin cloth wound around his hips" (English translation based on Carmack and Mondloch 1983:196, 253; Christenson 2003b).

Such practices can also be traced to the Classic Period in hieroglyphic texts and images. The Temple of the Inscriptions from Palenque describes the gifts of clothing and jewelry given by the site's rulers to the patron gods on each major period ending (Macri 1988:116–17). These include headdresses, necklaces, ear flares, and "dressings" (Stuart 2006:166–67). Numerous inscriptions also discuss the ritual bathing of deity effigies (Stuart, Houston, and Robertson 1999:ii–50). Finally, effigies were housed in temples analogous to human structures, described with terms such as *wayib* (dormitory) (Houston and Stuart 1989), *otoot* (house) (Stuart 1987:33–38), and *pibnaah* (steam bath) (Stuart 1987:38–39; Houston 1996).

As in later periods, Classic Maya patron gods were also fed. Yaxchilan Lintel 35 describes the patron deities of that site eating two sacrificed noblemen from Calakmul (Houston, Stuart, and Taube 2006:123). Tortuguero Monument 6 possibly describes patron gods consuming chocolate and *pulque*, an alcoholic beverage (Gronemeyer and MacCleod 2010:45). The Temple of the Inscriptions at Palenque refers to a gathering of lords in which patron gods consumed some sort of beverage.

Archaeological evidence at La Corona points to ritual god feeding as well. Every structure excavated in the Coronitas group has turned up midden deposits that point to the large-scale and long-term consumption of food in the area (see figure 5.2). Excavations on Structure 13R-9 and the back patio it shares with 13R-10 (Acuña 2006, 2009; Patterson, Garza, and Miguel 2012; Ponce and Cajas 2012) recovered massive amounts of ceramics, including many polychromes. Also recovered were animal bones and ceramic drums. Behind Structure 13R-10, Carlos Fernández (2011) excavated a *chultun* (a human-made pit dug into bedrock) that was filled with over 6,000 sherds, including utilitarian vessels, fancy serving vessels, and drums (Caroline Parris, personal communication 2012). It also contained over 1,100 animal remains, including deer, turtle, bird, domestic dog, opossum, large rodent, fish, and mollusks. The good preservation of these animal remains, the lack of taphonomic activity such as rodent gnawing (Fridberg and Cagnato 2012), and the ability to refit sherds from different levels of the chultun (Caroline Parris, personal communication 2014) all indicate that they were probably deposited all at once, in a single event. Other food remains included maize; seeds from the tomato family, including possibly chili seeds; amaranth seeds; and seeds of leafy greens (Fridberg and Cagnato 2012). A deposit next to the chultun included over 400 sherds, many of which were large water jars and food-processing basins (Caroline Parris, personal communication 2012). Over 700 animal remains were recovered, including deer, peccary, opossum, birds, turtles, and mollusks, as well as two teeth of a large feline (Fridberg and Cagnato 2012). Another midden deposit was located next to Structure 13R-7 (Perla Barrera 2013). It too contained numerous vessels, many of them fancy, including Fine Gray Ware, and a small number of animal bones. These data indicate that the structures along the northern side of the Coronitas group were a venue for large-scale food consumption.

On the patron deity temples themselves, midden deposits were recovered along the back terraces and ceramics were also left on the front terrace platforms. In her analysis, Caroline Parris (personal communication 2012) found that in the midden deposits, 13 percent of the identifiable vessels were plates, 16 percent were jars, 53 percent were bowls, and 18 percent were high-status drinking vessels (vases and Fine Gray bowls). Of the vessels recovered from the front terraces, the identifiable assemblage consisted of 72 percent jars, 22 percent bowls, and 6 percent plates. This high percentage of jars and bowls suggests that liquids were served at the front of the temples. The fact that both fancy and more utilitarian liquid serving vessels were recovered points to the presence of both elites and nonelites. Individual celebrants probably brought their vessels with them. They were served liquids from the abundant jars on the front terraces. After performing god-feeding rituals, participants then discarded their individual vessels off the back of the temples, where they accumulated as middens. Most of the serving jars remained in place at the front of the temples, perhaps as a way of commemorating the abundance of the feast. The small percentage of plates both on the front and the back of these temples suggests that while meat consumption was an important aspect of ritual feasting in Coronitas—as seen by the faunal remains in nearby middens—actual god-feeding rituals may have involved mostly liquids rather than solid foods, possibly because of the ease with which liquids could be smeared on deity effigies (as opposed to solid foods, which could not be so obviously "consumed"). Another possibility is that low-status celebrants did not use ceramics to hold solid foods but rather tortillas or the leaves of unwrapped tamales.

The evidence from archaeology, inscriptions, Native histories, and modern ethnographies indicates that patron deities—and later, patron saints—were believed to belong to the entire community where they resided. They were believed to protect and sustain their home communities and, in return, their effigies were bathed, clothed, sheltered, and fed. The feeding of patron deities involved ritual feasts in which humans and gods both participated in the consumption of food. The durability of these practices and beliefs across many generations indicates their importance and strength within the Maya understanding of the universe.

PATRON DEITY VENERATION AND MAYA RULERSHIP

The veneration of patron deities was tied to the authority of the Maya ruler. This is made explicit in the Popol Vuh. As discussed above, it describes the worship of Tohil as central to K'iche ethnic identity, even for nonruling groups. Somewhat contradictorily, the Nima K'iche rulers simultaneously claim sole responsibility for performing arduous fasts to supplicate the patron gods on behalf of the people: "They [cried] out in their hearts on behalf of their vassals and servants, as well as on behalf of their women and children. Thus each of the lords carried out his obligations. This was their way of showing veneration for their lordship . . . In unity they would go forth to bear the burden of the Quichés. For this was done for all" (Christenson 2003a:290–91). This passage implies that rulers were benevolent and that they fulfilled the important social function of supplicating the gods so that the nation could thrive.

But the passage does not end there. It goes on to claim that the benefits of rulership were ultimately the reward for this ritual service rather than the fruits of tyranny or conquest: "They did not achieve their lordship, their glory, or their sovereignty by deception or theft. They did not merely crush the canyons and the citadels of the small nations and the great nations. Great was the price that the nations gave in return. They sent jade and precious metal . . . They sent precious gems and glittering stones. They sent as well cotinga feathers, oriole feathers, and the feathers of red birds" (Christenson 2003a:291).

Thus, in this rhetoric, the rights and privileges of rulership were a direct result of the ruler's ritual service. Similar devices appear in Classic Maya monuments. In inscriptions referring to patron deity veneration, rulers took all the credit for properly carrying out rituals for the care and maintenance of patron gods, ignoring the participation of other community members. In addition, rulers claimed close, personal connections to patron deities, probably to argue that they were uniquely suited to carry out certain ritual responsibilities due to their familiarity with the gods. Some inscriptions describe the king-god relationship as like the one between parent and child. We see the phrase *ubaah uhuuntahn* (his precious thing) describing patron gods at Palenque (Houston and Stuart 1996:294). The same phrase may also appear on El Encanto Stela 1 of Tikal (Martin 2000a:53). This phrase is usually used in parentage statements to describe a mother's love for her child. As Stephen D. Houston and David Stuart argue (1996:294), the idea is probably to express the loving care offered by the king for the patron god effigies. At Caracol, Palenque, and La Corona, we also see the phrase *ubaah uch'ab yahk'abil*, usually expressing the relationship between father and son, used to describe the relationship between king and patron god. Finally, on the Temple of the Inscriptions at Palenque, a passage records that the ruler "satisfies the hearts of his gods" (*utimiw yohl uk'uhil*) (Houston, Stuart, and Taube 2006:189) with gifts of clothing, jewels, and a new temple. Although not as explicit as the Popol Vuh, Yaxchilan Hieroglyphic Stairway 3 draws a connection between ritual service to a patron god and royal authority. The text describes the accession of a ruler who receives the royal headband, a key symbol of royal power, during the ceremony. This headband is called *Bolon Tzak K'ahk' Chaak* (Many Conjurings of [Aj] K'ahk [O] Chaak), an important Yaxchilan patron deity. The name of the headband thus suggests that the office of kingship was intimately tied to the ritual responsibility of conjuring the site's main patron deity.

The rhetorical devices employed in the Popol Vuh and on Classic Maya monuments emphasized both the ways that patron gods benefited the whole community and the ways in which rulers were uniquely positioned to supplicate them. This allowed rulers to negotiate the contradictory situation in which they were required to present themselves as exceptional while at the same time members of their home communities, with the best interests of all people at heart.

This strategy for negotiating contradictions would have been especially important during times of political uncertainty, community conflict, or dynastic upheaval. This may explain the interesting phenomenon of patron deity introduction and accumulation. A good example can be seen on the Tikal Marcador text, which tells of events surrounding the *entrada* event of 378 CE. Although there is debate in the scholarly community about what exactly happened at this time (Braswell 2003), we know that the site went through some important dynastic events. A foreign warlord arrived at Tikal and the ruler died on the same day. The new ruler was the son of a foreigner named "Spearthrower Owl." It has been suggested that these events represent a takeover of Tikal by Teotihuacan (Stuart 2000). The Marcador text indicates that on the same day these events took place, a god arrived at Tikal named Waxaklajun Ubaah Kaan ("Eighteen Images of the Snake") (Stuart 2000:493–94; Taube 2000). Although this god would eventually appear in iconography and inscriptions at a variety of Maya sites, this is the earliest known reference to him in the Maya area. The deity's introduction is thus correlated with these dynastic changes, and the god subsequently became important at Tikal and at other sites. This did not mean a replacement of older Tikal patron deities, however. It merely added a new god to the mix.

A similar pattern can be observed in the inscriptions of Copan, although without explicit explanation. At certain points throughout the site's history, new patron deities appeared, while old deities continued to be venerated. Chante' Ch'oktaak and Bolon K'awiil were first mentioned in 542 CE during the reign of the eighth ruler. Chante' Ajaw was first mentioned in 613 CE during the reign of the eleventh ruler. K'uy Nik(?) Ajaw and Mo' Witz Ajaw were first mentioned in 715 CE, during the reign of the thirteenth ruler. Finally, Tukun Witz Ajaw and Chan Bate' were first mentioned during the reign of the sixteenth ruler. These accumulated patron gods all persisted up until the end of the hieroglyphic record and in inscriptions of Ruler 16 were referred to as the "guardians of Copan," as discussed above. This process was probably common at Classic Maya sites, resulting in the long deity lists seen in many inscriptions.

I propose that the sudden introduction of new patron deities at Classic Maya sites was a strategy employed by rulers to compete with the claims to authority of rival candidates to the throne. As discussed above, ancestor veneration was an important religious practice during the Classic Period (and today) that allowed practitioners to claim certain rights based on heredity. In order to suppress these competing claims, rulers with tenuous authority could replace rival ancestor cults with new patron deity cults. Since patron deity veneration was discursively linked to the well-being of the entire community, the introduction of new patron deities at the expense of one particular lineage could be justified. Thus, the ruler could remove a potential rival while at the same time originating and encouraging new discourses of community cohesion linked to his religious authority. A good example of this process can be seen in the history of patron deity veneration at La Corona.

PATRON DEITY INTRODUCTION AND ACCUMULATION AT LA CORONA

As discussed, Structure 13R-5 of the Coronitas group was dedicated as a patron deity shrine in 677 by La Corona ruler K'inich ? Yook. Structures 13R-2, 13R-3, and 13R-4 were dedicated as shrines to three other patron deities by his father, Chakaw Nahb Chan, in 658. Because of the rich hieroglyphic record at La Corona, it is possible to reconstruct several generations of this dynasty's family tree (Ringle 1985:152–53; Martin 2008). The family ruled La Corona nearly continuously from 625 CE until after 745 CE (figure 5.3).

Irregularities in the historical record suggest, however, that this family did not exert royal authority for the entirety of La Corona's history. The panel found in Structure 13R-5 discusses the arrival of a person named Tahn K'inich Lajua' to La Corona in 314 CE. While this panel was carved under the authority of K'inich ? Yook, the text implies that this early settler was not a member of his lineage but instead belonged to a different family. The royal or elevated status of Tahn K'inich Lajua' can be inferred from his name. *K'inich* refers to the Sun god and is typical in Classic Maya royal names.

K'inich ? Yook's family apparently traced its lineage to a ruler nicknamed "Vulture" who ruled during the early sixth century. His reign was associated with the introduction of a patron deity. La Corona Panel 6 (previously known as the Dallas Altar) depicts the arrival of Vulture's wife at La Corona (Martin 2008). She stands on a palanquin that also carries the large effigy of a Teotihuacan-style deity (Taube 2000). Such palanquins are also depicted at Tikal, where they are known to represent captured patron deities of other sites (Martin 1996, 2000b). The historical record does not give any information about the period immediately following Vulture's reign, from approximately 550 to 625 CE. This suggests that his lineage lost power at the site once again, as they did not later commemorate rulers from this time.

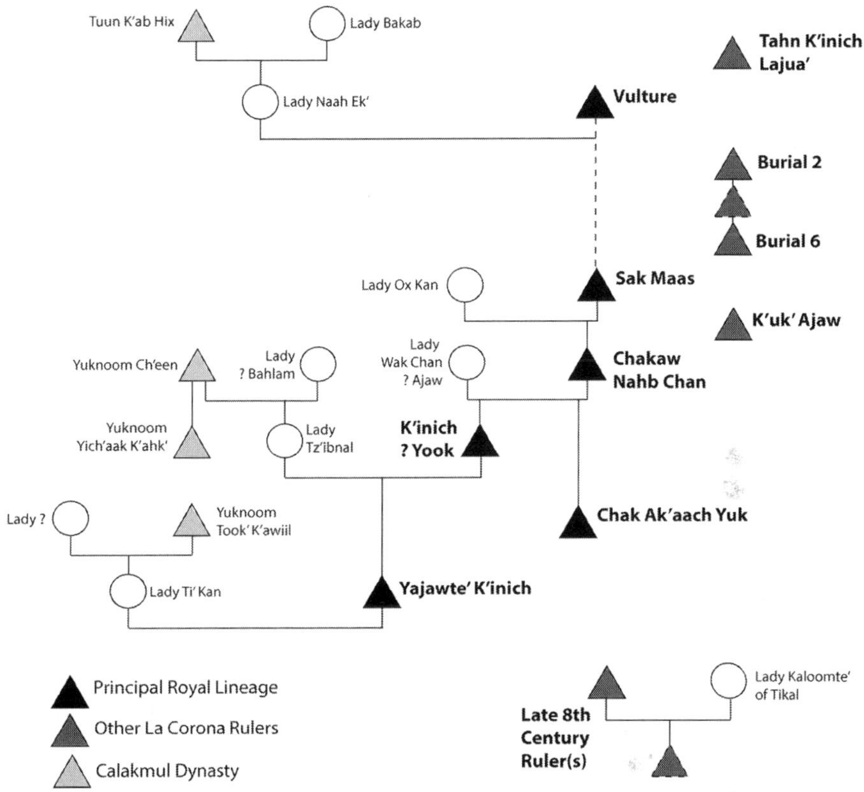

FIGURE 5.3. *The family tree of La Corona's main royal lineage and other La Corona rulers.*

Vulture's lineage regained authority at La Corona when Sak Maas came to power in 625 CE. Sak Maas appears to have introduced the patron god Ikiiy, since the two are closely associated in the text of Hieroglyphic Stairway A (David Stuart, personal communication 2012). Sak Maas died a violent death in 656 CE (Grube in Grube, Martin, and Zender 2002:85) after the apparent coup of a man named K'uk' Ajaw.

K'uk' Ajaw himself died violently two years later, in 658 CE, the same day that Chakaw Nahb Chan, the son of Sak Maas, came to power. His short-lived rule presents another irregularity in the royal succession of La Corona. After defeating his father's usurper, Chakaw Nahb Chan built temples for three new patron deities named Yaxal Ajaw, K'an Chaak, and Chak Wayib Chaak (Guenter 2005). This temple dedication took place only thirty-five days after Chakaw Nahb Chan's violent accession. These temples correspond to Structures 13R-2, 13R-3, and 13R-4, as discussed earlier in this chapter. Chakaw Nahb Chan's son K'inich ? Yook dedicated his own patron deity temple in 677 CE, corresponding to Structure 13R-5. His brother and son ruled after him until approximately 745 CE, when the hieroglyphic record falls silent again for four decades. When it resumes, the new ruler appears to belong to a different lineage.[1]

There are thus three instances in the history of La Corona in which the main royal family came to power after a different lineage had been in control: the early sixth century, 625 CE, and 658 CE. And on each occasion, a new patron deity (or deities) was promoted. This pattern alone suggests that the introduction of new patron deities was a strategy employed by rulers of La Corona in times of political upheaval. But archaeological excavations reveal that at least one of these introduction events took place at the direct expense of competing ancestor cults.

Excavations in 13R-2 and 13R-4 exposed the back terrace walls of early platforms. I refer to this construction phase as the "Mam Phase." While it was not extensively explored, a midden that had accumulated behind the Mam Phase platform of 13R-2 contained ceramic material dating to the mid-sixth century (Caroline Parris, personal communication 2012). Following these early platforms, a series of new construction episodes took place on all three structures. First, an 8-meter pyramidal platform was constructed on 13R-4. A similarly sized platform was next constructed on 13R-3, followed by a third on Structure 13R-2 (figure 5.4). While these platforms were built sequentially, not all at once, they appear to date to the mid- to late sixth century, with the 13R-4 platform built around 550 CE and the 13R-2 platform constructed sometime around 600 CE or slightly later. I refer to this major period of construction activity as the "Muk Phase." The purpose of these platforms became apparent upon deeper excavation: tombs were discovered under the Muk Phase of Structures 13R-2 and 13R-4. (A similar tomb is probably buried under 13R-3, but excavation was not conducted due to safety concerns). Crucially, these tombs correspond to the period of La Corona history between Vulture and Sak Maas, when the epigraphic record is silent and a different lineage probably ruled the community.

The tomb under Structure 13R-2 (Burial 6) was unlooted but had suffered from collapse, water damage, and animal activities. Nevertheless, important information was recoverable (Baron 2012). The tomb had been cut in bedrock below the central axis of the Muk Phase platform above. The occupant of the tomb was an adult, probably a male (Patterson 2012:374). He was laid with his head to the east and his bones were treated with red pigment. He was

Figure 5.4. *South profile of Structure 13R-2 showing principal phases of construction.*

buried with the bodies of a turtle and a crocodile as well as hundreds of locally available fresh water mollusks (Baron, Fridberg, and Canuto 2011). Fifteen ceramic vessels were also recovered, although some of them may originally have been placed above the tomb itself. The burial was sealed with a wooden roof that has since rotted away. On top of this wood was placed a woven mat, the impression of which survives in the fill above. After placing this mat and offerings, mourners covered the tomb with a large deposit of lithic flakes. While approximately 7,000 lithics were recovered, it is estimated that the total amount of lithics was between 20,000 and 30,000.

The features of this tomb suggest strongly that the occupant was a ruler of La Corona. His bones were treated reverentially with red pigment. Woven mats were symbols of royal authority among the Maya and similar lithic deposits have been found with royal tombs at other sites in the region (Demarest et al. 2003; Moholy-Nagy 1997). The construction of an 8-meter funerary shrine over the tomb also attests to the high status of the individual. Notably, he was not buried with many exotic wealth items. Only small amounts of marine shell were recovered and jade was not recovered at all. This suggests that this ruler did not have strong foreign connections, even though rulers of La Corona's main royal family had a close relationship with Calakmul, a powerful royal court located in Campeche (Martin 2008; Canuto and Barrientos Q. 2011). This, along with the silence of the epigraphic record about this period, suggests that this ruler was from a different lineage.

The tomb under Structure 13R-4 (Burial 2) was unfortunately looted. However, it had similar features to those seen in Burial 6 (Baron 2011). The tomb was also cut into bedrock and recovered bones had also been treated with red pigment. The funerary platform constructed over the tomb was also 8 meters high. Given the proximity of Burials 2 and 6, it is likely that these two occupants were members of the same lineage. They were both probably rulers of La Corona who reigned during the late sixth century but did not belong to the site's most successful royal lineage. Their funerary shrines (Structures 13R-2 and 13R-4 along with 13R-3) were constructed sequentially, as each ruler died. Their descendants and family members would have used these shrines to carry out ancestor veneration rituals, in order to established continued claims to hereditary rights.

But in 625 CE, Sak Maas, from Vulture's lineage, acceded to power at La Corona, introducing the patron god Ikiiy to bolster his claims. The accession of Sak Maas's son did not occur smoothly, however, as K'uk' Ajaw carried out his short-lived coup. When Chakaw Nahb Chan eventually did accede to power, he did so after the violent death of K'uk' Ajaw. And thirty-five days later, Chakaw Nahb Chan dedicated three new shrines for his patron deities.

The final phase of Structures 13R-2, 13R-3, and 13R-4 corresponds to this event. While the previous Muk Phase consisted of a sequence of platforms, the final phase, nicknamed the "K'uh Phase," was a single architectural program that united the three platforms (figure 5.4). The K'uh Phase consisted of new front stairways and façades on the three buildings, with the new architecture only measuring about a meter thick. The K'uh Phase did not extend onto the back terraces of the platforms, leaving the Muk Phase terraces exposed. The superstructures of the three shrines were made from perishable materials, as evidenced by the presence of daub and the lack of recovered vault stones. This rather shoddy architecture is consistent with a construction phase completed in just thirty-five days. Thus, the archaeological record appears to show that Chakaw Nahb Chan, almost immediately upon his accession to power, replaced funerary shrines of a rival lineage with the temples of three patron deities.

I propose that the dedication of patron deity shrines at La Corona was a strategy employed by rulers of the site's main royal lineage to gain political authority. It is clear from the epigraphic record that this family contended with other elite lineages for control of the community. As at other Maya sites, ancestor veneration would have played a role in this struggle. By venerating important deceased ancestors, elite lineages made claims to hereditary rights to royal authority. The erasure of competing ancestor cults negated the claims of rival lineages, framing them as non-authoritative pretenders to power. By replacing these competing ancestor cults with patron deity cults, rulers ideally situated themselves in the contradictory position of leadership. This position required the ruler to be, in some ways, unique and apart from the rest of the community, thereby justifying his claims to tribute and status, yet simultaneously part of and concerned with the well-being of the community, thereby inducing followers to obey. The belief that patron deities belonged to and served the entire populace, regardless of lineage, reinforced ethnic similarities between ruler and followers. Yet the ruler's claims to a close, affective relationship with these gods emphasized his unique ritual responsibilities and the debt owed to him by the community.

But as Kurnick notes in her introduction, it is not enough to identify the rhetorical claims of Maya rulers. In order to understand the creation and maintenance of political authority, it is necessary to investigate whether these claims and strategies were successful. In the case of La Corona, it appears that they were. The many midden assemblages of the Coronitas group indicate that feasting events and god-feeding rituals were an important and long-lasting tradition. The participation of nonelites in these rituals points to the overall success of the royal strategy of introducing new patron deities. By participating in these events, commoners and other elites gave their implicit consent to the authority of the community's rulers.

It is interesting to note that many of the midden assemblages in the Coronitas group are dated to the late eighth century or later, at a time in which the main La Corona royal family appears to have lost power once again. Thus, the patron deities that were originally introduced to bolster the claims of one lineage over another came to be naturalized and accepted as a part of local identity, regardless of which dynasty ruled. This is a similar pattern to that seen at Ceibal, described above, where GI-K'awiil remained as patron god in spite of dynastic changes. The rhetorical stance taken by Chakaw Nahb Chan, that patron gods served everyone and that their caregivers were thus worthy of authority, was successful for him but ultimately unsuccessful for his descendants. An alternative royal lineage was equally capable of caring for the patron gods of the community and was therefore worthy of support when it eventually gained power in the late eighth century. The slow accumulation of new deities at Maya sites may reflect this pattern. New rulers introduced new patron gods, like Lewis Carroll's Red Queen, running just to stay in place.

CONCLUSION

In this chapter, I have given a review of the importance of patron deity veneration among the Classic Maya and its role in the creation and maintenance of political authority. I have demonstrated that patron deities were just one of a series of different supernatural categories recognized by the Maya. They differed from more general deities in their special relationships with particular communities and they differed from ancestors in their active intervention in human affairs. While the Classic Maya practiced ancestor veneration as a means of claiming hereditary rights, patron deities were believed to look after the well-being of the entire community. In order to supersede the claims of competing elite lineages, Maya rulers took steps to neutralize the power of rival ancestor cults and simultaneously promoted themselves as having a special relationship with the patron deities of the community. In many cases, Maya rulers even introduced new deities as a way of further reinforcing their authority over their followers.

This process can readily be seen in the archaeological and epigraphic record at La Corona. Throughout the site's history, periods of civil conflict and dynastic change resulted in the introduction of new patron gods by the main royal lineage of the community. And in some cases, these deities were given temples built directly atop the now defunct ancestor shrines of a competing lineage. This strategy appears to have been successful, as there is evidence showing the participation of nonelites in patron deity veneration rituals. In the later history of the site this ruling lineage became a victim of its own success by failing to adequately differentiate itself from other potential rulers. Thus, any ruler who cared for patron gods was worthy of support, no matter which lineage he belonged to.

These strategies and their results reveal some of the complexities of Classic Maya rulership. It was not sufficient for rulers to be unique, nor to be similar to other members of the community. To maintain authority, rulers had to be both unique and similar. And strategies that began as a means of negotiating this contradiction may have ultimately led to different results over generations of reinterpretation. As at La Corona, many Maya communities display a gradual accumulation of patron deities as new gods were introduced through time. But as the veneration of these gods became a routinized aspect of community religious life, it was no longer sufficient for the maintenance of political authority by particular rulers. Instead, these leaders were forced to introduce more new gods, or to adopt new strategies altogether, as the need arose. By examining patron deity veneration, therefore, we gain a glimpse into the highly complex and contradictory nature of political authority during the Classic Period. Maya rulers were forced to support their claims to authority through a never-ending process of negotiation and reassessment.

ACKNOWLEDGMENTS

I would like to thank Marcello Canuto and Tomás Barrientos, directors of the La Corona Regional Archaeology Project, for their support over the years that I worked at La Corona. I would also like to thank Diana Fridberg, Clarissa Cagnato, Caroline Parris, and Erin Patterson for sharing the results of their artifact analyses with me and all the other members of the project for years of fruitful collaboration. The research described in this chapter was made possible by a Wenner-Gren Foundation Dissertation Fieldwork Grant (8260), the University of Pennsylvania Department of Anthropology, the Penn Museum, and the Louis J. Kolb Society.

NOTE

1. This assessment is based on the fact that the main La Corona royal family was strongly allied to Calakmul and married princesses from its royal line on three separate occasions (Martin 2008). The later ruler of the site, however, married a woman from Tikal, Calakmul's traditional enemy (Barrientos et al. 2011).

REFERENCES

Acuña, Mary Jane. 2006. "CR-ES: Excavaciones de Sondeo en los Grupos A, B y C de La Corona." In *Proyecto Arqueológico El Perú-Waka': Sub-Proyecto La Corona,*

Informe no. 2, temporada 2006, edited by Marcello A. Canuto, Mary Jane Acuña, Ellen E. Bell, Stanley H. Guenter, and Damien B. Marken, 34–55. Guatemala City: Instituto de Antropología e Historia.

Acuña, Mary Jane. 2009. "Operación CR 11A: Limpieza de Trinchera de Saqueo en la Estructura 13R-9." In *Proyecto Regional Arqueológico La Corona: Informe final, temporada 2008*, edited by Marcello A. Canuto and Tomás Barrientos Q., 109–28. Guatemala City: Instituto de Antropología e Historia.

Baron, Joanne. 2011. "Operaciones CR12, CR14 y CR15: Excavaciones en las Estructuras 13R-3, 13R-4, y 13R-2 de Grupo Coronitas." In *Proyecto Regional Arqueológico La Corona: Informe final, temporada 2010*, edited by Tomás Barrientos, Marcello A. Canuto, and Mary Jane Acuña, 249–76. Guatemala City: Instituto de Antropología e Historia.

Baron, Joanne. 2012. "Operaciones CR14, CR15 y CR17: Excavaciones en las Estructuras 13R-2, 13R-3, 13R-4, y 13R-5." In *Proyecto Regional Arqueológico La Corona: Informe final, temporada 2011*, edited by Tomás Barrientos, Marcello A. Canuto, and Jocelyne Ponce, 231–64. Guatemala City: Instituto de Antropología e Historia.

Baron, Joanne P. 2013. "Patrons of La Corona: Deities and Power in a Classic Maya Community." PhD diss., University of Pennsylvania.

Baron, Joanne P., Diana Fridberg, and Marcello Canuto. 2011. "'Entró el agua': Utilización de especies acuáticas en contextos mortuorios de La Corona, Guatemala." Paper presented at the 23rd Encuentro Internacionál de Investigadores de Cultura Maya, Campeche, Mexico, November 18.

Barrientos, Tomás, Marcello Canuto, Joanne Baron, Yann Desailly-Chanson, and Bruce Love. 2011. "El Reino de Sak Nikte': Nuevos datos sobre la historia, cronología, asentamiento y medio ambiente en La Corona." In *XXIV Simposio de investigaciones arqueológicas en Guatemala*, edited by Bárbara Arroyo, Lorena Paiz Aragón, Adriana Linares Palma, and Ana Lucia Arroyave. Guatemala City: Ministerio de Cultura y Deportes / Instituto de Antropología e Historia / Asociación Tikal.

Baudez, Claude-François. 2002. *Une histoire de la religion des Mayas: Du panthéisme au panthéon*. Paris: Albin Michel.

Braswell, Geoffrey E., ed. 2003. *The Maya and Teotihuacan: Reinterpreting Early Classic Interaction*. Austin: University of Texas Press.

Bunzel, Ruth Leah. 1959. *Chichicastenango: A Guatemalan Village*. Seattle: University of Washington Press.

Cancian, Frank. 1965. *Economics and Prestige in a Maya Community: The Religious Cargo System in Zinacantan*. Stanford: Stanford University Press.

Canuto, Marcello A., and Tomás Barrientos Q. 2011. "La Corona: Un acercamiento a las políticas del reino Kaan desde un centro secundario del noroeste del Petén." *Estudios de Cultura Maya* 37: 11–43.

Canuto, Marcello A., Stanley Guenter, Evangelia Tsesmeli, and Damien Marken. 2006. "El reconocimiento de La Corona, 2005." In *Proyecto Arqueológico El Perú-Waka': Informe no. 3, temporada 2005*, edited by Héctor Escobedo and David A. Freidel, 455–68. Guatemala City: Instituto de Antropología e Historia.

Carmack, Robert M., and James L. Mondloch. 1983. *El Título de Totonicapán: Texto, traducción y comentario*. Mexico City: Universidad Nacional Autónoma de México.

Christenson, Allen J. 2001. *Art and Society in a Highland Maya Community: The Altarpiece of Santiago Atitlán*. Austin: University of Texas Press.

Christenson, Allen J. 2003a. *Popol Vuh: The Sacred Book of the Maya*. New York: O Books.

Christenson, Allen J. 2003b. "K'iche'-English Dictionary and Guide to Pronunciation of the K'iche'-Maya Alphabet." Accessed April 9, 2014. http://www.famsi.org/mayawriting/dictionary/christenson/quidic_complete.pdf.

Demarest, Arthur A. 1992. "Ideology in Ancient Maya Cultural Evolution: The Dynamics of Galactic Polities." In *Ideology and Pre-Columbian Civilizations*, edited by Arthur A. Demarest and Geoffrey Conrad, 135–57. Santa Fe: School of American Research Press.

Demarest, Arthur, Kim Morgan, Claudia Wolley, and Héctor Escobedo. 2003. "The Political Acquisition of Sacred Geography: The Muciélagos Complex at Dos Pilas." In *Maya Palaces and Elite Residences: An Interdisciplinary Approach*, edited by Jessica Joyce Christie, 120–53. Austin: University of Texas Press.

Fernández, Carlos Enrique. 2011. "Operación CR16: Excavaciones en la Estructura 13R-10." In *Proyecto Regional Arqueológico La Corona: Informe final, temporada 2010*, edited by Tomás Barrientos, Marcello A. Canuto, and Mary Jane Acuña, 277–304. Guatemala City: Instituto de Antropología e Historia.

Fields, Virginia M., and Dorie Reents-Budet. 2005. *Lords of Creation: The Origins of Sacred Maya Kingship*. Easthampton, MA: Scala.

Freidel, David A., and Linda Schele. 1988. "Kingship in the Late Preclassic Maya Lowlands: The Instruments and Places of Ritual Power." *American Anthropologist* 90(3): 547–67.

Freidel, David A., Linda Schele, and Joy Parker. 1993. *Maya Cosmos: Three Thousand Years on the Shaman's Path*. New York: William Morrow.

Fridberg, Diana N., and Clarissa Cagnato. 2012. "Estudios de plantas e animales en La Corona." Paper presented at the 26th Simposio de Investigaciones Arqueológicas en Guatemala, Guatemala City, July 16–20.

Gonlin, Nancy. 2007. "Ritual and Ideology among Classic Maya Rural Commoners at Copan, Honduras." In *Commoner Ritual and Ideology in Ancient Mesoamerica*, edited by Nancy Gonlin and Jon C. Lohse, 83–121. Boulder: University Press of Colorado.

Gronemeyer, Sven, and Barbara MacCleod. 2010. "What Could Happen in 2012: A Re-Analysis of the 13-Bak'tun Prophecy on Tortuguero Monument 6." *Wayeb Notes* 34: 1–68.

Grube, Nikolai, Simon Martin, and Marc Zender. 2002. *The Proceedings of the Maya Hieroglyphic Workshop: Palenque and Its Neighbors*, edited by Phil Wanyerka. Austin: University of Texas.

Guenter, Stanley. 2005. "La Corona Find Sheds Light on Site Q Mystery." *PARI Journal* 6(2): 16–18.

Hellmuth, Nicholas M. 1987. *Monster und Menschen in der Maya-Kunst: Eine Ikonographie der alten Religionen Mexikos und Guatemalas*. Graz: Akademische Druck- und Verlagsanstalt.

Houston, Stephen D. 1996. "Symbolic Sweatbaths of the Maya: Architectural Meaning in the Cross Group at Palenque, Mexico." *Latin American Antiquity* 7(2): 132–51.

Houston, Stephen D., and Takeshi Inomata. 2009. *The Classic Maya*. Cambridge: Cambridge University Press.

Houston, Stephen D., John Robertson, and David Stuart. 2001. *Quality and Quantity in Glyphic Nouns and Adjectives*. Research Reports on Ancient Maya Writing 47. Washington, DC: Center for Maya Research.

Houston, Stephen, and David Stuart. 1989. "The Way Glyph: Evidence for 'Co-essences' among the Classic Maya." Research Reports on Ancient Maya Writing 30. Washington, DC: Center for Maya Research.

Houston, Stephen, and David Stuart. 1996. "Of Gods, Glyphs, and Kings: Divinity and Rulership among the Classic Maya." *Antiquity* 70(268): 289–312.

Houston, Stephen, David Stuart, and Karl Taube. 2006. *The Memory of Bones: Body, Being, and Experience among the Classic Maya*. Austin: University of Texas Press.

Houston, Stephen D., S. Symonds, David Stuart, and Arthur Demarest. 1992. "A Civil War of the Late Classic Period: Evidence from Hieroglyphic Stairway 4." Unpublished manuscript.

Inomata, Takeshi. 2006. "Plazas, Performers, and Spectators: Political Theaters of the Classic Maya." *Current Anthropology* 47(5): 805–42.

Joyce, Arthur A., and Errin T. Weller. 2007. "Commoner Rituals, Resistance, and the Classic-to-Postclassic Transition in Ancient Mesoamerica." In *Commoner Ritual and Ideology in Ancient Mesoamerica*, edited by Nancy Gonlin and Jon C. Lohse, 143–84. Boulder: University Press of Colorado.

Lacadena, Alfonso, and Søren Wichmann. 2004. "On the Representation of the Glottal Stop in Maya Writing." In *The Linguistics of Maya Writing*, edited by Søren Wichmann, 103–62. Salt Lake City: University of Utah Press.

Lounsbury, Floyd G. 1980. "Some Problems in the Interpretation of the Mythological Portion of the Hieroglyphic Text of the Temple of the Cross at Palenque." In *Third Palenque Round Table, 1978*, edited by Merle Green Robertson, 99–115. Austin: University of Texas Press.

Lucero, Lisa J. 2003. "The Politics of Ritual: The Emergence of Classic Maya Rulers." *Current Anthropology* 44(4): 523–58.

Macri, Martha J. 1988. "A Descriptive Grammar of Palenque Mayan." PhD diss., University of California, Berkeley.

Marcus, Joyce. 1978. "Archaeology and Religion: A Comparison of the Zapotec and Maya." *World Archaeology* 10(2): 172–91.

Marcus, Joyce. 1983. "Zapotec Religion." In *The Cloud People: Divergent Evolution of the Zapotec and Mixtec Civilizations*, edited by Kent V. Flannery and Joyce Marcus, 345–51. New York: Academic Press.

Marcus, Joyce. 1992. *Mesoamerican Writing Systems: Propaganda, Myth, and History in Four Ancient Civilizations*. Princeton: Princeton University Press.

Martin, Simon. 1996. "Tikal's 'Star War' Against Naranjo." In *Eighth Palenque Roundtable, 1993*, edited by Martha J. Macri and Jan McHargue, 223–36. San Francisco: Pre-Columbian Art Research Institute.

Martin, Simon. 2000a. "At the Periphery: The Movement, Modification, and Re-Use of Early Monuments in the Environs of Tikal." In *The Sacred and the Profane: Architecture and Identity in the Maya Lowlands. 3rd European Maya Conference, University of Hamburg, November 1998*, edited by Pierre Robert Colas, Kai Delvendahl, Marcus Kuhnert, and Annette Schubart, 51–61. Markt Schwaben: Anton Saurwein.

Martin, Simon. 2000b. "Nuevos datos epigraficos sobre la guerra maya del Clásico." In *La guerra entre los antiguos mayas: Memoria de la Primera Mesa Redonda de Palenque*, edited by Silvia Trejo, 107–24. Mexico City: Instituto Nacional de Antropología e Historia / Consejo Nacional Para la Cultura y las Artes.

Martin, Simon. 2008. "Wives and Daughters on the Dallas Altar." Mesoweb. Accessed June 28, 2013. http://www.mesoweb.com/articles/martin/Wives&Daughters.pdf.

Martin, Simon, and Nikolai Grube. 2000. *Chronicle of the Maya Kings and Queens: Deciphering the Dynasties of the Ancient Maya*. New York: Thames & Hudson.

Mathews, Peter. 1979. "Notes on the Inscriptions of 'Site Q.'" Unpublished manuscript.

McAnany, Patricia A. 1995. *Living with the Ancestors: Kinship and Kingship in Ancient Maya Society*. Austin: University of Texas Press.

Moholy-Nagy, Huttula. 1997. "Middens, Construction Fill, and Offerings: Evidence for the Organization of Classic Period Craft Production at Tikal, Guatemala." *Journal of Field Archaeology* 24(3): 293–313.

Oakes, Maud. 1951. *The Two Crosses of Todos Santos: Survivals of Mayan Religious Ritual*. New York: Pantheon.

Otzoy, Simón, trans. 1999. *Memorial de Sololá: Edición facsimilar del manuscrito original*. Guatemala City: Comisión Interuniversitaria Guatemalteca de Conmemoración del Quinto Centenario del Descubrimiento de América.

Patterson, Erin. 2012. "Analásis de restos esqueléticos: Temporada 2011." In *Proyecto Regional Arqueológico La Corona: Informe final, temporada 2011*, edited by Tomás Barrientos, Marcello A. Canuto, and Jocelyne Ponce, 373–89. Guatemala City: Instituto de Antropología e Historia.

Patterson, Erin, Elisandro Garza, and Leticia Miguel. 2012. "Operaciones CR18 y CR19: Excavaciones en el Patio Norte Del Grupo 13R-II." In *Proyecto Regional Arqueológico La Corona: Informe final, temporada 2011*, edited by Marcello A. Canuto and Jocelyne Ponce, 319–34. Guatemala City: Instituto de Antropología e Historia.

Perla Barrera, Divina. 2013. "Operación CR117: Excavaciones en la Estructura 13R–7." In *Proyecto Regional Arqueológico La Corona: Informe final, temporada 2012*, edited by Tomás Barrientos Q., Marcello A. Canuto, and Jocelyne Ponce, 221–50. Guatemala City: Instituto de Antropología e Historia.

Ponce, Jocelyne, and María Antonieta Cajas. 2012. "El Grupo 13R-II de La Corona: El contexto arqueológico de La Escalinata Glífica 2." Paper presented at the 26th Simposio de Investigaciones Arqueológicas en Guatemala, Guatemala City, July 20.

Proskouriakoff, Tatiana. 1978. "Olmec God and Maya God-Glyphs." In *Codex Wauchope: A Tribute Roll*, edited by Marco Giardino, Barbara Edmonson, and Winifred Creamer, 113–17. New Orleans: Tulane University.

Redfield, Robert, and Alfonso Villa Rojas. 1962. *Chan Kom: A Maya Village*. Chicago: University of Chicago Press.

Reina, Ruben. 1966. *The Law of the Saints*. New York: Bobbs-Merrill.

Ringle, William. 1985. "Notes on Two Tablets of Unknown Provenance." In *Fifth Palenque Round Table, 1983*, edited by Virginia M. Fields and Merle Green Robertson, 151–58. San Francisco: Pre-Columbian Art Research Institute.

Ringle, William. 1988. *Of Mice and Monkeys: The Value and Meaning of T1016, the God C Hieroglyph*. Research Reports on Ancient Maya Writing 18. Washington, DC: Center for Maya Research.

Sachse, Frauke. 2004. "Interpreting Maya Religion: Methodological Remarks on Understanding Continuity and Change in Maya Religious Practices." In *Continuity and Change: Maya Religious Practices in Temporal Perspective. Fifth European Maya Conference, University of Bonn, December 2000*, edited by Daniel Grana-Behrens, Christian M. Prager, Frauke Sachse, Stefanie Teufel, and Elizabeth Wagner, 1–21. Markt Schwaben: Anton Saurwein.

Schele, Linda, and David Freidel. 1990. *A Forest of Kings: The Untold Story of the Ancient Maya*. New York: Morrow.

Schele, Linda, and Peter Mathews. 1998. *The Code of Kings: The Language of Seven Sacred Maya Temples and Tombs*. New York: Simon & Schuster.

Schele, Linda, and Mary Ellen Miller. 1986. *The Blood of Kings: Dynasty and Ritual in Maya Art*. New York: George Braziller.

Schellhas, Paul. 1904. *Representations of Deities of the Maya Manuscripts*. Papers of the Peabody Museum of Archaeology and Ethnology 4. Cambridge, MA: Harvard University.

Siebers, Hans. 1999. *"We Are Children of the Mountain": Creolization and Modernization among the Q'eqchi'es*. Amsterdam: Center for Latin American Research and Documentation.

Siegel, Morris. 1941. "Religion in Western Guatemala: A Product of Acculturation." *American Anthropologist* 43(1): 62–76.

Stuart, David. 1987. *Ten Phonetic Syllables*. Research Reports on Ancient Maya Writing 14. Washington, DC: Center for Maya Research.

Stuart, David. 2000. "'The Arrival of Strangers': Teotihuacan and Tollan in Classic Maya History." In *Mesoamerica's Classic Heritage: From Teotihuacan to the Aztecs*, edited by Davíd Carrasco, Lindsay Jones, and Scott Sessions, 465–513. Boulder: University Press of Colorado.

Stuart, David. 2001. "Las ruinas de La Corona, Petén, y la identificación del 'Sitio Q.'" Paper presented at the 15th Simposio de Investigaciones Arqueológicas en Guatemala, Guatemala City.

Stuart, David. 2005. "Ideology and Classic Maya Kingship." In *A Catalyst for Ideas: Anthropological Archaeology and the Legacy of Douglas Schwartz*, edited by Vernon L. Scarborough, 257–85. Santa Fe: School of American Research Press.

Stuart, David. 2005. *The Inscriptions from Temple XIX at Palenque*. San Francisco: Pre-Columbian Art Research Institute.

Stuart, David, Stephen D. Houston, and John Robertson. 1999. "Recovering the Past Classic Maya Language and Classic Maya Gods." In *Notebook for the XXIIIrd Maya Hieroglyphic Forum at Texas*. Austin: Department of Art and Art History, College of Fine Arts, and Institute of Latin American Studies, University of Texas at Austin.

Taube, Karl Andreas. 1992. *The Major Gods of Ancient Yucatan*. Washington, DC: Dumbarton Oaks.

Taube, Karl. 2000. "The Turquoise Hearth: Fire, Self Sacrifice, and the Central Mexican Cult of War." In *Mesoamerica's Classic Heritage: From Teotihuacan to the Aztecs*, edited by Davíd Carrasco, Lindsay Jones, and Scott Sessions, 269–340. Boulder: University Press of Colorado.

Thompson, J. Eric S. 1950. *Maya Hieroglyphic Writing: An Introduction*. Washington, DC: Carnegie Institution of Washington.

Townsend, Richard Fraser. 1979. *State and Cosmos in the Art of Tenochtitlan*. Washington, DC: Dumbarton Oaks.

Valladares, León. 1957. *El hombre y el maíz: Etnografía y etnopsicología de Colotenango*. Second edition. Mexico City: B. Costa-Amic.

Villagutierre Soto-Mayor, Juan de. 1983. *History of the Conquest of the Province of the Itza: Subjugation and Events of the Lacondon and Other Nations of Uncivilized Indians in the Lands from the Kingdom of Guatemala to the Provinces of Yucatan in North America*. Edited by Frank E. Comparato. Translated by Robert D. Wood. Culver City, CA: Labyrinthos.

Vogt, Evon Z. 1993. *Tortillas for the Gods: A Symbolic Analysis of Zinacanteco Rituals*. Norman: University of Oklahoma Press.

Warren, Kay B. 1978. *The Symbolism of Subordination: Indian Identity in a Guatemalan Town*. Austin: University of Texas Press.

Watanabe, John M. 1990. "Saints to Shibboleths: Image, Structure, and Identity in Maya Religious Syncretism." *American Ethnologist* 17(1): 131–50.

Watanabe, John M. 1992. *Maya Saints and Souls in a Changing World*. Austin: University of Texas Press.

Wisdom, Charles. 1940. *The Chorti Indians of Guatemala*. Chicago: University of Chicago Press.

Wright, Mark A. 2011. "A Study of Classic Maya Rulership." PhD diss., University of California, Riverside.

6

Entangled Political Strategies

Rulership, Bureaucracy, and Intermediate Elites at Teotihuacan

Tatsuya Murakami

It is now widely acknowledged that no polity is a homeostatic system with equilibrium (Brumfiel 1992) but instead consists of individuals and collectivities with varying interests and practical capacities. There are multiple sources of power (Mann 1986) forming distinct but overlapping social fields (Bourdieu 1990) in which different sets of rules and resources embody multifaceted social relations (e.g., McGuire 1983; Paynter and McGuire 1991; Sewell 1992). Contradiction, defined as opposition of structural principles (Giddens 1979:141–45), therefore, exists in any societal formation and is actively negotiated by varying social segments. In a critical assessment of the dual-processual model (Blanton et al. 1996), David B. Small (2009) demonstrates the varying social contexts in which exclusionary and corporate strategies were employed in an ancient Greek polity (see also Beekman, this volume). Small breaks down the dual-processual model into several analytical domains, including ideology, institutions (contexts), and behavior. As critiqued by several scholars (e.g., Campbell 2009; Smith 2011; Yoffee 2005: 177–79; see also Inomata, this volume; Joyce et al., this volume), political dynamics cannot be subsumed in a single dimension of leadership strategies. Rather, there can be ideological multiplicity, various discourses, varying practices or behaviors, and social and physical contexts associated with certain ideologies where specific sets of practices are socially expected, promoted, or constrained. Thus, we need to pay attention to the fact

DOI: 10.5876/9781607324164.c006

that multiple and contradictory principles become contextually defined and situationally operative (Flanagan 1989:261). Ultimately, "it is the practice of social life" that sets up and perpetuates equalities and inequalities (Josephides 1985:140; see also Inomata, this volume).

As reiterated by Sarah Kurnick in the introduction of this volume, similarities and differences (or equalities and inequalities) between the rulers and the ruled need to be simultaneously achieved for the successful operation of polities (Ferguson and Mansbach 1996; for the logical coexistence of both hierarchy and equality, see Dumont [1977]). These differences and similarities can be conceptualized broadly as some dimensions of political authority and a shared identity (or imagined community), respectively (Campbell 2009). A network of ideology/discourse, practice, and human and material resources constitute political authority and a shared identity. This indicates that both political authority and a shared identity have material dimensions or are mediated by material culture, including portable objects and built environment (Smith 2011), which can be gleaned in the urban architecture of Teotihuacan, the capital of a regional state in Central Mexico (ca. 150–650 CE).

The city of Teotihuacan consists of grand-scale monumental structures and other buildings along the Street of the Dead (hereafter the central precinct) and the surrounding residential area (figure 6.1). Similarities can be observed in the canonical orientation of buildings and standardized construction materials as well as several components of architectural complexes such as rooms, temples, and courtyards (Murakami 2013, 2014). Differences are noted in varying scales and the degree of embellishment of these buildings. This general observation on the architectural similarities and differences provides a useful starting point from which we can delve into historically contingent processes of the creation of an imagined community and social distinctions (Murakami 2014). This chapter examines how these architectural similarities and differences were shaped by strategic actions of and the negotiation among different social segments, resulting in the creation of social integration and distinctions. Specifically, I focus on the changing nature of the relationship between rulers, bureaucracy, and intermediate elites and demonstrate that the similarities and differences observed in urban architecture were produced and reproduced through complexly entangled political strategies employed by different social actors.

RULERSHIP AT TEOTIHUACAN

The consolidation of a central authority can clearly be seen in the explosive growth of monumental structures toward the end of the Tzacualli phase (ca.

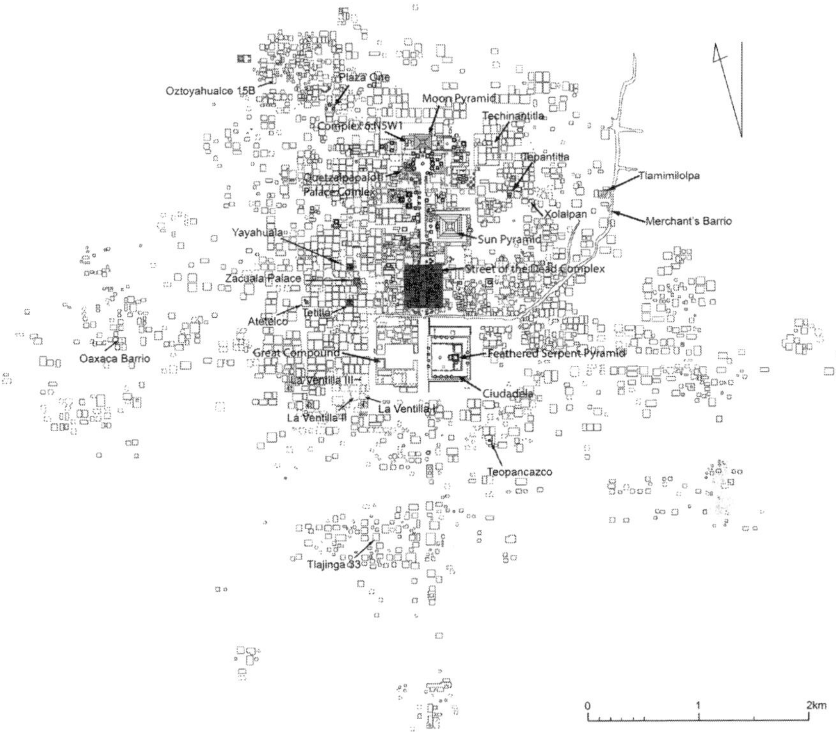

FIGURE 6.1. *Location of architectural complexes mentioned in the text (redrawn and modified after René Millon 1973).*

1–150 CE) or at the beginning of the Miccaotli phase (ca. 150–250 CE) (figure 6.2) (Cowgill 1997, 2000; R. Millon 1981; Murakami 2010, 2015; Sugiyama 2004; Sugiyama et al. 2013). The canonical orientation was likely established by this time (Sugiyama 2004). The alignment of the Moon Pyramid and Cerro Gordo (a mountain standing on the northern limit of the Teotihuacan Valley) (Tobriner 1972), the presence of an artificial cave under the Sun Pyramid (Heyden 1975, 1981), and the east-west axis of the Sun Pyramid, which is aligned to the sunset point on the initial day of the Maya Long Count calendar (R. Millon 1993; see also Cowgill 2000; Dow 1967; Šprajc 2000), all suggest that these monumental structures were closely associated with the creation of the world (Headrick 2007). While the representation of cosmic themes might have enhanced a corporate solidarity (Blanton et al. 1996:6), the construction of these major monuments probably served to legitimize and disseminate the central authority through the mobilization of a large labor

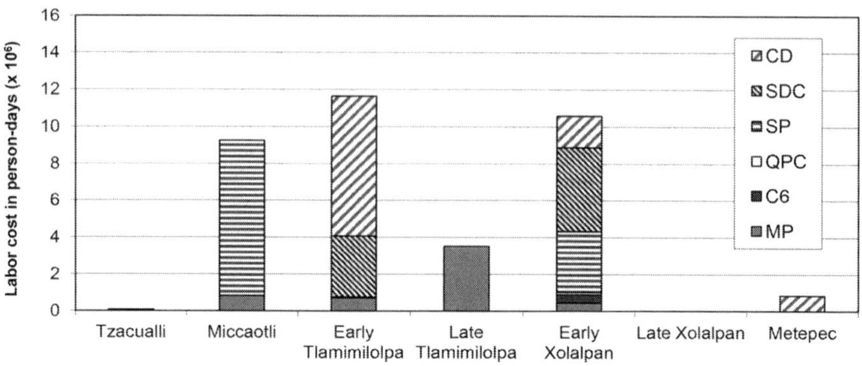

FIGURE 6.2. *Diachronic changes in total labor costs for the central precinct (CD: Ciudadela; SDC: Street of the Dead Complex; SP: Sun Pyramid; QPC: Quetzalpapalotl Palace Complex; C6: Complex 6:N5W1; MP: Moon Pyramid).*

force (Murakami 2010) and the institutionalized violence as seen in sacrificial burials that accompanied these monuments (Sugiyama 2004; Sugiyama and López Luján 2007). Considering the large size of major plazas, including the Street of the Dead, a wide audience likely participated in sacrificial and other rituals, and these public spectacles provided a basis to enhance sovereign power (Foucault 1995; Murakami 2014). Although material evidence for ruling elites, such as rulers' portraits and royal tombs, has not been uncovered to date, it seems reasonable to assume that the body of ruling elites was directly experienced in these rituals.

The association between major monuments and rulership became clearer when the Feathered Serpent Pyramid (FSP) (figure 6.3) was built at the Ciudadela in the Miccaotli-Tlamimilolpa transition (around 250 CE). Sculptures on the facades are interpreted as a scene representing the Feathered Serpent carrying on his back a headdress in the form of a primordial crocodilian monster, or the Teotihuacan equivalent of Aztec *cipactli*, which represents the first day of the ritual calendar (Sugiyama 1992, 2005; see also Taube 1986). Taking into account that the headdress was an emblem of rulership in other Mesoamerican societies, Saburo Sugiyama (1992, 2005) argues that the scene represents the creation of a new era and the succession of a ruler, both of which were brought by the Feathered Serpent. Along with the message embedded in the façades, over 200 sacrificed victims accompanied the construction (Sugiyama 2005). Rulership backed by military institutions was sacralized and promoted widely among city residents and beyond who would

FIGURE 6.3. *Feathered Serpent Pyramid at the Ciudadela.*

have participated in the ritual. René Millon (1993) and others (Cowgill 1983; Sugiyama 2004) see the construction of the Ciudadela as the culmination of the despotic rulership.

It is likely that the nature of rulership underwent a significant change by the Early Xolalpan phase (R. Millon 1988, 1993; Sugiyama 1998) or earlier (Cowgill 1998). Sacrificial burials have not been found from the rebuilt portions of major pyramids (Cabrera et al. 1991:88), and such an absence might attest to changes in the material and ritual manifestation of rulership. This change is probably associated with a termination ritual conducted at the FSP during the Late Tlamimilolpa or Early Xolalpan phase. Sugiyama (1998:158–61) demonstrates that the construction of the Adosada Platform abutted to the frontal façade of the FSP at the Ciudadela was accompanied by the demolition and burning of the old temple atop the FSP, the looting of burials, and the defacement of the façades of the FSP. He proposes that all these events were institutionally organized acts that served as the desecration of the FSP and the termination of the original ritual meanings for political ends. Sugiyama (1998) suggests that this possible termination program is indicative of political discord or replacement of rulership. René Millon (1988, 1993) postulates that the despotic rule provoked a reaction and rejection, leading to the establishment of institutional checks on the glorification of personal power and/or collective leadership.

After the Early Xolalpan phase, major pyramids were never rebuilt and construction activities were centered on administrative and residential buildings (figure 6.4), as I will discuss shortly. This may or may not signify the decline of rulership, but what we can see here is the changing network of ideology, practice, and resources. Construction as a practice, the use of a large labor force, and architectural conspicuous consumption were disconnected from the production of a central authority with or without ideological changes. Evidence suggests some continuities in the representation of militaristic rulership. For example, during the Late Xolalpan phase (450–550 CE), a pottery workshop was constructed at the north side of the Ciudadela, where theater-type censers (figure 6.5, top left) were produced (Múnera 1985; Rattray 2001). The central figure or mask in the center is interpreted as warrior (Sugiyama 2002), with some figures wearing nose pendants and earspools, which are possible symbols of the central authority. The censers were widely distributed in the surrounding apartment compounds and were used in funerary rituals or for other purposes. This might indicate changes in practices and technologies of authorization, not necessarily the discursive meaning of rulership.

THE DEVELOPMENT OF BUREAUCRACY

Possible changes in the nature of rulership during the Early Xolalpan phase were likely accompanied by the development of bureaucracy at Teotihuacan.

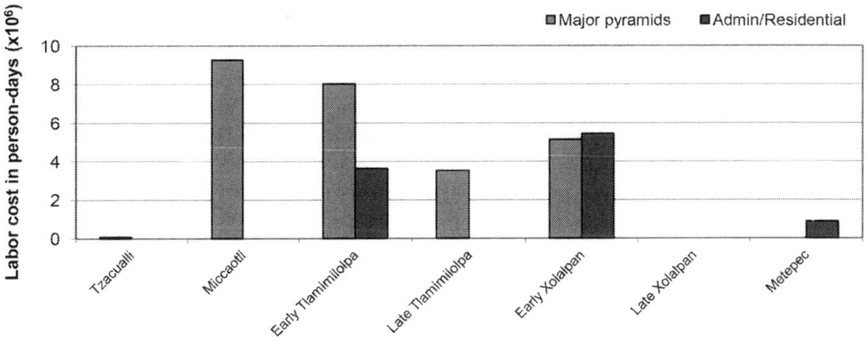

FIGURE 6.4. *Diachronic changes in labor costs for major pyramids and administrative/residential structures within the central precinct.*

Although identifying bureaucracy in the archaeological record is not straightforward (Murakami n.d.), architectural evidence from the central precinct indicates changes in the central administrative organization.

IDENTIFYING ADMINISTRATIVE FACILITIES

It is not an easy task to identify specialized administrative facilities at Teotihuacan and other sites in Mesoamerica mainly because the same buildings often have multiple functions (e.g., Inomata and Houston 2001). At Teotihuacan, architectural form is highly standardized across the city, and this complicates the identification of administrative facilities. Each architectural complex, a discrete group of buildings usually surrounded by walls, has both residential quarters and courtyards or plazas associated with temples (figures 6.6, 6.7), which may have served as ceremonial and/or social gathering areas. This means that there were no recognizable (at least for us) specialized facilities for administration. Administrative activities could have been carried out in both courtyard units associated with temples and rooms. Therefore, morphological traits alone do not provide reliable criteria for isolating the administrative function of buildings; rather, the location, size, internal layout, and associated artifacts and features have been used to infer the function of each complex and courtyard unit (Cabrera and Gómez 2008; Cowgill 1983, 1997, 2008; Gómez 2000; Gómez and Hernández 1999; Manzanilla 1996, 2009).

Further complicating the issue of identifying administrative facilities is that there is little evidence to suggest the extent to which political spheres were differentiated from religious and other spheres, unlike the Maya region and

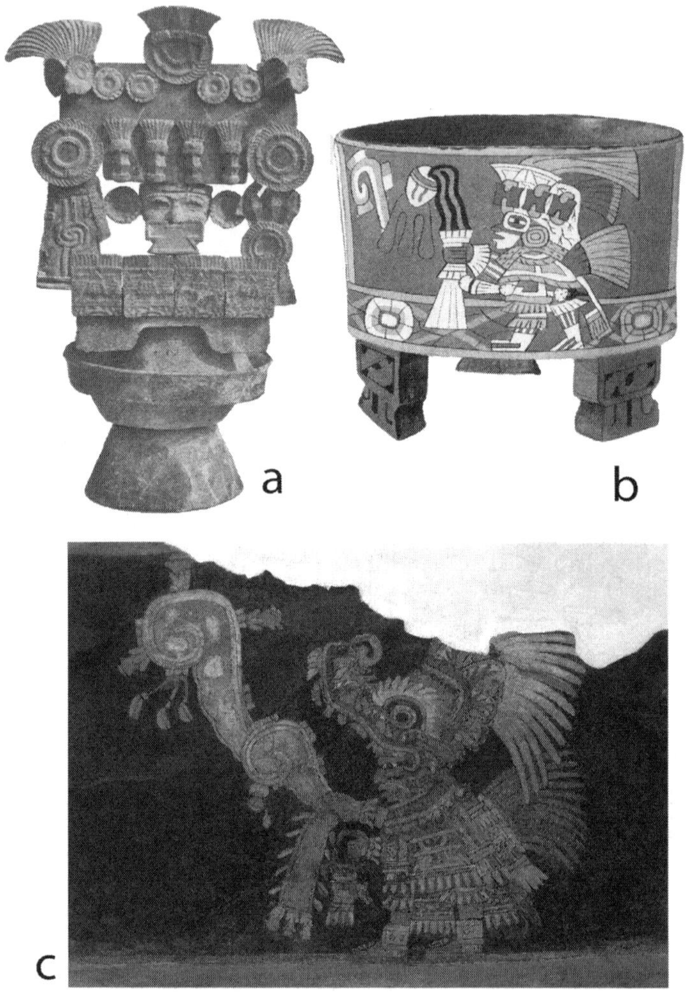

Figure 6.5. *Human representations during the Xolalpan and Metepec phases: (a) theater-type censer (after Séjourné 1966:figure 9, courtesy of Fondo de Cultura Económica); (b) stuccoed tripod vessel (after Séjourné 1966:figure 75, courtesy of Fondo de Cultura Económica); (c) profile figure with priestly attire in the mural of the Tepantitla apartment compound.*

Postclassic polities (see Baron, this volume; Pollard, this volume). In other words, we do not know for sure whether there were specialized administrators separate from priestly and other institutions, such as the military. Iconographic

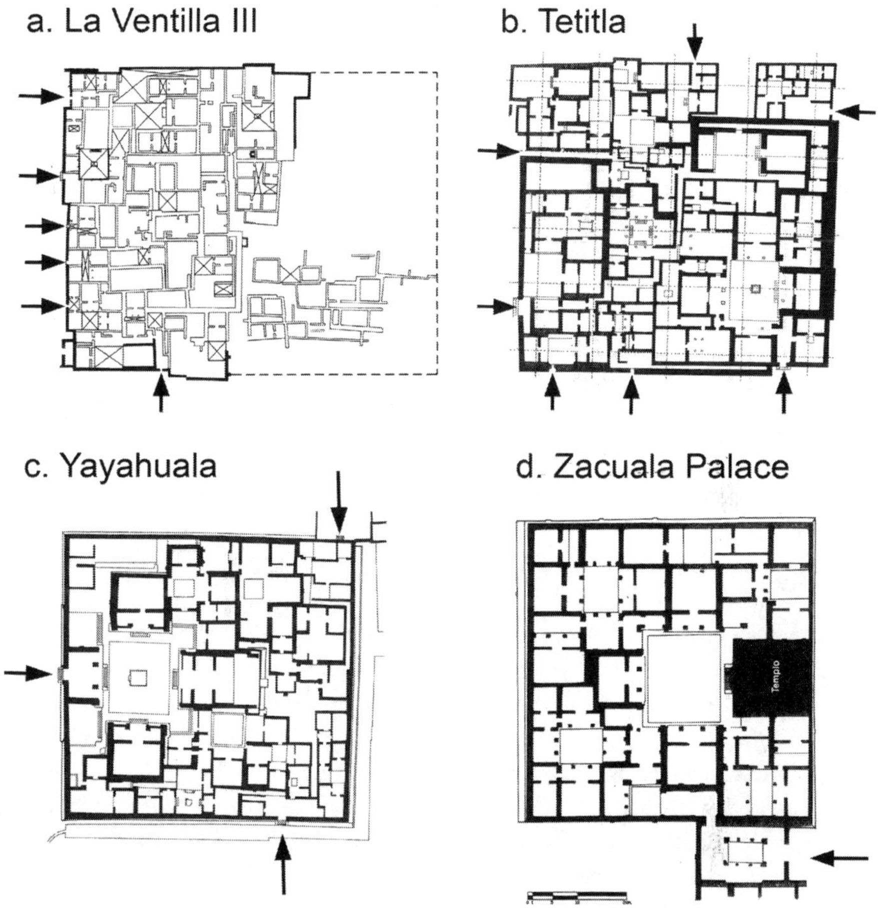

FIGURE 6.6. *Layout of some apartment compounds, arrows indicate entrances: (a) modified after Cabrera and Gómez 2008:figure 7; (b) modified after Manzanilla 2004:figure 5.6, courtesy of John Wiley and Sons; (c) modified after Manzanilla 2004:figure 5.3, courtesy of John Wiley and Sons; (d) modified after Cabrera and Gómez 2008:figure 3.*

studies show that priestly and military figures are prominent in murals, and there is little doubt that they participated in the state administration; although it is possible that priestly and military institutions were not conceived as separate and distinct from each other (Cowgill 1992:212–13). However, as Linda Manzanilla (1992) points out, it is likely that political hierarchies were largely conceived in religious terms. This does not mean that state administrators were all priests but that political decision-making processes occurred in religious settings, both physically and organizationally. Thus, the overwhelming number of ritual facilities within the central precinct does not imply that this zone was used mainly for religious purposes; governmental functions and political activities were likely carried out in these facilities (Cowgill 1983:332).

Based on the location, size, quality, and complexity of architectural complexes, George L. Cowgill (1983) proposes that the North and South Palaces of the Ciudadela, the Street of the Dead Complex (SDC) (figure 6.7), and other complexes were the major administrative foci, with possible shifts in importance through time (see also R. Millon 1973). Among these complexes, I argue that the SDC is the most plausible candidate for the central administrative facilities. The SDC is a mega-complex located between the Sun Pyramid and the Ciudadela, consisting of five three-temple complexes, room structures around the temple structures, and the street segmented by four transverse platforms forming three sunken courtyards (Wallrath 1967; figure 6.7). Only some portions of the complex have been excavated, including the Viking Group, the East Plaza Complex, the area of the "Excavations of 1917," the West Plaza Complex, and the Complex of the Superimposed Structures (see Morelos 1982, 1993).

The SDC and other excavated architectural complexes within the central precinct are characterized by the near absence of burials underneath floors in their residential quarters. This contrasts with apartment compounds outside the central precinct and may suggest that the SDC housed institutionally affiliated groups, such as government officials, their retainers, and servants. The majority of excavated apartment compounds seem to have been organized into houses and that members of each compound, or house, shared ritual practices (specifically mortuary rituals) that can be distinguished from those of other compounds, thereby perpetuating a specific identity through time (Clayton 2009). Thus, the absence of burials at the SDC (and other complexes) suggests that hereditary groups did not inhabit the complex (see Cabrera and Gómez 2008:49; Gómez 2000:596–602). It is possible that personnel of the SDC were recruited from outside the central precinct and that they stayed within the complex for the duration of their appointments.

These observations do not preclude the possibility that residents of the SDC and other complexes received some special mortuary treatment and were buried somewhere else. However, the North and South Palaces at the Ciudadela contain burials, suggesting that these complexes housed hereditary groups such as royal families or priests (see Cowgill 1983, 1997; R. Millon 1973). Due to these differences regarding the presence of burials, it is likely that there is a clear difference in the nature of social groups among different architectural complexes within the central precinct.

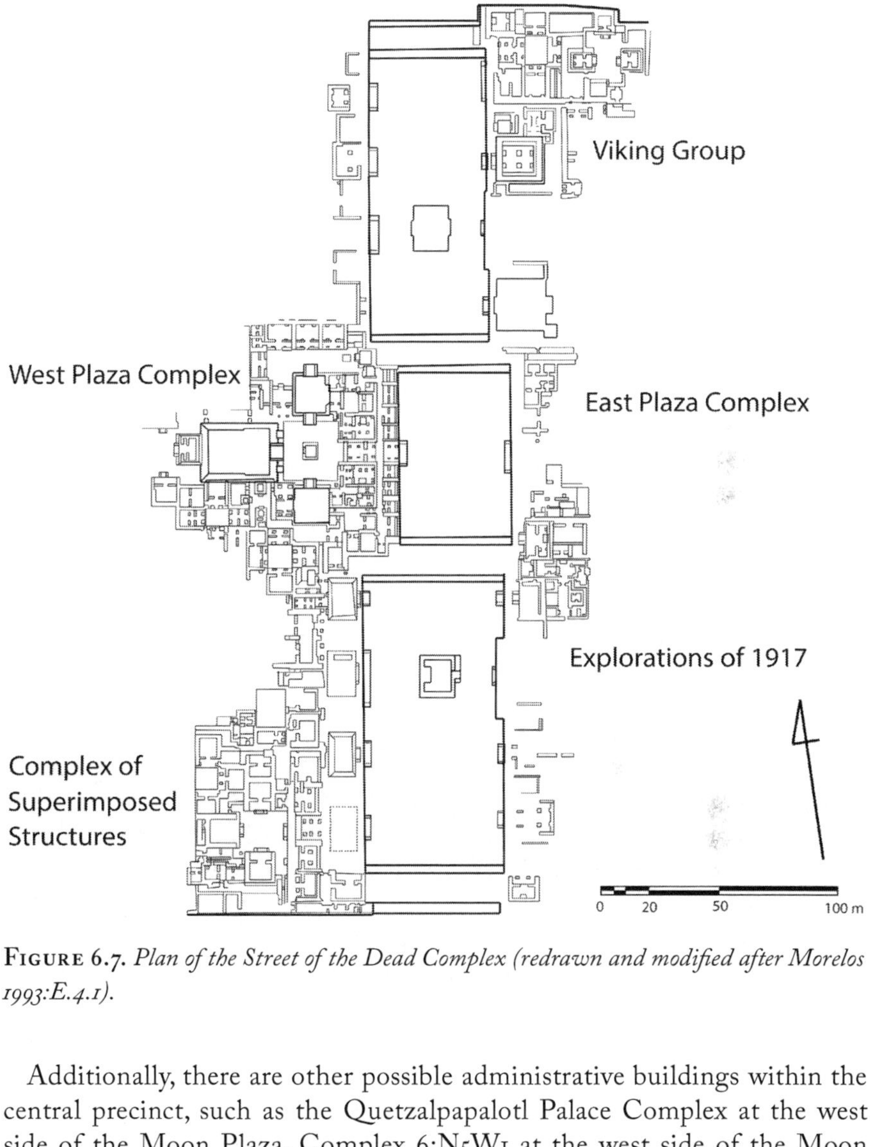

FIGURE 6.7. *Plan of the Street of the Dead Complex (redrawn and modified after Morelos 1993:E.4.1).*

Additionally, there are other possible administrative buildings within the central precinct, such as the Quetzalpapalotl Palace Complex at the west side of the Moon Plaza, Complex 6:N5W1 at the west side of the Moon Pyramid, and possibly other unexcavated complexes. The nature of social groups in these complexes is poorly understood, but it is likely that some administrative activities were carried out there. The presence of multiple administrative facilities might attest to a relatively high degree of internal differentiation of administrative organization into multiple institutions, although it is not clear to what extent these institutions were specialized or independent and how they were related to each other (e.g., Cowgill 1992). It is possible that there were multiple orders, such as civil, judicial, military, and religious, as seen in the Aztec empire (see also Pollard, this volume). Annabeth Headrick (2007) proposes that the institution of the ruler, lineages, and the military order shaped the dynamic of power in the city. If so, royal families and lineage and military leaders may have formed the upper echelons of the bureaucracy.

High-level administrative decision making would have taken place in royal palaces (e.g., Christie and Sarro 2006; Inomata and Houston 2001), but the location of royal palaces remains controversial at Teotihuacan. René Millon (1973) and Cowgill (1983) think that the North and South Palaces at the Ciudadela were the seat of the rulers, but Cowgill (1983) also suggests the possibility that the royal residence was moved to the SDC afterward (see also Sanders and Evans 2006). Manzanilla (2006; Manzanilla and López Luján 2001) argues that the Xalla Complex, to the east of the Moon Plaza, was the royal palace. In any case, due to this unsolved issue, the spatial and organizational relationship between the rulers and possible administrative organization is not clearly understood.

The Evolution of Administrative Buildings

There are diachronic changes in the size and labor expenditure for administrative buildings, which suggest the expansion of administrative organization and possibly an increased degree of bureaucratization. All the complexes mentioned above were built during the Early Tlamimilolpa phase (ca. 250–300 CE), with rebuilding episodes in the subsequent phases. There is little evidence of administrative buildings before the Early Tlamimilolpa (i.e., the Tzacualli and Miccaotli phases; ca. 1–250 CE) largely because, except for major pyramids, most structures were razed to build new architectural complexes during the Early Tlamimilolpa phase. There is a possible elite residential quarter in an area where the Ciudadela was to be constructed, but its layout is not well understood (Cabrera 1991:35; 1998; Cabrera et al. 1991b:83–84; Gazzola 2009). Therefore, I focus on changes from the Tlamimilolpa to later phases.

There are two major construction stages at the SDC and they are dated to the Early Tlamimilolpa and Early Xolalpan phases (Morelos 1993; Sánchez 1991), although there are limited ceramic data to confirm this (see Cabrera and Andrade 2004:284; R. Millon 1973:55). Matthew Wallrath (1967:115, 119) originally suggested that the original complex may have been smaller, and excavation data seem to confirm it (Morelos 1993:106). If so, the east-west dimension of the complex likely measured around 250 meters in the first stage and was extended to around 350 meters in the second stage. There was probably no change in the north-south dimension (ca. 380 meters). Thus, the total area of the SDC was likely expanded from ca. 9.5 hectares to ca. 13 hectares. Moreover, excavations at the West Plaza Complex revealed that a number of room structures were constructed in the second stage in an area where there were open spaces during the first construction stage (Morelos 1993:84, 90). All this suggests that there were fewer room structures at the first construction stage, although this needs to be examined through further excavations.

The second construction stage, dated to the Early Xolalpan phase, corresponds to most structures now exposed at the SDC. The floor level was raised on average ca. 2.10 meters from the floor of the first construction stage (Morelos 1993:19, 82). A number of room structures were built on this raised floor. The SDC is surrounded by walls (1.8–2.2 meters thick) and embankments likely built during the second construction stage (Wallrath 1967:117–18). Cowgill (1983:339) estimates that the SDC housed around 800 to 1,600 persons, or probably more. This increased number of administrators may correspond to the increased number of official positions, which is an indication of an intensified internal differentiation or bureaucratization.

A substantial change in the layout is also reported from the Quetzalpapalotl Palace Complex (QPC) and the Complex 6:N5W1. There are two major construction stages at the QPC, which are dated to the Early Tlamimilolpa and Early Xolalpan phases (Acosta 1964; Koga 2005; R. Millon 1973:57; Müller 1978:30). At the second stage, the floor level was raised about 4 meters, burying previous temple and room structures (Acosta 1964:plano 6). A similar trend can be seen at the Complex 6:N5W1, where the floor level was raised 2 meters from the previous level, with several temple and room structures being built atop the new floor during the Early Xolalpan phase (Carballo 2005:89). The North and South Palaces at the Ciudadela also show some rebuilding episodes after their original construction in the Early Tlamimilolpa phase, and the floor level was raised from ca. 70 centimeters to 150 centimeters, probably during the Early Xolalpan phase (Cabrera 1991:planos 2–4; Cabrera et al. 1991:87–88). While the same layout was likely kept throughout the rebuilding episodes at the North and South Palaces, a new residential compound was added at the west side of the North Palace, suggesting an increase in the number of residents within the Ciudadela (Cabrera 1991: 39–40, 1998:158).

Resource Allocation for Administrative Buildings

The expansion of administrative organization can be seen more clearly in the changing resource allocation for construction within the central precinct. Energetic analysis (for specifics of the method, see Murakami 2010) has revealed decentralization processes in the use of labor and material resources, which suggests changes in internal power relations among ruling elites (figures 6.2 and 6.4). During the Tzacualli and Miccaotli phases, power was highly centralized and labor investment was concentrated in a single structure: the Sun Pyramid (ca. 90 percent of the total labor costs within the central precinct). In the Early Tlamimilolpa phase, power became less centralized, as seen in more proportionate labor allocation among different architectural complexes. However, construction activities still focused on ceremonial structures, as exemplified by the erection of the FSP and the Ciudadela (ca. 65 percent of the total labor). As mentioned above, excavations at the FSP revealed burials of around 200 sacrificed victims, and Sugiyama (2005) convincingly demonstrates that the erection of the FSP represents the creation of a new era and the accession of the ruler.

By the Early Xolalpan phase, the process of decentralization within the governmental institutions was likely intensified. The SDC stands as the most important architectural complex in terms of labor investment (ca. 43 percent of the total labor). Furthermore, as figure 6.4 shows, investment in administrative and residential structures increased during the Early Xolalpan phase; about 24 percent of the total labor costs were invested for administrative/residential structures in the Early Tlamimilolpa phase, whereas the proportion of this cost increased to 51 percent in the Early Xolalpan phase. An emphasis on structures of primarily administrative (and residential) function during the Early Xolalpan phase departs from an earlier emphasis on ceremonial structures (the Sun Pyramid and the FSP in the Ciudadela) and probably speaks to the increased power of the inhabitants of those structures (government officials, institutions, and/or the factions of those institutions) and/or the increased importance of administrative activities. In summary, all these observations suggest an increase in size, complexity, and possibly power of the administrative organization during the Early Xolalpan phase.

Bureaucrats and Intermediate Elites

As discussed above, it is likely that bureaucrats at Teotihuacan were recruited from outside the central precinct, and this implies that there was a close connection between administrative officials and some lineages, or houses, at apartment compounds, walled enclosures with several residential units inside (figure 6.6). The most likely candidates for bureaucrats are members of intermediate elite apartment compounds or higher ranked intermediate elite compounds, which are generally thought to have been neighborhood centers (Manzanilla 2006; R. Millon 1976, 1981). These intermediate elite compounds have a larger central courtyard and temple structures than those of other apartment compounds, and their internal rooms are profusely decorated with murals. Studies of these murals at some apartment compounds (e.g., C. Millon 1973; Headrick 2007) show that the decorative themes include those related to state ideology. Furthermore, a set of greenstone earspools, a nose pendant, and beads, possible symbols of state officials (Cabrera 2002), were also uncovered from a burial at La Ventilla B (LVB 21) in the Early Tlamimilolpa context (Rattray 1997:lamina III).

Somewhat paralleled to the expansion of bureaucracy in the Xolalpan phase, mural depictions of priestly and/or armed personnel (figure 6.5, bottom) increased at intermediate elite apartment compounds (e.g., Miller 1973; C. Millon 1973; R. Millon 1992). Accordingly, the production of stuccoed tripod vessels depicting these personnel (figure 6.5, top right) increased during the Xolalpan phase (Rattray 2001). This might attest to the close association between state bureaucracy and some intermediate elites as well as the proliferation of bureaucrats/intermediate elites. Although residents in administrative buildings possibly included servants in addition to administrators, a relatively large portion of social groups in the city was involved in administrative duties (see Cowgill 1983:339). It is possible that bureaucrats were also recruited from lower status apartment compounds to form lower echelons of the bureaucracy, as seen in the Late Postclassic Basin of Mexico (Fargher et al. 2011; Hicks 1999). Manzanilla (2001:177) points out that each apartment compound has at least one burial with very rich offerings, including slate discs, theater-type censers, and tripod vessels, among other items. This suggests the possibility that these persons with rich offerings were formerly state bureaucrats.

URBAN CONSTRUCTION AND ENTANGLED POLITICAL STRATEGIES

The changing relationship among governmental institutions, along with the development of bureaucracy during the Early Xolalpan phase or earlier, was probably a consequence of social transformations during the Tlamimilolpa phase, which substantially altered the urban landscape surrounding the central precinct. The adoption of apartment compounds marks the start of this urban transformation, and over 2,000 apartment compounds were constructed over the course of one hundred years or so (R. Millon 1981). Considering the conformity of the orientation of the apartment compounds, R. Millon (1993; see also Cowgill 2000) states that the decision to build such compounds derived from a strong and effective centralized authority. The creation of an orderly laid-out city was perhaps an extension of the construction of the central precinct, which embodied an ideology associated with cosmic themes (Cowgill 2003). Furthermore, the reduction of basal units of urban populace by aggregating several residential units in a single compound would have reduced the burden of the internal administration of the city (R. Millon 1981:212). Thus, the urban renewal project was likely predicated on the ideological and practical interests of ruling elites.

René Millon (1993:29) postulates that the state must have sponsored the building of apartment compounds by organizing the supply of building materials. My study of construction materials (Murakami 2010) generally supports this view, which suggests that the state regulated labor forces and that lime and cut stone blocks were procured centrally by the state and distributed to the urban populace. This indicates a strong infrastructural power of the state, which is defined as its ability to penetrate into civil life (Mann 1984). The exercise of strong infrastructural power is generally associated with developed bureaucracy since a complex administrative system is required to administer the wide distribution of public goods (Blanton and Fargher 2008). Archaeological evidence at Teotihuacan is consistent with such a general trend, and the urban renewal project probably resulted in the expansion of bureaucratic organization mentioned above.

However, it is unlikely that urban renewal was the sole result of the decisions of ruling elites. To achieve the ideological and practical goals of ruling elites, it would not be necessary to widely distribute costly construction materials such as lime. I suggest that there was a demand for such construction materials by urban residents. From functionalist perspectives, bureaucracy is usually formed to implement political goals of rulers, but it also needs to meet the demands of major social groups, from which the rulers want to mobilize resources. Thus, to the extent that the state relies on internal revenues (Blanton and Fargher 2008), bureaucracy is required to provide and regulate public services. Based on the comparative study of bureaucracies, Shmuel Noah Eisenstadt (1963:281–87) characterizes "service-oriented" bureaucracies by their dependence on the rulers along with their partial incorporation into various social groups. Archaeological evidence at Teotihuacan seems consistent with this view, as discussed above. This suggests the possibility that decisions in the central authority reflect the interests of certain social groups, from which bureaucrats were recruited. In this kind of political organization, the distinction between top-down and bottom-up decision-making processes becomes somewhat blurred yet is certainly distinct from democratic regimes. Nonetheless, we can envision something like an amalgam of strategic actions by rulers, bureaucrats, and possibly intermediate elites, and the negotiation among these social groups would have resulted in the urban renewal project. It is intriguing to reconstruct the initial process of urban renewal in order to understand the nature of this negotiation. Although data are elusive in this respect, I summarize below currently available data and illustrate that the urban renewal project was likely initiated through the negotiation between the state (the rulers and bureaucracy) and social groups closely related to state institutions.

Initial Process of the Urban Renewal Project

While most excavated apartment compounds were founded during the Late Tlamimilolpa phase (ca. 300–350 CE) (see R. Millon 1981:206), there are some compounds that were founded in the Early Tlamimilolpa (ca. 250–300 CE), which include several in the La Ventilla district (La Ventilla I, II, A, and B) (see Gómez 2000; Rattray 1997), Tlajinga 33 (Widmer 1987), and possibly some compounds in the Oaxaca barrio (Croissier 2007; Spence 1992). It is possible that there was a time lapse between the construction of the first apartment compounds and that of later ones. Deep excavations at a portion of La Ventilla II (Delgado n.d.) revealed that a residential unit built in the Early Tlamimilolpa phase was rebuilt once during the same phase. This suggests that the first compound was built early in the Early Tlamimilolpa phase and that there were one or two generations of time lapse between the first La Ventilla II and other compounds built in the Late Tlamimilolpa phase. At Tlajinga 33, a lower status compound in a periphery of the city, some small-scale modifications of buildings, as well as a superimposition of a floor, were observed during the Early Tlamimilolpa phase (Widmer 1987:330–36), and this also suggests that the compound was built early in the Early Tlamimilolpa phase.

The possible time lapse between the construction of first and later apartment compounds suggests that the urban renewal consisted of at least two steps: introduction of the compounds by a limited number of people and the subsequent (probably rapid) spread of the compounds to the great majority of urban residents. Considering their relatively high labor costs (Murakami 2010), I suggest the possibility that only privileged people were allowed to construct typical apartment compounds early in the Early Tlamimilolpa phase. The La

Ventilla district is located just west of the Great Compound, and it is possible that residents in the district were closely affiliated with governmental institutions (see Gómez 2000). In fact, a burial with greenstone ornaments has been uncovered from one of these early compounds, as mentioned above.

It is doubtful, however, that the residents at Tlajinga 33 were also privileged. It is possible that they emulated the new style of living and constructed the compound by themselves (Murakami 2013). Randolph J. Widmer (1987; Widmer and Storey 1993:102) suggests that only a compound-level organization was required for major construction activities at Tlajinga 33, based on its disconformity of orientation and the poor execution of structures. Construction materials and techniques are different from those of compounds in the urban core. For example, the majority of raw materials used were available in nearby areas, such as river cobbles and earth, and lime plaster was probably not used for these early buildings.

This suggests that lime and other construction materials, widely distributed later, were demanded by relatively powerful people (or so-called intermediate elites) in the initial stage of urban renewal. Elite residences both within and outside the central precinct probably provided a model or an idea of the ideal housing, which was adopted by most urban residents in subsequent phases. As my study suggests (Murakami 2010, 2013, 2014), a grand-scale urban renewal was made possible by the active intervention of the state in the procurement and distribution of construction materials, resulting in highly standardized construction materials and techniques.

In summary, the canonical orientation, an orderly layout, and the reorganization of basal units of urban populace would reflect strategies of ruling elites, whereas the use of costly construction materials and techniques was likely derived from strategies of intermediate elites and other social groups. These varying strategies were mediated by state bureaucracy, which exercised a strong infrastructural power to implement the demands of both ruling elites and major social groups. Thus, as Cowgill (2003) suggests, urban renewal represents a mix of both top-down and bottom-up processes, but these decision-making processes were entangled in a complex way.

CONCLUSIONS: SOCIAL INTEGRATION, SEPARATION, AND THE DIALECTIC OF CONTROL

Urban architecture provided varying social fields that constituted both differences and similarities among various social segments at Teotihuacan. The production of the central authority was predicated on the mobilization of ideology, which connected cosmic themes with institutionalized violence in a substantive way, and the mobilization of human and material resources, which enhanced bodily experience of sovereign power. These two different levels or kinds of mobilization intersected at the very act of monument building, thereby perpetuating the solid network of ideology, practice of authorization, and resources. Thus, monumental construction does not only reflect the power of ruling elites but was an essential component of the practice of authorization and subjection (Smith 2003, 2011). And, in this light, we can clearly see why monumental structures were often rebuilt continuously. Moreover, the meanings inscribed in these monumental structures were probably enacted continuously through ritual performance in spacious plazas within the central precinct (Murakami 2014).

The urban renewal project was probably an extension of the same practice of authorization and subjection but at a greater scale and with different consequences. Ideological and practical interests of varying social groups were actively negotiated, resulting in the use of highly standardized construction materials and techniques. I suggested that the creation of the notion of the ideal housing and collective demands for such housing is the key to understanding this process. In a sense, standardized apartment compounds can be interpreted as a material manifestation of the dialectic of control or relations of autonomy and dependence (Giddens 1979:145–49). In other words, subject populations controlled to some extent the distribution of resources, thereby reinforcing the reciprocal relations between the state and its subjects and perhaps promoting a corporate ideology. I argued that state bureaucracy played a central role in this process of negotiation. By incorporating various individuals in the administration of the city (and beyond), bureaucracy and major social groups were well integrated to form a civil society. It should be emphasized, however, that this social integration rested on the separation of the lowest status residents from the standard "culture" of housing. Archaeological evidence points to the fact that there were people who did not have access to standardized construction materials and techniques, some of them living in insubstantial structures. This indicates that the production of similarities at one level may reinforce difference at another level of social interaction (and vice versa). Therefore, we must acknowledge multiple scales or levels in the production of similarities and differences (e.g., between rulers and bureaucrats, between state elites and subject population, etc.). In fact, it is possible that the creation of similarities through the urban renewal project had a profound impact on the nature of rulership and the relationship between the rulers and bureaucracy during the Early Xolalpan and subsequent phases.

As mentioned at the outset of this chapter, multiple and contradictory principles become contextually defined and situationally operative (Flanagan 1989:261). We should pay close attention to varying contexts and situations (or social fields, in more general terms) without losing sight of the totalizing and individualizing effects of the state system (Foucault 1982). Overall, the similarities and differences between the rulers and the ruled at Teotihuacan were achieved not as a sole result of rulers' political strategies but through entangled political strategies among varying social groups and at multiple scales of social interaction.

ACKNOWLEDGMENTS

I would like to thank Sarah Kurnick and Joanne Baron for inviting me to contribute to this volume and two anonymous reviewers for their invaluable comments on an earlier draft of this chapter. Part of the research presented here was funded by the National Science Foundation Dissertation Improvement Grant (BCS-0836716), Arizona State University (the Graduate and Professional Student Association and the School of Human Evolution and Social Change), and Sigma Xi (ASU Chapter).

REFERENCES

Acosta, Jorge R. 1964. *El Palacio del Quetzalpapalotl*. Mexico City: Instituto Nacional de Antropología e Historia.

Blanton, Richard, and Lane Fargher. 2008. *Collective Action in the Formation of Pre-Modern States*. New York: Springer.

Blanton, Richard E., Gary M. Feinman, Stephen A. Kowalewski, and Peter N. Peregrine. 1996. "A Dual-Processual Theory for the Evolution of Mesoamerican Civilization." *Current Anthropology* 37(1): 1–14.

Bourdieu, Pierre. 1990. *The Logic of Practice*. Translated by Richard Nice. Stanford: Stanford University Press.

Brumfiel, Elizabeth M. 1992. "Breaking and Entering the Ecosystem—Gender, Class, and Faction Steal the Show." *American Anthropologist* 94(3): 551–67.

Cabrera Castro, Rubén. 1991. "Secuencia arquitectónica y cronología de La Ciudadela." In *Teotihuacan 1980–1982: Nuevas interpretaciones*, edited by Rubén Cabrera Castro, Ignacio Rodríguez García, and Noel Morelos García, 31–60. Mexico City: Instituto Nacional de Antropología e Historia.

Cabrera Castro, Rubén. 1998. "La cronología de la Ciudadela en su secuencia arquitectónica." In *Los ritmos de cambio en Teotihuacán: Reflexiones y discusiones de su cronología*, edited by Rosa Brambila Paz and Rubén Cabrera Castro, 143–66. Mexico City: Instituto Nacional de Antropología e Historia.

Cabrera Castro, Rubén, and David Andrade. 2004. "Los edificios con bandas entrelazadas de Teotihuacan: Discusión de su cronología y de sus antecedentes." In *La costa del Golfo en tiempos teotihuacanos: Propuestas y perspectivas: Memoria de la Segunda Mesa Redonda de Teotihuacan*, edited by María Elena Ruiz Gallut and Arturo Pascual Soto, 279–306. Mexico City: Instituto Nacional de Antropología e Historia.

Cabrera Castro, Rubén, and Sergio Gómez Chávez. 2008. "La Ventilla: A Model for a Barrio in the Urban Structure of Teotihuacan." In *Urbanism in Mesoamerica/ El Urbanismo en Mesoamérica*, vol. 2, edited by Alba Guadalupe Mastache, Robert H. Cobean, Angel García Cook, and Kenneth G. Hirth, 37–83. University Park: Pennsylvania State University / Mexico City: Instituto Nacional de Antropología e Historia.

Cabrera Castro, Rubén, Ignacio Rodríguez G., and Noel Morelos G, eds. 1991. *Teotihuacan 1980–1982: Nuevas interpretaciones*. Mexico City: Instituto Nacional de Antropología e Historia.

Cabrera Castro, Rubén, Saburo Sugiyama, and George L. Cowgill. 1991. "The Temple of Quetzalcoatl Project at Teotihuacan: A Preliminary Report." *Ancient Mesoamerica* 2(1): 77–92.

Cabrera Cortés, Oralia. 2002. "Ideología y política en Teotihuacan: Ofrendas de rocas semipreciosas de la Pirámide de la Serpiente Emplumada." In *Ideología y política a través de materiales, imágenes y símbolos: Memoria de la Primera Mesa Redonda de Teotihuacan*, edited by María Elena Ruiz Gallut, 75–99. Mexico City: Universidad Nacional Autónoma de México / Instituto Nacional de Antropología e Historia.

Carballo, David M. 2005. "State Political Authority and Obsidian Craft Production at the Moon Pyramid, Teotihuacan, Mexico." PhD diss., University of California, Los Angeles.

Campbell, Roderick B. 2009. "Toward a Networks and Boundaries Approach to Early Complex Polities: The Late Shang Case." *Current Anthropology* 50(6): 821–48.

Christie, Jessica Joyce, and Patricia Joan Sarro, eds. 2006. *Palaces and Power in the Americas: From Peru to the Northwest Coast*. Austin: University of Texas Press.

Clayton, Sarah. 2009. "Ritual Diversity and Social Identities: A Study of Mortuary Behaviors at Teotihuacan." PhD diss., Arizona State University.

Cowgill, George L. 1983. "Rulership and the Ciudadela: Political Inferences from Teotihuacan Architecture." *In Civilization in the Ancient Americas: Essays in Honor of Gordon R. Willey*, edited by Richard M. Leventhal and Alan L. Kolata, 313–43. Albuquerque: University of New Mexico Press / Cambridge, MA: Peabody Museum of Archaeology and Ethnology.

Cowgill, George L. 1992. "Social Differentiation at Teotihuacan." In *Mesoamerican Elites: An Archaeological Assessment*, edited by Diane Z. Chase and Arlen F. Chase, 206–20. Norman: University of Oklahoma Press.

Cowgill, George L. 1997. "State and Society at Teotihuacan, Mexico." *Annual Review of Anthropology* 26: 129–161.

Cowgill, George L. 1998. "Nuevos datos del Proyecto Templo de Quetzalcóatl acerca de la cerámica Miccaotli-Tlamimilolpa." In *Los ritmos de cambio en Teotihuacán: Reflexiones y discusiones de su cronología*, edited by Rosa Brambila Paz and Rubén Cabrera Castro, 185–99. Mexico City: Instituto Nacional de Antropología e Historia.

Cowgill, George L. 2000. "The Central Mexican Highlands from the Rise of Teotihuacan to the Decline of Tula." In *The Cambridge History of the Native Peoples of the Americas*, vol. 2, *Mesoamerica, Part 1*, edited by Richard E. W. Adams and Murdo J. MacLeod, 250–317. Cambridge: Cambridge University Press.

Cowgill, George L. 2003. "Teotihuacan: Cosmic Glories and Mundane Needs." In *The Social Construction of Ancient Cities*, edited by Monica L. Smith, 37–55. Washington, DC: Smithsonian Institution Press.

Cowgill, George L. 2008. "Teotihuacan as an Urban Place." In *Urbanism in Mesoamerica/El Urbanismo en Mesoamérica*, vol. 2, edited by Alba Guadalupe Mastache, Robert H. Cobean, Angel García Cook, and Kenneth G. Hirth, 85–112. University Park: Pennsylvania State University / Mexico City: Instituto Nacional de Antropología e Historia.

Croissier, Michelle M. 2007. "The Zapotec Presence at Teotihuacan, Mexico: Political Ethnicity and Domestic Identity." PhD diss., University of Illinois at Urbana-Champaign.

Delgado, Jaime. n.d. "Excavación de Interiores: Aposento Este del Conjunto 'Bordes Rojos.'" Unpublished manuscript.

Dow, James W. 1967. "Astronomical Orientations at Teotihuacan: A Case Study in Astroarchaeology." *American Antiquity* 32: 326–34.

Dumont, Louis. 1977. *From Mandeville to Marx: The Genesis and Triumph of Economic Ideology*. Chicago: University of Chicago Press.

Eisenstadt, Shmuel Noah. 1963. *The Political Systems of Empires*. London: Free Press of Glencoe.

Fargher, Lane F., Verenice Y. Heredia Espinoza, and Richard E. Blanton. 2011. "Alternative Pathways to Power in Late Postclassic Highland Mesoamerica." *Journal of Anthropological Archaeology* 30: 306–26.

Ferguson, Yale H., and Richard W. Mansbach. 1996. *Polities: Authority, Identities, and Change*. Columbia: University of South Carolina Press.

Flanagan, James G. 1989. "Hierarchy in Simple 'Egalitarian' Societies." *Annual Review of Anthropology* 18: 245–66.

Foucault, Michel. [1977] 1995. *Discipline and Punish: The Birth of the Prison.* Translated by Alan Sheridan. New York: Vintage.

Foucault, Michel. 1982. "The Subject and Power." *Critical Inquiry* 8(4): 777–95.

Gazzola, Julie. 2009. "Características arquitectónicas de algunas construcciones de fases tempranas en Teotihuacán." *Arqueología* 42: 216–33.

Giddens, Anthony. 1979. *Central Problems in Social Theory: Action, Structure and Contradiction in Social Analysis.* Berkeley: University of California Press.

Gómez Chávez, Sergio. 2000. "La Ventilla: Un barrio de la antigua ciudad de Teotihuacan." Professional thesis, Escuela Nacional de Antropología e Historia.

Gómez Chávez, Sergio, and Jaime Núñez Hernández. 1999. "Análisis preliminar del patrón y la distribución espacial de entierros en el Barrio de La Ventilla." In *Prácticas funerarias en la Ciudad de los Dioses: Los entierros humanos de la antigua Teotihuacan*, edited by Linda Manzanilla and Carlos Serrano, 81–148. Mexico City: Instituto Universidad Nacional Autónoma de México / Instituto de Investigaciones Antropológicas.

Headrick, Annabeth. 2007. *The Teotihuacan Trinity: The Sociopolitical Structure of an Ancient Mesoamerican City.* Austin: University of Texas Press.

Heyden, Doris. 1975. "An Interpretation of the Cave Underneath the Pyramid of the Sun in Teotihuacan, Mexico." *American Antiquity* 40(2): 131–47.

Heyden, Doris. 1981. "Caves, Gods, and Myths: World-View and Planning in Teotihuacan." In *Mesoamerican Sites and World-Views*, edited by Elizabeth P. Benson, 1–35. Washington, DC: Dumbarton Oaks.

Hicks, Frederic. 1999. "The Middle Class in Ancient Central Mexico." *Journal of Anthropological Research* 55(3): 409–27.

Inomata, Takeshi, and Stephen D. Houston, eds. 2001. *Royal Courts of the Ancient Maya.* 2 vols. Boulder: Westview.

Josephides, Lisette. 1985. *The Production of Inequality: Gender and Exchange among the Kewa.* London: Tavistock.

Koga, Yuko. 2005. "The Transition of a Residential Compound in Teotihuacan, Mexico: An Analysis of the Construction in the Palace 3 through 3D Survey Data." (In Japanese.) *América Antigua* 8: 1–30.

McGuire, Randall H. 1983. "Breaking Down Cultural Complexity: Inequality and Heterogeneity." In *Advances in Archaeological Method and Theory 6*, edited by Michael B. Schiffer, 91–142. New York: Academic Press.

Mann, Michael. 1984. "The Autonomous Power of the State: Its Origins, Mechanisms and Results." *European Journal of Sociology* 25(2): 185–213.

Mann, Michael. 1986. *The Sources of Social Power*. Vol. 1, *A History of Power from the Beginning to A.D. 1760*. Cambridge: Cambridge University Press.

Manzanilla, Linda. 1992. "The Economic Organization of the Teotihuacan Priesthood: Hypotheses and Considerations." In *Art, Ideology, and the City of Teotihuacan: A Symposium at Dumbarton Oaks, 8th and 9th October 1988*, edited by Janet Catherine Berlo, 321–38. Washington, DC: Dumbarton Oaks.

Manzanilla, Linda. 1996. "Corporate Groups and Domestic Activities at Teotihuacan." *Latin American Antiquity* 7(3): 228–46.

Manzanilla, Linda. 2001. "Gobierno corporativo en Teotihuacan: Una revisión del concepto 'palacio' aplicado a la gran urbe prehispánica." *Anales de Antropología* 35: 157–90.

Manzanilla, Linda. 2004. "Social Identity and Daily Life at Classic Teotihuacan." In *Mesoamerican Archaeology: Theory and Practice*, edited by Julia A. Hendon and Rosemary A. Joyce, 124–47. Malden, MA: Wiley-Blackwell.

Manzanilla, Linda. 2006. "Estados corporativos arcaicos: Organizaciones de excepción en escenarios excluyentes." *Cuicuilco* 13(36): 13–45.

Manzanilla, Linda. 2009. "Corporate Life in Apartment and Barrio Compounds at Teotihuacan, Central Mexico: Craft Specialization, Hierarchy, and Ethnicity." In *Domestic Life in Prehispanic Capitals: A Study of Specialization, Hierarchy, and Ethnicity*, edited by Linda R. Manzanilla and Claude Chapdelaine, 21–42. Memoirs of the Museum of Anthropology No. 46. Ann Arbor: University of Michigan

Manzanilla, Linda, and Leonardo López Luján. 2001. "Exploraciones en un posible palacio de Teotihuacan: El Proyecto Xalla 2000–2001." *Mexicon* 13(3): 58–61.

Miller, Arthur G. 1973. *The Mural Painting of Teotihuacán*. Washington, DC: Dumbarton Oaks.

Millon, Clara. 1973. "Painting, Writing, and Polity in Teotihuacan, Mexico." *American Antiquity* 38(3): 294–314.

Millon, René. 1973. *Urbanization at Teotihuacan, Mexico.* Vol. 1, *The Teotihuacan Map, Part 1, Text*. Austin: University of Texas Press.

Millon, René. 1976. "Social Relations in Ancient Teotihuacan." In *The Valley of Mexico: Studies in Pre-Hispanic Ecology and Society*, edited by Eric R. Wolf, 205–48. Albuquerque: University of New Mexico Press.

Millon, René. 1981. "Teotihuacan: City, State, and Civilization." In *Supplement to the Handbook of Middle American Indians*, vol. 1, *Archaeology*, edited by Victoria Bricker and Jeremy A. Sabloff, 198–243. Austin: University of Texas Press.

Millon, René. 1988. "The Last Years of Teotihuacan Dominance." In *The Collapse of Ancient States and Civilizations*, edited by Norman Yoffee and George L. Cowgill, 102–64. Tucson: University of Arizona Press.

Millon, René. 1992. "Teotihuacan Studies: From 1950 to 1990 and Beyond." In *Art, Ideology, and the City of Teotihuacan: A Symposium at Dumbarton Oaks, 8th and 9th October 1988*, edited by Janet Catherine Berlo, 339–430. Washington, DC: Dumbarton Oaks.

Millon, René. 1993. "The Place Where Time Began: An Archaeologist's Interpretation of What Happened in Teotihuacan History." In *Teotihuacan: Art from the City of the Gods*, edited by Kathleen Berrin and Esther Pasztory, 17–43. New York: Thames & Hudson.

Morelos García, Noel. 1982. "Exploraciones en el área central de la Calzada de los Muertos al norte del Río San Juan, dentro del llamado Complejo Calle de los Muertos." In *Memoria del proyecto arqueológico Teotihuacan, 80–82*, edited by Rubén Cabrera Castro, Ignacio Rodríguez García, and Noel Morelos García, 271–317. Mexico City: Instituto Nacional de Antropología e Historia.

Morelos García, Noel. 1993. *Proceso de producción de espacios y estructuras en Teotihuacan*. Mexico City: Instituto Nacional de Antropología e Historia.

Müller, Florencia. 1978. *La cerámica del centro ceremonial de Teotihuacán, México*. Mexico City: Instituto Nacional de Antropología e Historia.

Múnera Bermúdez, Luis Carlos. 1985. "Un taller de cerámica ritual en la Ciudadela, Teotihuacán." MA thesis, Escuela Nacional de Antropología e Historia.

Murakami, Tatsuya. 2010. "Power Relations and Urban Landscape Formation: A Study of Construction Labor and Resources at Teotihuacan." PhD diss., Arizona State University.

Murakami, Tatsuya. 2013. "Persistent Technology, Changing Social Relations: Urban Architecture at Teotihuacan." Paper presented at the 35th Coloquio de Antropología e Historia Regionales, Zamora, Mexico.

Murakami, Tatsuya. 2014. "Social Identities, Power Relations, and Urban Transformations: Politics of Plaza Construction at Teotihuacan." In *Mesoamerican Plazas: Arenas of Community and Power*, edited by Kenichiro Tsukamoto and Takeshi Inomata, 34–49. Tucson: University of Arizona Press.

Murakami, Tatsuya. 2015. "Replicative Construction Experiments at Teotihuacan, Mexico: Assessing the Duration and Timing of Monumental Construction." *Journal of Field Archaeology* 40(3): 263–282.

Murakami, Tatsuya. n.d. "Identifying Bureaucracy in the Archaeological Record: Dimensions of State Power and Urban Construction at Teotihuacan." Unpublished manuscript.

Paynter, Robert, and Randall H. McGuire. 1991. "The Archaeology of Inequality: Material Culture, Domination, and Resistance." In *The Archaeology of Inequality*, edited by Randall H. McGuire and Robert Paynter, 1–27. Oxford: Blackwell.

Rattray, Evelyn Childs 1997. *Entierros y ofrendas en Teotihuacan: Excavaciones, inventario, patrones mortuorios*. Mexico City: Universidad Nacional Autónoma de Mexico.

Rattray, Evelyn Childs. 2001. *Teotihuacan: Ceramics, Chronology and Cultural Trends*. Mexico City: Instituto Nacional de Antropología e Historia / Pittsburgh: University of Pittsburgh.

Sanders, William T., and Susan Toby Evans. 2006. "Rulership and Palaces at Teotihuacan." In *Palaces and Power in the Americas: From Peru to the Northwest Coast*, edited by Jessica Joyce Christie and Patricia Joan Sarro, 256–84. Austin: University of Texas Press.

Séjourné, Laurette. 1966. *Arqueología de Teotihuacan: La cerámica*. Mexico City: Fondo de Cultura Económica.

Sewell, William H., Jr. 1992. "A Theory of Structure: Duality, Agency, and Transformation." *American Journal of Sociology* 98(1): 1–29.

Small, David. 2009. "The Dual-Processual Model in Ancient Greece: Applying a Post-Neoevolutionary Model to a Data-Rich Environment." *Journal of Anthropological Archaeology* 28(2): 205–21.

Smith, Adam T. 2003. *The Political Landscape: Constellation of Authority in Early Complex Polities*. Berkeley: University of California Press.

Smith, Adam T. 2011. "Archaeology of Sovereignty." *Annual Review of Anthropology* 40: 415–32.

Spence, Michael W. 1992. "Tlailotlacan, a Zapotec Enclave in Teotihuacan." In *Art, Ideology, and the City of Teotihuacan: A Symposium at Dumbarton Oaks, 8th and 9th October 1988*, edited by Janet Catherine Berlo, 59–88. Washington, DC: Dumbarton Oaks.

Sprajc, Ivan. 2000. "Astronomical Alignments at Teotihuacan, Mexico." *Latin American Antiquity* 11(4): 403–15.

Sugiyama, Nawa, Saburo Sugiyama, and Alejandro Sarabia G. 2013. "Inside the Sun Pyramid at Teotihuacan, Mexico: 2008–2011 Excavations and Preliminary Results." *Latin American Antiquity* 24(4): 403–32.

Sugiyama, Saburo. 1992. "Rulership, Warfare, and Human Sacrifice at the Ciudadela: An Iconographic Study of Feathered Serpent Representations." In *Art, Ideology, and the City of Teotihuacan: A Symposium at Dumbarton Oaks, 8th and 9th October 1988*, edited by Janet Catherine Berlo, 205–30. Washington, DC: Dumbarton Oaks.

Sugiyama, Saburo. 1998. "Termination Programs and Prehispanic Looting at the Feathered Serpent Pyramid in Teotihuacan, Mexico." In *The Sowing and the Dawning: Termination, Dedication, and Transformation in the Archaeological and Ethnographic Record of Mesoamerica*, edited by Shirley Boteler Mock, 146–64. Albuquerque: University of New Mexico Press.

Sugiyama, Saburo. 2002. "Militarismo plasmado en Teotihuacan." In *Ideología y política a través de materiales, imágenes y símbolos: Memoria de la Primera Mesa Redonda de Teotihuacan*, edited by María Elena Ruiz Gallut, 185–209. Mexico City: Universidad Nacional Autónoma de México / Instituto Nacional de Antropología e Historia.

Sugiyama, Saburo. 2004. "Governance and Policy at Classic Teotihuacan." In *Mesoamerican Archaeology: Theory and Practice*, edited by Julia A. Hendon and Rosemary A. Joyce, 97–123. Oxford: Blackwell.

Sugiyama, Saburo. 2005. *Human Sacrifice, Militarism, and Rulership: Materialization of State Ideology at the Feathered Serpent Pyramid, Teotihuacan*. Cambridge: Cambridge University Press.

Sugiyama, Saburo, and Leonardo López Luján. 2007. "Dedicatory Burial/Offering Complexes at the Moon Pyramid, Teotihuacan: A Preliminary Report of 1998–2004 Explorations." *Ancient Mesoamerica* 18: 127–46.

Taube, Karl A. 1986. "The Teotihuacan Cave of Origin: The Iconography and Architecture of Emergence Mythology in Mesoamerica and the American Southwest." *Res* 12: 51–82.

Tobriner, Stephen. 1972. "The Fertile Ground: An Investigation of Cerro Gordo's Importance to the Town Plan and Iconography of Teotihuacan." In *Teotihuacan: XI Mesa Redonda*, 103–15. Mexico City: Sociedad Mexicana de Antropología.

Wallrath, Matthew. 1967. "The Calle de los Muertos Complex: A Possible Macro-Complex of Structures Near the Center of Teotihuacan." In *Teotihuacan: XI Mesa Redonda*, 113–22. Mexico City: Sociedad Mexicana de Antropología.

Widmer, Randolph J. 1987. "The Evolution of Form and Function in a Teotihuacan Apartment Compound: The Case of Tlajinga 33." In *Teotihuacán: Nuevos datos, nuevas síntesis, nuevos problemas*, edited by Emily McClung de Tapia and Evelyn Childs Rattray, 317–68. Mexico City: Universidad Nacional Autónoma de Mexico.

Widmer, Randolph J., and Rebecca Storey. 1993. "Social Organization and Household Structure of a Teotihuacan Apartment Compound: S3W1:33 of the Tlajinga Barrio." In *Prehispanic Domestic Units in Western Mesoamerica: Studies of the Household, Compound, and Residence*, edited by Robert S. Santley and Kenneth G. Hirth, 87–104. Boca Raton, FL: CRC Press.

Yoffee, Norman. 2005. *Myths of the Archaic State: Evolution of the Earliest Cities, States and Civilizations*. Cambridge: Cambridge University Press.

7

Landscapes, Lordships, and Sovereignty in Mesoamerica

Bryce Davenport and
Charles Golden

We take a materialist view of power and authority in this chapter, recognizing, as Sarah Kurnick (this volume:3) insightfully states in her opening chapter, that "the exercise of power is an intensely physical process that operates through the built environment." Our discussion focuses on the construction, experience, and ontology of landscapes as a component of rulership in Mesoamerica that emerges from daily experience. In particular, we are interested in the perimetric bounding of landscapes and the role of boundary creation and maintenance in the substantiation of rulership and the constitution of political communities in pre-Columbian Mesoamerica. Mesoamerican sovereigns enacted their status and hierarchical positions in no small part through the performance of landscape boundaries, marking territories within which they participated as legitimate, moral monarchs of a political community. In such performances Mesoamerican rulers manifested their authority and power by acting in ways that were fundamentally grounded in and in accord with the greater population's quotidian practice and knowledge of how spaces were delimited and transformed into places.

In framing our approach to borders in terms of landscapes, we emphasize political strategies as explicit social relationships with bounded places, not simply relationships *in* places that are spatially expressed. The development of modern European and American legal understandings of territoriality derives from

DOI: 10.5876/9781607324164.c007

Renaissance and Enlightenment cartography and property law (Olwig 1996; Cosgrove 1999; Harley 1988), and archaeologists frequently express resistance, even antipathy, to the notion that control of territory was a significant concern of many pre-Columbian peoples in Mesoamerica. Even for the expansive Aztec state, Michael E. Smith suggests that polities "were defined not in terms of territory or space—as they are in the modern world—but in terms of personal obligations" (Smith 2012:158), a concept of state often formulated as "hegemonic" in contrast to "territorial" (Beekman 1996). Much the same argument has been made for the Classic Period Maya lowlands, where the performances of state and the need to reinforce and perform the kingdom are taken as indicative of a deeply interpersonal relationship between ruler and ruled (Demarest 1992; Houston 2006; Houston and Inomata 2009:150–62; Hull 2003; Inomata 2006a, 2006b; Looper 2001, 2003, 2009), typically without a clear connection drawn between these political relationships and the delimitation of landscape.

We suggest a role for boundary marking in Mesoamerican political practice that was predicated on exactly those interpersonal relations that so frequently form the contrast to territorial approaches. In turn, this highlights the emic ambiguity between political institutions and local identity and (potentially) removes the contradictions of similarity and difference inherent in authority from open negotiation. In this sense, rulers and polities co-constituted the political landscapes of pre-Columbian Mesoamerica. However, as we have emphasized, territory in the abstract is not a useful category—the formation and operation of political landscapes and borders are historically contingent processes.

The central Mexican *altepetl,* the Yucatecan *cah* (municipal community), the *chinamit* of highland Guatemala, and the *ñuu* of the Mixteca Alta in Oaxaca are all indigenous terms that linked places to people. The construction of kinship, mutual interpersonal and political obligations, responsibility, and subjugation were deeply intertwined with places and the experience of a shared physical environment (Akkeren 2000:24; Braswell 2001:319–25, 2004:133–36; Carmack 1981:83; Hill 1996:64; Hare 2000:84; Hill and Monaghan 1987:74; Licate 1980; Restall 1997, 1998:46–50; Smith 1989, 2012). However, the political importance of landscape does not inherently lead to a political concern with demarcation of bounded territories; indeed, the literature on Mesoamerican polities tends to emphasize political centers rather than peripheries.

Maya capitals, with their clustered pyramids and houses, or the royal palaces and central temples of the altepetl in central Mexico, stand as iconic symbols of these political units in the academic literature. In part, this is because, from indigenous perspectives, they served as the "heads" of political bodies, centers that metonymically evoked the bounded polity as a whole (Hanks 1990:393). Yet a research bias is also at work here because, from the perspective of archaeologists, they are eminently visible, even as ruins, and are thus attractive as sites for excavation. Such center-focused scholarship creates dichotomies between center and periphery, and by extension, between ruler and subject. These dyads inherently suggest dialectical contradictions between space and power, as conceived hierarchically around the seat of royal authority and heterarchically organized subordinate populations in the more dispersed world of commoners.

We argue instead that the ontology of space in Mesoamerica—the bringing into being of place through bodily movement and action—requires a greater emphasis on the edges as well as the center. The bounding of space, not just the centering of place, structured the relationships between rulers and subjects in Mesoamerica. The demarcation of bounded landscapes made manifest the power and authority of rulers not because of a center-periphery hierarchical relationship but rather because the delimitation of places from the microscale of the household and *milpa* up to the macroscale of the state were understood as essentially identical practices. Simply put, they differed in scale but not in kind.

To ground this discussion we draw on ethnohistoric, epigraphic, and archaeological case studies from the Mixteca Alta of Oaxaca, Mexico, and the Maya regions of Mexico and Central America (figures 7.1, 7.2). The comparison of regionally, culturally, and temporally distinct regions is intended as a preliminary and suggestive exploration of commonalities in Mesoamerican rulership. We are keenly aware that such a juxtaposition does not provide full coverage of Mesoamerica, nor does it fit more popular *pars pro toto* cultural combinations like Aztec and Maya or Maya and Teotihuacan (for a fruitful recent study, see Vail and Hernandez 2010). We select these cases because of the evidential strength from richly attested pre-Columbian epigraphic traditions, copious native language colonial documentation, and consequently, strong claims for employing direct historical methods linking ethnographic, historical, and archaeological data in both areas.

BOUNDING LANDSCAPES, EXPERIENCING BORDERS

We take a landscape perspective in this paper because doing so pulls together the threads of bodily movement across extensive spaces and the participation of social groups in formulating not just conceptions, beliefs, and

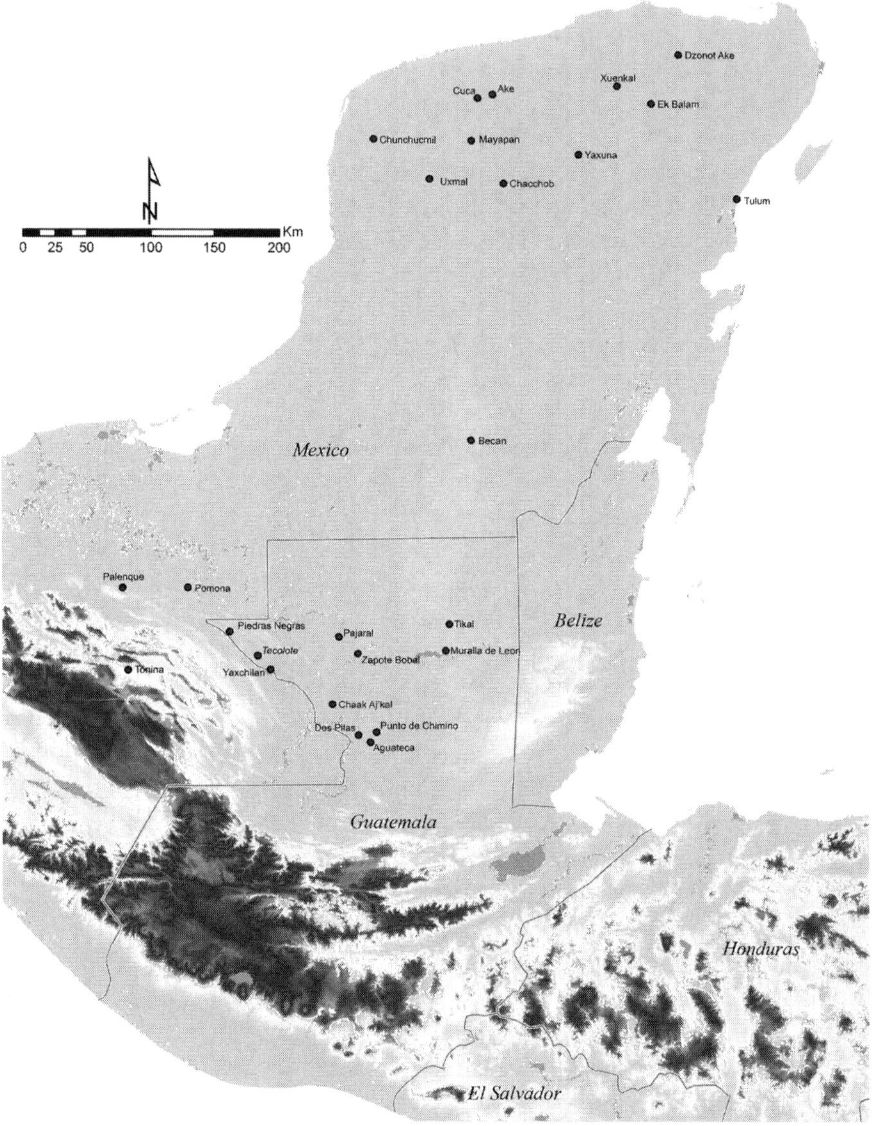

FIGURE 7.1. *Map of the Maya area.*

ideologies of place but the fundamental creation of place. The recursive constitution of place and landscape has a voluminous literature, and this is not a forum to offer an extensive review. In brief, rather than a "natural" setting,

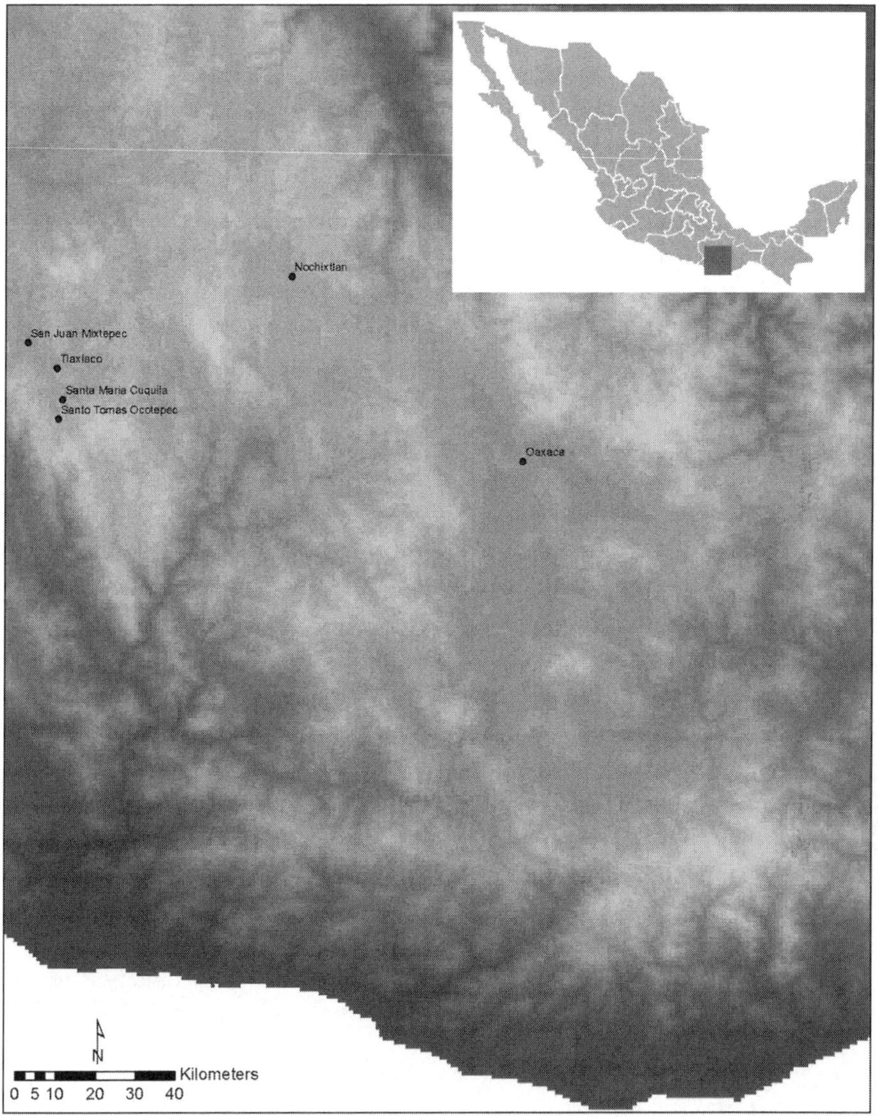

FIGURE 7.2. *Detail map of Oaxaca showing selected sites in the Mixteca Alta.*

landscapes are the spatial and temporal arrangement of social relationships, particularly as they relate to issues of power and authority (Knapp and Ashmore 1999). They require work to create, maintain, or transform. Human activity takes place in space and time, and landscapes contour potential action, even as they are inscribed by previous activity (Cosgrove 1984; Ingold 1993; Lefebvre 1991; Smith 2003). These landscapes-as-palimpsests are not received by an agent viewing an external environment. They are the product of lived experience as humans engage with the concrete possibilities and limitations of her or his circumstances—everything from the placement of features such as roads, plots, and homes to questions of identity and inclusiveness that are predicated on them.

It is the movement, experience, and action of bodies upon, across, and through landscapes that gives much of the context of lived human experience. Bodily practice will, over time, alter the shape, meaning, and understanding of a landscape. We argue that this is not, as Pierre Bourdieu might suggest, the "misrecognition of the limits of cognition" or the "recognition of legitimacy through misrecognition of arbitrariness" (Bourdieu 1977:164, 168). Such a perspective implies a passive belief by community members in social structures created as an outcome of the production of landscapes. Rather, the performance of space and place, the enactment of landscape, actively creates an epistemologically complete and ontologically valid bodily experience across scales (Lefebvre 1991:38–46; Smith 2003:73). It is something that is real, not something that is misrecognized.

Landscapes have concrete impacts on societies and environments because they require constant maintenance, and part of that process is the establishment of limits. As with all components of landscape, bordered places and borderlands exist as experiential realities because they are maintained and reinforced by bodies that perform them. Moreover, the acts of bordering are performed as bodily experience from the level of the individual ("personal space") to the household and house, from the village to the polity as a whole. The performance of boundaries becomes a primary prerogative and method of organizing governing institutions, not necessarily in contradiction to the actions of individuals but rather in emulation or co-option of individual and small group performance.

In modern states, the limits of a given political landscape are defined with regard to, and extend out from, a political, economic, or cultural center toward a space conceived of as the edge. The most extreme expression of this principle can be found in the ideal of the modern nation-state, where juridical, political, economic, and even moral prerogatives are explicitly linked to and profoundly defined by the control of what are legally defined as fixed borders (Anderson and O'Dowd 1999; Brunet-Jailly 2005; Cunningham and Heyman 2004; Hannerz 1997; Kearney 2004; Newman 2006; Rumford 2006; Van Houtum and Struever 2002; Walters 2006). Although borders may structure the daily practice and behavior of people who live in border zones, political boundaries are impositions from the political center, often with no relation to local concerns. Tension and contradictions between centers of power and authority and their borders and frontiers are an inherent outcome of this construction of state landscapes.

A consideration of the bounding of territorial landscapes in modern states is therefore conceptually useful here primarily as a contrast to the construction of delimited landscapes in pre-Columbian societies such as those of the Mixteca and the Maya area. Critics are right to point out that a territorial approach to Mesoamerican civilizations may carry unwarranted assumptions of homogenous control, absolute space, and temporal stasis that are not appropriate in a pre-Columbian context (Chance 1996; Hoekstra 1990; Smith 2005; Tomaszewski and Smith 2010). Others have argued that even the most nuanced studies of territorially defined polities are based exclusively on ethnographic and ethnohistoric data and therefore reflect elements either transplanted by or in reaction to colonial encounters (Wolf 1957, 1986; Monaghan 1995).

Indeed, a common theme of colonial era land documents in Mesoamerica is the metric quality of boundaries based on European cartographic conventions for the measurement, occupation, and control of pre-social space (Cosgrove 1992; Harley 1992), leading to the abundance of primordial titles used in Spanish courts to substantiate claims to ownership and sometimes to justify new land grabs (Hamann 2012; Hanks 2010; Restall 1998; Terraciano 2001). We agree that such juridical notions of fixed landscapes in Mesoamerica were a product of the colonial administration and the economics of an *encomienda* system that assigned labor rights to Spanish settlers, *indios hidalgos*, indigenous communities, and individuals based on notions of fixed and (ideally) unchanging boundaries. Within the legal documents of the colonial period there are, however, strong indications of a pre-Columbian notion of bounding ownership and authority that extend back at least to the Classic Period (ca. 250–900 CE), if not earlier. There seems to be a deeply indigenous conception of bounded landscapes that are at once experienced as fixed and real, even as they are dynamic and performed places (Farriss 1978:202). Borders were, and often still are, performed through word and deed rather than encoded in legal documents, and the same processes at work in the house were extended to larger political structures. The emergence of polity borders from daily practice is critical to our arguments on the concomitant identification between ruler and territory.

DELIMITING SPACE, CREATING PLACE THROUGH SPEECH AND MOVEMENT

In Mesoamerica the delimitation of bounded spaces practiced at the political edge of modern towns or pre-Columbian polities traditionally finds its model in the home and the agricultural field, the milpa. Evon Vogt (1965) argues that for Zinacantecos of modern Chiapas, the political structure of the community at all scales replicates that of the house and takes the form of an "aggregate of aggregates . . . an orderly replication of increasing structural scale (Vogt 1962, 1965:344; see also Rosaldo 1968). Politics in practice is rarely so "orderly," but we do suggest that a scalar understanding of bounded space and political practice is central to understanding Mesoamerican rulership.

As William F. Hanks suggests for Maya communities in Yucatan, all domestic organization is founded on the *haál*, the perimeter or outer boundary, which "divides the inner, private space from the outer, public one" (Hanks 1990:324). The perimeter with the center point forms the quincunx so central to Mesoamerican thought and imagery in all periods. Bounded space creates a whole place, a landscape that is complete, unsegmented, and defined by the edges. Indeed, the domestic landscape is a replica of the ordered universe. Hanks (1990:335–36) argues that this space extends from the laying out of the household altar up to the level of the entire domestic landholding and, by extension, to the community beyond. Movement of the body through space and time is paralleled in spoken and written language, which partakes in the work of boundary making. In highland and lowland Maya languages, couplets and other more expansive narrative parallelisms mark event boundaries in processions that move the listener through time and space (Gossen 1974a; Hofling 1993:178). In Mixtec examples, households are explicitly identified with activity before structure. Feeding and clothing define a corporate group, acts at once of cosmogenic importance and as basic tokens of affection (Monaghan 1995:356). In part, this is a feature of how little time is spent in the house itself, tying the agricultural activities in far-flung fields directly into the demarcation of social space and the production of social substance. The boundaries that are drawn by inclusion or exclusion in these domestic spheres are then reinforced by communal activities that play out across the broader landscape—building houses, working fields, and hosting fiestas as cargo. Outside the perimeter of the altar, the house, and the community is a space-time that is not unified, that is fractured and dangerous, animalistic, amoral, and inhuman (Hanks 1990:349; Taube 2003:464; Wisdom 1940:421–22).

This is a process of creating boundaries in space-time with physical movement of the body, and the linguistic evocation of movement is echoed in understandings of how the world itself was created. In the K'iche Popul Vuh, the sky and earth are staked out at their corners and measured, just as a maize field traditionally was for cultivation (Christenson 2004:56; Tedlock 1996, 220). In Zinacantán, this replication of bounded space at different scales is recognized from the smallest to the largest order, since the universe as a whole is "like a house, like a table [altar]" (Vogt 1993:11; see also Taube 2003:462). This ontology is mirrored by other Maya language communities, including the Chortí, for whom the maize field, altars, and world are identified with one another (Wisdom 1940:430).

In delimiting boundaries, the concern ethnographically and ethnohistorically is not with the identification of distinct internal features of the landscape but rather in demarcating lines with no width that extend between points, delimiting the edges of the landscape (Carmack 1995:40–43; Hanks 2010:289–90). People gave life to these borders in writing and in performances. Hanks (2010) calls particular attention to what he calls "tour guide" perambulations of the features of boundary markers, in which officials, neighbors sharing the boundary, and others proceed in steps. The Yaxkukul surveys of Yucatan evoke the performance of territorial limits: "Southward I go counting stone markers; it goes all the way until it arrives at the foot of Mul Ac; there's a marker there" (Hanks 2010:300).

Again, bounded places could be enacted through both bodily motion and the performative word that moves the speaker and audience through space and time (Gossen 1974a; Hofling 1993:178). Toponyms and personal names in Mixtec codices were brought into relief with the present through recitations and public display, a tradition that continued with oral litigation in the Spanish courts. Colonial documents on borders are thus better viewed not as static records of a past, but as repositories for spoken performances that were conceived of as perpetually in action and which recreated the borders even when they could not be walked (Hanks 2010:283–314). "Like the practices of prayer, land documents were world-making, even if that world was subject to contestation and revision" (Hanks 2010:289), a reality that is mirrored in pre-Columbian texts (Houston and Stuart 1998; Hull 2003:375–76; Stuart 1996, 1998). Visual and verbal metonymy also played a critical role in the performance of territory, making "objects of landowners and humanizing features of the land" (Restall 1997:199; see also Roys 1967:63–66). This is more than simple rhetoric—punning names and performs those locations, bringing them into being as places. The pieces that act to embody the whole are things of the highest ranking order (Hanks 1990:393).

Colonial period documents also make it patently clear, however, that boundaries were contestable and required reinscription and maintenance. People, aware of this danger, sought multiple routes to literally solidify boundaries and make them material through perpetual performance. In some instances, durable stone features—walls, stones, cenotes, and more—marked boundaries. Villages evacuated during the colonial era reductions also retained social salience for the purposes of delimiting space for decades or centuries after their occupants departed (Hanks 2010:306; Kowaleski et al. 2009:310; Spores and Balkansky 2013:125). There was, however, also resistance to the placement of boundary stones for fear those stones might be moved or become the cause of disagreements over the "real" borders between location-based communities (*cah*) and demarcations of the edges of forests (Restall 1998:92–94; cf. Restall 1998:125–28). Thus, while physical markers could act as significant features of delimiting landscapes, performance, word, and ritual acts that often leave no enduring material sign were more important still (Farriss 1984:148; Stephens 1848:265–67; Hanks 2010:287).

The inscription of place and delimitation of landscapes was, and is, more than a claim of ownership in Mixtec and Maya communities. Bounded space is inextricably linked to moral behavior, authority, and legitimacy. For the Chamula of highland Chiapas, the internal boundaries and outer limits of the community are critically important for interpersonal interaction; beyond those boundaries the places are delimited not by precise notions of space but by the morality or amorality of the people outside of Chamula (Gossen 1974a:18). In Yucatan, the laying out of boundary lines is conjoined linguistically by the term *toh*, which means "straight" and "truth" and historically carries implications of virtue, justice, and correct moral behavior (Barrera Vasquez 1980:801; Hanks 1990:357; Taube 2003:465).

When forced to live outside of properly bounded places, humans become animal-like, amoral, and uncivilized (Taube 2003). Outside of the limits of the house, people are exposed, their behavior potentially dangerous, like the wilds of the forest (Haviland and Haviland 1982, 1983:353). In the Chilam Balam of Chumayel, when the Itza were forced out of Chichen Itza they lost their status as civilized people and "went beneath the trees, beneath the bushes, beneath the vines, to their misfortune" (Roys 1933:136). In the Mixteca, the mythical *tiumi*, or "people of the wilds," are described as living without households as both cause and consequence of their primitiveness (Monaghan 1995:32).

The distinction between moral or immoral behavior, human versus inhuman behavior, need not be agentive in the sense suggested by Anthony Giddens (1984). The inadvertent transgression of delimited boundaries may be considered immoral no matter the intent of the transgressor (Hanks 1990:324; Danziger 2010). In no small part because they are ignorant of boundaries, wild animals wandering outside of human-forged spatial boundaries, and transgressing those boundaries, are improper and amoral (Burkhart 1986:113; Taube 2003:469).

Thus, a body or bodies able to actively delimit the landscape are inherently imbued with a significant authority: they have the power to move as moral beings along the perilous edges of controlled and controllable space and to define who is encompassed and who is excluded by these bounded places, to define who is human and who is other. To bring order to these spaces and bring places into being are "inherently good and ethically correct human acts" (Taube 2003:465).

BOUNDING PRE-COLUMBIAN MAYA KINGDOMS

We have discussed above the identity of power and authority across scales of bounded landscapes, beginning with the household altar, expanding to the house, the milpa, and the larger political community of which they are a part. At each scale, bounding creates a singular and coherent moral landscape that represents a world in proper order—one that requires work to maintain, but which only some bodies are empowered to delimit and create. As we focus now specifically on pre-Columbian Maya kingdoms, we are challenged by the same issues raised by Joanne Baron (this volume) in her discussion of commoner participation in patron deity veneration: we believe that similar processes were at work across all hierarchical status levels, but our most robust evidence comes from the noble and royal contexts that have yielded rich textual and iconographic data.

Yet, data from commoner households across the Maya area suggest that daily practice and ritual behavior guided delimitation of houses and houselots much as in historical and modern communities. Archaeological excavations have typically focused on place making rituals that center the house, making it a social and moral place, particularly through the interment of burials and caches beneath interior floors (e.g., McAnany 1995). Finding the limits of the domestic space outside the house structure itself can be more challenging simply because the material signs of such boundaries may not be so obvious.

However, in some Maya cities, such as Chunchucmil and Mayapan in Yucatan, the bounded limits of the household unit, or small groups of households and even neighborhoods, are conspicuously marked by stone walls and walkways (Hare and Masson 2012; Hutson et al. 2004; Hutson and Stanton 2007; Magnoni et al. 2012). Even where such boundaries are not obviously set in stone, it is possible to reconstruct the repeated movements of household members in and around architectural spaces and look at discard patterns of artifacts to infer the delimited landscapes made real by these quotidian practices (e.g., Arnauld et al. 2012; Hutson et al. 2007; Hutson and Stanton 2007; Lemonnier 2012; Morton 2012; Robin 2002; Stockett 2005).

Scaling up the performance of delimiting houses to the more imposing spaces of royal residences, we can also see hints of household-level rituals from palatial inscriptions that record dedication ceremonies in which royal residences and other buildings were enlivened as social places through fire or censing ritual (Stuart 1998). David Stuart (1998) suggests that, by analogy with modern and historically documented rituals, the censing of these pre-Columbian royal buildings involved feeding not just the center but the four corners of the house. So, too, the working and bounding of the milpa finds its way into royal inscriptions as a trope of rulership. Sovereigns do not simply supervise ritual or political events; they work them and cultivate them as one would work and cultivate a milpa (Stuart 2011:2; 2005; Taube 2003:464). Even in the elite epicenters of Classic Period sites, however, not every structure bears such dedicatory inscriptions. Nonetheless, James A. Doyle (2013; see also Powell 2010) has demonstrated that the same logic and geometry applied to laying out the four corners of the commoner household and the milpa are writ large on the monumental buildings at the heart of Maya cities. Thus, just as commoners delimited their milpas, houses, and neighborhoods on one scale, so, too, kings and queens enacted and delimited their royal households, with their milpas being the courtly city and the polity writ large.

At this polity-level scale too, moral places had to be brought into being and bounded, formed out of amoral, asocial space to encompass the political community (Houston et al. 2003; Sharer and Golden 2004). Such moral authority implies a social contract between ruler and ruled that almost certainly mirrored obligations between humans and the vivified world of nonhuman beings (that which Euro-Americans tend to gloss as "supernatural") in which substantive reciprocal obligations needed to be met to maintain a world in order (Houston et al. 2003; Monaghan 1995, 1998; Tokovinine 2008). Beyond the borders within which legitimate moral authority extended, power might still be expressed, but such expressions would not have involved the same social contract and instead required hegemonic relationships with other figures of power and authority, or the exercise of military power, to maintain (Golden and Scherer 2013).

We can see archaeological and epigraphic evidence for the creation and performance of large-scale political landscapes delimited by the performance of rulers and their courtiers. Boundary making varied from polity to polity depending on the nature of the political hierarchy, relationships with neighboring polities, and underlying geography and environmental factors such as vegetation (cf. Beekman 1996:136). Some boundaries left profound material marks on the landscape, as with the walled borderland settlements and roadways that served as boundary markers in Yucatan (Kurjack and Andrews 1974), while others were more ephemeral. Indeed, even within the same polity, boundary marking took dramatically different forms along different territorial limits (Golden et al. 2008; Golden and Davenport 2013; Golden and Scherer 2013; Scherer and Golden 2009).

Perhaps the most famous, and enigmatic, of boundary features in the Maya lowlands is a system of earthworks that encompasses portions of the immediate hinterland surrounding epicentral Tikal (Webster et al. 2007). Soil and rock were scooped from the ground and piled alongside the trench that was formed. In some places the channel dips several meters below the original surface of the earth, and the adjacent berm rises similarly above the ground. In other sections the berm is barely visible and the ditch less than two meters deep.

Because the physical form of the earthworks does not completely encircle epicentral Tikal, Jay E. Silverstein, David Webster, and their colleagues (Silverstein et al. 2009; Webster et al. 2007) are divided over what, if any, function they may have served. Because they do not fully encircle the city, and in many locations are quite low, they do not make sense as defensive features. In some places they may have served to manage drainage, but this function does not make sense for all extant sections; and because they do not form a solid perimeter, there are doubts about their role as boundary markers delimiting a territory of some sort. Webster and colleagues (2007:60) also suggest that the earthworks may simply be incomplete, a labor abandoned mid-construction.

However, the earthworks need not have formed a complete durable and material perimeter for the purposes of engaging ruler and ruled in communal acts of boundary making. Even the labor required for occasional additions to the earthworks would be sufficient for such purposes (Golden and Scherer 2013:163). Further, it seems plausible that, as in the ethnohistoric cases discussed above, a stepwise progression of ruler, courtiers, and other community members could have inscribed the territory as much as the actual construction of the earthworks. Thus, although they may appear unfinished to modern archaeological eyes, for the political community of Tikal they were completed in word and motion, marking the edges of the moral community.

Much as at Tikal, research in the Usumacinta River region has revealed another mode of delimiting the kingdom: a boundary wall system along the northern limits of the Yaxchilan kingdom (figure 7.3). Walls and hilltop redoubts cross from east to west, comprising part of an architectural landscape that includes the palaces of border lords at sites such as La Pasadita and Tecolote (Golden et al. 2008; Golden and Scherer 2013; Scherer and Golden 2009, 2014). The walls, defensive positions, and broken terrain constituted a formidable martial landscape and give the impression of permanence.

Whatever function the wall systems of the Yaxchilan kingdom had, it is not only their durable materiality that participated in the bounding of the moral landscape of the polity. The personal performance of the ruler, his courtiers, and the populace were required to constitute, activate, and perpetually maintain (or redefine) the limits of the kingdom. Like the earthworks of Tikal, participation by many members of the populace in building, maintaining, and manning the defensive positions of the Yaxchilan kingdom's wall engaged ruler and ruled in the creation of landscape.

For Yaxchilan, however, the walls were reinforced by the emplacement of palatial border sites with monuments depicting the ruler of Yaxchilan and his subordinates dancing, scattering offerings, dominating captives, and receiving them as tribute. The texts on such royal monuments are not necessarily or centrally concerned with the biographic history of the sovereign or other individuals depicted thereon. Such inscriptions are instead primarily concerned with "the placement, creation, and activation of ritual things and spaces" (Stuart 1998:375). They are devices that aided the body of the ruler in creating the moral space-time that centered the kingdom and created place from space (Monaghan 1998).

Such inscribed monuments were particularly potent because they united the image and self of the ruler in perpetual performance (Houston and Stuart 1998; Houston, Taube, and Stuart 2006:72–81; Stuart 1996). Like the colonial era documents, the texts on these royal monuments were performed. They were enacted by ritually charged actors who may have been the depicted ruler but may also have been a surrogate—perhaps a ritual specialist or royal descendant of the depicted monarch—competent to present a literate style of history (Gossen: 1974b: 398–99; Hull 2003:375–76). Because the actions depicted on these monuments are ongoing, and the people portrayed are perpetually present, the implication is that the ruler and his border lords perpetually enact the border (Houston and Stuart 1998; Hull 2003; Golden 2010; Golden and Scherer 2013; Scherer and Golden 2014; Stuart 1996).

The limits of the territory were danced and fought and performed into being by the ever-present, ever-living bodies of the ruler and his subordinate depicted as the epitome of controlled human behavior. The depicted captives

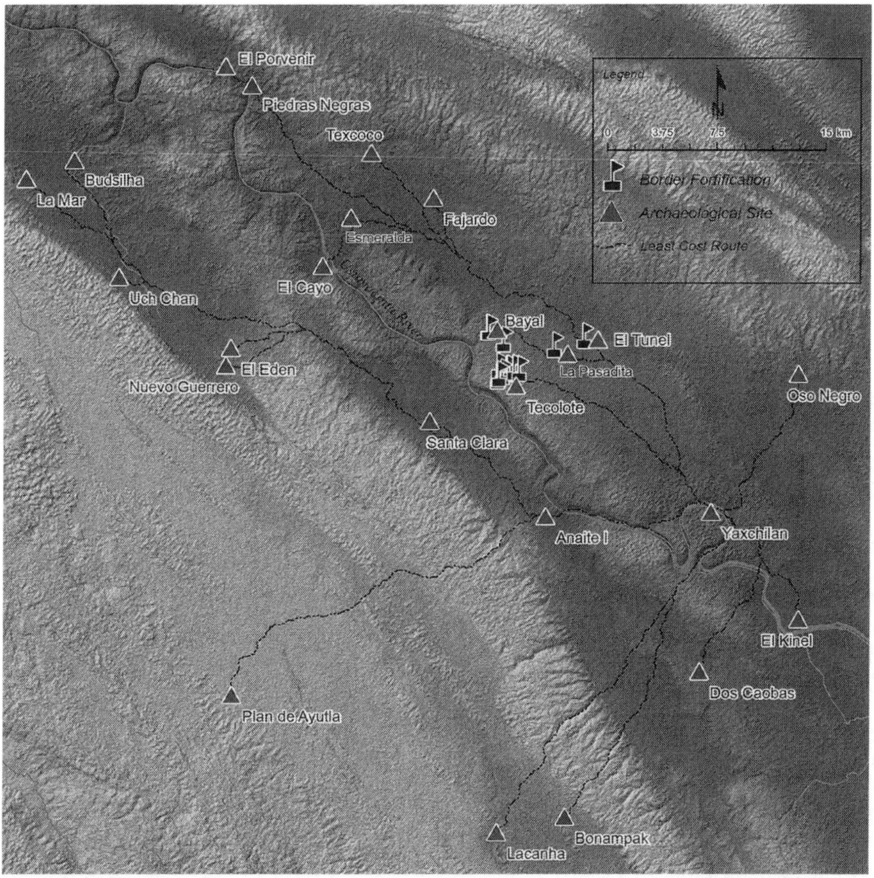

FIGURE 7.3. *Map of the region between Piedras Negras, Guatemala, and Yaxchilan, Mexico, showing border sites and fortifications along the northern border of the Yaxchilan kingdom, in what today is Guatemala, north of the sites of Tecolote, La Pasadita, and El Tunel. This system may continue to the west in Mexico, but field research is pending there (map by Charles Golden).*

are twisted and writhing, animalistic beings from outside the moral landscape of the kingdom (Houston, Taube, and Stuart 2006:202–26; Taube 2003), who stand as metonymic symbols of their places of origin outside the boundaries of the community. Thus, on these ever-present, ever-active sculptures, the limits of the kingdom were performed by kings, nobles, and captives, replicating the distinction between milpa and forest, and spaces in the house and outside the house at smaller scales. As at Tikal, the Yaxchilan kingdom is not entirely encircled and delimited by obvious material signs like walls and monuments. However, it is a reasonable hypothesis to suggest that other material indices of the royal domain may be found in future research or, if not, that such territorial limits were nonetheless repeatedly performed and reinscribed in ways that simply left relatively little in the way of a durable record.

EMBODYING RULERS IN THE MIXTECA ALTA

In Oaxaca, the linkage between ruler and bounded landscape is even more overt than in examples from the Maya region, and, correspondingly, the complications of this political strategy are more clearly defined. Rulers maintained exclusive relations over and through the landscape; however, as in the Maya area, these relationships are not unique to rulers but rather a part of a common genre of political idiom. Postclassic codices and colonial documents alike depict marriage alliances, genealogies, and personal identity from across social strata in the Mixteca in terms of *ñuu*, glossed variously as anything from "city-state" to simply "settled place." The word is pervasive in Mixtec, and the Alta region was known locally as *ñuu dzahui* or "the place of rain." However, there is a clear tradition across sources of ñuu also referring specifically to sociopolitical units, and more recent research has clarified that ñuu in this sense are best understood as "potentially autonomous states" (Terraciano 2001:347–48). These coherent territories bound multiple local communities (*siqui*, broadly commensurate with the Nahua *calpolli* and Spanish *barrio*) through shared historical claims to land and governing institutions.

Ñuu were centered, both conceptually and pragmatically, on the royal household; today the defining feature of the smallest modern community in the region is still the municipal palace. The lords of these establishments—*yya* (male) or *yya dzehe* (female)—held hereditary rights to tracts of land, labor obligations, and tribute. Although some areas were also held in common by the ñuu, siqui, and individual households, across much of the Mixteca, the royal estate co-opted corporate systems of allocation as part of the yya's prerogative (Terraciano 2001:206). The proliferation of land-tenure systems underscores the distinctions between political borders and property lines—however these plots were arranged, they still "belonged" to the ñuu and explicitly formed part of the ruler's estate (Spores and Balkansky 2013:110).

This estate, the *añiñe*, was based on the same organizational template as any other Mixtec household, with structures abutting an open-air patio that was used for ritual performance as well as being the functional space for most activity. The household landscape was discontinuous, with the house structure serving as the integrative nexus for working close terraces and far-flung fields and bringing together kin for marriage, important festivals, and resolving conflicts; these activities were scaled up to include greater segments of the population in the añiñe.

Houses in the Mixteca are said to be "cooked" during their construction to separate them from wild lands (Monaghan 1995:34), indicating not only physical transformation of the landscape but also the affective action that continually reconstitutes the household. The conceptual separation of the house from the world outside is replicated with the añiñe as premier household, establishing a focal point for the community and the locus of boundary making activities—reciting the glyphic toponyms of subject communities from codices, arbitrating disputes, and bringing together representative nobility from across the ñuu for feasts, marriages, and other integrative events. The performance of boundary activities within the royal house created the ñuu as the royal household, linking statecraft with smaller scale and everyday activity.

During the colonial period, añiñe were symbolically and legally the centers of their communities as the repositories for land documents such as title deeds and plot boundaries, and in pre-Columbian contexts, the image of the royal household, both structure and ruling couple, frequently represents the ñuu as a whole. Kevin Terraciano (2001:165) describes the *teccalli* as a close Nahuatl analogue of the añiñe, "as much to a lordly establishment . . . as a physical structure, a sociopolitical entity as an actual residence." Households can be understood as landscape-oriented territorial strategies, a set of actions that mark inclusive and exclusive space; in turn, we can connect these practices to the production of community and state boundaries as distinct from our more familiar cartographic abstractions.

As discrete territories, ñuu were remarkably persistent through both time and political reorganization. Stephen A. Kowalewski and colleagues' (2009) comprehensive survey of the Alta found that many of the major Postclassic and early colonial centers had roots stretching back to the Early Classic, despite a period of wide-scale abandonment at the end of the Late Classic. Ñuu also survived as distinct entities even while joined into *yuhuitayu*, a concept that describes both dynastic alliance through marriage and the polity formed by the communities so linked (Pohl, Monaghan, and Stiver 1997:206). The term *yuhuitayu* was a pun that invoked both the seat of rulership—a reed mat, or *yuhui*—and the royal couple, *tayu*, as metonymic devices for the domain as a whole (Terraciano 2001:158). The articulation of ñuu within yuhuitayu meant that governance was localized through both semantic naturalization and affinal relation. The marriage of rulers did not erase local identities but appropriated their forms of representation to conflate yya and yya dzehe with the bounded landscapes they ruled.

Since Alfonso Caso's (1938a, 1960a) early explorations, many scholars have directed their efforts toward identifying archaeological sites with toponyms from the Mixtec codices. Place-names in this region were highly localized, at a scale smaller than seen in colonial Nahuatl documents such as the Codex Mendoza (Byland and Pohl 1994:36). The linguistic and visual representation of place in the Mixteca indelibly linked socially defined space to immediate physical geography—the hills, towns, rivers, and plains of this rugged terrain (Smith 1973a). Ñuu and yuhuitayu were concrete entities, correlated with specific features on the landscape, and their boundaries were likewise defined in terms of places rather than abstract boundary limits (figure 7.4). In colonial documents, toponyms are sometimes appended with alphabetic glosses or cross symbols to indicate this border status (Smith 1998:82). In contrast to the ethnographic evidence from Yucatan, noted above, boundary lines do not seem to have been a concern; whether this is a regional preference, a response to colonial legal requirements, or simply a practice for which we no longer have evidence in the Mixteca is unclear.

Archaeologically and ethnohistorically, we find outpost settlements, ballcourts, marketplaces, cave shrines, small cardinal mound groups, and defensive fortifications as some of the anthropogenic features that have been recognized as boundary markers for polities from the Early Classic Period onward (Kowalewski et al. 2009:310, 324; Pohl, Monaghan, and Stiver 1997). As in the examples of Tikal and Yaxchilan, the manifestation of these border activities was not uniform within or between polities, and oral histories surrounding unmodified geological features and the absence of settlement between centers can also appear as boundary strategies in some instances. Although we now have considerable insight into the glyphic identification of many major archaeological sites in the region, the possible correlations between modern municipal boundaries and pre-Columbian territories are much less secure.

To name a place in the Mixteca, either verbally or visually, was to integrate it into a system of governance that was fundamentally genealogical. Claims to ñuu and yuhuitayu were inherited, and the Mixtec codices have a particularly historical bent among the surviving manuscripts from across pre-Columbian Mesoamerica. These elite narratives legitimized the authority of the yya both over and through places. Bruce E. Byland and John M. D. Pohl (1994:39) argue that "one of the keys to interpreting the codices is to understand that persons associated with place signs also serve as symbols for their communities by virtue of the fact that they are the lords of these towns." The reverse also

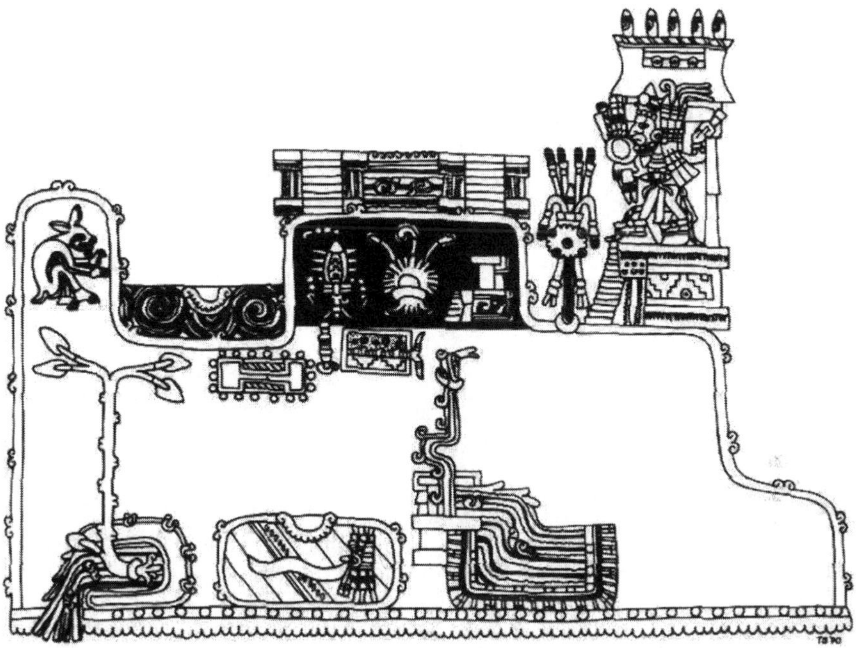

FIGURE 7.4. *Detail from page 22 of the Codex Zouche-Nuttall showing the toponyms of subsidiary and border settlements inside of the glyph for the ñuu (drawing taken from Byland and Pohl 1994:figure 20, courtesy of University of Oklahoma Press).*

may have been true, with minor nobles being named as places rather than persons in early colonial documents (Smith 1998:34). In this light, maps and genealogies in the Mixteca are one and the same, and rulers and territories co-constitute each other in the political life of the region.

The implications that conflating yya with ñuu as a bounded, performed place are illustrated through a historical case study of border negotiation in Santa María Cuquila, a community in the modern *municipio* of Tlaxiaco, known in Mixtec as Ñucuiñe, or "Town of the Tiger." Mary Elizabeth Smith (1998) has traced Ñucuiñe's glyphic toponym through both pre-Columbian and colonial sources (figure 7.5). A 1584 legal document describes the boundaries of Ñucuiñe with territories controlled by other yuhuitayu; these borders retained their integrity through several legal challenges and were recognized by a royal grant in 1707 (Ruiz Medrano 2010:323). However, in the early eighteenth century, the royal couple died and left an heir too young to rule. Nine-year-old Doña Teresa moved to Tepejillo in the Mixteca Baja with her uncle, taking

Figure 7.5. *Detail of the Lienzo de Ocotepec, an early colonial document showing the boundaries between Santo Tomas Ocotepec and Santa Maria Cuquila. Both geomorphological features and other settlements are employed to this effect (drawing taken from Mary Elizabeth Smith 1998:figure 34, courtesy of Vanderbilt University).*

Cuquila's legal titles with her as personal property—a common practice in the region. Almost immediately, the rulers of surrounding ñuu filed suit against the *cabildo* of Cuquila, claiming their own hereditary rights to lands that were no longer defended by local royalty (Ruiz Medrano 2010:330). Without either primordial documents or royal heirs, Cuquila's lands quickly shrank in a tumultuous series of legal battles, raids, and assassinations.

The link between ruler and ruled through shared space also constituted a ñuu as a moral community. The capacity of these boundaries to mark the limits of legitimate authority is still very much an active concern in these areas—as John Monaghan (1995), Ethelia Ruiz Medrano (2010), and others have shown—historically and ethnographically, the communities of Mixteca Alta, and especially the Tlaxiaco region, have remained geographically isolated to the extent that each pueblo has its own dialect and mestizo populations and institutions are not prevalent. This relative isomorphism between kinship, language, and landscape cements not only the cohesion of the ñuu but the urgency of defending territorial borders as more than lines on a map. As seen in the example of Cuquila, high levels of intercommunity conflict characterize Oaxaca, in contrast to other primarily indigenous areas in Latin America (Dennis 1987; Ruiz Medrano 2010; Spores and Balkansky 2013:215). Records of these events make it clear that above and beyond opportunities for political and economic development, challenges to territorial integrity are also challenges to identity by groups outside of the moral fabric of the community, paralleling the example of Chamula (Gossen 1974a; Monaghan 1995:27). While our archaeological knowledge of conflict in this region is relatively scarce in comparison to the rich legal record of the colonial and national periods, it is clear from the localized nature of both codices and fortifications that these are long-standing patterns.

In pre-Columbian and early colonial contexts, the royal household formed the institutional focus of many of the morally constitutive actions we find ethnographically—labor obligations, feasting, and maintaining boundaries. These practices outline the ways in which ñuu were conceived of and performed as bounded landscapes from the earliest colonial records, and the language, objects, and locations deployed all point to a continuation of pre-Hispanic systems of territoriality. The primary colonial context of border performance was litigation over these prerogatives in courts—an extension of the former oratory practice that signaled rulership across Mesoamerica. Raids, rituals, and markets continue to be important boundary activities today (Pohl, Monaghan, and Stiver 1997; Ruiz Medrano 2010), and are couched in the connection that modern communities have with their antecedents. In turn, yya are still recognized as fundamental to the landscape; modern accounts ascribe them generative powers over the terrain, and modern Cuquila uses the glyph for their ancestral yuhuitayu as the seal of the pueblo (Ruiz Medrano 2010:248). Significantly, in contrast to examples from Chiapas and Yucatan, the high levels of intercommunity conflict in the Mixteca, whether legal or armed, continue to be the foremost vector of boundary inscription—competing claims and transgressions cement the historical continuity of borders while prescribing appropriate actions at the edges between moral communities. Leadership, past and present, revolved around organizing border activity in a process that simultaneously defined the territory and the ruler.

This tight link between rulers and territories in the Mixteca allowed yya to present themselves as foundational to local identity, even while claiming fundamentally different origins from the populace. For yuhuitayu, this was necessarily the case: half of the emblematic couplet came from a nonlocal dynasty. The conceptual friction between being close enough to rule but far enough to be authoritative is elided, but not without generating a new set of vulnerabilities. John K. Chance (2010; Menegus Bornemann 2005) evaluates the difference between pre-contact yuhuitayu and later colonial *cacicazgos* granted by the Spanish crown by noting that the suite of rights and responsibilities accorded to rulers became defined exclusively in terms of property ownership. Seignorial rights, and by extension the management of the ñuu, left the purview of the yya. In some communities, this opened up paths of resistance for commoners to repudiate hereditary labor obligations, while in others (such as Cuquila), absent owners were unable to defend their newly defined and diminished rights. While the Spanish legal system restricted the channels of negotiation and condensed the fluid political structure, it is clear that the boundaries of the landscape were the primary field of political contestation and underlay other claims to legitimacy throughout the Mixteca.

The new relationship to land as property disrupted the parallels between statecraft and household, and many rulers took to living in Spanish centers for access to the courts and colonial administration. This "absentee landlordism" provoked outrage from members of the ñuu—rulers were dwelling outside of their moral communities, quite literally, living immorally. Pre-Columbian and early colonial governance not only extended household patterns of boundary making, they relied on them for coherence. Reduplication of ordered, bounded, and hierarchically arranged places across scales gave these communities incredible resilience through time while also undercutting the institutions of broader governance, as new legal regimes and elite settlement patterns took hold.

SOME PROBLEMS OF CONTRADICTIONS IN BOUNDED LANDSCAPES

Despite our argument that the power and authority vested in rulers to delimit territories of the moral community was emergent from smaller scale practices of daily household life, there is obviously a glaring dichotomy that we have not delved into: many bodies in the populace at large were vested with the authority to delimit household altars, the house, and the milpa, but only a very few bodies were empowered to delimit the polity. This distinction between the power afforded to different bodies in setting limits at different scales was a point of potential contradiction. Indeed, such distinctions often became lines of political fracture along which Mesoamerican polities shattered.

One method found across Mesoamerica to distinguish these bodies is to ground hereditary claims in a primordial genesis, coeval with the territory itself. Scenes of birth from caves, trees, and rivers ensconced the ruling lineages as landscape features, naturalizing their authority. In some instances, the places of origin appear to have been tropes more than geography. At the time of the Spanish arrival in Mesoamerica, for instance, the Nahuatl Chicomoztoc and Tollan, the "place of the seven caves" and "among the reeds" served as sources of legitimate origin (Gillespie 1989; Smith 2012). So, too, the K'iche lords of Q'umarkaj (Carmack 1981; Christenson 2007) came out of a vague "east," with Tulan (Tollan) a later stop on their rise to power. In Yucatan, the Chilam Balam of Chumayel requires the performer to engage with the language of Zuyua, a place also mentioned in highland Maya documents with no known geographic specificity but a clear connection to rulership (Roys 1967; Stross 1983). In the Classic Period, the rulers of Palenque's dynasty looked for their origin to a place called Toktahn, though whether this is an as yet unidentified physical place or an otherwise intangible place of origin like Chicomoztoc remains unclear (Stuart and Stuart 2008:113).

The genealogy of the Mixtecs was, instead, locally grounded and readily identifiable. The codices name an area called Yute Coo, "River of the Serpent," in the Nochixtlan Valley as the place of origin for many of the original dynasties of major kingdoms (Byland and Pohl 1994:116). The sixteenth-century Chontal lords of Acalan-Tixchel similarly located their origins in a specific location, on the shrine island of Cozumel, an origin from which they claimed no small part of their authority (Restall 1998:58–59). Mixtec nobles distinguished themselves from commoners as having originated from sacred trees rather than the earth (Jansen 1982b). Unlike the lordly peregrinations claimed by the Nahuas of central Mexico, social stratification was also localized in the Mixteca, having taken place at a ñuu known as Apoala (Terraciano 2001:255). This distinct primordial genesis for rulers and ruled extended the hereditary claims of rulers back to a time when the landscape itself was being created, naturalizing their authority at the same time that it necessitated territorial control as a prerequisite for governance. For the K'iche lords of the Popul Vuh, the distinction from non-K'iche peoples and non-lordly classes was not based on the substance of creation—for all humans were formed from maize—but rather on descent from foundational ancestors and the distinct locations of communities in the aftermath of their dispersal across the landscape (Christenson 2007).

What unifies these examples is that they all speak to the creation of fundamentally different sorts of bodies for rulers. These were authoritative and powerful bodies modeled out of different substances emerging from different places, or generationally distinct and descended through closed lineages. Such different royal bodies were needed to delimit extensive political territories and mark the landscapes internal and external to the moral community of the polity.

Yet, as our case studies have emphasized, such territoriality as a political strategy is a system of power and authority that arose out of complementarity with commoner practice, not from contradictions with it. Organizing the local community and state on the principles of the milpa and household made the structural positions of leaders not only appropriate but necessary for the definition of a coherent moral space and order. The contradictions of kind, rather than scale, that emerged out of these power relationships were thus inimical to the logic of extending household and local community space outward to the maximal edges of the polity and eventually participated in the cyclical breakdown of Mesoamerican political systems (Golden and Scherer 2013). Such systems typically did not disappear but returned to their basic organizational scale of the household and local community.

CONCLUSIONS

The editors of this volume have asked authors to engage and wrestle with the role of contradictions in the perception and practice of power and authority in Mesoamerican rulership. In focusing on the delimiting of landscapes as a central component of power and authority in Mesoamerica, however, we see more consistency than contradictions. In saying that the enactment of rulership and the expression of power and authority were in accord with the quotidian practice of the populace we are not claiming that there were not fundamental differences at work across social classes. However, in considering the role of human-landscape interactions as instruments of power and authority, these differences were not in kind but rather scalar in terms of economic input (the sorts of material and human power involved) and the number of bodies involved (whether a few members of a household or the entire populace of a kingdom).

Power and authority in Mesoamerica were not about "belief" in Max Weber's (1978:213) sense (see Kurnick, this volume: chapter 1). Belief from such a perspective suggests, in a rather Marxist sense, ideology that can be penetrated to reveal an underlying truth. In Mesoamerican thought, however, there is only the basic truth of action: it is practice—not intent, not belief—that is central. Farmers in the milpa must "not only have faith but 'show, express' faith" (Hanks 1990:362). Rulers and subjects participated in the formation of bounded political spaces for which the ruler served as the metonymic head, an appropriate moral position, and one identical in terms of position and practice (though on a much smaller scale) to that of the head of household who lays out the altar, the boundaries of the houselot, and the milpa.

In the logic of bounding space, the ontological foundations of the landscape and human relationships to landscape and to other humans were the same at every scale; heads of household, heads of community, and heads of kingdoms occupied necessarily replicated positions with regard to the template for ordered space. Crucial here is the notion that places are brought into a moral being through human intervention—boundary making is a fundamentally social activity. Consequently, we do not find grand contradictions as the basis for governance in pre-Columbian Mesoamerica. Rather, while the contradictions we identify emerged from the scalar differences in bounding landscape, they were not instrumental in building or maintaining power but, over the long term, were inherent tensions that led to collapse (Golden and Scherer 2013).

ACKNOWLEDGMENTS

We wish to thank Sarah Kurnick and Joanne Baron for the invitation to participate in this volume and their guidance as editors. We also wish to thank the anonymous reviewers for their constructive criticism, which has helped us to hone our arguments, though any remaining failures of fact or logic are solely our own. Field research in Oaxaca was supported by a Sachar Award from Brandeis University and aided immensely by the generosity of Ethelia Ruiz Medrano, Marcus Winter, and the Instituto Nacional de Antropología e Historia of Mexico. Field research providing archaeological data in the Yaxchilan border zone was conducted by the Sierra del Lacandón Regional Archaeology Project, directed by Charles Golden, Andrew Scherer, and Rosaura Vasquez, with support from the Foundation for the Advancement of Mesoamerican Studies, Inc. (grants 02020, 05027, and 07043), the National Geographic Society (grants 7575-04 and 7636-04), the National Science Foundation (grants 0406472 and 0715463), Dumbarton Oaks Research Library, H. John Heinz III Charitable Trust Grants for Latin American Archeology, the J. M. Kaplan Fund through the World Monuments Fund, Wagner College, Baylor University, the Theodore and Jane Norman Fund and the Jane's Fund from the Latin American and Latino Studies program at Brandeis University, and Brown University. Golden and Scherer thank the Fundación Defensores de la Naturaleza for their ongoing support and assistance and the Instituto de Antropología e Historia of Guatemala for permission to conduct this research.

REFERENCES

Akkeren, Ruud van. 2000. *Place of the Lord's Daughter: Rab'inal, Its History, Its Dance-Drama*. Leiden: Research School CNWS.

Anderson, James, and Liam O'Dowd. 1999. "Borders, Border Regions and Territoriality: Contradictory Meaning, Changing Significance." *Regional Studies* 33(7): 593–604.

Arnauld, M. Charlotte, Dominique Michelet, Boris Vannière, Philippe Nondédéo, and Eva Lemonnier. 2012. "Houses, Emulation, and Cooperation Among the Rio Bec Groups." In *The Neighborhood as a Social and Spatial Unit in Mesoamerican Cities*, edited by M. Charlotte Arnauld, Linda R. Manzanilla, and Michael E. Smith, 202–28. Tucson: University of Arizona Press.

Barrera Vasquez, Alfredo, ed. 1980. *Diccionario Maya Cordemex: Maya-Español, Español-Maya*. Mérida: Ediciones Cordemex.

Brunet-Jailly, Emmanuel. 2005. "Theorizing Borders: An Interdisciplinary Perspective." *Geopolitics* 10(4): 633–49.

Barth, Fredrik, ed. 1969. *Ethnic Groups and Boundaries: The Social Organization of Culture*. Boston: Little Brown.

Basso, Keith H. 1996. *Wisdom Sits in Places: Landscape and Language Among the Western Apache*. Albuquerque: University of New Mexico Press.

Beekman, Christopher S. 1996. "Political Boundaries and Political Structure: The Limits of the Teuchitlan Tradition." *Ancient Mesoamerica* 7(1): 135–47.

Bourdieu, Pierre. 1977. *Outline of a Theory of Practice*. Translated by Richard Nice. Cambridge: Cambridge University Press.

Bourdieu, Pierre. 1990. The Logic of Practice. Translated by Richard Nice. Stanford: Stanford University Press.

Burkhart, Louise M. 1986. "Moral Deviance in Sixteenth-Century Nahua and Christian Thought: The Rabbit and the Deer." *Journal of Latin American Lore* 12(2): 107–39.

Braswell, Geoffrey E. 2001. "Post-Classic Maya Courts of the Guatemalan Highlands: Archaeological and Ethnohistorical Approaches." In *Royal Courts of the Ancient Maya*, vol. 2, *Data and Case Studies*, edited by Takeshi Inomata and Stephen D. Houston, 308–44. Boulder: Westview.

Braswell, Geoffrey E. 2004. "A Forest of Trees: Postclassic K'iche'an Identity and the Anthropological Problem of Ethnicity." In *Maya Ethnicity: The Construction of Ethnic Identity from Preclassic to Modern Times*, edited by Frauke Sachse, 125–40. Markt Schwaben: Anton Saurwein.

Byland, Bruce E., and John M. D. Pohl. 1994. *In the Realm of 8 Deer The Archaeology of the Mixtec Codices*. Norman: University of Oklahoma Press.

Carmack, Robert M. 1981. *The Quiche Mayas of Utatlan: The Evolution of a Highland Guatemala Kingdom*. Norman: University of Oklahoma Press.

Carmack, Robert M. 1995. *Rebels of Highland Guatemala: The Quiche-Mayas of Momostenango*. Norman: University of Oklahoma Press

Caso, Alfonso. 1960. "The Historical Value of the Mixtec Codices." *Boletín de Estudios Oaxaqueños* 16: 1–7.

Caso, Alfonso. 1938. *Exploraciones en Oaxaca, quinta y sexta temporadas, 1936–1937*. Publicación 34. Mexico City: Instituto Panamericano de Geografía e Historia.

Chance, John K. 2010. "From Lord to Landowner: The Predicament of the Late Colonial Mixtec Cacique." *Ethnohistory* 57(3): 445–66.

Chance, John K. 1996. "The Barrios of Colonial Tecali: Patronage, Kinship, and Territorial Relations in a Central Mexican Community." *Ethnology* 35(2): 107–39.

Christenson, Allen J. 2007. *Popol Vuh: The Sacred Book of the Maya*. Norman: University of Oklahoma Press.

Cosgrove, Denis E. 1984. *Social Formation and Symbolic Landscape*. London: Croom Helm.

Cosgrove, Denis. 1992. "Mapping New Worlds: Culture and Cartography in Sixteenth-Century Venice." *Imago Mundi* 44(1): 65–89.

Cosgrove, Denis E. 1999. *Mappings*. London: Reaktion.

Cunningham, Hilary, and Josiah Heyman. 2004. "Introduction: Mobilities and Enclosures at Borders." *Identities-Global Studies in Culture and Power* 11(3): 289–302.

Danziger, Eve. 2010. "On Trying and Lying: Cultural Configuration of Grice's Maxim of Quality." *Intercultural Pragmatics* 7(2): 199–219.

Demarest, Arthur A. 1992. "Ideology in Ancient Maya Cultural Evolution: The Dynamics of Galactic Polities." In *Ideology and Pre-Columbian Civilizations*, edited by Arthur A. Demarest and Geoffrey W. Conrad, 135–58. Santa Fe: School of American Research Press.

Dennis, Philip A. 1987. *Intervillage Conflict in Oaxaca*. New Brunswick, NJ: Rutgers University Press.

Doyle, James A. 2013. "Early Maya Geometric Planning Conventions at El Palmar, Guatemala." *Journal of Archaeological Science* 40(2): 793–98.

Farriss, Nancy M. 1978. "Nucleation versus Dispersal: The Dynamics of Population Movement in Colonial Yucatan." *Hispanic American Historical Review* 58(2): 187–216.

Farriss, Nancy M. 1984. *Maya Society under Colonial Rule: The Collective Enterprise of Survival*. Princeton, NJ: Princeton University Press.

Flynn, Donna K. 1997. "'We are the border': Identity, Exchange, and the State along the Benin-Nigeria Border." *American Ethnologist* 24(2): 311–30.

Galemba, Rebecca B. 2009. "Culture of Contraband: Contesting (Il)legality at the Mexico-Guatemala Border." PhD diss., Brown University.

Gavrilis, George. 2010. "Conflict and Control on the Ottoman-Greek Border." In *Understanding Life in the Borderlands: Boundaries in Depth and in Motion*, edited by I. William Zartman, 40–57. Athens: University of Georgia Press.

Geertz, Clifford. 1980. *Negara: The Theater State in Nineteenth-Century Bali*. Princeton, NJ: Princeton University Press.

Gerhard, Peter. 1970. "A Method of Reconstructing Pre-Columbian Political Boundaries in Central Mexico." *Journal de la Société des Américanistes* 59(1): 27–41.

Giddens, Anthony. 1984. *The Constitution of Society: Outline of the Theory of Structuration*. Berkeley: University of California Press.

Gillespie, Susan D. 1989. *The Aztec Kings: The Construction of Rulership in Mexica History*. Tucson: University of Arizona Press.

Golden, Charles. 2010, "Frayed at the Edges: The Re-Creation of Histories and Memories on the Frontiers of Classic Period Maya Polities." *Ancient Mesoamerica* 21(2): 373–84.

Golden, Charles, and Andrew K. Scherer. 2013. "Territory, Trust, Growth, and Collapse in Classic Period Maya Kingdoms." *Current Anthropology* 54(4): 397–434.

Golden, Charles, Andrew K. Scherer, A. René Muñoz, and Rosaura Vasquez. 2008. "Piedras Negras and Yaxchilan: Divergent Political Trajectories in Adjacent Maya Polities." *Latin American Antiquity* 19(3): 249–74.

Gorenstein, Shirley. 1985. *Acambaro: Frontier Settlement on the Tarascan-Aztec Border*. Nashville: Vanderbilt University Publications in Anthropology No. 32.

Gossen, Gary H. 1974a. *Chamulas in the World of the Sun: Time and Space in a Maya Oral Tradition*. Cambridge, MA: Harvard University Press.

Gossen, Gary H. 1974b. "To Speak with a Heated Heart: Chamula Canons of Style and Good Performance." In *Explorations in the Ethnography of Speaking*, edited by Richard Bauman and Joel Sherzer, 398–416. Cambridge: Cambridge University Press.

Hamann, Byron Ellsworth. 2012. "Sacred Geography in the Nochixtlan Valley." *Ancient Mesoamerica* 23(1): 25–45.

Hanks, William F. 2010. *Converting Words: Maya in the Age of the Cross*. Berkeley: University of California Press.

Hanks, William F. 1990. *Referential Practice: Language and Lived Space among the Maya*. Chicago: University of Chicago Press.

Hannerz, Ulf. 1997. "Borders." *International Social Science Journal* 49(154): 537–48.

Hare, Timothy S. 2000. "Between the Household and the Empire: Structural Relationships within and among Aztec Communities and Polities." In *The Archaeology of Communities: A New World Perspective*, edited by Marcello A. Canuto and Jason Yaeger, 78–101. New York: Routledge.

Hare, Timothy S., and Marilyn A. Masson. 2012. "Intermediate-Scale Patterns in the Urban Environment of Postclassic Mayapan." In *The Neighborhood as a Social and Spatial Unit in Mesoamerican Cities*, edited by M. Charlotte Arnauld, Linda R. Manzanilla, and Michael E. Smith, 229–60. Tucson: University of Arizona Press.

Harley, J. Brian. 1988. "Maps, Knowledge, and Power." In *The Iconography of Landscape: Essays on the Symbolic Representation, Design and Use of Past Environments*, edited by Denis Cosgrove and Stephen D. Daniels, 277–312. Cambridge: Cambridge University Press.

Harley, J. Brian. 1992. "Rereading the Maps of the Columbian Encounter." *Annals of the Association of American Geographers* 82(3): 522–42.

Haviland, Leslie K., and John B. Haviland. 1982. "Inside the Fence": The Social Basis of Privacy in Nabenchauk." *Estudios de Cultura Maya* 14: 323–51.

Haviland, Leslie K., and John B. Haviland. 1983. "Privacy in a Mexican Indian Village." In *Public and Private in Social Life*, edited by Stanley I. Benn and Gerald F. Gaus, 341–62. London: Croom Helm.

Hill, Robert M., and John Monaghan. 1987. *Continuities in Highland Maya Social Organization: Ethnohistory in Sacapulas, Guatemala*. Philadelphia: University of Pennsylvania Press.

Hoekstra, Rik. 1990. "A Different Way of Thinking: Contrasting Spanish and Indian Social and Economic Views in Central Mexico (1550–1600)." In *The Indian Community of Colonial Mexico: Fifteen Essays on Land Tenure, Corporate Organizations, Ideology and Village Politics*, edited by Arij Ouweneel and Simon Miller, 60–86. Amsterdam: CEDLA.

Hofling, Charles Andrew. 1993. "Marking Space and Time in Itzaj Maya Narrative." *Journal of Linguistic Anthropology* 3(2): 164–84.

Houston, Stephen D. 2006. "Impersonation, Dance, and the Problem of Spectacle among the Classic Maya." In *Archaeology of Performance: Theaters of Power, Community, and Politics*, edited by Takeshi Inomata and Lawrence S. Coben, 135–55. Lanham, MD: AltaMira.

Houston, Stephen D., and Takeshi Inomata. 2009. *The Classic Maya*. Cambridge: Cambridge University Press.

Houston, Stephen D., and David Stuart. 1998. "The Ancient Maya Self: Personhood and Portraiture in the Classic Period." *Res* 33: 73–101.

Houston, Stephen, David Stuart, and Karl Taube. 2006. *The Memory of Bones: Body, Being, and Experience among the Classic Maya*. Austin: University of Texas Press.

Houston, Stephen D., Héctor Escobedo, Mark Child, Charles Golden, and René Muñoz. 2003. "The Moral Community: Maya Settlement Transformation at Piedras Negras, Guatemala." In *The Social Construction of Ancient Cities*, edited by Monica L. Smith, 212–53. Washington, DC: Smithsonian Institution Press.

Howitt, Richie. 2001. "Frontiers, Borders, Edges: Liminal Challenges to the Hegemony of Exclusion." *Australian Geographical Studies* 39(2): 233–45.

Hull, Kerry Michael. 2003. "Verbal Art and Performance in Ch'orti' and Maya Hieroglyphic Writing." PhD diss., University of Texas at Austin.

Hutson, Scott R., and Travis W. Stanton. 2007. "Cultural Logic and Practical Reason: The Structure of Discard in Ancient Maya Houselots." *Cambridge Archaeological Journal* 17(2): 123–44.

Hutson, Scott R., Aline Magnoni, and Travis W. Stanton. 2004. "House Rules? The Practice of Social Organization in Classic Period Chunchucmil, Yucatan, Mexico." *Ancient Mesoamerica* 15(1): 75–92.

Hutson, Scott R., Travis W. Stanton, Aline Magnoni, Richard Terry, and Jason Craner. 2007. "Beyond the Buildings: Formation Processes of Ancient Maya Houselots and Methods for the Study of Non-Architectural Space." *Journal of Anthropological Archaeology* 26(3): 442–73.

Ingold, Tim. 1993. "The Temporality of the Landscape." *World Archaeology* 25(2): 152–74.

Inomata, Takeshi. 2006a. "Overture: An Invitation to the Archaeological Theater." In *Archaeology of Performance: Theaters of Power, Community, and Politics*, edited by Takeshi Inomata and Lawrence S. Coben, 11–44. Lanham, MD: AltaMira.

Inomata, Takeshi. 2006b. "Plazas, Performers, and Spectators: Political Theaters of the Classic Maya." *Current Anthropology* 47(5): 805–42.

Jansen, Maarten E. 1982. *Huisi Tacu: Estudio interpretativo de un libro mixteco antiguo: Codex Vindobonensis Mexicanus I*. 2 vols. Amsterdam: CEDLA.

Jusionyte, Ieva. 2012. "Writing on the Margins of the State: News Production in an Argentine Border Town." PhD diss., Brandeis University.

Kearney, Michael. 2004. "The Classifying and Value-Filtering Missions of Borders." *Anthropological Theory* 4(2): 131–56.

Kowalewski, Stephen A., Andrew K. Balkansky, Laura R. Stiver Walsh, Thomas J. Pluckhahn, John F. Chamblee, Verónica Pérez Rodríguez, Vernice Y. Heredia Espinoza, and Charlotte A. Smith. 2009. *Origins of the Ñuu: Archaeology in the Mixteca Alta, Mexico*. Boulder: University Press of Colorado.

Knapp, A. Bernard, and Wendy Ashmore. 1999. "Archaeological Landscapes: Constructed, Conceptualized, Ideational." In *Archaeologies of Landscape:*

Contemporary Perspectives, edited by Wendy Ashmore and A. Bernard Knapp, 1–30. Malden, MA: Blackwell.

Landa, Diego de. 1978. *Yucatan Before and After the Conquest.* Translated by William Gates. New York: Dover.

Lefebvre, Henri. 1991. *The Production of Space*. Oxford: Blackwell.

Lemonnier, Eva. 2012. "Neighborhoods in Classic Lowland Maya Societies: Their Identification and Definition from the La Joyanca Case Study (Northwestern Peten, Guatemala)." In *The Neighborhood as a Social and Spatial Unit in Mesoamerican Cities*, edited by M. Charlotte Arnauld, Linda R. Manzanilla, and Michael E. Smith, 181–201. Tucson: University of Arizona Press.

Licate, Jack A. 1980. "The Forms of Aztec Territorial Organization." In *Historical Geography of Latin America: Papers in Honor of Robert C. West*, edited by William V. Davidson and James J. Parsons, 27–45. Baton Rouge: Louisiana State University Press.

Lockhart, James. 1992. *The Nahuas after the Conquest: A Social and Cultural History of the Indians of Central Mexico, Sixteenth Through Eighteenth Centuries*. Palo Alto: Stanford University Press.

Looper, Matthew G. 2001. "Dance Performances at Quiriguá." In *Landscape and Power in Ancient Mesoamerica*, edited by Rex Koontz, Kathryn Reese-Taylor, and Annabeth Headrick, 113–135. Boulder: Westview.

Looper, Matthew G. 2003. *Lightning Warrior: Maya Art and Kingship at Quirigua*. Austin: University of Texas Press.

Looper, Matthew G. 2009. *To Be Like Gods: Dance in Ancient Maya Civilization*. Austin: University of Texas Press.

Magnoni, Aline, Scott R. Hutson, and Bruce H. Dahlin. 2012. "Living in the City: Settlement Patterns and the Urban Experience at Classic Period Chunchucmil, Yucatan, Mexico." *Ancient Mesoamerica* 23(2): 313–43.

McAnany, Patricia A. 1995. *Living with the Ancestors: Kinship and Kingship in Ancient Maya Society*. Austin: University of Texas Press.

Menegus Bornemann, Margarita. 2005. "El cacicazgo en Nueva España." In *El cacicazgo en Nueva España y Filipinas*, coordinated by Margarita Menegus Bornemann and Rodolfo Aguirre Salvadaor, 13–69. Mexico City: Centro de Estudios sobre la Universidad / Universidad Nacional Autónoma de México / Plaza y Valdés.

Monaghan, John. 1994. "Irrigation and Ecological Complementarity in Mixtec Cacicazgos." In *Caciques and Their People: A Volume in Honor of Ronald Spores*, edited by Joyce Marcus and Judith Francis Zeitlin, 143–62. Ann Arbor: Museum of Anthropology, University of Michigan.

Monaghan, John. 1995. The *Covenants with Earth and Rain*. Norman: University of Oklahoma Press.

Monaghan, John. 1998. "The Person, Destiny, and the Construction of Difference in Mesoamerica." *Res* 33: 137–46.

Morphy, Howard. 1995. "Landscape and the Reproduction of the Ancestral Past." In *The Anthropology of Landscape: Perspectives on Place and Space*, edited by Eric Hirsch and Michael O'Hanlon, 184–209. Oxford: Clarendon.

Morton, Shawn G. 2012. "Ritual Procession and the Creation of *Civitas* Among the Ancient Maya: A Case Study from Naachtun, Guatemala." *Canadian Journal of Archaeology* 36(1): 141–65.

Munn, Nancy D. 1996. "Excluded Spaces: The Figure in the Australian Aboriginal Landscape." *Critical Inquiry* 22(3): 446–65.

Newman, David. 2006. "Borders and Bordering: Towards an Interdisciplinary Dialogue." *European Journal of Social Theory* 9(2): 171–86.

Olwig, Kenneth R. 1996. "Recovering the Substantive Nature of Landscape." *Annals of the Association of American Geographers* 86(4): 630–53.

Pohl, John M. D., John Monaghan, and Laura R. Stiver. 1997. "Religion, Economy, and Factionalism in Mixtec Boundary Zones." In *Códices y documentos sobre México: Segundo simposio*, vol. 1, edited by Salvador Rueda Smithers, Constanza Vega Sosa, and Rodrigo Martínez Baracs, 205–32. Mexico City: Dirección General de Publicaciones del Consejo Nacional para la Cultura y las Artes / Instituto Nacional de Antropología e Historia.

Powell, Christopher. 2010. "The Shapes of Sacred Space: A Proposed System of Geometry Used to Lay Out and Design Maya Art and Architecture and Some Implications Concerning Maya Cosmology." PhD diss., University of Texas at Austin.

Reese-Taylor, Kathryn. 2002. "Ritual Circuits as Key Elements in Maya Civic Center Design." In *Heart of Creation: The Mesoamerican World and the Legacy of Linda Schele*, edited by Andrea Stone, 143–65. Tuscaloosa: University of Alabama Press.

Restall, Matthew. 1997. *The Maya World: Yucatec Culture and Society, 1550–1850*. Stanford: Stanford University Press.

Restall, Matthew. 1998. *Maya Conquistador*. Boston: Beacon.

Robin, Cynthia. 2002. "Outside of Houses: The Practices of Everyday Life at Chan Noohol, Belize." *Journal of Social Archaeology* 2(2): 245–68.

Rosaldo, Renato I., Jr. 1968. "Metaphors of Hierarchy in a Mayan Ritual." *American Anthropologist* 70(3): 524–36.

Roys, Ralph L. 1967. *The Book of Chilam Balam of Chumayel*. Norman: University of Oklahoma Press.

Ruiz Medrano, Ethelia. 2010. *Mexico's Indigenous Communities: Their Lands and Histories, 1500–2010*. Translated by Russ Davidson. Boulder: University Press of Colorado.

Rumford, Chris. 2006. "Introduction: Theorizing Borders." *European Journal of Social Theory* 9(2): 155–69.

Sack, Robert David. 1986. *Human Territoriality: Its Theory and History*. Cambridge: Cambridge University Press.

Scherer, Andrew K., and Charles Golden. 2009. "Tecolote, Guatemala: Archaeological Evidence for a Fortified Late Classic Maya Political Border." *Journal of Field Archaeology* 34(3): 285–304.

Scherer, Andrew K., and Charles Golden. 2014. "War in the West: History, Landscape, and Classic Maya Conflict." In *Embattled Bodies, Embattled Places: War in Pre-Columbian Mesoamerica and the Andes*, edited by Andrew K. Scherer and John W. Verano, 57–92. Washington, DC: Dumbarton Oaks.

Sharer, Robert J., and Charles W. Golden. 2004. "Kingship and Polity: Conceptualizing the Maya Body Politic." In *Continuities and Changes in Maya Archaeology: Perspectives at the Millennium*, edited by Charles W. Golden and Greg Borgstede, 23–50. New York: Routledge.

Silverstein, Jay E., David Webster, Horacio Martinez, and Alvaro Soto. 2009. "Rethinking the Great Earthwork of Tikal: A Hydraulic Hypothesis for the Classic Maya Polity." *Ancient Mesoamerica* 20(1): 45–58.

Simala, Kenneth I., and Maurice Amutabi. 2005. "Small Arms, Cattle Raiding, and Borderlands: The Ilemi Triangle." In *Illicit Flows and Criminal Things: States, Borders, and the Other Side of Globalization*, edited by Willem van Schendel and Itty Abraham, 201–25. Bloomington: Indiana University Press.

Smith, Adam T. 2003. *The Political Landscape: Constellations of Authority in Early Complex Polities*. Berkeley: University of California Press.

Smith, Mary Elizabeth. 1973. *Picture Writing from Ancient Southern Mexico: Mixtec Place Signs and Maps*. Norman: University of Oklahoma Press.

Smith, Mary Elizabeth. 1998. *The Codex López Ruiz: A Lost Mixtec Pictorial Manuscript*. Nashville: Vanderbilt University Publications in Anthropology No. 51.

Smith, Michael E. 1989. "Cities, Towns, and Urbanism: Comment on Sanders and Webster." *American Anthropologist* 91(2): 454–60.

Smith, Michael E. 2012. *The Aztecs*. Third edition. Malden, MA: Wiley-Blackwell.

Smith, Monica L. 2005. "Networks, Territories, and the Cartography of Ancient States." *Annals of the Association of American Geographers* 95(4): 832–49.

Southall, Aidan. 1988. "The Segmentary State in Africa and Asia." *Comparative Studies in Society and History* 30(1): 52–82.

Staudt, Kathleen. 1998. *Free Trade? Informal Economies at the U.S.-Mexico Border*. Philadelphia: Temple University Press.

Stephens, John L. 1848. *Incidents of Travel in Yucatan*. Vol. 2. New York: Harper.

Stross, Brian. 1983. "The Language of Zuyua." *American Ethnologist* 10(1): 150–64.

Stuart, David. 1996. "Kings of Stone: A Consideration of Stelae in Classic Maya Ritual and Representation." *Res* 29/30: 148–71.

Stuart, David. 1998. "'The Fire Enters His House': Architecture and Ritual in Classic Maya Texts." In *Function and Meaning in Classic Maya Architecture*, edited by Stephen D. Houston, 373–425. Washington, DC: Dumbarton Oaks.

Stuart, David. 2005. "Ideology and Classic Maya Kingship." In *A Catalyst for Ideas: Anthropological Archaeology and the Legacy of Douglas Schwartz*, edited by Vernon L. Scarborough, 257–85. Santa Fe: School of American Research Press.

Stuart, David. 2007. "The Captives on Piedras Negras, Panel 12." *Maya Decipherment: Ideas on Ancient Maya Writing and Iconography* (blog). https://decipherment.wordpress.com/2007/08/18/the-captives-on-piedras-negras-panel-12/.

Stuart, David. 2011. "Some Working Notes on the Text of Tikal Stela 31." Accessed March 1, 2014. http://www.mesoweb.com/stuart/notes/Tikal.pdf.

Stuart, David, and George Stuart. 2008. *Palenque: Eternal City of the Maya*. London: Thames & Hudson.

Tambiah, Stanley J. 1976. *World Conqueror, World Renouncer*. Cambridge: Cambridge University Press.

Taube, Karl. 2003. "Ancient and Contemporary Maya Conceptions About Field and Forest." In *The Lowland Maya Area: Three Millennia at the Humane Wildland Interface*, edited by A. Gómez-Pompa, M. F. Allen, S. L. Fedick, and J. J. Jiménez-Osornio, 461–92. New York: Food Products Press.

Terraciano, Kevin. 2001. *The Mixtecs of Colonial Oaxaca: Ñudzahui History, Sixteenth Through Eighteenth Centuries*. Stanford: Stanford University Press.

Tokovinine, Alexandre Andreevich. 2008. "The Power of Place: Political Landscape and Identity in Classic Maya Inscriptions, Imagery, and Architecture." PhD diss., Harvard University.

Tomaszewski, Brian M., and Michael E. Smith. 2010. "Polities, Territory and Historical Change in Postclassic Matlatzinco (Toluca Valley, central Mexico)." *Journal of Historical Geography* 37(1): 22–39.

Vail, Gabrielle, and Christine Hernández, eds. 2010. *Astronomers, Scribes, and Priests: Intellectual Interchange between the Northern Maya Lowlands and Highland Mexico in the Late Postclassic Period.* Washington, DC: Dumbarton Oaks.

Van Houtum, Henk, and Anke Strüver. 2002. "Borders, Strangers, Doors and Bridges." *Space and Polity* 6(2): 141–46.

Vogt, Evon Z. 1965. "Structural and Conceptual Replication in Zinacantan Culture." *American Anthropologist* 67(2): 342–53.

Walters, William. 2006. "Borders/Control." *European Journal of Social Theory* 9(2): 187–203.

Weber, Max. 1978. *Economy and Society: An Outline of Interpretive Sociology*. Edited by Guenther Roth and Claus Wittich. Berkeley: University of California Press.

Webster, David, Timothy Murtha, Kirk D. Straight, Jay Silverstein, Horacio Martinez, Richard E. Terry, and Richard Burnett. 2007. "The Great Tikal Earthwork Revisited." *Journal of Field Archaeology* 32(1): 41–64.

Wisdom, Charles. 1940. *The Chorti Indians of Guatemala*. Chicago: University of Chicago Press.

Wolf, Eric R. 1986. "The Vicissitudes of the Closed Corporate Peasant Community." *American Ethnologist* 13(2): 325–29.

Wong, Diana. 2005. "The Rumor of Trafficking: Border Controls, Illegal Migration, and the Sovereignty of the Nation-State." In *Illicit Flows and Criminal Things: States, Borders, and the Other Side of Globalization*, edited by Willem von Schendel and Itty Abraham, 69–100. Bloomington: Indiana University Press.

8

Ruling "Purépecha Chichimeca" in a Tarascan World

Helen Perlstein Pollard

The study of the social evolution of centralized, large-scale polities in Mesoamerica has been dominated historically by a focus on isolating powerful causes of change; asking why certain trajectories appeared when and where we can document them (e.g., Fargher et al. 2011; Martin, this volume; Yoffee 2005). The big "why" questions turn to social and natural forces that operate at relatively large spatial and temporal scales that are amenable to archaeological data. Here, the editors have charged us to consider the "how" questions of the relationship between rulers and the ruled and present a model of political strategies that contains "the negotiation of contradictions" at its core (Kurnick, this volume). In this chapter, I will examine the Tarascan empire, a society only recently centralized when the Spanish conquered Mesoamerica. This relatively late time frame is advantageous for scholarship, giving us access to well-preserved archaeological remains and historical documents recorded by Spanish friars just a few generations after state formation. This data indicates that elites in the Tarascan empire readily manipulated local and foreign ethnic identities, allowing them to shift regional worldviews or "schemas" (Sewall 1996) to support simultaneously greater social inequality and greater ethnic solidarity in a social transformation that resulted in a new state.

Unlike other core regions of Mesoamerica, central Michoacán did not have a long history of city-states and empires during the Classic and Early Postclassic

DOI: 10.5876/9781607324164.c008

Period (200–1100 CE) but was politically and economically peripheral to powerful polities to the east and west. However, in the last centuries before European conquest a highly centralized state emerged in the Lake Pátzcuaro Basin—a state that was rapidly transformed into an expanding empire. This contemporary of the Aztecs, known to the indigenous population as the *Irechequa Tzintzuntzani* (kingdom of the lord of Tzintzuntzan), and to Spaniards and later scholars as the Tarascan empire, provides an opportunity to explore how elites and their factions managed, defended, and legitimized the transformation of their authority into power by means of both sixteenth-century documents and the archaeological record.

SOVEREIGNTY, LEGITIMACY, AND ETHNICITY

In Mesoamerica, especially as recounted in the mythic histories of ruling elites during the Postclassic Period, political strategies were tangled in issues of both class and ethnicity, often operating at multiple temporal and spatial scales (Stark and Chance 2008). In the Tarascan case, the political structure of the state, and the empire that expanded between 1350 CE and 1522 CE, is primarily known from documents and limited archaeological research within the imperial lands, including studies of the nature of Tarascan warfare, frontier fortresses, and the Tarascan-Aztec conflicts (figure 8.1). While these sources generally present a picture of a highly centralized, hierarchical polity, Purépecha-language documents and more nuanced analyses of the Relación de Michoacán (1541) raise important questions about how this new state, identity, and system of authority emerged and the degree to which the centralized model was a product of power struggles before or following the Spanish conquest (Castro Gutiérrez 2007; Castro Gutiérrez and Monzón García 2008; Espejel Carbajal 2008; Haskell 2008; Martínez Baracs 2005; Monzón et al. 2009; Roskamp 2012; Stone 2004).

The primary document describing the Tarascan empire for the Spaniards is the Relación de Michoacán (Alcala 1980),[1] recorded in the capital of Tzintzuntzan in 1538–1540 by a Franciscan friar acting as scribe and interpreter for the state high priest (*petámuti*) and given to the first viceroy in 1541. The second part of the document contains the retelling of the official history of how the ruling dynasty came to create and rule the state—that is, how a group of nomadic, hunter-gatherer, warrior Chichimecs moved into Purépecha territory in the thirteenth century, joining other Nahua-speaking earlier migrants. Due to their superior skills and powerful patron deity, they married into local Purépecha elite families and, over the next century, came to dominate them.

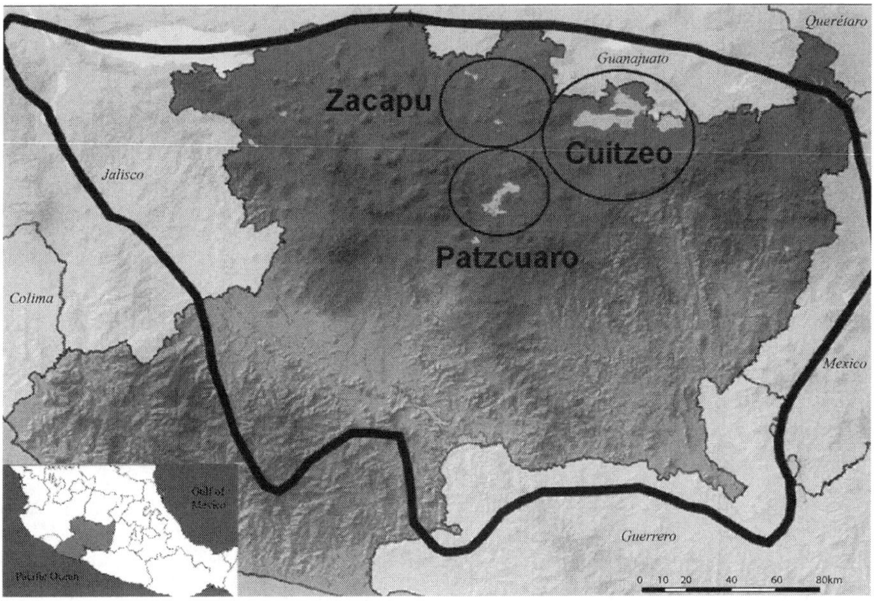

FIGURE 8.1. *Extent of the Tarascan empire and major lake basins referred to in text.*

This process produced what David L. Haskell (2008) calls a "cultural logic of hierarchy," as the once Chichimec leaders, now the Uanacase-Uacúsecha royal dynasty, ruled over Purépecha and Nahua elites and commoners. Only a personally felt supernatural link to Curicaueri could legitimate ruler status. While the local earth deities remain part of the state pantheon, and indeed are among the most powerful and ubiquitous supernatural beings, they are subordinated to the celestial deities. The original exchange of deer meat for fish that accompanied the Chichimec hunters' and Purépecha fishers' negotiation of the marriage that produced Tariacuri is replaced over time by the status markers that "nobles eat meat" and "commoners eat fish" (Relación de Michoacán and *Relaciones geográficas* in Martínez Gonzalez 2009).

As the empire expanded, additional ethnic/cultural groups were incorporated into the Tarascan domain. Other primary documents include the *Relaciones geográficas* of 1579–1581 (Acuña 1987) and local land titles (Albiez-Wieck 2011; Beltrán 1994; Carrasco 1986; Cerda Farías 2002; Kuthy 1996; Paredes Martínez and Terán 2003; Roskamp 1998). The most notable consistency in these documents is how often the lands are said to have been given to the community by the great King Tzitzipandáquare (1465–1490 CE), including communities in the geopolitical core that were part of the original state and were continuously occupied since the Late Preclassic Period. These purported gifts of land thus ignored the historical claims of these settlements in favor of the legitimacy of royal decree. Newer populations fleeing Aztec expansion also obtained land grants directly from the king in return for military service (Roskamp 2010).

Recent years have seen new, complete editions of two sixteenth-century Purépecha dictionaries and grammars (Gilberti 1989; Lagunas 1983) and the discovery and transcription of a third (Warren 1991), along with the careful analysis of several other relevant sixteenth-century Spanish documents (Aguilar González 2005; Albiez-Wieck 2011; Castro Gutiérrez 2007; Kuthy 1996; López Sarralangue 1965; Roskamp and César Villa 2003; Warren 1985). Finally, with the assistance of linguists, the first documents written in Purépecha have been translated and published (Castro Gutiérrez and Monzón García 2008; Monzón 2005; Monzón, Roskamp, and Warren 2009) and detailed historical linguistics of Nahua are more available (e.g., Kaufman 2001). These new sources and analyses have made it possible to better understand (1) how Purépecha-speakers conceptualized power (table 8.1) and the meaning of many state political offices (table 8.2); (2) the degree of multiethnicity in the empire, including non-Purépecha elites holding positions of power; and (3) the degree to which the imperial history as presented in the Relación de Michoacán simplified and ignored the role of elite factionalism in the creation and maintenance of the state.

BACKGROUND TO TRANSFORMATION

The Tarascan empire was the second largest in Mesoamerica (more than 75,000 square kilometers) and was ethnically dominated by a population the Spaniards called Tarascos, who spoke a language known as Tarasco or Purépecha. But while the empire only emerged in the two centuries before the Europeans' arrival, Purépecha culture can be identified at least 2 millennia earlier. The massive transformations this cultural tradition underwent, along with the emergence of a centralized state and an expansionist empire, have dominated the archaeology and ethnohistory of this region for the last century (Espejel 2007; Michelet 2008; Michelet et al. 2005; Pollard 1993).

The Purépecha heartland was located in central and northern Michoacán, especially in the Zacapu, Cuitzeo, and Pátzcuaro Lake basins (figure 8.1). The available evidence confirms the presence of a distinguishable Purépecha cultural tradition in the Pátzcuaro Basin by the Late Preclassic Period and suggests that it is likely that these populations were cultural descendants of the earlier Chupícuaro tradition (Arnauld et al. 1993; Carot 2005; Pollard 2005,

Table 8.1. Concepts of governance in the Tarascan state.

Concept	*Definition*
camahchacuhpeni	to govern; to group with others; to congregate over a territory (space); jurisdiction over others
camachacuhpecha	the government; "those who have the hands and arms of their forces, and command the submission of the commoners for the benefit and sign of friendship with 'los buenos' (the good ones). And to humble and to subjugate (oppressing) 'los malos' (the bad ones) harshly" (Lagunas 1983:250).
chechexequa	authority; majesty; that which induces fear in a body
chemazqua	that which induces fear repeatedly over time
ureguandani	principal; lord; he who speaks first; the first
hapingata	servant/slave; that which is possessed
camahchacungari	subject; someone whose body was grouped
vapatzequa	barrio; a bundle of large objects (firewood) from below; a space lower in the hierarchy (subordinate) where firewood exists (subjects exist)
yrenariquareponi	barrio; to live together in the place of origin
irechequa	the lord's place; the Tarascan kingdom

Source: from Castro Gutiérrez and Monzón García 2008; Pollard 1993.

2008). These Loma Alta phase populations (table 8.3) inhabited both lacustrine and non-lacustrine settlements and practiced canal irrigation with intensified agricultural production dominated by maize. In the Pátzcuaro Basin, at least one settlement was twenty hectares, including stone architecture. At the type site in the Zacapu Basin, sunken plaza/platform architecture appeared during the Loma Alta 2b phase (250–350 CE). This architecture included a central altar, walls of worked stone, and stairways made with basalt and clay brought from almost 10 kilometers away. A new burial tradition also appeared in which richness of interment is directly related to proximity to platform centrality. These burial deposits are currently the best evidence for the timing of the emergence of social ranking, documenting the existence of small-scale, socially ranked agrarian societies. Long-distance exchange in Pachuca obsidian and Thin Orange pottery suggests indirect linkages to Teotihuacan.

During the Epiclassic Lupe phase there was an increase in the number of settlements and larger populations, and some of these communities included plazas and ballcourts. The elite were buried in group tombs that were similar to each other in their methods of construction and their uses over multiple generations. Grave goods included precious items imported from other

Table 8.2. Major political positions of the Tarascan state.

Political position	*Definition*
irecha (yrecha)	lord; king; head of uacúsecha lineage (cazonci)
cazonci	king; ruler over irecha
carachacapacha	nobles; live in court, collect tribute and organize troops from home communities; governors of the four quarters of the empire
achaecha	other members of nobility who act as advisors; local nobles; called "Don" in Colonial Period
angámecha	leaders of towns and villages, called caciques or señores, "those who stand at the door"
angatacuri	governor or prime minister
capitán	military leader in time of war
quangariecha	heads of military units in time of war
minister of tribute	officer in charge of tribute collectors
ocámbecha	bosses; people who have others under their control; tribute collectors (ureguandani: boss of barrio)
mayordomos	heads of groups that stored and distributed tribute, produced crafts and service within the palace (thirty-four named in Relación de Michoacán)
petámuti	chief priest
priests	hierarchy of ten levels below the petámuti serving in temples dedicated to the state religion

Source: from Castro Gutiérrez and Monzón García 2008; Pollard 1993.

Table 8.3. Cultural sequence of central Michoacán.

Period	*Local phases*
Late Postclassic	Tariacuri (1350–1525 CE)
Middle Postclassic	Late Urichu (1000/1100–1350 CE)
Early Postclassic	Early Urichu (900–1000/1100 CE)
Epiclassic	Lupe-La Joya (600/700–900 CE)
Middle Classic	Jaracuaro (500–600/700 CE)
Early Classic	Loma Alta 3 (350–500 CE)
Late/Terminal Preclassic	Loma Alta 2 (100 BCE–350 CE)

regions of Mesoamerica that, along with cranial deformation and dental mutilation, distinguished these families from the rest of the population. These items reveal the elite's role as intermediaries with distant powers to the east and west. Grave goods also include projectile points, atlatls, maces, and war attire, showing the importance of the warrior identity for elite men.

During the Early Postclassic (Early Urichu phase) (900–1100 CE), the number of sites increased and the number of hectares occupied almost doubled in the lake basins of central and northern Michoacán as the climate of the Medieval Warm Period (Medieval Climate Anomaly) brought marked drops in lake levels. Small settlements were now located on newly exposed islands and in marsh zones, while many other communities occupied the *malpaís* zones (eroded lava flows) with terraces, mounds, and retaining walls in dense, large settlements with hundreds of stone structures. Elite burials were richer in grave goods, some of which appear to be ritual paraphernalia imported from Tula or in Toltec style (e.g., flutes, censers).

STATE EMERGENCE

The Middle Postclassic or Late Urichu phase (1100–1300 CE) includes the two centuries during which the Tarascan state formed and to which the historically recorded accounts of state emergence and ethnic affiliation pertain. In these centuries the number of sites in the region increased and the area of occupation again doubled. As in the Early Urichu phase, settlement expanded onto islands as the lake level remained low, but also markedly expanded in upland zones and onto the malpaís in defensible locations. Nevertheless, basic resources such as obsidian, basalt, and pottery were being produced, distributed, and consumed in patterns unchanged since the Loma Alta phase. In the last decades of this phase lake levels rose again (in the Lake Pátzcuaro Basin more than 14 meters), reaching their Contact Period levels. This resulted in the abandonment of low-lying communities and flooded agricultural land and the relocation of marsh production zones. Given the size of the population in the region, and the existence of sociopolitical elites in the larger communities, competition over expanding, diminishing, and shifting resources must have become fierce. For example, in the Zacapu Basin the Postclassic Period was marked by a 50 percent increase in sites and a shift to the malpaís above Zacapu, where up to 20,000 people inhabited thirteen sites covering 5 square kilometers (Michelet 2008; Michelet et al 2005). In addition, obsidian production from the Zináparo zone was reorganized and prismatic blade technology was introduced (Darras 2008).

Thus, during the Early and Middle Postclassic Periods, the Purépecha cultural heartland came to be composed of several competing small polities. This was a transition period when settlements shifted and elite mortuary patterns changed. Both the archaeological and ethnohistoric records suggest that patterns of leadership and control were in flux.

TARASCAN STATE STRUCTURE

During the Late Postclassic or Tariacuri phase, after low-lying sites were flooded, settlements shifted to the new, higher lakeshore and upland areas of high agricultural fertility. Tzintzuntzan was the largest of over ninety Tarascan settlements located around Lake Pátzcuaro (figure 8.2). Of the basin's estimated total population of 80,000 in 1522 (Gorenstein and Pollard 1983), Tzintzuntzan had about 35,000, with several secondary and tertiary administrative centers, each with 5,000 to 15,000 people (Pollard 1993, 2008). By the fifteenth century Tzintzuntzan was a primary regional center not only because of its population size, but also because of its control of the administrative, tributary, market, religious, and social hierarchies. Throughout the Tarascan heartland, population density reached its zenith, and the largest and most populous settlements within any single region, whether ceremonial centers or cities, also date to the Late Postclassic (Cerda Farías 2002; Macías Goytia 1990; Macías Goytia and Vackimes Serret 1988; Michelet 2008; Michelet et al. 2005; Pollard 2004, 2008).

Given the denser occupations, occurring during a time when previously irrigable lands were flooded, new economic mechanisms were required to support local populations. The core of the Tarascan state in the Pátzcuaro Basin was not viable economically on purely local terms, and it thrived only by the exchange of goods and services through local and regional markets and various state institutions (Pollard 1993). While documents indicate the existence and location of markets, the tributary relationships of many communities, and the nature of goods acquired by state long-distance merchants, detailed sourcing analyses of archaeological collections are clarifying the complex nature of the production, distribution, and consumption patterns of obsidian, pottery, shell, and metal objects (see Darras 2008; Hosler 2009; Maldonado 2008; Pollard 2005, 2008). Analyses of obsidian artifacts, for example, suggest that while Zináparo obsidian production was widely dispersed and exchanged in local and regional markets (Darras 2008), much of the production or distribution of prismatic blades from the Ucareo sources was under state control (Pollard 2008). Metal objects of gold, silver, copper, and bronze alloys were produced within the empire and used for ritual, status, and utilitarian purposes (Hosler

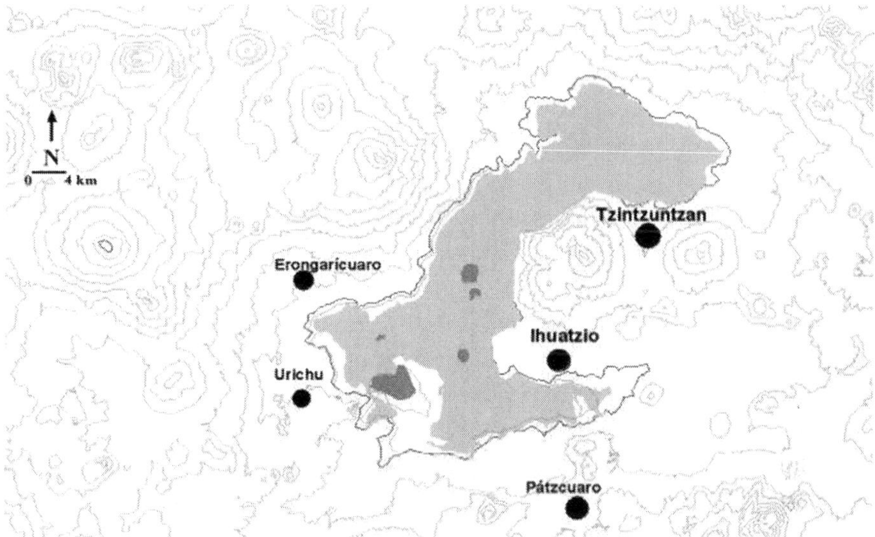

FIGURE 8.2. *Major Late Postclassic urban sites in the Lake Pátzcuaro Basin.*

2009; Pollard 1993; Roskamp 1998). Some of the mining, smelting, and production of objects was carried out by full-time craft specialists and tenants under the direct control of the state (Pollard 2008). The production of ingots took place at smelting centers in the Balsas River drainage and some of the crafting of objects took place in the Tarascan capital, possibly within the king's palace. Other metals or smelted ingots were obtained through tribute, particularly for gold and silver, especially from the frontier zones of the southeast and the west, where there is some evidence of independent production and distribution in local or regional markets. Those markets were associated with elite administrators' residences, probably reflecting redistribution of state goods to officeholders. Limited metal sourcing suggests artifacts were produced from ores mined in the Balsas Basin and adjacent Jalisco (Hosler 2009).

The sources of revenue for the state included (1) basic goods (especially maize, beans, chili, cotton, salt, and firewood) and scarce goods (e.g., turquoise, gold, silver, copper, feathers) collected by a hierarchy of officials at the local and regional level, and (2) labor on the king's fields and for public works. A separate group of officials (*quengue*) oversaw the state storehouses for this tribute. Other strategic, but statewide, tribute included men serving in military campaigns. Populations located along the frontiers served their tribute in both manning fortresses and providing basic supplies for warriors. Recent research indicates that unlike most of the empire, in the Pátzcuaro Basin the local tribute collectors (*ocámbecha*) were probably organizers of tribute-in-labor, not goods (Aguilar González 2005, 2012) (table 8.2).

The royal dynasty officially allocated all access to land, water, forests, and mineral resources, although in practice access to land was distributed within communities by traditional kin ties and land was acquired by kings for support of state administrators (*angámecha*) and state temples. In addition, there were state copper mines, obsidian mines, forests, fisheries, and craft workshops. The documents are unclear about the degree to which they were seen as resources traditionally held by specific communities or resources to which communities were allowed access by the king. Sixteenth-century documents suggest the latter, but, if so, this was a change in the ideology of resource ownership that would only have emerged with the unification of the state in the Middle Postclassic Period (e.g., Acuña 1987). The royal dynasty did claim large landholdings in the southeast portion of the Pátzcuaro Basin and smaller parcels in many other communities (e.g., Beltrán 1994; Martínez Baracs 2005; Warren 1985).

According to the Relación de Michoacán, the division between noble and commoner was absolute, as lineages did not cross class boundaries and marriages were within one's class. Among the nobility, a distinction was made among the royal dynasty, the upper nobility, and the lower nobility; commoners varied by ethnicity (although overwhelmingly Purépecha in the highland lake basins), occupation, and if they were slaves (generally war captives) (Carrasco 1986; García Alcaraz 1976). The royal dynasty was located in the capital (Tzintzuntzan) and at the sacred religious center of Ihuatzio (figure 8.3); members of the upper and lower nobility were found in at least eleven settlements in the Pátzcuaro Basin. Elites and commoners located in secondary and tertiary centers of the Tarascan heartland consumed the same goods, as did the residents in the capital, sharing Tarascan elite/commoner identity and participating in a single social system (Pollard 2008) (figure 8.4).

The establishment of a new ideology that made the Pátzcuaro Basin the center of cosmic power accompanied the creation of the Tarascan state (Espejel Carbajal 2008; Monzón 2005; Pollard 1993, 2008; Alcala 1980). The patron gods of the now dominant ethnic elite were elevated to celestial power while various regional deities and worldviews—themselves products of generations of change—were elevated, incorporated, or marginalized. The clearest evidence of this process involved the joining of the ethnic Chichimec or Uacúsecha deity Curicaueri with the ethnic "islander" or Purépecha goddess Xarátanga. In the prophetic language of a great epic, the Relación de Michoacán states, "Curicaueri will conquer this land, and you for your part will stand with one foot on the land and one on the water . . . and we shall become one people"

FIGURE 8.3. *Local elite identity in burial 9 at Urichu. Spouted polychrome vessel and several bronze and shell earrings.*

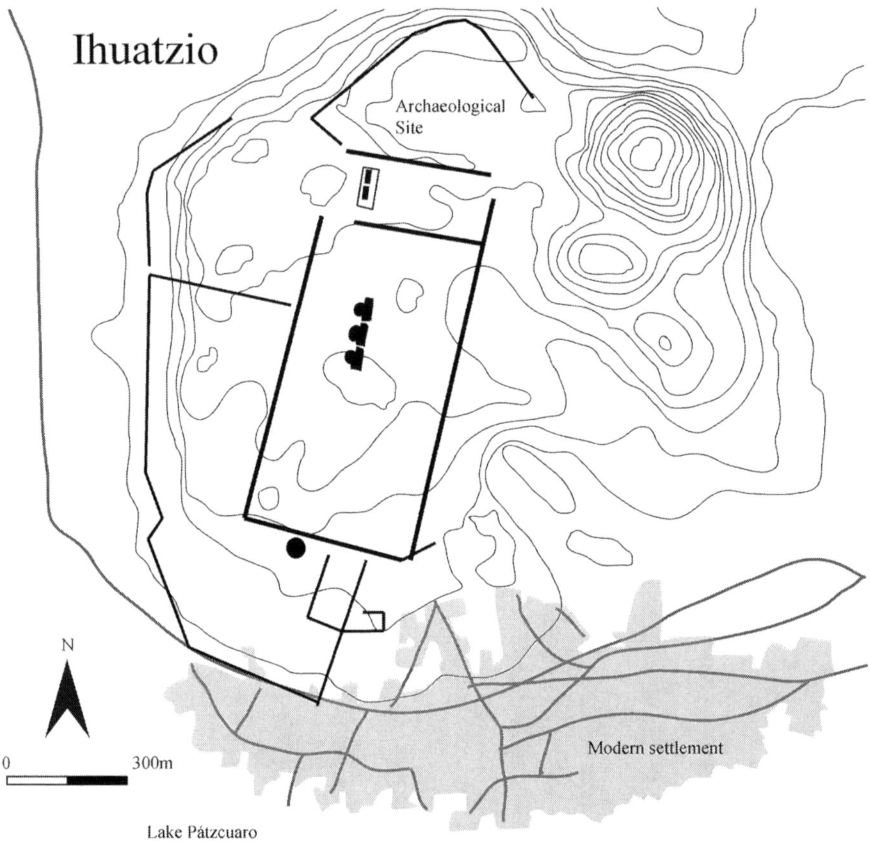

FIGURE 8.4. *Ritual center of Ihuatzio.*

(Alcala 1980:40, my translation). While the culture hero Tariacuri was the son of a Chichimec leader and the daughter of the Purépecha lord of the island of Xarácuaro, his god is Curicaueri, and over the course of the Relación this patron deity comes to represent the protector of all the people (Martínez Gonzalez 2009:55, 58). Indeed, his god and the other celestial deities are considered the powers of Tarascan sacred kingship, while the earthly deities, especially Xarátanga and Cuerauaperi, the mother goddess who controls rain and springs, are considered "foreign"—that is, non-Chichimec. In kinship terms, the celestial (Chichimec) deities are patrilines (fathers and brothers) and the earthly deities are marriage partners, or in-laws (Martínez Gonzalez 2009).

Thus, Tariacuri is *both* a lineal descendant of Chichimecs and "Islanders," a ruler who can unite all people, and also the human representation of the celestial sun, Curicaueri, with whom he has established a supernatural link. In the complex story of Tariacuri, recounted in the Relación, he is characterized as first Chichimec, then Islander, and eventually his designated "heirs," his two nephews, become patrons of Curicaueri and Xarátanga, respectively.

Taríacuri's prophetic dream of a unified state mandated by his god is interpreted in the following decades as the "event" that delegitimized all previous and competing claims to authority. Each Tarascan king (*irecha*) must personally establish this link to the supernatural to be considered legitimate, but only those of the Uacúsecha line are eligible. This union of deities can also be seen in Tarascan ritual architecture. A specialized pyramid form, the *yácata*, consisting of a keyhole shape, was constructed at major religious centers associated with the Tarascan sun god, Curicaueri. The greatest number (five) was located in Tzintzuntzan, but at Ihuatzio there were three yácatas as well as two rectangular pyramids associated with Xarátanga, adjacent to a ballcourt (figure 8.3). Ihuatzio is the only ritual center that was aligned to the cardinal directions, with a north-south principal orientation. It is also the only major Tarascan center with astronomically oriented structures in the basin. Directly east of the plaza with the two rectangular pyramids are three small hills (los Coyotes, or *iuatsi)*. A line projected east from the corridor between the two rectangular pyramids falls midway between the two northern hills; when viewed this way the hills bracket one lunar phase cycle on either side of the equinox (Anthony Aveni, personal communication 1989). The sighting of the sun or Venus along this line was reported as part of major state religious celebrations (Pollard 2003:373). Stone *chacmool* sculptures, associated with human sacrifice, were placed in front of the yácatas at Tzintzuntzan and Ihuatzio, scenes of major ceremonies celebrating the state and cosmic order.

The transformation associated with the emergence of a politically unified Pátzcuaro Basin and its expansion throughout and then beyond the Tarascan heartland involved a shift in elite identity from one primarily associated with imported finished goods from distant powerful centers and control of prestige goods networks, as documented for the Classic and Early Postclassic elites, to an identity primarily associated with locally produced, distinctively Tarascan goods and control of tributary, military, political, and ideological networks in the Late Postclassic (Pollard 2008). Thus, the emergence of a new political economy was also associated with a new state religion and a new regional elite identity.

For the Purépecha (commoners) of central and northern Michoacán, this new society was a major transformation on the macro level but also permitted continuities on the household and village scale. The social continuity represented by the long cultural tradition from the Preclassic to the Postclassic is visible in ceramic technology, ceramic designs and the use of negative (resist) on polychrome pottery, types of figurines, mortuary patterns, basic technology, diet, and household organization of labor. These traditions emphasize the degree of continuity at the level of the household, despite major changes in the political economies that took place during those two thousand years.

"PURÉPECHA CHICHIMECS"

While the legendary histories record several episodes of migration of non-Purépecha populations into the region from the *bajío* (lowlands) to the north and northwest, these population movements are not visible in the archaeological record of either the Zacapu or Pátzcuaro Basins to which they refer (Michelet et al. 2005; Pollard 2008). In the legend recorded in the Relación de Michoacán, these migrants are described and illustrated as northern nomadic hunters of deer and followers of their patron deity, Curicaueri, to whom they were obliged to offer wood for ritual fires. But the evidence from the region of Zacapu, stretching from the Lerma River to the northwest edge of the Pátzcuaro Basin, provides no support for these cultural "Chichimecs." What is documented, however, is the spread of the Loma Alta and Lupe ceramic traditions along parts of the Lerma and southern Guanajuato (table 8.3), followed by widespread abandonment of these settlements at the close of the Epiclassic and beginning of the Postclassic Periods (900–1000 CE) (Pereira et al. 2005). Some of these abandonments are matched by the appearance of Postclassic sites occupied by what has been interpreted as the descendants of these population movements (Michelet et al. 2005). During the Middle Postclassic, significant cultural changes become visible in (1) settlement nucleation in malpaís defendable sites with walls and terraces; (2) ritual architecture separated from residential zones and no construction of ballcourts; (3) new artifacts, including polychrome pottery, ceramic pipes, copper and alloyed metal tools, and locally produced prismatic obsidian blades; and (4) a new mortuary pattern distinct from earlier phases. While these changes occurred at the time and place of the legendary arrival of "Chichimecs," they better reflect the cultural continuities and changes in a rapidly shifting sociopolitical (and natural) environment that was non-Chichimec. Christine L. Hernández and Dan M. Healan (2008) have demonstrated the ability of archaeology to detect ethnic variation within the Tarascan domain, strengthening the "absence of evidence" as reflecting the true absence of "Chichimecs."

In the Pátzcuaro Basin to the south there is greater continuity in commoner material culture, especially in pottery, but the Late Postclassic is marked by the unification of the basin polities, the creation of a new common elite culture and a suite of traits marking the existence of the state, and a series of status markers used to assign sociopolitical rank among the elites. By the fifteenth century these traits are found throughout the empire at all state administrative installations and include (Pollard 1993, 2008):

1. The specialized pyramid form, the yácata, consisting of a keyhole shape, associated with the Tarascan/Chichimec sun god, Curicaueri (Cabrera Castro 1987).
2. The basalt chacmool sculpture, associated with human sacrifice.
3. An ossuary at Tzintzuntzan with skull racks here and elsewhere.
4. Notched/grooved human long bones associated with ritual spaces (Pereira 2005).
5. Ceramic pipes in large quantities in ritual spaces.
6. Metal artifacts of copper, bronze, gold, silver, and other alloys used for tools, ritual paraphernalia, and elite status markers.
7. Spouted vessels and spout-handled vessels, often with resist decoration, associated with use for a cacao drink (Pollard et al. 2013).
8. Obsidian lip plugs with inlays of turquoise, gold, amber, and other valuable rare materials in various sizes, depending on the political status of the wearer. The king provided the lip plug to men on assuming office and removed it when the individual was removed from office.
9. Cotton spindle whorls found in elite residences and elite female burials.
10. Large quantities of obsidian prismatic blades and segments associated with ritual plazas, structures, and elite residences.

While few of these traits are unique to the Late Postclassic Tarascans, they are unique in the cultural history of central and northern Michoacán and not part of the "Chichimec" traditions to the north. With the exception of the ceramic styles, they are closest to the Early Postclassic traditions of Tula (Healan 2012). Yet, unlike their Aztec counterparts, nowhere in the ethnohistory or historical records do Tarascan nobles link themselves to Toltec royal dynasties or ethnicities, and in several episodes of the Relación de Michoacán, the narrator refers (sometimes with disdain) to Nahua practices they do not follow, such as named and numbered days of the 260-day ritual calendar used to determine auspicious times for military campaigns (for a variant interpretation of this episode, see Roskamp 2012).

Understanding the "choice" to call on a "Chichimec" or Uacúsecha heritage while materializing the state with a selection of central Mexican state practices, and simultaneously identifying as ethnic Purépecha, can only make any sense by referring now to the newly restudied and newly translated documents that emphasize the large presence of Nahua populations within the Tarascan empire at the same time that Aztecs are seen as enduring enemies. The most surprising document dates to 1543, in which an earlier document is summarized in Purépecha (Monzón et al. 2009). In it a Nahua lord claims to be a descendant of one of twenty Nahua merchants who came to the military aid of the Tarascan king Tzitzipandáquare in "reconquering" Tzintzuntzan to his rule. In return, they are rewarded with rights and privileges, including the right to settle in a barrio of the capital, the right to noble status, and land and labor in the empire for them and their descendants. When the Spaniards moved the capital of Michoacán in 1540 from Tzintzuntzan to Pátzcuaro, the native nobility objected (Warren and Monzón García 2004), especially these Nahua nobles, who feared losing their special status in the move. What is not clear from this document is whether all or most long-distance traders were Nahua nobles. Other documents suggest the earlier presence of Nahua populations, including specialized metallurgists and Nahua nobles who held political office in Tancítaro and Uruapan (state administrative centers) (Albiez-Wieck 2011; Roskamp 1998, 2010).

The issue of ethnic Nahua populations within the imperial territory both before and after the Late Postclassic Period needs to be understood within the context of more than a century of military hostilities that dominated the Tarascan/Aztec relationship. While never a closed frontier, by the sixteenth century, parallel lines of Tarascan and Aztec fortified citadels defined the eastern border of the Tarascan empire (see Pollard and Smith 2003). Local groups on both sides of the border, including Otomí and Matlatzinca populations, became tributaries of these empires, generally manning the citadels and providing warriors. One result of this restricted interaction was the ease with which each government could develop negative stereotypes of their enemies (Pollard 1993:172). For the Tarascans, their language made them very vulnerable when crossing Aztec territory, and Nahua merchants and formal interpreters were used as messengers (*uaxanoti*) housed in the capital when communication with the Aztecs was necessary. The Irechequa Tzintzuntzani was clearly multiethnic, especially with Nahua nobles and commoners who had moved into Michoacán from the north and northeast during the Epiclassic and Early Postclassic Periods. Those traits, beliefs, and practices that were incorporated into the emerging Tarascan state from Nahua, Toltec, and/or Matlatzinca cultures were due to interaction and emulation from these earlier periods. To the extent that "Aztec Nahua" refers to the Middle and Late Postclassic Periods, these peoples were contemporaries. Indeed there are a number of ritual practices shared by Tarascan, Matlatzinca, and Nahuatl elites that suggest they all shared some roots in Early Postclassic north central Mexican concepts of sacred rulership, despite variations by the fifteenth century.

In contrast, the Tarascan ruling dynasty and related lineages that made up most of the Uacúsecha in general—the lower and upper nobility—were Purépecha speakers and self-identified culturally as Purépecha. They were able to hold office by the sacred authority and duty to maintain the worship of Curicaueri—women and non-Purépecha were unfit for this task. In the depiction of the family tree of the ruling dynasty (Relación de Michoacán folio 140r), the founder is shown holding a bloodstained blade used by *axamencha* (sacrificers), a role limited to rulers (Afanador-Pujol 2010). I believe the calls to special Chichimec heritage advanced the claims of legitimacy of the Uanacase branch over other ruling elites of the Pátzcuaro Middle Postclassic polities—that is, as part of the internal factional fights among qualified elite lineages that apparently lasted throughout the fifteenth century. The fierceness and success of Chichimec warfare served the Uanacase well in their construction of power. Indeed, their very concepts of power, rulership, and class (table 8.1) incorporate physical control and fear. Of the ten known state rituals, at least two of them foregrounded this theme on a yearly basis, including *Hanciuanscuaro* (the imprisoning of rebels) and *Purecatacuaro* (the initiation of warriors) (Pollard 1993:145).

The sixteenth-century documents already used in this analysis demonstrate that Tarascan rulers could and did shift between reference to their Chichimec heritage or their Purépecha heritage to legitimize access to political power and communication with supernatural beings, especially Curicaueri. However, all of these documents were written after the Colonial Period process of transformation had begun. This means that it is difficult to know how these multiple aspects of identity were actually used before factions of indigenous nobles and Spaniards began using "history" to prove why one lord or lineage should become irecha or retain power. Reading these texts always makes me wish I had samples of histories in the same way I can sample assemblages of artifacts. What the documents do reveal, however, is how nimble, flexible, and political were the categories of ethnicity, heritage, allies, and enemies.

Despite this, they took as their model of state-building the traits of a powerful Nahua culture to the east. Central Michoacán had long had indirect ties to Toltec ideas and practices, as revealed by imported ritual goods (censers, flutes), "warrior" burials with mosaic shields (Pollard 2008), and, particularly between 900–1000 CE, by the flow of people and obsidian to Tula (Healan 2012). This model of political hierarchy also included the notion of multiethnic communities and states that were highly centralized. As ironic as it may seem now, while

Nahua populations were gradually assimilating to Purépecha culture and language, the Purépecha rulers were incorporating Nahua models of governance. In this process, as Eric R. Wolf notes, "Old ideas were rephrased to fit different circumstances, and new ideas were presented as age-old truths" (1999:275).

SUMMARY

The emergence of the Tarascan state late in the prehistory of Mesoamerica (after 1350 CE), in a region where states had never existed previously, has provided us with the opportunity to use both archaeological and documentary sources to bear on the topic of pre-Columbian elite political strategies. These sources present a complex, and somewhat counterintuitive, pattern of ruling elites who claim an immigrant Chichimec heritage to justify their co-option of the native Purépecha nobility, while at the same time presenting themselves as fully ethnically Purépecha. Moreover, they have materialized the state and its institutions using a template from the Toltec world of Epiclassic and Early Postclassic north central Mexico. This was balanced by essential continuities in patterns of production, distribution, and consumption of basic commodities and maintenance of local social and political relationships, as the Chichimec patron deity, Curicaueri, became the Tarascan solar deity, creator of sacred kingship and husband of Purépecha goddess Xarátanga, and son-in-law of the great Purépecha Cuerauaperi, earth mother and rainwater deity.

These strategies allowed Tarascan rulers to overcome the contradictions inherent in political authority. Ethnic similarities to Purépecha subjects legitimized royal claims to power through proper veneration of Curicaueri, while Chichimec identity simultaneously distinguished these same rulers from rival elites. The use of material culture of Nahua origin also allowed rulers to express their similarities to this distant and prestigious form of governance while simultaneously maintaining open hostilities with the neighboring Aztec empire. In the ecologically and politically unstable world of the Postclassic, both commoners and elites alike saw benefits in following this new form of society and internalizing it as the only true society they had ever known.

ACKNOWLEDGMENTS

I would like to thank the volume editors, Sarah Kurnick and Joanne Baron, for their patience and suggestions in revising this chapter, and the two anonymous reviewers whose comments markedly improved the organization and content.

NOTE

1. There are several modern editions of this document; for conciseness I have used only the 1980 edition.

REFERENCES

Acuña, René, ed. 1987. *Relaciones geográficas del siglo XVI: Michoacán*, vol. 9. Mexico City: Universidad Nacional Autónoma de México.

Afanador-Pujol, Angélica J. 2010. "The Tree of Jesse and the 'Relación de Michoacán': Mimicry in Colonial Mexico." *Art Bulletin* 92(4): 293–307.

Aguilar González, José Ricardo. 2005. "Tzintzuntzan Irechequa: Política y sociedad en el Estado Tarasco." Licenciatura thesis, Universidad Michoacana, Morelia.

Aguilar González, José Ricardo. 2012. "Los [uh]cambecha y el sistema tributario en el Estado Tarasco: tradiciones interpretativas sobre la Relación de Michoacán." In *Abriendo caminos: El legado de Joseph Benedict Warren a la historia y a la lengua de Michoacán un Homenaje al Dr. J. Benedict Warren*, edited by L. Enkerlin Pauwells, 241–74. Morelia: Instituto Nacional de Antropología e Historia.

Albiez-Wieck, Sarah. 2011. "Contactos exteriores del Estado Tarasco: Influencias desde dentro y fuera de Mesoamérica." PhD diss., Rheinische Friedrich-Wilhelms-Universitat zu Bonn.

Alcala, Fray Jerónimo de. [1541] 1980. *La Relación de Michoacán, versión paleográfica*. Edited by Francisco Miranda. Morelia: Fimax Publicistas.

Arnauld, Marie Charlotte, Patricia Carot, and Marie-France Fauvet-Berthelot. 1993. *Arqueología de las Lomas en la cuenca lacustre de Zacapu, Michoacán, México*. Mexico City: Centro de estudios mexicanos y centroamericanos.

Beltrán, Ulises. 1994. "Estado y sociedad tarascos en la época prehispánica." In *El Michoacán antiguo: Estado sociedad tarascos en la época prehispánica*, edited by Brigitte Boehm de Lameiras, Ricardo Sánchez González, and Ulises Beltrán, 31–163. Zamora: El Colegio de Michoacán / Gobierno del Estado de Michoacán.

Cabrera Castro, Rubén. 1987. "Tzintzuntzan: Décima temporada de excavaciones." In *Homenaje a Román Piña Chan*, edited by M. C. Serra Puche, 531–65. Mexico City: Universidad Nacional Autónoma de México / Instituto de Investigaciones Antropológicas.

Carot, Patricia. 2005. "Reacomodos demográficos del Clásico al Posclásico en Michoacán: El retorno de los que se fueron." In *Reacomodos demográficos del Clásico al Posclásico en el centro de México*, edited by Linda Manzanilla, 103–21. Mexico City: Universidad Nacional Autónoma de México / Instituto de Investigaciones Antropológicas.

Carrasco, Pedro. 1986. "Economía política en el reino Tarasco." In *La Sociedad indígena en el centro y occidente de México*, edited by Pedro Carrasco, 63–102. Zamora: El Colegio de Michoacán.

Castro Gutiérrez, Filipe. 2007. "Luis de Castilleja y Puruata: Un noble de 'mano poderosa' entre dos epocas del gobierno indígena." *Estudios de Historia Novohispana* 37: 17–50.

Castro Gutiérrez, Felipe, and Cristina Monzón García. 2008. "El lenguaje del poder: Conceptos tarascos en torno a la autoridad." In *Símbolos de poder en Mesoamérica*, edited by Guilhem Olivier, 31–46. Mexico City: Universidad Nacional Autónoma de México.

Cerda Farías, Igor. 2002. *La Relación geográfica de Tiripetío, 1580. Transcripción, estudio y notas*. Morelia: Universidad Michoacana de San Nicolás de Hidalgo.

Darras, Véronique. 2008. "Estrategias para la producción de navajas de obsidiana en la región de Zacapu y la vertiente del Lerma (Michoacan, México) entre el Epiclásico y el Posclásico Tardío." *Ancient Mesoamerica* 19(2): 243–64.

Espejel Carbajal, Claudia. 2007. "Etnohistoria y Arqueología Tarasca." Report submitted to FAMSI. Accessed June 28, 2013. http://www.famsi.org/reports/06041es/index.html.

Espejel Carbajal, Claudia. 2008. *La justicia y el fuego: Dos claves para leer la Relación de Michoacán*. 2 vols. Zamora: El Colegio de Michoacán.

Fargher, Lane F., Verenice Y. Heredia Espinoza, and Richard E. Blanton. 2011. "Alternative Pathways to Power in Late Postclassic Highland Mesoamerica." *Journal of Anthropological Archaeology* 30: 306–26.

García Alcaraz, Agustín. 1976. "Estratificación social entre los tarascos prehispánicos." In *Estratificación social en la Mesoamérica prehispánica*, edited by Pedro Carrasco and Johanna Broda, 221–24. Mexico City: Centro de Investigaciones Superiores / Instituto Nacional de Antropología e Historia.

Gilberti, R. P. Fr. Maturino. [1559] 1989. *Diccionario de la lengua tarasca o de Michoacán*. Morelia: Fimax Publicistas.

Gorenstein, Shirley, and Helen Perlstein Pollard. 1983. *The Tarascan Civilization: A Late Prehispanic Cultural System*. Nashville: Vanderbilt University Publications in Anthropology No. 28.

Haskell, David L. 2008. "The Cultural Logic of Hierarchy in the Tarascan State." *Ancient Mesoamerica* 19(2): 231–41.

Healan, Dan M. 2012. "The Archaeology of Tula, Hidalgo, Mexico." *Journal of Archaeological Research* 20(1): 53–115.

Hernández, Christine L., and Dan M. Healan. 2008. "The Role of Late Pre-Contact Colonial Enclaves in the Development of the Postclassic Ucareo Valley, Michoacan, Mexico." *Ancient Mesoamerica* 19(2): 265–82.

Hosler, Dorothy. 2009. "West Mexican Metallurgy: Revisited and Revised." *Journal of World Prehistory* 22(3): 185–212.

Kaufman, Terrence. 2001. "The History of the Nawa Language Group from the Earliest Times to the Sixteenth Century: Some Initial Results." Last modified March 2001. http://www.albany.edu/pdlma/Nawa.pdf.

Kuthy-Saenger, Maria de Lourdes. 1996. "Strategies of Survival, Accommodation and Innovation: The Tarascan Indigenous Elite in Sixteenth Century Michoacan." PhD diss., Michigan State University.

Lagunas, Fray Juan Baptista de. [1574] 1983. *Arte y diccionario con otras obras en lengua Michuacana. Edición facsimilar*. Edited by J. Benedict Warren. Morelia: Fimax Publicistas.

López Sarralangue, Delfina Esmeralda. 1965. *La nobleza indígena de Pátzuaro en la época virreinal*. Mexico City: Universidad Nacional Autónoma de México / Instituto de Investigaciones Historicas.

Macías Goytia, Angelina. 1990. *Huandacareo: Lugar de juicios, tribunal*. Mexico City: Instituto Nacional de Antropología e Historia.

Macías Goytia, A., and K. Vackimes Serret. 1988. "Tres Cerritos, Cuitzeo, Michoacán." In *Primera reunión sobre las sociedades prehispánicas en el centro-occidente de México*, vol. 1, *Cuaderno de Trabajo*, 161–64. Mexico City: Instituto Nacional de Antropología e Historia.

Maldonado, Blanca E. 2008. "A Tentative Model of the Organization of Copper Production in the Tarascan State." *Ancient Mesoamerica* 19(2): 283–97.

Martínez Baracs, Rodrigo. 2005. *Convivencia y utopía. El gobierno indio y español de la "ciudad de Mechuacan," 1521–1580*. Mexico City: Fondo de Cultura Económico.

Martínez González, Roberto. 2009. "Dioses propios y ajenos: Deidades patronas y realeza sagrada entre los purépechas del siglo XVI." *Revista Española de Antropología Americana* 39(1): 53–76.

Michelet, Dominique. 2008. "Living Differently: The Sites of the Milpillas Phase (1250–1450 AD) in the Malpaís de Zacapu (Michoacán)." In *Urbanism in Mesoamerica/El Urbanismo en Mesoamérica*, vol. 2, edited by Alba Guadalupe Mastache, Robert H. Cobean, Angel García Cook, and Kenneth G. Hirth, 593–620. University Park: Pennsylvania State University / Mexico City: Instituto Nacional de Antropología e Historia.

Michelet, Dominique, Grégory Pereira, and Gérald Migeon. 2005. "La llegada de los Uacúsechas a la región de Zacapu, Michoacán: Datos arqueológicos y discusión."

In *Reacomodos demográficos del Clásico al Posclásico en el centro de México*, edited by Linda Manzanilla, 137–53. Mexico City: Universidad Nacional Autónoma de México / Instituto de Investigaciones Antropológicas.

Monzón, Cristina, Hans Roskamp, and Benedict Warren. 2009. "La memoria de don Melchor Caltzin (1543): Historia y legitimación en Tzintzuntzan, Michoacán." *Estudios de Historia Novohispana, México* 40: 21–55.

Paredes Martínez, Carlos, and Marta Terán, eds. 2003. *Autoridad y gobierno indígena en Michoacán: Ensayos a través de su historia*, vol. 1. Zamora: El Colegio de Michoacán, Centro de Investigaciones y Estudios Superiores en Antropología Social / Instituto Nacional de Antropología e Historia / Universidad Michoacana de San Nicolás de Hidalgo.

Pereira, Grégory. 2005. "The Utilization of Grooved Human Bones: A Reanalysis of Artificially Modified Human Bones Excavated by Carl Lumholtz at Zacapu, Michoacán, Mexico." *Latin American Antiquity* 16(3): 293–312.

Pereira, Grégory, Gérald Migeon, and Dominique Michelet. 2005. "Transformaciones demográficas y culturales en el centro-norte de México en vísperas del Posclásico: Los sitios del Cerro Barajas (Suroeste de Guanajuato)." In *Reacomodos demográficos del Clásico al Posclásico en el centro de México*, edited by Linda Manzanilla, 123–36. Mexico City: Universidad Nacional Autónoma de México / Instituto de Investigaciones Antropológicas.

Pollard, Helen Perlstein. 1993. *Tariacuri's Legacy: The Prehispanic Tarascan State*. Norman: University of Oklahoma Press.

Pollard, Helen Perlstein. 2003. "Central Places and Cities in the Core of the Tarascan State." In *Urbanization in Mesoamerica/El Urbanismo en Mesoamérica*, vol. 1, edited by William T. Sanders and Alba Guadalupe Mastache, 345–90. University Park: Pennsylvania State University / Mexico City: Instituto Nacional de Antropología e Historia.

Pollard, Helen Perlstein. 2004. "El imperio tarasco en el mundo mesoamericano." *Relaciones* 25(99): 115–42.

Pollard, Helen Perlstein. 2005. "Michoacán en el Mundo Mesoamericano Prehispánico: Erongarícuaro, Michoacán y los Estados Teotihuacano y Tarasco." In *El antiguo occidente de México: Nuevas perspectivas sobre el pasado prehispánico*, edited by Eduardo Williams, Phil C. Weigand, Lorenza López Mestas, and David Grove, 283–303. Zamora: El Colegio de Michoacán.

Pollard, Helen Perlstein. 2008. "A Model of the Emergence of the Tarascan State." *Ancient Mesoamerica* 19(2): 217–30.

Pollard, Helen Perlstein. Forthcoming. "La jerarquía y heterarquía en el mundo prehispánico tarasco: La transformación dentro de una tradición." In *Nuevas miradas sobre los antiguos michoacanos (México): Un diálogo interdisciplinario*, edited by Hans Roskamp and Sarah Albiez-Wieck.

Pollard, Helen Perlstein, Joshua Lieto, and A. Dan Jones. 2013. "The Curious Case of the Spouted Vessels: Detection of Cacao in Tarascan Pottery." Paper presented at the Midwest Mesoamericanist Meeting, Chicago, March 16.

Pollard, Helen Perlstein, and Michael E. Smith. 2003. "The Aztec-Tarascan Border." In *The Postclassic Mesoamerican World*, edited by Michael E. Smith and Frances F. Berdan, 87–90. Salt Lake City: University of Utah Press.

Roskamp, Hans. 1998. *La historiografía indígena de Michoacán: El Lienzo de Jucutacato y los títulos de Carapan*. Leiden: CNWS.

Roskamp, Hans. 2010. "Los nahuas de Tzintzuntzan-Huitzitzilan, Michoacán: Historia, mito y legitimación de un señorío prehispánico." *Journal de la Société des Américanistes* 96(1): 75–106.

Roskamp, Hans. 2012. "Memories of a Kingdom: The Tarascan and Nahua Foundation of Pre-Hispanic Tzintzuntzan, West Mexico." In *Mesoamerican Memory: Enduring Systems of Remembrance*, edited by Amos Megged and Stephanie Wood, 113–27. Norman: University of Oklahoma Press.

Roskamp, Hans, and Guadalupe César Villa. 2003. "Iconografía de un pleito: El Lienzo de Aranza y la conflictividad política en la sierra tarasca, siglo XVII." In *Autoridad y gobierno indígena en Michoacán*, vol. 1, edited by Paredes Martínez, Carlos, and Marta Terán, 217–39. Zamora: El Colegio de Michoacán / Centro de Investigaciones y Estudios Superiores en Antropología Social, Instituto Nacional de Antropología e Historia / Universidad Michoacana de San Nicolás Hidalgo.

Sewall, William H., Jr. 1996. "Historical Events as Transformations of Structures: Inventing Revolution at the Bastille." *Theory and Society* 25(6): 841–81.

Smith, Michael E., and Frances F. Berdan, eds. 2003. *The Postclassic Mesoamerican World*. Salt Lake City: University of Utah Press.

Stark, Barbara L., and John K. Chance. 2008. "Diachronic and Multidisciplinary Perspectives on Mesoamerican Ethnicity." In *Ethnic Identity in Nahua Mesoamerica: The View from Archaeology, Art History, Ethnohistory, and Contemporary Ethnography*, edited by Frances F. Berdan, John K. Chance, Alan R. Sandstrom, Barbara L. Stark, James Taggart, and Emily Umberger, 1–37. Salt Lake City: University of Utah Press.

Stone, Cynthia L. 2004. *In Place of Gods and Kings: Authorship and Identity in the Relación de Michoacán*. Norman: University of Oklahoma Press.

Warren, J. Benedict. 1985. *The Conquest of Michoacan: The Spanish Domination of the Tarascan Kingdom in Western Mexico, 1521–1530*. Norman: University of Oklahoma Press.

Warren, J. Benedict, ed. 1991. *Diccionario grande de la lengua de Michoacán: Tarasco-español.* Morelia: Fimax Publicistas.

Warren, J. Benedict, and Cristina Monzón. 2004. "Carta de los principales de Patzcuaro al obispo Vasco de Quiroga, 10 de marzo de 1549." *Relaciones* 25(99): 177–212.

Wolf, Eric R. 1999. *Envisioning Power: Ideologies of Dominance and Crisis.* Berkeley: University of California Press.

Yoffee, Norman. 2005. *Myths of the Archaic State: Evolution of the Earliest Cities, States, and Civilizations.* Cambridge: Cambridge University Press.

9

Reflections on the Archaeopolitical

Pursuing the Universal within a Unity of Opposites

Simon Martin

A central question, indeed a perennial quandary, for those investigating ancient societies is how do we divine political meaning from the scant remains left to us? How can leveled buildings and abandoned artifacts betray extinct systems of authority and one-time strategies of control? How do we justify interpretations of the past that can only exist here in the present? These are quests that animate the contributors to this volume and, in one guise or another, are addressed and readdressed by every generation of scholars. As time goes by, knowledge grows and understanding is enriched. Yet we know that this is not simply a product of ever-larger accumulations of data, but also of the changing conceptual frameworks within which they are interpreted. Their shifting parameters point to the ways that knowledge exists within paradigmatic matrices in the Kuhnian (1962) sense, in which both the questions we ask and the answers we get are under the influence of deeper tides.

In this concluding chapter, I will be looking at some key themes raised in preceding ones, situating them within a broader theoretical context that encompasses the past, present, and future prospects of research into ancient politics. Historical reflection allows us to perceive where we stand on time's arrow: simultaneously cognizant of the intellectual inheritance bequeathed to us; engaged with the social, cultural, and political ideas that suffuse our own academic age; and casting our eyes forward to the ground on which further possibilities yet lie.

DOI: 10.5876/9781607324164.c009

In her introductory chapter, Sarah Kurnick asks how rulers establish their authority in ways that both separate them from, and integrate them with, their subject communities; the two capacities sitting within the same person in a contradictory yet fruitful manner. Contradiction is a much-discussed term in social studies and it obliges us to consider the logical status of paradoxes. Immanuel Kant (1999) saw antimonies—statements that are incompatible yet equally true—as evidence that the world we know through our senses can never be reconciled with pure reason. In his dissent from this, Georg Wilhelm Friedrich Hegel (1991:93) argued that reality itself arises from contradictory forces, a unity of opposites in which knowledge and truth only emerge from dialectical exchange.[1] A "unity of opposites" is a fine characterization of the social sciences, which are shot through with conceptual polarities; with individual-society, universal-particular, mental-material, and form-function some of the first that come to mind.

The underlying aim of much recent work has been to reconcile these dichotomous tendencies, and Kurnick's chapter sets out to "advance a model [of political authority] that is all-inclusive yet allows for the great inherent variability in human practices." Contradiction serves as a cross-cultural theme, yet she asks each author to "ascertain and delineate the specific acts and practical actions . . . among a particular group in a particular place during a particular time" (3).

Politics can be seen not simply as the pursuit and maintenance of status and resources but as a power-inflected process that works to resolve, ameliorate, or mask inherent and constantly arising contradictions. Imbalances in social position and material wealth are to be found in every complex society, but any idea that this is a truly stable situation is disabused by the innumerable ways in which such distinctions are sustained or reinforced. Indeed, consciously or not, whole armories of ideology and impositions of social constraint are mustered to achieve this end.

REASSESSING ARCHAEOPOLITICS

We have direct experience of the political in our own lives and consequently possess both discursive and practical knowledge of how power relations engage us as subjects and participants. But what is essential about the nature of politics and what is dependent on a particular context of time and place? What principles within the politics of the present can be safely projected into the past?

In his chapter about Ceibal, Takeshi Inomata is concerned with the uncritical application of Western models of politics to past societies. He points to how both familiarity and unthinking ethnocentrism can lead us to misidentify modern constructs as universals: "An important contribution of archaeology should be disclosing . . . the historical situatedness of our taken-for-granted ideas about humanity and human society" (p. 38). For example, he critiques the Western emphasis on the individual, rational actor, arguing instead that human beings often act in ways that lack real intentionality. Rationality is often applied retrospectively as people try to explain their own actions. Similarly, in their discussion of territoriality in the pre-Columbian past, Bryce Davenport and Charles Golden caution against taking the modern nation-state—with "juridical, political, economic, and even moral prerogatives . . . explicitly linked to and profoundly defined by the control of what are legally defined as fixed borders" as a model for political landscapes of the past (184). This is the kind of retrospective application to which archaeologists frequently join in voicing their objections but implicitly adhere to nonetheless—a point I will return to later.

To create a context for these debates, we need to consider the intellectual tools available to us and therefore how political anthropology—the domain of archaeopolitics—distinguishes itself from political science. The latter is predicated on the notion of a common heritage to Western thought and experience, tracing its origins back to the Enlightenment and further through an illustrious line of Renaissance and Classical thinkers. Its overriding mission is to understand the workings of the modern world via a conception of the "state" that is both historically real and a transcending abstraction. Political anthropology lacks this metahistorical purpose. In studying a vast array of societies dispersed across space and time, it asks not what the past contributes to the present but how plastic and context-dependent social formations and distributions of power can be, alert to how culture complicates or disrupts the idea of human universals.

This interest in politics outside the Western metahistory—that is, in the ethnographic present and the archaeological past—is much more recent, not emerging with purpose until the mid-twentieth century. Yet crucially, this coincided with the rehabilitation of the Victorian idea of universal sociocultural evolution (White 1949; Steward 1955) and a resuscitation of the typologies that gave it shape and order (Sahlins and Service 1960; Service 1962; Fried 1967). As a result, analysis was initially yoked to the same teleological enterprise and charged with providing a prequel to the modern. A concern with regional histories was regularly subordinated to the greater purpose of classification within an evolutionary scheme. Ethnographically known peoples were viewed as "contemporary ancestors" whose modest social and material complexity offered a snapshot of our own past.[2] An archaeology dedicated to process sought the origins of institutions, most especially the "early state"—an entity that, however qualified, could never escape its reference point in the contemporary world. Processualist archaeology played to its material strengths, focusing on how the systematics of evolutionary stages were etched into the ground (see Smith 2003:33–45). Here, the location and scale of settlements, their architectural taxonomies, and the distributions of artifactual assemblages were not simply the traces of political lives but direct stigmata of societal organization. As a result, political vision narrowed to a mechanical one in which the actualism of events, people, and the ideas that motivated them were not only seen to be beyond reach, but beyond relevance—consigned to the status of epiphenomena.[3]

Critiques of this neoevolutionary program and its archaeological analogues are by now familiar and came not only from the vanguard of post-processualism but from those holding to an enduring cultural-historical sensibility, since joined by a generation that has absorbed and expanded the argument (e.g., Hodder 1982, 1986; Gailey and Patterson 1987; Kohl 1987; Shanks and Tilley 1987; Shennan 1993:53; Yoffee 1993, 2005; Kehoe 1998; Chapman 2003:42–45; Smith 2003; Pauketat 2007; Campbell 2009). The neoevolutionary program had been undermined on both theoretical and evidential grounds. Where direct testing against historical data was possible, it revealed the deeply blurred reality between the discretely drawn types of stage theory (e.g., Feinman and Neitzel 1984). The substantive charge, in the end, was that one-time heuristic models had ossified into "things in the world" (Wolf 1982:3; Kohl 1984:127–29; Roscoe 2000:116), generating an order to the past that was not so much exposed as imposed. A laudable ambition to understand social change in more rigorous ways had elevated the scientific to such a lofty pedestal that it had occluded the ostensible subjects of the endeavor: the people behind the artifacts, the ideas behind the distributions.

In the wake of this critique, a renewed program for exploring the social and political in the ancient world was required. It was clear that this would need to include (a) a shift in focus from disembodied systems to a peopled past; (b) a concern with ideational as much as material aspects of social life; (c) an orientation toward society as historical and contingent; (d) an engagement with politics on the level of practical effects; and (e) an approach toward internal rather than externally imposed change.[4] This effort would be expressed in a particular group of theoretical concerns, a revised set of thematic interests, a revisiting of material and spatial engagements, and a renewed concern with documents and representations.

A Theoretical Ground

The work of three theorists, Michel Foucault, Pierre Bourdieu, and Anthony Giddens, would have a telling impact on this rebuilding exercise, and it is no surprise that they are referenced by a number of the authors in this book. Foucault is recognized for his contributions to the contemporary concept of power (e.g., Foucault 1978, 1979, 1980, 2003, 2007), taking a historical approach that emphasized its indivisible links to knowledge. For him, power is generated as one individual acts upon another, which, in so doing, develops into an autonomous and self-generating phenomenon. The institutions that govern us—which are neither benign nor malign—emerge, counterintuitively, less as sources of power than its products. Foucault fulfilled the post-neoevolutionary agenda for a more pervasive idea of politics, but his resolutely impersonal strictures of regulation hardly satisfied the goal of a peopled past, as Inomata, in particular, remarks.

Several of the contributors to this volume have grappled with the applicability of Foucault's ideas to the ancient world, generating some diverse responses. Foucault is cited in Tatsuya Murakami's chapter on Teotihuacan, where his models of regulation and disciplinary order constitute a subtext to how power structures were manifested architecturally in that city. Foucault had argued against essentialism, insisting that there are no fixed norms to human beliefs or behavior and that each epoch establishes its own values. Central to his vision of disciplinary "biopower" was its invention in the post-Enlightenment era, marking a radical departure from the sovereign control over life and death that preceded it. It was only by disputing the temporal situatedness of his concept of discipline over sovereign subjects—denying its confinement to the modern era—that Giorgio Agamben (1998) converted it into a trans-historical idea. Inomata, though generally critical of the tendency to retrofit Foucault into historical contexts, sees value in his diffuse, collective notions of power, distinguished from that focused on a central emblematic ruler. In a similar questioning of Foucault's temporal divide, Kurnick asks whether the distinction between discipline and punishment are not modes of domination that actually coexist in all societies.

To realize the aim of a peopled past it would be necessary to step away from Foucault and employ some other strands of anthropological and sociological thinking, and this is where the theories of practice from Bourdieu (1977, 1990) and structuration from Giddens (1979, 1984) come to the fore. The essence of both is a recursiveness in which individuals and society, agents and structures, are never isolated but constantly act upon and modify the other. Kurnick and Inomata rightly highlight that this central recursive relationship between agency and structure is too little explored in most archaeological applications. For Bourdieu, it takes place through gradual and often unconscious innovations in daily life, amendments to the internalized dispositions he calls habitus. Giddens has a different emphasis in focusing on knowledgeable actors who more consciously and strategically try to shape their place in the world. It is hard to overestimate the influence of these agency approaches to current anthropology and archaeology—largely fulfilling a prediction of paradigmatic status (Ortner 1984:127). Even so, one could be forgiven for thinking that the tangle of propositions identified with agency today indicate that it has become something of a banner under which a wide range of humanistic concerns gather (see Dobres and Robb 2000; Dornan 2002).

Bourdieu (1977:164) saw a similar temporal watershed to Foucault, with the concept of habitus situated in modern times and contrasted with doxa—in which practices are so engrained that they lack real intentionality and political orders are mistaken for natural ones—which he considered to be the norm among ancient societies. Adam T. Smith (2001) questions Bourdieu's blanket ascription of doxa to antiquity, comparing it to a false consciousness and a view that risks stereotyping everyone who is temporally and culturally remote from us as an "Other." In their chapter on pre-Columbian political landscapes, Davenport and Golden similarly critique Bourdieu's related notion of "misrecognition of arbitrariness," arguing that it denies local agents the ability to perceive their own engagement with landscape and the production of meaning within it. For them, communities have an active understanding of the relationship between physical and social, which is experienced bodily and interpreted discursively.

Giddens's (1979:2) structuration theory was explicitly devised to address the sociology of Western capitalism and socialism and only later, and somewhat vaguely, ascribed universal qualities (Giddens 1984). The modern focus of Giddens's model frequently passes without comment by the scholars who use it (for exceptions, see Last 1995:152; Knapp 2010:196), though its greater sense of volition and scope for innovation is often contrasted with Bourdieu's more cognitively constrained notion of habitus. If Foucault's idea of disciplinary power was bereft of personal agency, then, in turn, neither Giddens nor Bourdieu were overly concerned with the exercise of power. To be sure, forms of constraint and domination nominally pervaded their treatments of agency-structure dualities, but their greater focus always lay in "how to go on." While agency approaches are clearly versatile tools, they have "holes" (Ortner 2006:129), and some important ones appear wherever political issues are at stake. As originally conceived, they are well suited to understanding how a status quo is perpetuated, but much less so the workings of competition, resistance, or transformation, including new forms of subjection. They barely address the dynamics of politics, nor explore the pragmatics of how personal or institutional power is reified as hierarchy.[5] Perhaps the most vocal complainant here has been Nicos Mouzelis (1995:100–26), who describes the absence of an adequate conception of hierarchy in agency models as "like swimming in an empty pool" (126). Hierarchy is indispensable to any full political analysis because it is the prime structural condition enabling and constraining action, with social status and role affecting both what types of actions are feasible and the scale of their effects.

The issue is whether the dualistic conflation of subject and object in Bourdieu and Giddens makes hierarchy inherently problematic, as Mouzelis would have it, or whether hierarchy can be accommodated by recognizing its integral role in social structure as real life (Williams 1977:108–10; Sewell 1992:20–21).[6] In regard to the latter, John C. Barrett (2001:161) characterizes polities and their differential empowerment as "the structuring of large-scale and vertically ranked political systems within which certain elites worked explicitly to define the conditions under which other forms of agency could operate." In other words, the terms of agency-structure relationships differ, allowing more powerful agents to secure their positions and profit by ensuring that the system restricts the opportunities of others. All individuals have agency, but some have more agency than others. But how do these asymmetries come about in the first place and how do elites sustain their structural advantages and therefore political power? How is power itself to be understood within an agency-led perspective?

This takes us to an important but under-specified feature of Giddens's work: his model of structure as composed of two parts, "rules" and "resources," the latter described as "the media through which power is exercised" (Giddens 1979:91). Commentators have long pointed to how elites succeed by harnessing and manipulating resources in the widest sense—everything from raw materials to recondite knowledge—but the innovation here is to fuse them to their mobilizing ideas within a single model of structure.[7] This proposal has been refined and expanded by William H. Sewell (1992:9–13), who recasts rules as "schemas" to evade the implication of rigidity and express a more adaptive and inventive potential. Most importantly, he insists on a recursive relationship between the two components not found in Giddens. For Sewell, there can be no schemas without the resources that make them possible, and, in turn, resources are recognized as resources only because they are created or utilized by schemas. As with the capacity for agency, resources are universal. All actors possess capacities of mind and material, however vast or meager they might be.

From here, Sewell develops this rationale to show how a duality of schemas and resources can generate inequalities, and how the unpredictability in their relationship through time opens a mechanism for transformation (Sewell 1992:16–19). It is their purposeful allocation, including the transposability of schemas from one set of resources to another, which allows power to be distributed disproportionately and used to enact practical domination.[8] Of the chapters in this volume, only Helen Perlstein Pollard's makes reference to Sewell's construct. Her interest lies in how elites in the Postclassic Tarascan state mobilized material objects and discourses of ethnogenesis as resources to create hierarchical distinctions between different social segments. Sewell's understanding of how mental and material resources are joined recursively to ideas offers additional range to what agency approaches can achieve in analytical terms—not by overlying a separate concept of power but by expanding the logic of some of the existing features of the concept. It is especially important to see a model of power in practice that does more than provide a definition based on effects, concluding with its familiar, though true, underpinning in violence. There is a great deal more to explain about how practical political effects are achieved, taking account of how they are manufactured within webs of motivations, norms, capacities, strategies, methods, and tangible materials.

Thematic Directions

Theories of power and agency established a grounding for the post-neoevolutionary program, but shifts of topic and theme have been hardly less significant. Major influences here have been the intellectual traditions that have always taken an analytical and historical perspective on politics—namely, the various shades of Marxism and the sociology of Max Weber. Thus, the realms of ideology, authority, legitimacy, sovereignty, conflict, and order, for example, have moved to the foreground, largely displacing objects of analysis such as the state, city, government, economy, religious organizations, and so forth (see especially Baines and Yoffee 1998). With no small debt to Foucault, the political is no longer taken to be a discrete activity emanating from just a central source but is also a flow of power relations crosscutting and permeating society as a whole, linking its many active domains in both durable and dynamic configurations.

That ideology has taken so prominent a place among these topics is little wonder, given its inherent promise to fuse the cultural and political, with the added attraction that its symbolic expression might be open to archaeological, historical, and iconological investigation (see Kurnick's overview of the topic). Ideology has multiple definitions but minimally describes a set of interrelated ideas that condition how social participants interpret their world and conduct political action. There are still two major senses in which it is used: either as a Marxist false consciousness (Marx and Engels 1970)—a knowing conspiracy of the powerful to mystify and entrench their position by duping the wider public—or a more encompassing conception of a social and political worldview (e.g., Conrad and Demarest 1984; Miller and Tilley 1984; Demarest and Conrad 1992). In this second sense, a nexus of ideas legitimize authority, including collective processes of naturalization in which a constructed political artifact projects itself as some innate and unquestionable order to the world. Although the first sense has been richly critiqued (e.g., Abercrombie, Hill, and Turner 1980), it is still a vein that maintains a strong influence in anthropological understandings of exploitation. Most of the chapters in this volume, when they use the term, adhere to the second definition of ideology, as does most recent work on the topic. However, over time this form has acquired a worryingly diffuse series of applications. Almost every aspect of social operation has been described as ideological in nature, rendering the term at best slippery, at worst devoid of distinctive meaning. While it remains a useful and at times essential term, it is one that demands explicit qualification.

Ideology plays a major role in Murakami's contribution, but there it is largely broken down from a monolithic single entity to pluralistic "ideologies," each addressed to a specific purpose and realm. This is not necessarily antithetical to his concern for an encompassing "state ideology" that operates on a higher, or at least more overtly political, level. Davenport and Golden express the more radical view that ideology is entirely secondary to performed action: "it is practice—not intent, not belief—that is central." This draws liberally on the referential practice for which William F. Hanks (1990) is best known, which explores how people orient themselves according to the people and things around them rather than to a set of guiding notions.

Looking at political society from an ideological perspective offered one way out of the evolutionary mind-set, and a notable effort in this direction was the model of dual-processualism (Blanton et al. 1996; see also Kurnick, this volume).[9] This examines modes of leadership and distinguishes an exclusionary network strategy from a more inclusive corporate strategy—which is to say, regimes centered on individuals who concentrate power as opposed to regimes that distribute it among a collective elite. Dual-processualism necessarily features in Murakami's chapter on Teotihuacan since this great metropolis was the model's exemplar of corporate governance. Yet his reanalysis serves to highlight how recent data argues for a more complex picture and an interpenetration of strategic practice throughout all levels of society.[10] Similarly, Christopher S. Beekman's chapter questions dual-processualism's claim that corporate and exclusionary strategies could not coexist. He shows that in the Tequila valleys of Jalisco, lineage self-aggrandizement and rituals of community cohesion existed side by side, often in the same architectural spaces. Public performances were used to mitigate the "cognitive dissonance" that this would have produced. Both contributors concur with a wider skepticism toward dual-processualism's utility—principally because it fails to explicate the relationship between its two strategies, its analytical ambition quickly dissolving into a pair of totalizing categories following the style, if not the goals, of the neoevolutionists (Yoffee 2005:177–79; Campbell 2009:822). More generously, it might be best to see the model in historical terms as an intermediate step, a halfway house on the path to more elemental understandings.

For the most part, a reorientation toward the thematic in political life had left one object untouched or, better perhaps, hidden in plain sight. The pinnacle of neoevolutionary pyramids and the core feature of social scientific thought since the Enlightenment, the *state* has deep foundations and a tenacious hold on our collective imagination. Yet Robert H. Lowie (1927), as others before him, thought that the emergence of what we call states in history introduced no "qualitative transformations to human society" (Kohl 1987:27), while Arthur R. Radcliffe-Brown (1940: xxiii) called the state a "fiction of the philosophers," claiming that only governments as groups of empowered actors truly exist. But the most serious challenges have come from within the spiritual home of the state—political science—which began to wonder if the object that had consumed so much of its energies was quite what it seemed. In one influential assessment, the success of the state stems from its very lack of substance—that its purpose is to serve as an artful façade or "mask" obscuring the real functioning of politics (Abrams 1988). What is real is not the state but the *idea* of a state, which works to legitimize otherwise unacceptable forms of domination. Even those political scientists who believe that the state is more just than an idea see an entity of extreme variation, filled with so many complexities and contradictions that it is "largely useless for theory-building" (Ferguson and Mansbach 1996:10). If these doubts and caveats are valid for the modern state, how much more so must they be of the ancient one, an object entirely dependent on backward projection? As Yale H. Ferguson (2002:83–84) puts it, "Where we differ strongly with most archaeologists and anthropologists is with regard to their persistent use of the term 'state' to refer to a host of different polities in the ancient and medieval (pre-Westphalian) worlds . . . It is the political equivalent of talking about the wheeled carts on Roman roads being automobiles."

Smith (2003:78–102) reaches this same conclusion in his comprehensive, not to say surgical, extirpation of the archaic state from anthropological and archaeological thought. Even those who similarly reject stage theories feel the need to retain the state as a real and necessary artifact (e.g., Chapman 2003; Yoffee 2005). Yet Smith assails it on several fronts, concluding that it is an illusion that impedes the necessary reflection on what early complex societies actually did and how they were constituted: "In placing the State at the heart of investigations into early complex polities, political analysis—the investigation of the formation, administration, and transformation of civil relationships—is replaced by a political cladistics in which typological classification suffices for explanation" (Smith 2003:81). This is in part because the significance accorded the state in neoevolutionary models was not heuristic at all; it was openly considered the end result of a qualitative leap forward crossing a "great divide" (Fried 1967:236; Service 1975:3–10). Smith is among those who dispute the reality of this historical boundary, whose arbitrary criteria artificially cleave state from non-state within the series of contingent transformations that produce greater social and political complexity. The object offered in place of the archaic state is the "early complex polity," an entity concentrated on a governing authority formed through mutually sustaining relations of power and legitimation. This triumvirate of authority, power, and legitimacy becomes the pivot from which to transfer analytical attention away from type/form and toward content, an attempt to peer within the "black box" and perceive the relational principles that constitute political life (see also Campbell 2009; Johansen and Bauer 2011; Smith 2011).

The steady rise of polity as a term of choice in the study of ancient politics has been (a) a way of traversing the contentious transition between chiefdom and state (without denying the viability of either); (b) an attempt to sidestep evolutionary issues altogether; or, now, (c) an overt challenge to the utility of the archaic state concept. The current volume duly reflects the lexical shift in its chapters, while its bibliographical entries, by contrast, abound with titles incorporating state/states—a clear reflection of the word's conceptual legacy.

What we often find in Mesoamerica are forms of political cohesion that challenge the assumptions inherent to many universalistic types, compelling us to define local configurations of community. Arthur A. Joyce et al. (this volume:59), for example, note that the Río Viejo polity, while exhibiting many of the features that archaeologists have traditionally used to identify archaic states, was in fact a fragile political formation that lasted only a century or two:

> Río Viejo exhibits many of the hallmarks that archaeologists have traditionally attributed to the kinds of politically centralized and tightly integrated societies normally defined as states. In the case of Río Viejo, these characteristics include a five-tiered settlement hierarchy, urbanism, monumental public architecture, and rulers who were sufficiently powerful to sponsor large labor projects and public ceremonies. Yet a closer reading of the evidence shows that people in outlying communities . . . exhibited considerable independence from the regional center in ritual practices and architectural techniques and styles. In contrast to traditional archaeological models of complex political formations as strongly hierarchical and tightly integrated, our view of the later Formative Río Viejo polity is that it was neither highly integrated nor significantly coercive. While Río Viejo challenges assumptions about complex polities, it was far from being an isolated case.

Both Murakami and Pollard, on the other hand, continue to apply the term *state* to their subjects of Teotihuacan and the Tarascan empire, respectively. These large, centralized polities have the scale and presence we commonly associate with modern nation-states. Davenport and Golden, on the other hand, seem to want to reclaim *state* as a neutral term for comparative purposes, but it would be preferable for the authors of all three of these chapters to explicitly define and defend their usage in light of the theoretical currents that have moved against it.

Of late, interest in legitimatized authority has coalesced around the idea of sovereignty. Although a number of contributors to this volume refer to sovereigns or sovereignty, their conceptual grounding remains largely unexamined. Debated since Classical times, sovereignty is traditionally defined as supreme authority over a specific territory and its population (e.g., Hinsley 1966). It has always had a presence in political science but has recently blossomed within a political anthropology shedding its origins in colonialist ethnography and staking ground outside its familiar terrains of kingship and kinship. Vital here is the aforementioned work by Agamben and his understanding of sovereignty as a single constituting/constituted power rooted in violence (Humphrey 2004; Hansen and Stepputat 2006). Sovereign will is imposed through judgments and sanctions to which it is not itself subject (murder is a crime but capital punishment is justice). Given, however, that violence underpins all political power, especially the illegitimate, the truly distinguishing qualities of sovereignty lie in its two forms of corporality—vested in the person of a ruler or in a communal body politic—and its implied possession of some moral dimension speaking to an idealized or transcendent identity.

Whether it draws on a potent mythology, antique tradition, or legal statute all depends on a legitimacy that ultimately rests in public acceptance, or at least acquiescence. Sovereignty is now forwarded as an agenda within archaeology that involves "practical regimes of authorization and subjection . . . the embodied regimens, rituals, habits, and activities that reproduce, and undo, sovereignty in interactions from the spectacular to the everyday" (Smith 2011:419).

What remains to be more thoroughly developed is a view of the pragmatics of sovereignty that lies between high ideals and base violence. There is more to sustaining authority than ideological beguilement and the threat, or use, of brute force. The successful mobilization of resources in their widest sense can be considered a given, but this is not a phenomenon that can go unexamined (as several authors in this volume show). We need to know more about how leaders use their resources to energize the agency of subjects who, in proffering up *their* resources, reflexively generate the empowerment of leaders. It is here that the previously noted addition of schemas as ideas dedicated to this end offers a productive tool. Ideology may supply an overarching framework, but practical politics work on the microscale engineering of stimulus: with action and compliance motivated by the fear of retribution and the promise of reward, not simply by how to go on. Schemas are crafted to the production and utilization of every resource, be it human, material, or informational—supplying the necessary discursive knowledge of how to use them to furnish power.

Because agency theories see structure as an undifferentiated whole for analytical purposes, they cannot offer insights into social divisions of the kind that isolate the elite from the masses. We therefore need to keep attending to status and role, meaning that the functionalism of Parsons (1951) has a part to play and is not entirely upstaged or eclipsed by practice and structuration (Mouzelis 1995). Similarly, we need to pursue the means by which status distinctions were realized throughout the political community. Worldwide, the elite are consistently adept at sustaining their differentiation through the "dramaturgy of power" (Cohen 1981; Wengrow 2001:169), part of which is expressed in elaborate public performances (see Inomata and Coben 2006). This performative aspect of politics is emphasized in several chapters of this volume. Thus, at Ceibal, Inomata sees in its grand plazas evidence for spectacles of violence that were important in shaping social differentiation at the very beginning of settled life at the site. For Beekman, the control of such open performative spaces enabled the socially powerful to compete for recruits, whether for descent groups or community associations. While for Davenport and Golden, the public demarcation of boundaries by performance was central to establishing territorial claims. The elaborate and institutionalized feasting described by both Joyce et al. and Joanne Baron were similarly acts of drama with their own scripts and stage directions.

All social actors seek to make the most of their structural position, and we should not assume that only the elite possessed discursive consciousness and critical reflection. We also need to move away from the assumption that elites were in some way immune to the processes of naturalization. There is little reason to doubt that they believed themselves specially selected to rule by means of bloodline and divine will, judging themselves uniquely capable in the bargain. What agency brings to the table here is a more holistic view of power in society that is neither top-down nor bottom-up. Rulers obviously cannot exist in isolation but are embedded in a social matrix where all participants are contributing agents, and all events performed by the ruler "connote collective actions" (Houston and Escobedo 1997:467). Monarchs need not only armies but also porters, fan-bearers, potters, farmers, and laborers, each contributing to the political community to the extent that their differing access to resources permit: "Recognition of this requires de-privileging the position of elites in archaeological and historical analyses and reconsidering a multiplicity of actors in a multiplicity of arenas." (Porter 2010:168)

Inomata (this volume:35) is also interested in the integrative function of monarchy and "an important implication we might draw from broad cross-cultural studies is that the central property of the divine king is . . . his symbolic nature as the embodiment of the political community." While all authors acknowledge the role of commoners in the ongoing negotiation of authority, several also move beyond the simple dichotomy with rulers to discuss other interest groups. Joyce et al. discuss the tensions between the centralizing motives of the rulers at Río Viejo, as opposed to the regional elite that resisted this. Murakami discusses the rise of a class of bureaucrats who were tasked with the administration of the Teotihuacan polity and their intermediary relationship between rulers and commoners at the site. Baron and Beekman both discuss competing elite lineages within communities and the ramifications of this competition for other community members. In dealing with the only multiethnic system under discussion here, Pollard describes how different ethnic groups held different statuses within the Tarascan polity and how the manipulation of ethnic identity was a key tool in the creation of the empire.

The Materiality of Politics

The call to switch from static understandings of political structure to those of ongoing acts of authorization, regularization, and subjugation is, to varying degrees of emphasis, supported by all the authors in this volume. But how is this archaeology of practice distinguished from its predecessors? To address such a question we must begin with its approach toward the "archaeological record," a notion that sounds stable enough but in fact differs significantly depending on the paradigm in play (Patrik 1985). John C. Barrett (2001) critiques the label itself for its implication of coherence and narrative; he sees nothing in the taphonomic processes of deposition that resembles a text of the kind pursued in hermeneutic archaeology (Hodder 1986:122–24, 1988; for critiques, see Keesing 1987:169 and Preucel 1991:23). For Barrett, an agency-led archaeology sees material remains not as the vestiges of past social practices, the vast majority of which leave no trace, but of the facilities that enabled them.

This perspective joins a rich contemporary tradition in which architecture and artifacts are seen as collaborators with humans in the making of social acts, ranging from the spectacular and episodic to the prosaic and routine.[11] This link between practices and materials appears in Bourdieu (1977), who describes how both the animate and inanimate contribute to processes of socialization (Miller 2005:6). "Materiality" has come to define recent thinking on this topic—which is not a theory of things so much as a theory of the way things are enmeshed in human lives, reaching beyond the mundanely practical to the cognitive, emotional, and sensual (e.g., Miller 1998, 2005; Boivin 2004, 2008; Hodder 2012; Renfrew 2004; Meskell 2005a, 2005b). Objects occupy space and have weight, form, size, color, and texture but are also set in time, decaying rapidly or imperceptibly, discarded or renewed—some long outliving their creators or appropriators, others made and unmade within a day. Archaeology retrieves the durable portion of what was once a far richer material world and asks it questions of function and meaning. A commonsensical division between the practical and the symbolic quickly breaks down, as the closer one looks, the distinction can only be one of emphasis. A question of function demands that we address meaning in the hands of whom, to what purpose, and directed at whom?

An explicit effort to fuse politics with the object world came in the model of "materialization," which describes the "transformation of ideas, values, stories, myths and the like into a physical reality—a ceremonial event, a symbolic object, a monument, or a writing system" (DeMarrais, Castillo, and Earle 1996:16). The argument here is that ideologies do not reside "in people's heads" and that to come into being they must be realized in some tangible form beyond language. The construct seeks to register the role of meaningful objects in the furtherance of power but sees them working reflectively rather than reflexively, with materializations still vehicles at the command of a higher mental order (Pauketat 2001:85).[12] This differs from a political materiality, which considers how practices create, manipulate, or engage objects for specific effects, while they simultaneously reproduce the conditions and necessity for those practices (see Johansen and Bauer 2011:12–16; Smith 2011:425–26). Objects and built environments pattern human actions by means of their physicality and spatiality, structuring to some extent how they should be handled and moved within and between, resisting many, though never all, alternatives.[13]

We have already noted the manufacture and control of ceramics at Monte Albán that allowed elites to structure debts and obligations within and beyond the polity (Joyce et al., this volume). This depended on assigning value to objects that, like fired clay, have no intrinsic worth or scarcity and must be deliberately empowered to achieve their effects. This is a very common, conceivably universal expression of materiality—analogous to how we decide that small metal disks constitute money. To choose another example from Michoacán (Pollard, this volume), portable objects such as ceramic pipes, metal ornaments, spouted vessels, obsidian blades and ornaments, and cotton spindle whorls allowed a newly unified elite class to mark their status within the context of the newly unified state. When Murakami describes the relationship between the bureaucratic requirements of the Teotihuacan polity and the physical facilities that housed them, we need to contemplate the self-generating properties of those institutional forms—that is, not only how needs generate facilities by means of a certain kind of mental model, but the way facilities condition and operationalize the conduct of their users, thus engendering additional needs and operations. Any built environment has this same reflexive potential—not simply as products but as producers of meaning.

In such contexts, objects and spaces can be seen as active rather than passive contributors, taking us close to ascribing them agency—the notion that the material can achieve autonomy from its makers and act on its own account. Object agency is associated with Alfred Gell (1998), who concentrated on effects generated in the mind of the viewer, a perspective that is altogether more palatable to realists than that of Bruno Latour (2005), whose version implies a sentience compatible with animism. Every intentionally made or selected artifact is imbued with sense and purpose, but once let loose into the world, its interpretation depends on how successfully it conforms to cultural understandings and systems of coding, themselves dependent on the strength of social forces that work to maintain them. There may well be a dominant reading, but this can erode over time if the "interpretive community" (Fish 1980) to which it speaks changes or the message lost entirely if that community is decisively disrupted or displaced.[14] Objects can be co-opted and can acquire new meanings, with the patina of time making them all the more compliant to revisionism. These are convoluted processes of semiosis, not agency, and the manner in which materials appear so agent-like is more a comment on how we are cognitively predisposed to see the world (e.g., J. L. Barrett 1998; Boyer 2001). Political materiality envelops acculturated participants in a "semiosphere" (Lotman 1990) of meaningful places and things that subliminally condition as much as they openly propound.[15]

A final aspect of materiality, though one overlapping with other thematic concerns, is landscape. In his compelling case for the constitutive role of landscape in all forms of political authority, Smith (2003) notes not only its obvious spatial dimensions but its role as an anchor for historical experience, meaning, representation, and therefore belonging. Landscape, which includes built or otherwise modified environments, is not natural space but a human production like any other artifact, though here its limits are as much conceptual as they are pragmatic. The only chapter to address landscape directly is that by Davenport and Golden, whose topic of territoriality highlights how the recent emphasis on elite networks in Mesoamerican archaeology has come at the expense of examining bounded and possessed spaces. The essence of this argument is that political relations and perceptions operate at different scales and that a concentration on diffuse webs of political allegiance at the regional or pan-regional level are not appropriate to lower levels—where the logics of local sovereignty works very differently and physical contact with a sustaining environment provokes different mental constructs.

Beyond the Archaeological

Recovering practices may be a new generalized goal, but it does not magically render the archaeological record more transparent or meaningful. Indeed, a move away from perceiving imprints of sociopolitical order to an engagement between the material and immaterial, ascribing value and importance to even fleeting acts and perceptions, sets the bar for archaeological inference even higher. Investigators therefore remain as reliant as ever on external sources of information that inspire, expand, support, or corroborate interpretation. I refer here to the contributions of analogy on one hand and the analysis of word and image on the other.

All statements about the past are either explicitly or implicitly analogical in character. We can assign meaning to the unknown only by comparison with the known (Wylie 1985).[16] But analogy is as problematic as it is indispensable (Clark 1951; Hawkes 1954; Ascher 1961; Gould and Watson 1982). The criteria by which a given parallel is selected, applied, and assessed can never be consistent or truly objective. Analogies fall into general and specific categories. The former is universalistic and consists of choosing a counterpart deemed appropriate by its environmental or cultural resemblance, while the latter is particularistic, referencing descendent or otherwise related societies. In the first case, the problem lies in the subjectivity of the selection, which introduces all sorts of a priori assumptions; in the second ("direct historical analogy"), the greater concern is essentialism, the presumptive notion that a defined cultural group possesses some inherent characteristics that persist through time. The sources used can vary enormously, from societies deep in the prehistoric past to those rich in historical documentation, to contemporary people open to observation and interlocution—each with its own subjectivities. Processualism was wary of analogy despite its regard for a neoevolutionary logic that would seem to make it a highly compatible line of reasoning. The preference was to employ parallels for the purpose of hypothesis forming, but not to use them to seek confirmation or validation of results. Post-processualism was generally much more open to the debt owed to comparative data, switching from the traditional role of neutral observers to one of active engagement in living communities. This approach is popular in Mesoamerica because of the survival of some socially relevant indigenous documents from the early Spanish occupation and a greater number produced by and for the colonial administrations. The existence of many "traditional" societies (leaving the problematic use of that label and the way anthropologists act as its arbiters to one side) also offers opportunities for ethnographic fieldwork.

Ethnohistorical and ethnographic analogies take a significant role in the chapters by Beekman, Baron, and Davenport and Golden, where they serve to contextualize arguments and establish precedents. The modern and historical Náyari are used by Beekman to interpret the purposes of architectural spaces and artifactual remains in the Tequila valleys of Jalisco, not through overt commonalities of form but through perceived commonalities of practice. In documented tensions between the concepts of lineage and community in modern towns, as well as rituals that concern fertility and the seasonal cycle, Beekman detects persuasive analogues for his archaeological material. Baron uses colonial and contemporary accounts of Maya ritual practice, and specifically the beliefs and rituals involving Catholic saints, to trace antecedents in ancient Maya patron deities. By establishing indigenous reinterpretations of imposed Christian concepts, she supports both her general arguments about the links between present and past usage and the specific political roles that the supernatural takes in community and kin competition. Especially rich literary sources and living traditions in Oaxaca allow Davenport and Golden to explore indigenous concepts with considerable time-depth. These strong continuities open comparative vistas that seem to shed light on other parts of Mesoamerica, where they discern analogous concepts of territoriality and boundary making.

Word and image, having languished under the same epiphenomenal tag as ideology under processualism, made a comeback under post-processualism. While open to the possibilities of "reading" ancient art in a manner akin to their readings of architectonics and other material as text (see above), practitioners were riven by doubts about its validity as a decontextualized source (e.g., Tilley 1991; Johnson 2010:111). Within Mesoamerica, this left most of the relevant research to be conducted by less theoretically directed epigraphers and iconologists, usually as part of multidisciplinary programs. It was within this context that the revolutionary decipherment of Maya script took place, and major advances were made in the understanding of motifs and narrative art in that tradition and elsewhere. Indeed, the very limited impact of openly post-processualist theory in the region (with the notable exception of gender studies) was in no small measure because the high point of its intrinsically subjective hermeneutics coincided with the actual reading of art and writing. While European prehistory was enlivened by phenomenological interpretations of its landscapes, mounds, and monuments, the names of Maya buildings and their functions—often with that of their owner or commissioning king included for good measure—were being read with demonstrable clarity. For Baron, hieroglyphic texts are a vital connective tool with which to illuminate and contextualize material remains. There is no space here to discuss the wider ramifications of these developments, but they share close correspondences to the material and text advances that revolutionized the study of Ancient Egypt and Mesopotamia in the nineteenth century.

An engagement with political practice has, as anticipated, brought a renewed enthusiasm for studying written documents and symbolic and narrative images. Indeed, if one looks at recent work exploring the constitution of ancient political relations through practice, one is struck by the degree to which their focal points are not architectural or artifactual finds per se, but narrative texts and images (e.g., Smith 2001; Wengrow 2001; Campbell 2009). On one level this engagement of archaeology with epigraphy and iconology is the kind of synergistic approach we should expect within the ambit of anthropological archaeology, but on another it points to the difficulty of pursuing the ephemera of ideas, experience, and events outside such communicative technologies. Semiotic systems were in large part expressly devoted to memorializing practices. Elsewhere, in architectonic analysis, there can still be disquieting leaps of faith, as the content and orientation of a cache or alignment of a building takes on the mantle of weighty evidence pointing to one form of political system or another. Emphasis is usually placed on a search for meaning, yet the essential problem is often not too few potential meanings but too many. The task for the investigator is to limit the inherent ambiguity of the record, to see how the best available evidence can restrict the free play of speculation.

NATURE OF THE UNIVERSAL

The final part of this chapter takes a different tack, looking beyond the past and present of investigating ancient politics to ask what lines of inquiry might contribute to its future. Of all the oppositions noted at the outset of this chapter, none is more fundamental than the contrast between its positivist and idealist orientations—separating those aspects of the field subject to natural laws from those that can only be intuited through the human mind. This is the central dialectic of social science, without which the field would collapse into sterile data collection on the one hand and tether-less postulation on the other. These oscillations from one side of the dichotomy to the other, enacted over spans of decades, can be seen as a macroscale mirror to the to-and-fro reasoning that researchers perform at the level of personal psyche. Each domain offers a check and a control on the other, and in their sharply contrasting, often conflicting, mappings of phenomena there arise new possibilities for making sense of human engagement with the world and each other. Each side of the equation is in a constant state of development, however punctuated progress may be, and as a result, constantly revivifies the interaction.

Although the balance between positivism and idealism in social studies has shifted through time, it has lately been strongly skewed to the latter, exerting a powerful influence over what ideas are productive or permissible in paradigmatic terms.[17] This raises the question of whether the current idealist preeminence is permanent or simply a stage in the ongoing process of knowledge formation. Could we be approaching the point where scientific epistemologies return to the arena, and this time as protagonists in the debate rather than simply as sources of metaphor?

As we have seen, contemporary configurations of the archaeopolitical shift attention from idealized types to a series of elemental articulations. What both share, however, is their universalistic ambition. Where there was once a ubiquity of forms scattered across the world and through time (e.g., band, tribe, chiefdom, state), there is now a ubiquity of relational principles (e.g., authority, power, legitimacy, sovereignty). This universal currency of political life is seen to underlay all societies, no matter their size, antiquity, or myriad of cultural particularities. But a necessary question must follow: Where do we locate the universal in this analysis? Is it to be found in impersonal processes—patterns that spill from the logics of mathematics or physics—or is it inherently embodied? If we assert the latter then we have not resolved the matter, only brought the problematic issue of "nature" into play. Anthropology has always struggled with its dual mission to understand both body and mind, vacillating between a vision of humans as the highest form of ape, and therefore part of the natural order, and as unique cultural beings that exist somewhere above or beyond it.

To explore extracultural explanation in society is to invite a charge of reductionism. This is ironic, since an accusation designed to admonish anthropologists is one that scientists find themselves at ease with, given their avowed interest in reducing surface complexities to core principles, a key tenet of all scientific method and "more a virtue than a sin" (Laland and Brown 2011:66). If we identify recurring behaviors in human societies worldwide, and therefore espouse universalism, we are obliged to search out a source beyond the idiosyncrasies of local cultures, turning to fields that deal with the macropatterning of people and the world.

Complexity and Chaos

A number of mechanistic strands from the natural sciences have influenced recent thinking on social life. One example is heterarchy, an idea that was originally developed to explain certain neurological functions (McCulloch 1945) that has now been taken up for its sociological implications (Crumley 1979, 1987, 1995, 2003). Countering some deep-seated assumptions about the ubiquity of hierarchy, heterarchy describes forms of organization in which elements are unranked or capable of being ranked in different ways.[18] Political formations certainly appear to combine hierarchical and heterarchical orders. The latter is evident, for example, in the interaction of parallel institutions or in the shifts in power relations between autonomous entities, although many are as easily explained as nested or competing hierarchies (Yoffee 2005:179).

Heterarchy is one of several concepts to fall under the general sobriquet of complexity theory (Crumley 2001, see also Kehoe 1998:216–18). This reimagining of systems thinking emerged from attempts to better understand bioevolutionary change and argues for previously unrecognized processes of "self-organization" (Kauffman 1993, 1995; Casti 1994; Lansing 2003). As such, it stresses the ways in which systems develop holistically and collaboratively rather than by the individual roles of components, this "self-creation" emerging from nonhierarchical communication between all of their elements (Luhmann 1995). Complexity theory is not without its problems, but its ideas engender useful reflection on certain types of political issue. Models of political formation, maintenance, and reproduction usually place emphasis on intentionality—on structures as the realized ambitions of individuals or groups. We are familiar with actions having unintended consequences, but complexity goes further to question whether structures are the products of planning in any straightforward sense, opening the door to ways in which they emerge and are regulated by self-organizing principles. Anthropologists and historians alike are much concerned with personal motivations, cost-benefit analysis, and rational choice, for example, and these continue to be factors we can associate with knowledgeable agents at the microscale. Yet complexity posits that intentions coexist with "systems effects" at the micro- and macroscale that are neither designed nor under any sentient control.

Another approach often considered under the umbrella of complexity is chaos theory, which began as a branch of mathematics but has since been identified in a range of scientific disciplines (Waldrop 1992). Chaos, or nonlinear dynamics, describes how minuscule variations in the initial conditions of processes lead to radically different outcomes. As a result, wherever the starting conditions of a given system cannot be fully known, there are significant limits to predicting its future behavior. The popular notoriety of chaos can detract from serious attention to its principles and it can be misapplied—it is not, for example, a synonym for stochastic behavior—but its effects are consistent with what we see in highly unpredictable phenomena such as history (McCloskey 1991; Reisch 1991; Shermer 1993, 1995) and, in a pioneering collected volume, archaeology (Beekman and Baden 2005).[19] Despite a determined search for covering laws to history (Hempel 1942), none have been demonstrated, blocking all conventional attempts to absorb historical studies within the domain of science. Because humans both act and perceive effects and reflexively respond by adapting their behavior, society functions as a constant exercise in feedback (e.g., Giddens 1979:25). While we can trace the trajectory of a social system through time to a given present, chaos casts severe doubt on our ability to deduce exactly why it took one path rather than another or predict how it would develop in the future. The value of the approach therefore lies less in its ability to prescribe fresh avenues of research than the ways it poses restrictions to what we can know of the past—limits that even an unimaginably large dataset could not overcome. Chaos is a science of unpredictability that steers our attention toward problems that are solvable and away from those that are, more than likely, not.

Applying these modes of thinking to human societies past or present smacks of antihumanism. We intuitively resist the idea that our existence amounts to the play of impenetrable statistical probabilities and the whims of unseen hands, yet we can recognize the synergy they present with the autonomous power structures of Foucault, for example, who was interested in precisely these kinds of disembodied processes. Foucault's victims, the "docile bodies" of his disciplinary biopower, demonstrate his awareness of the real life beyond the abstractions. It is to this kind of corporality that we should now move.

Biology and Society

There is no questioning that the power of culture dominates our experience and perception of the world. But this has led to a widely held, but actually quite radical, proposition that cultural development has so superseded natural processes that it renders them all but redundant. In John Locke's well-worn metaphor of the *tabula rasa*, the human brain is conceived as a blank slate onto which our mental superstructure is uniquely inscribed anew through active and passive learning. To become civilized is to somehow leave biology at the door.

But a swathe of empirical data from cognitive and genetic research dispute these assumptions, establishing a prefigured mind that challenges us to find new ways of understanding the relationship between human nature and human culture. A range of biological specializations and subfields, including human sociobiology, evolutionary anthropology, and evolutionary psychology, has developed to explore the relationships between the innate and the acquired (for an overview, see Laland and Brown 2011). Their studies produce no deterministic laws reducing people to programmed automata but rather a growing appreciation that it is the coevolution of genes, culture, and environment that has produced the rich diversity of human expression we see in both past and present.[20] At the heart of sociobiology and its sister disciplines is the recognition that our genus, *Homo*, has spent 99.5 percent of its past living in small groups of hunter-gatherers and that our minds and bodies alike have been shaped by that lifestyle and its imperatives. Cultural evolution may have vastly outstripped its biological counterpart in recent millennia, but the embedded traits and propensities we once relied upon for survival in a "state of nature" have not disappeared and remain with us in the radically different milieu of the modern world. Our environment is so transformed that these traits may no longer have functional roles, their original purposes obscured or altered by the dazzling power of culture (Tooby and Cosmides 1992). The one-time charge of determinism misunderstands the extraordinarily intricate and malleable interplay between biology and culture (Boyd and Richardson 1985, 2005), where to exclude either renders us helpless to explore some of the more profound issues in social and political life.

If we are to answer the truly important social questions—why human societies are hierarchical; why conflict occurs but not all the time, why individuals will risk their lives for the sake of others; why ethnocentrism is pervasive and hard to overcome; why materialism matters so much and is so rarely satisfied—then we need to look into our own deep past. Here, it is disciplines outside anthropology—most notably, the fields of political science and international relations—which have taken up Darwinian approaches to these problems and produced persuasive and logically consistent responses (e.g., Masters 1983, 1989, 1990; Thayer 2000, 2004). Darwinian evolution operates at the level of ultimate causation, not on the proximate causation at which historical actions or events are manifested.[21] It speaks instead to elemental features of the human motivational complex, which are outwardly diverse but ultimately reducible to the familiar goals of somatic survival and reproductive success.

Aiding the move toward dialectical exchange is the recognition that biological evolution is more complex, contingent, and probabilistic that many specialists once believed (see Levins and Lewontin 1985), and this understanding of evolution as a historical process has opened new points of contact with the humanities. Nicole Boivin (2008) has made a bold and innovative effort to demonstrate how decisive the implications of these developments can be for social studies. One she highlights is "niche construction," which was developed to describe how animals do not only exploit environments but shape them to their own specifications with demonstrable evolutionary consequences (Lewontin 2000:51–55). This has obvious applications to humankind—the niche constructors par excellence (Laland, Odling-Smee, and Feldman 2001; Laland and Brown 2006). This ability to determine the conditions of existence is critical because it alters selection pressures and provides a motor for the coevolution of people, places, and things. Archaeology has spent a great deal of time examining the impact of environmental effects on social development and not nearly enough on how those same environments are very often the result of human modification stretching back for millennia. Yet the issue of coevolution runs deeper when we consider the potential for technology to reflexively shape the cognitive capacities of hominids—in effect, materiality producing a "self-made" species (Kingdon 1993; Boivin 2008:190–97). This is especially relevant given that the pace of certain evolved traits has proved to be significantly faster than expected—some operating on the short timescales relevant to complex society (Laland and Brown 2006:101) and even, through epigenetics, in gene-expression changes within a single lifetime. Culture itself is increasingly seen in evolutionary scholarship as *both* a manifestation and a facilitator of human self-construction, a merging of mind and body that renders many long-standing disagreements somewhat moot.

CONCLUDING REFLECTIONS

The aim of this chapter has been to seek a broader setting for the preceding contributions, to show how they are linked by common threads and shared concerns and that, while they may be geographically circumscribed, they are not theoretically isolated. They address questions of broad relevance to current thinking about political practice as it has developed in recent years, taking inspiration from a range of subject areas—theoretical, thematic, material, analogical, textual, and imagistic. They collectively offer a time capsule of where the study of Mesoamerican archaeopolitics currently stands, conscious of the enabling and constraining effect of current paradigms, working within local, regional, and worldwide traditions, yet also innovating and moving the field forward.

My chapter is loosely structured as a historical narrative, describing how contemporary archaeopolitics emerged from the post-processualist critique of processualism and seeks alternative ways to conceive of past lifeways. To the degree that it takes a stand of its own, it is that the universalism inherent in that vision cannot be left as a disembodied abstraction. We are compelled to explain why human communities that were widely distributed across the globe and through time generated recurring patterns of power articulations and practice. There are doubtless several factors at work, but the most obvious is simply our common humanity. But this is not some vague notion of human nature but a very specific instantiation of the long evolution of mind that allowed us to navigate and shape our environment and fellow humans, as they shaped us. The political cannot be subsumed within the humanities but, like all questions of social study, straddles an epistemological divide of central importance to the discipline.

The social sciences are, in this understanding, innately dialectical because they encompass two logically incompatible components. Their friction, expressed as contradiction, is a source for the working versions of reality that need to find some accommodation between them. Latour (1993) usefully paints the scientific-humanistic dialectic not as communication or negotiation but as a series of "translations." This captures the idea that such exchanges cannot be perfect. Each gains some impression of the other's conceptual realm but never a verbatim one. Since they lack a common vocabulary, share no grammatical or syntactical principles, their dialogue is unpredictable and inventive. Calls to dissolve the boundary between science and the humanities have an immediate appeal: they appear redolent of remaking our crusty, sedimented categorizations and breaking through to new conceptual territories. But on closer inspection, what they generally propose are strategies for rethinking existing translations and engineering new ones.

Hegel (1991) saw his dialectic as the explanation for the churn of intellectual paradigms and the successive revolutions in systems of knowledge. It was the meeting of contradictions that led to an unfolding process of renewal and creation. As soon as we seem to have reached resolution—the identification of some timeless and essential truth—it is dispelled by the realization that it is, after all, just another artifact of our consciousness, another contradiction to solve. The cycle is initiated once more, the onward march of a world ever reinventing itself.

ACKNOWLEDGMENTS

I would like to thank the editors for their invitation to contribute to this volume and their diligence and expertise in bringing it to fruition. I would also like to thank the two anonymous reviewers for their helpful comments and suggestions, and additionally, those received from Stephen Houston and Joel Skidmore.

NOTES

1. For a summary of how the unity of opposites concept has been employed within different strands of philosophy, see McGill and Parry (1948).

2. This term is most often associated with Elman R. Service (1968, 1975), although it was earlier ascribed to William I. Thomas (in Dorsey 1931:21).

3. For an exception to the general tenor of processualism regarding ideology, see Flannery (1972).

4. See Hodder 1982, 1986; Tilley 1982; Miller and Tilley 1984.

5. The key texts (Bourdieu 1977, 1990; Giddens 1979, 1984) show only a handful of references to *hierarchy* and most of these are unrelated to political concerns.

6. For a discussion of Raymond Williams and his contribution to practice theory, see Ortner (1984:149).

7. Resources take a wide variety of forms but fall into categories that Giddens called "authoritative" and "allocative," recast and clarified by Sewell as "human" and "nonhuman": "Nonhuman resources are objects, animate or inanimate, naturally occurring or manufactured, that can be used to enhance or maintain power; human resources are physical strength, dexterity, knowledge, and emotional commitments that can be used to enhance or maintain power, including knowledge of the means of gaining, retaining, controlling, and propagating either human or nonhuman resources" (Sewell 1992:9).

8. Barrett (2001:149–50) explains this point, although without the input of schemas per se: "Agency is always situated in the structural conditions which facilitate its actions because agency requires a medium through which to work. Practice is therefore structured by the resources which are its medium and its outcome. These resources extend from material and symbolic resources to traditions of execution and expression. The effectiveness of the mobilization of such resources in practice depends partly upon the degree of control and knowledgeability exercised by the agent, partly upon the power of the agent over these resources, and partly upon the agent's expertise to communicate effectively."

9. For another ideologically driven perspective, see Joyce and Winter (1996), which also focuses on elite strategies of control.

10. This is part of a wider sea change in the perception of Teotihuacan, which questions whether impressionistic evaluations of art and architecture can offer reliable equations to a political system, including doubts that political leadership was as impersonal as long assumed (see Taube 2000).

11. Here we might note Inomata and Coben (2006), for case studies worldwide on the intersection of human performance with designed spaces and dedicated paraphernalia.

12. In response to this and similar approaches, a group of scholars, following Renfrew (2004), elaborated a highly recursive notion of "material engagement" under the broader aegis of cognitive archaeology (see Malafouris 2004; Knappett 2004).

13. For this kind of reflexivity in Maya architecture, see Martin (2001:168–69).

14. For interpretive communities in Mesoamerica, see Martin 2006.

15. I use this term in a more restrictive sense than Lotman intended. Rather than a whole world of human-made meaning, I apply it only to the object world of a given society.

16. A broad definition appears in Ascher (1961:317): "In its most general sense interpreting by analogy is assaying any belief about non-observed behavior by referral to observed behavior which is thought to be relevant."

17. There are a good number of overviews of this history as well as more detailed treatments of its phases. See, for example, relevant sections of Vincent (1990), Kehoe (1998), Trigger (2006), and Johnson (2010).

18. For treatments of heterarchy in the Maya region, see Potter and King (1995), Scarborough, Valdez, and Dunning (2003), and Becker (2004).

19. For a concise history of the tentative efforts to understand history through nonlinear dynamics, see Shermer (1995:59–69).

20. The initial programmatic claims of Wilson (1975) were quickly rejected by Sahlins (1976), although his charges of biological determinism were in turn rebutted by Alexander (1977, 1979). Weaknesses within Wilson's original exposition were critiqued from within biology, although these have subsided with the growing consensus about the mechanisms at work in sociobiology (see Losco 2011:81).

21. To illustrate this contrast: the proximate cause of thirst is that you have gone without drinking for a while, while the ultimate cause of thirst is that our metabolism requires water and the sensation has evolved to motivate a sufficient intake (see Gat 2006).

REFERENCES

Abercrombie, Nicholas, Stephen Hill, and Bryan S. Turner. 1980. *The Dominant Ideology Thesis.* London: Allen & Unwin.

Abrams, Philip. 1988. "Notes on the Difficulty of Studying the State." *Journal of Historical Sociology* 1(1): 58–89.

Agamben, Giorgio. 1998. *Homo Sacer: Sovereign Power and Bare Life.* Translated by Daniel Heller-Roazen. Stanford: Stanford University Press.

Alexander, Richard D. 1976. Review of *The Use and Abuse of Biology: An Anthropological Critique of Sociobiology*, by Marshall D. Sahlins. *American Anthropologist* 79(4): 917–20.

Alexander, Richard D. 1979. *Darwinism and Human Affairs.* Seattle: University of Washington Press.

Ascher, Robert. 1961. "Analogy in Archaeological Interpretation." *Southwestern Journal of Anthropology* 17(4): 317–25.

Baines, John, and Norman Yoffee. 1998. "Order, Legitimacy, and Wealth in Ancient Egypt and Mesopotamia." In *Archaic States*, edited by Gary M. Feinman and Joyce Marcus, 199–260. Santa Fe: School of American Research Press.

Barrett, John C. 2001. "Agency, the Duality of Structure, and the Problem of the Archaeological Record." In *Archaeological Theory Today*, edited by Ian Hodder, 140–62. Cambridge: Polity Press.

Barrett, Justin L. 1998. "Cognitive Constraints on Hindu Concepts of the Divine." *Journal for the Scientific Study of Religion* 37(4): 608–19.

Becker, Marshall J. 2004. "Maya Heterarchy as Inferred From Classic-Period Plaza Plans." *Ancient Mesoamerica* 15(1): 127–38.

Beekman, Christopher S., and William W. Baden, eds. 2005. *Nonlinear Models for Archaeology and Anthropology: Continuing the Revolution*. Aldershot: Ashgate.

Blanton, Robert E., Gary M. Feinman, Stephen A. Kowalewski, and Peter N. Peregrine. 1996. "A Dual-Processual Theory for the Evolution of Mesoamerican Civilization." *Current Anthropology* 37(1): 1–14.

Boivin, Nicole. 2004. "Mind over Matter? Collapsing the Mind-Matter Dichotomy in Material Culture Studies." In *Rethinking Materiality: The Engagement of Mind with the Material World*, edited by Elizabeth DeMarrais, Chris Gosden, and Colin Renfrew, 63–71. Cambridge: McDonald Institute for Archaeological Research.

Boivin, Nicole. 2008. *Material Cultures, Material Minds: The Impact of Things on Human Thought, Society, and Evolution*. Cambridge: Cambridge University Press.

Bourdieu, Pierre. 1977. *Outline of a Theory of Practice*. Translated by Richard Nice. Cambridge: Cambridge University Press.

Bourdieu, Pierre. 1990. *The Logic of Practice*. Translated by Richard Nice. Stanford: Stanford University Press.

Boyd, Robert, and Peter J. Richerson. 1985. *Culture and the Evolutionary Process*. Chicago: University of Chicago Press.

Boyer, Pascal. 2001. *Religion Explained: The Evolutionary Origins of Religious Thought*. New York: Basic Books.

Campbell, Roderick B. 2009. "Toward a Networks and Boundaries Approach to Early Complex Polities: The Late Shang Case." *Current Anthropology* 50(6): 821–48.

Casti, John L. 1994. *Complexification: Explaining a Paradoxical World through the Science of Surprise*. London: Abacus.

Chapman, Robert. 2003. *Archaeologies of Complexity*. London: Routledge.

Clark, J. Grahame D. 1951. "Folk-Culture and the Study of European Prehistory." In *Aspects of Archaeology in Britain and Beyond*, edited by W. F. Grimes, 49–65. London: Edwards.

Cohen, Abner. 1981. *The Politics of Elite Culture: Explorations in the Dramaturgy of Power in a Modern African Society*. Berkeley: University of California Press.

Conrad, Geoffrey W., and Arthur A. Demarest. 1984. *Religion and Empire: The Dynamics of Aztec and Inca Expansionism*. Cambridge: Cambridge University Press.

Crumley, Carole L. 1979. "Three Locational Models: An Epistemological Assessment for Anthropology and Archaeology." In *Advances in Archaeological Method and Theory*, vol. 2, edited by Michael B. Schiffer, 141–73. New York: Academic Press.

Crumley, Carole L. 1987. "A Dialectical Critique of Hierarchy." In *Power Relations and State Formation*, edited by Thomas C. Patterson and Christine W. Gailey, 155–69. Washington, DC: American Anthropological Association.

Crumley, Carole L. 1995. "Heterarchy and the Analysis of Complex Societies." In *Heterarchy and the Analysis of Complex Societies*, edited by Robert M. Ehrenreich, Carole L. Crumley, and Janet E. Levy, 1–5. Arlington: American Anthropological Association.

Crumley, Carole L. 2001. "Communication, Holism, and the Evolution of Sociopolitical Complexity." In *From Leaders to Rulers*, edited by Jonathan Haas, 19–33. New York: Kluwer Academic/Plenum Publishers.

Crumley, Carole L. 2003. "Alternative Forms of Social Order." In *Heterarchy, Political Economy, and the Ancient Maya: The Three Rivers Region of the East-Central Yucatán Peninsula*, edited by Vernon L. Scarborough, Fred Valdez, Jr., and Nicholas Dunning, 136–45. Tucson: University of Arizona Press.

Demarest, Arthur A., and Geoffrey W. Conrad, eds. 1992. *Ideology and Pre-Columbian Civilizations*. Santa Fe: School of American Research Press.

DeMarrais, Elizabeth, Luis J. Castillo, and Timothy K. Earle. 1996. "Ideology, Materialization and Power Strategies." *Current Anthropology* 37(1): 15–31.

Dobres, Marcia-Ann, and John E. Robb. 2000. "Agency in Archaeology: Paradigm or Platitude?" In *Agency in Archaeology*, edited by Marcia-Ann Dobres and John E. Robb, 3–17. London: Routledge.

Dornan, Jennifer L. 2002. "Agency and Archaeology: Past, Present, and Future Directions." *Journal of Archaeological Method and Theory* 9(4): 303–29.

Dorsey, George A. 1931. *The Story of Civilization: Man's Own Show*. New York: Halycon House.

Feinman, Gary, and Jill Neitzel. 1984. "Too Many Types: An Overview of Sedentary Prestate Societies in the Americas." *Advances in Archaeological Method and Theory* 7: 39–102.

Ferguson, Yale H. 2002. "The State Concept and a World of Polities Under Perpetual Siege." In *The State, Identity and Violence: Political Disintegration in the Post–Cold War Era*, edited by R. Brian Ferguson, 89–95. London: Routledge.

Ferguson, Yale H., and Richard W. Mansbach. 1996. *Polities: Authority, Identities, and Change.* Columbia: University of South Carolina Press.

Fish, Stanley. 1980. *Is There a Text in This Class? The Authority of Interpretive Communities*. Cambridge, MA: Harvard University Press.

Flannery, Kent V. 1972. "The Cultural Evolution of Civilizations." *Annual Review of Ecology and Systematics* 3: 399–426.

Foucault, Michel. 1978. *The History of Sexuality.* Vol. 1, *An Introduction*. Translated by Robert Hurley. New York: Pantheon.

Foucault, Michel. 1979. *Discipline and Punish: The Birth of the Prison*. Translated by Alan Sheridan. New York: Vintage.

Foucault, Michel. 1980. *Power/Knowledge: Selected Interviews and Other Writings, 1972–1977.* Edited by Colin Gordon. Brighton: Harvester Press.

Foucault, Michel. 2003. *"Society Must Be Defended": Lectures at the Collège de France, 1975–1976.* Edited by Mauro Bertani and Alessandro Fontana. Translated by David Macey. New York: Picador.

Foucault, Michel. 2007. *Security, Territory, Population: Lectures at the Collège de France, 1977–1978.* Edited by Michel Senellart. Translated by Graham Burchell. New York: Picador.

Fried, Morton H. 1967. *The Evolution of Political Society: An Essay in Political Anthropology.* New York: Random House.

Gailey, Christine W., and Thomas C. Patterson. 1987. "Power Relations and State Formation." In *Power Relations and State Formation*, edited by Thomas C. Patterson and Christine W. Gailey, 1–26. Washington, DC: American Anthropological Association.

Gat, Azar. 2006. *War in Human Civilization.* Oxford: Oxford University Press.

Gell, Alfred. 1998. *Art and Agency: An Anthropological Theory.* Oxford: Clarendon.

Giddens, Anthony. 1979. *Central Problems in Social Theory.* Berkeley: University of California Press.

Giddens, Anthony. 1984. *The Constitution of Society: Outline of the Theory of Structuration.* Berkeley: University of California Press.

Gould, Richard A., and Patty Jo Watson. 1982. "A Dialogue on the Meaning and Use of Analogy in Ethnoarchaeological Reasoning." *Journal of Anthropological Archaeology* 1(4): 355–81.

Hanks, William F. 1990. *Referential Practice: Language and Lived Space among the Maya.* Chicago: University of Chicago Press.

Hansen, Thomas Blom, and Finn Stepputat. 2006. "Sovereignty Revisited." *Annual Review of Anthropology* 35: 295–315.

Hawkes, Christopher. 1954. "Archaeological Theory and Method: Some Suggestions from the Old World." *American Anthropologist* 56(2): 155–68.

Hegel, Georg Wilhelm Friedrich. [1830] 1991. *The Encyclopaedia Logic, with the Zusätze: Part 1 of the Encyclopaedia of Philosophical Sciences with the Zusätze.* Translated by T. Geraets, W. A. Suchting, and H. S. Harris. Indianapolis: Hackett.

Hempel, Carl Gustav. 1942. "The Function of General Laws in History." *Journal of Philosophy* 39(1): 35–48.

Hinsley, Francis H. 1966. *Sovereignty.* New York: Basic Books.

Hodder, Ian. 1982. "Theoretical Archaeology: A Reactionary View." In *Symbolic and Structural Archaeology*, edited by Ian Hodder, 1–16. Cambridge: Cambridge University Press.

Hodder, Ian. 1986. *Reading the Past: Current Approaches to Interpretation in Archaeology*. Cambridge: Cambridge University Press.

Hodder, Ian. 1988. "Material Culture Texts and Social Change: A Theoretical Discussion and Some Archaeological Examples." *Proceedings of the Prehistoric Society* 54: 67–75.

Hodder, Ian. 2012. *Entangled: An Archaeology of the Relationship between Humans and Things*. Malden: Wiley-Blackwell.

Houston, Stephen D., and Hector Escobedo. 1997. "Descifrando la política Maya: Perspectivas arqueológicas y epigráficas sobre el concepto de los estados segmentarios." In *X Simposio de investigaciones arqueologicas en Guatemala, 1996*, edited by Juan Pedro Laporte and Héctor L. Escobedo, 463–81. Guatemala City: Museo de Arqueología y Etnología.

Humphrey, Caroline. 2004. "Sovereignty." In *A Companion to the Anthropology of Politics*, edited by David Nugent and Joan Vincent, 418–36. Oxford: Blackwell.

Inomata, Takeshi, and Lawrence S. Coben, eds. 2006. *Archaeology of Performance: Theaters of Power, Community, and Politics*. Lanham, MD: AltaMira.

Johansen, Peter G., and Andrew M. Bauer. 2011. "Reconfiguring the 'Political' in the Reconstruction of Past Political Production." In *The Archaeology of Politics: The Materiality of Political Practice and Action in the Past*, edited by Peter G. Johansen and Andrew M. Bauer, 1–19. Newcastle upon Tyne: Cambridge Scholars.

Johnson, Matthew. 2010. *Archaeological Theory: An Introduction*. Second edition. London: Wiley-Blackwell.

Joyce, Arthur A., and Marcus Winter. 1996. "Ideology, Power, and Urban Society in Pre-Hispanic Oaxaca." *Current Anthropology* 37(1): 33–47.

Kant, Immanuel. [1781] 1999. *Critique of Pure Reason*. Edited by Paul Guyer and Allen W. Wood. Cambridge: Cambridge University Press.

Kauffman, Stuart. 1993. *The Origins of Order: Self-Organization and Selection in Evolution*. Oxford: Oxford University Press.

Kauffman, Stuart. 1995. *At Home in the Universe*. Oxford: Oxford University Press.

Kehoe, Alice Beck. 1998. *The Land of Prehistory: A Critical History of American Archaeology*. New York: Routledge.

Kingdon, Jonathan. 1993. *Self-Made Man and His Undoing*. New York: Simon & Schuster.

Knapp, A. Bernard. 2010. "Beyond Agency: Identity and Individuals in Archaeology." In *Agency and Identity in the Ancient Near East: New Paths Forward*, edited by Sharon R. Steadman and Jennifer C. Ross, 193–200. London: Equinox.

Knappett, Carl. 2004. "The Affordance of Things: a Post-Gibsonian Perspective on the Relationality of Mind and Matter." In *Rethinking Materiality: The Engagement of*

Mind with the Material World, edited by Elizabeth DeMarrais, Chris Gosden, and Colin Renfrew, 43–51. Cambridge: McDonald Institute for Archaeological Research.

Kohl, Philip L. 1984. "Force, History, and the Evolutionist Paradigm." In *Marxist Perspectives in Archaeology*, edited by Matthew Spriggs, 127–34. Cambridge: Cambridge University Press.

Kohl, Philip L. 1987. "State Formation: Useful Concept or Idée Fixe?" In *Power Relations and State Formation*, edited by Thomas C. Patterson and Christine W. Gailey, 27–34. Washington, DC: American Anthropological Association.

Kuhn, Thomas S. 1962. "The Structure of Scientific Revolutions." *International Encyclopedia of Unified Science*. Vols. 1–2, *Foundations of the Unity of Science*. Chicago: University of Chicago Press.

Laland, Kevin N., and Gillian R. Brown. 2006. "Niche Construction, Human Behavior, and the Adaptive-Lag Hypothesis." *Evolutionary Anthropology* 15(3): 95–104.

Laland, Kevin N., and Gillian R. Brown. 2011. *Sense and Nonsense: Evolutionary Perspectives on Human Behaviour*. Second edition. Oxford: Oxford University Press.

Laland, Kevin N., John Odling-Smee, and Marcus W. Feldman. 2001. "Cultural Niche Construction and Human Evolution." *Journal of Evolutionary Biology* 14: 22–33.

Lansing, Stephen J. 2003. "Complex Adaptive Systems." *Annual Review of Anthropology* 32: 183–204.

Last, Jonathan. 1995. "The Nature of History." In *Interpreting Archaeology: Finding Meaning in the Past*, edited by Ian Hodder, Michael Shanks, Alexandra Alexandri, Victor Buchli, John Carman, Jonathan Last, and Gavin Lucas, 141–57. New York: Routledge.

Latour, Bruno. 1993. *We Have Never Been Modern*. Translated by Catherine Porter. Cambridge, MA: Harvard University Press.

Latour, Bruno. 2005. *Reassembling the Social: An Introduction to Actor-Network-Theory*. Oxford: Oxford University Press.

Levins, Richard, and Richard Lewontin. 1985. *The Dialectical Biologist*. Cambridge, MA: Harvard University Press.

Lewontin, Richard. 2000. *The Triple Helix: Gene, Organism, and Environment*. Cambridge, CA: Harvard University Press.

Losco, Joseph. 2011. "From Outrage to Orthodoxy? Sociobiology and Political Science at 35." *Politics and the Life Sciences* 30(1): 80–84.

Lotman, Yuri Mikhailovich. 1990. *Universe of the Mind: A Semiotic Theory of Culture*. Translated by Ann Shukman. London: I. B. Tauris.

Lowie, Robert H. 1927. *The Origin of the State*. New York: Harcourt, Brace.

Luhmann, Niklas. 1995. *Social Systems*. Palo Alto, CA: Stanford University Press.

Malafouris, Lambros. 2004. "The Cognitive Basis of Material Engagement: Where Brain, Body and Culture Conflate." In *Rethinking Materiality: The Engagement of Mind with the Material World*, edited by Elizabeth DeMarrais, Christopher Gosden, and Colin Renfrew, 53–61. Cambridge: McDonald Institute for Archaeological Research.

Martin, Simon. 2001. "Court and Realm: Architectural Signatures in the Classic Maya Southern Lowlands." In *Royal Courts of the Ancient Maya*, vol. 1, *Theory, Comparison, and Synthesis*, edited by Takeshi Inomata and Stephen D. Houston, 168–94. Boulder: Westview.

Martin, Simon. 2006. "On Pre-Columbian Narrative: Representation across the Word-Image Divide." In *A Pre-Columbian World*, edited by Jeffrey Quilter and Mary Miller, 55–105. Washington, DC: Dumbarton Oaks.

Marx, Karl, and Frederich Engels. 1970. *The German Ideology*. Edited by C. J. Arthur. New York: International Publishers.

Masters, Roger D. 1983. "The Biological Nature of the State." *World Politics* 35(2): 161–93.

Masters, Roger D. 1989. *The Nature of Politics*. New Haven: Yale University Press.

Masters, Roger D. 1990. "Evolutionary Biology and Political Theory." *American Political Science Review* 84(1): 195–210.

McCloskey, Donald. 1991. "History, Differential Equations, and the Problem of Narration." *History and Theory* 30(1): 21–36.

McCulloch, Warren S. 1945. "A Heterarchy of Values Determined by the Topology of Neural Nets." *Bulletin of Mathematical Biophysics* 7: 89–93.

McGill, V. J., and W. T. Parry. 1948. "The Unity of Opposites: A Dialectical Principle." *Science and Society* 12(4): 418–44.

Meskell, Lynn, ed. 2005a. *Archaeologies of Materiality*. Malden, MA: Blackwell.

Meskell, Lynn. 2005b. "Objects in the Mirror Appear Closer than They Are." In *Materiality*, edited by Daniel Miller, 51–71. Durham: Duke University Press.

Miller, Daniel, ed. 1998. *Material Cultures: Why Some Things Matter*. London: UCL Press.

Miller, Daniel. 2005. "Materiality: An Introduction." In *Materiality*, edited by Daniel Miller, 1–50. Durham: Duke University Press.

Miller, Daniel, and Christopher Tilley. 1984. "Ideology, Power and Prehistory: An Introduction." In *Ideology, Power and Prehistory*, edited by Daniel Miller and Christopher Tilley, 1–15. Cambridge: Cambridge University Press.

Mouzelis, Nicos P. 1995. *Sociological Theory: What Went Wrong? Diagnosis and Remedies*. London: Routledge.

Ortner, Sherry B. 1984. "Theory in Anthropology since the Sixties." *Comparative Studies in Society and History* 26(1): 126–66.

Ortner, Sherry B. 2006. *Anthropology and Social Theory: Culture, Power, and the Acting Subject*. Durham: Duke University Press.

Parsons, Talcott. 1951. *The Social System*. Glencoe, IL: Free Press.

Patrik, Linda E. 1985. "Is There an Archaeological Record?" *Advances in Archaeological Method and Theory* 8: 27–62.

Pauketat, Timothy R. 2000. "The Tragedy of the Commoners." In *Agency in Archaeology*, edited by Marcia-Anne Dobres and John A. Robb, 113–29. London: Routledge.

Pauketat, Timothy R. 2001. "Practice and History in Archaeology: An Emerging Paradigm." *Anthropological Theory* 1(1): 73–98.

Pauketat, Timothy R. 2007. *Chiefdoms and Other Archaeological Delusions*. Lanham, MD: AltaMira.

Porter, Anne. 2010. "Akkad and Agency, Archaeology and Annals: Considering Power and Intent in Third Millennium BCE Mesopotamia." In *Agency and Identity in the Ancient Near East: New Paths Forward*, edited by Sharon R. Steadman and Jennifer C. Ross, 166–80. London: Equinox.

Potter, Daniel R., and Eleanor M. King. 1995. "A Heterarchical Approach to Lowland Maya Socioeconomies." In *Heterarchy and the Analysis of Complex Societies*, edited by Robert M. Ehrenreich, Carole L. Crumley, and Janet E. Levy, 17–32. Arlington: American Anthropological Association.

Preucel, Robert W. 1991. "The Philosophy of Archaeology." In *Processual and Postprocessual Archaeologies: Multiple Ways Of Knowing the Past*, edited by Robert W. Preucel, 17–29. Carbondale: Southern Illinois University.

Radcliffe-Brown, Arthur R. 1940. "Preface." In *African Political Systems*, edited by M. Fortes and E. E. Evans-Pritchard, xi–xxiii. Oxford: Oxford University Press.

Reisch, George. 1991. "Chaos, History, and Narrative." *History and Theory* 30(1): 1–20.

Renfrew, Colin. 2004. "Towards a Theory of Material Engagement." In *Rethinking Materiality: The Engagement of Mind with the Material World*, edited by Elizabeth DeMarrais, Christopher Gosden, and Colin Renfrew, 23–31. Cambridge: McDonald Institute for Archaeological Research.

Richerson, Peter J., and Robert Boyd. 2005. *Not by Genes Alone: How Culture Transformed Human Evolution*. Chicago: University of Chicago Press.

Roscoe, Paul. 2000. "Costs, Benefits, Typologies, and Power." In *Hierarchies in Action: Cui Bono?*, edited by Michael W. Diehl, 113–33. Center for Archaeological Investigations, Occasional Paper No. 27. Carbondale: Southern Illinois University.

Sahlins, Marshall D. 1976. *The Use and Abuse of Biology: An Anthropological Critique of Sociobiology*. Ann Arbor: University of Michigan Press.

Sahlins, Marshall D., and Elman R. Service, eds. 1960. *Evolution and Culture*. Ann Arbor: University of Michigan Press.

Scarborough, Vernon L., Fred Valdez, Jr., and Nicholas Dunning, eds. 2003. *Heterarchy, Political Economy, and the Ancient Maya: The Three Rivers Region of the East-Central Yucatán Peninsula.* Tucson: University of Arizona Press.

Service, Elman R. 1962. *Primitive Social Organization.* New York: Random House.

Service, Elman R. 1968. "War and Our Contemporary Ancestors." In *War: The Anthropology of Armed Conflict and Aggression*, edited by Morton H. Fried, Marvin Harris, and Robert F. Murphy, 160–67. Garden City, NY: Natural History Press.

Service, Elman R. 1975. *Origins of the State and Civilization The Process of Cultural Evolution.* New York: W. W. Norton.

Sewell, William H. 1992. "A Theory of Structure: Duality, Agency, and Transformation." *American Journal of Sociology* 98(1): 1–29.

Shanks, Michael, and Christopher Tilley. 1987. *Social Theory and Archaeology.* Cambridge: Polity Press.

Shennan, Stephen. 1993. "After Social Evolution: A New Archaeological Agenda?" In *Archaeological Theory: Who Sets the Agenda?*, edited by Norman Yoffee and Andrew Sherratt, 53–59. Cambridge: Cambridge University Press.

Shermer, Michael. 1993. "The Chaos of History: On a Chaotic Model That Represents the Role of Contingency and Necessity in Historical Sequences." *Nonlinear Science Today* 2(4): 1–13.

Shermer, Michael. 1995. "Exorcising Laplace's Demon: Chaos and Antichaos, History and Metahistory." *History and Theory* 34(1): 59–83.

Smith Adam T. 2001. "The Limitations of Doxa: Agency and Subjectivity from an Archaeological Point of View." *Journal of Social Archaeology* 1(2): 155–71.

Smith Adam T. 2003. *The Political Landscape: Constellations of Authority in Early Complex Polities.* Berkeley: University of California Press.

Smith Adam T. 2011. "Archaeologies of Sovereignty." *Annual Review of Anthropology* 40: 415–32.

Steward, Julian H. 1955. *Theory of Culture Change: The Methodology of Multilinear Evolution.* Urbana: University of Illinois Press.

Taube, Karl A. 2000. *The Writing System of Ancient Teotihuacan.* Barnardsville, NC: Center for Ancient American Studies.

Thayer, Bradley A. 2000. "Bringing in Darwin: Evolutionary Theory, Realism, and International Politics." *International Security* 25(2): 124–53.

Thayer, Bradley A. 2004. *Darwin and International Relations: On the Evolutionary Origins of War and Ethnic Conflict.* Lexington: University Press of Kentucky.

Tilley, Christopher. 1982. "Social Formation, Social Structures and Social Change." In *Symbolic and Structural Archaeology*, edited by Ian Hodder, 26–38. Cambridge: Cambridge University Press.

Tilley, Christopher. 1991. *Material Culture and Text: The Art of Ambiguity*. London: Routledge.

Tooby, John, and Leda Cosmides. 1992. "The Psychological Foundations of Culture." In *The Adapted Mind: Evolutionary Psychology and the Generation of Culture*, edited by Jerome H. Barkow, Leda Cosmides, and John Tooby, 19–136. Oxford: Oxford University Press.

Trigger, Bruce G. 2006. *A History of Archaeological Thought*. Second Edition. Cambridge: Cambridge University Press.

Vincent, Joan. 1990. *Anthropology and Politics: Visions, Traditions, and Trends*. Tucson: University of Arizona Press.

Waldrop, Mitchell M. 1992. *Complexity: The Emerging Science at the Edge of Order and Chaos*. New York: Simon & Schuster.

Wengrow, David. 2001. "The Evolution of Simplicity: Aesthetic Labour and Social Change in the Neolithic Near East." *World Archaeology* 33(2): 168–88.

White, Leslie A. 1949. *The Science of Culture: A Study of Man and Civilization*. New York: Farrar, Straus.

Williams, Raymond. 1977. *Marxism and Literature*. Oxford: Oxford University Press.

Wilson, Edward O. 1975. *Sociobiology: The New Synthesis*. Cambridge, MA: Harvard University Press.

Wolf, Eric R. 1982. *Europe and the People Without History*. Berkeley: University of California Press.

Wylie, Alison. 1985. "The Reaction Against Analogy. *Advances in Archaeological Method and Theory* 8: 63–111.

Yoffee, Norman. 1993. "Too Many Chiefs? (or, Safe Texts for the '90s." In *Archaeological Theory: Who Sets the Agenda?*, edited by Norman Yoffee and Andrew Sherratt, 60–78. Cambridge: Cambridge University Press.

Yoffee, Norman. 2005. *Myths of the Archaic State: The Evolution of the Earliest Cities, States, and Civilizations*. Cambridge: Cambridge University Press.

Contributors

Sarah B. Barber is an associate professor of anthropology at the University of Central Florida. She received her PhD at the University of Colorado Boulder. Her current research focuses on the role of religion and long-distance exchange on the development of complex societies in Oaxaca.

Joanne Baron received her PhD in anthropology from the University of Pennsylvania. She is an assistant professor of global social sciences in the Bard Early College Network. Her research investigates political and economic relationships among the Classic Maya through archaeology and epigraphy. She has worked on archeological projects in Guatemala, Belize, and Honduras and is the director of the La Florida Archaeology Project in Guatemala.

Christopher S. Beekman received his PhD from Vanderbilt University in 1996. He is an associate professor at the University of Colorado Denver. His research interests include political systems and practices and social identity, particularly as revealed through research in western Mexico.

Jeffrey Brzezinski completed his MA in anthropology at the University of Central Florida in 2011 and his PhD in the Department of Anthropology at the University of Colorado Boulder in 2019. His research interests include the rise of complex societies in Mesoamerica, the negotiation of political authority during the Formative Period, and the role of religion in pre-Columbian political formations.

Bryce Davenport received his MA in anthropology from Brandeis University. After several years consulting as a geospatial analyst in both archaeological remote sensing projects and world heritage management work, he now serves as a statistical geographer for the United States Census Bureau. His research interests include premodern systems of exchange, the political economy of highland Mexico, and the integration of remote sensing technologies into archaeological investigation—most recently through contributions to The Western Maya Mountains Geospatial Project.

Charles Golden received his PhD from the University of Pennsylvania. He is an associate professor in the Department of Anthropology and Chair of the Latin American and Latino Studies Program at Brandeis University. He has worked in the Usumacinta River region since 1997, most recently as codirector of the Sierra del Lacandón Regional Archaeology Project in Petén, Guatemala, and the Proyecto Arqueológico Busilja-Chocolja in Chiapas, Mexico. His research interests concern the dynamic social and political boundaries between Maya kingdoms, human-environmental dynamics, and the cultural significance of temporal boundaries, history, and social memory for the ancient Maya.

Takeshi Inomata is a professor and Agnese Nelms Haury Chair at the School of Anthropology, University of Arizona. He earned a PhD from Vanderbilt University. Through the excavation of Aguateca and Ceibal, Guatemala, he has been examining social change, political organization, warfare, and households in Maya society.

Arthur A. Joyce earned his PhD from Rutgers University in 1991 and is a professor of anthropology at the University of Colorado Boulder. Since 1986 he has conducted interdisciplinary research in Oaxaca on issues of political dynamics, ideology, landscape, and ecology. He is author of *Mixtecs, Zapotecs, and Chatinos: Ancient Peoples of Southern Mexico* (2010) and editor of *Polity and Ecology in Formative Period Coastal Oaxaca* (2013).

Sarah Kurnick earned her PhD from the University of Pennsylvania. She is currently an assistant professor in the department of anthropology at the University of Colorado Boulder and codirector of the Punta Laguna Archaeology Project. Her primary interests include the role of the past in shaping the political present and how archaeology can benefit the public and foster social change.

Carlo J. Lucido earned his MA from the University of Central Florida. He has conducted archaeological excavations in Florida with the Tribal Historic Preservation Office of the Florida Seminole and in Mexico with the Proyecto Río Verde. His work in Oaxaca began in 2009, where he has excavated the acropolis at Rio Viejo. His research interests include trade, politics, and identity. His current research focuses on feasting and the use of monumental spaces during early political centralization in coastal Oaxaca, Mexico.

Simon Martin received his PhD from University College London and is currently an associate curator at the University of Pennsylvania Museum of Archaeology and Anthropology. His research focuses on the political structure and interactions of the Classic Maya, and he has conducted fieldwork at Calakmul, Campeche, Mexico, for over twenty years.

Tatsuya Murakami received his PhD from Arizona State University and is currently an assistant professor in the Department of Anthropology at Tulane University. His research focuses on the materiality of sociopolitical processes in central Mexico and uses practice-based and multidisciplinary approaches, including archaeometric methods. He codirects an archaeological project with Shigeru Kabata (Universidad de las Américas Puebla) at the Formative site of Tlalancaleca, Puebla, Mexico, investigating regional processes that led to the formation of the Teotihuacan state.

Helen Perlstein Pollard received her PhD from Columbia University in 1972. She is now professor emerita at Michigan State University, where she has worked since 1986. She has carried out extensive archaeological and ethnohistoric research in central and west Mexico since 1970, with a particular focus on Michoacan and the Tarascan empire. She is currently writing two monographs that will synthesize archaeological understandings of the emergence of Tarascan civilization for archaeologists and the general public.

Víctor Salazar Chávez studied at the Universidad Autónoma de San Luis Potosí, Mexico, where he earned a degree in archaeology in 2013. He is currently a doctoral student at George Washington University. His research interests are in the study of subsistence systems in the Early Formative Period in Mesoamerica, using zooarchaeological and paleobotanical evidence.

Index

Page numbers in italics indicate illustrations.